Ballads Without Words

Chopin and the Tradition of the Instrumental *Ballade*

James Parakilas

AMADEUS PRESS
Reinhard G. Pauly, General Editor
Portland, Oregon

For permission to reprint from the following works, grateful acknowledgment is hereby made to

European American Music, excerpts from Martin, *Ballade for Piano and Orchestra.* Copyright 1948 by Universal-Edition, Vienna.

Houghton Mifflin Co., excerpt from *The Poems of François Villon*, translated with an introduction by Galway Kinnell. Copyright 1955, 1977 by Galway Kinnell.

Penguin USA, excerpts from *The Penguin Book of Folk Ballads of the English-Speaking World*, edited by Albert B. Friedman.

University of Nebraska Press, excerpt from *Edvard Grieg: The Man and the Artist* by Finn Benestad and Dag Schjelderup-Ebbe, translated by William H. Halverson and Leland B. Sateren.

Except where otherwise noted, translations of foreign texts are by James Parakilas.

ISBN 0-931340-47-0
Printed in Singapore

AMADEUS PRESS
9999 S.W. Wilshire, Suite 124
Portland, Oregon 97225

Library of Congress Cataloging-in-Publication Data

Parakilas, James.
   Ballads without words : Chopin and the tradition of the
instrumental Ballade / James Parakilas.
      p.   cm.
   Includes bibliographical references and index.
   ISBN 0-931340-47-0
   1. Ballades (Instrumental music)--History and criticism.
2. Instrumental music--History and criticism. 3. Chopin, Frédéric,
1810-1849. Ballades, piano.   I. Title.
ML460.P34   1992
784.18'96--dc20   91-30216
                                                          CIP
                                                           MN

This book is dedicated, with appreciation and admiration,
to my colleague
ANN BESSER SCOTT.

Contents

List of Plates

Preface

This book grew out of my experience teaching Chopin's first Ballade to a class in nineteenth-century music at Bates College a number of years ago. I found that none of the available analytical approaches provided much insight into that overwhelming music. No traditional formal model, including sonata form, could satisfactorily account for even the complex phrase structures of the first theme of the work, and the simple title "*ballade*" did not point to a specific plot around which a programmatic interpretation could be constructed.

During a leave of absence from teaching, I began to search for a way to make sense of this Ballade. I first turned to Günther Wagner's study, *Die Klavierballade um die Mitte des 19. Jahrhunderts* (1976), and to the rich resources of the Library of Congress, examining the context of the other Chopin Ballades, other nineteenth-century piano *ballades*, and other instrumental works based on ballads. The amazing diversity of this repertory forced me to think abstractly about what ballads are and how instrumental works could be modeled on them. In the present study, as a result, I propose a model of the ballad in terms that can be applied equally to works like Chopin's that have the generic title "*ballade*" and those, like Dukas's *The Sorcerer's Apprentice*, that name a specific poetic ballad as inspiration.

The works covered in this book come from every part of Europe as well as the Americas. One notices, however, that a great many of the most impressive *ballades* of the nineteenth and early twentieth centuries were written by composers from what were then the margins of European culture: Chopin, Liszt, Grieg, Tchaikovsky, Dvořák, Bartók, and Janáček. To make sense of this phenomenon I consider the political meanings of the ballad in the century before World War I and describe individual instrumental *ballades* as composers' responses to the nationalist fervor of their times and the political realities that constrained their careers.

I hope that this book will provide both a context for understanding the complex nature of a single *ballade* and a basis for appreciating the historical importance of a musical genre that has not been surveyed comprehensively before now. The more *ballades* readers listen to, the more the subject will come alive for them. Fortunately, more and more *ballades* are available to be played and heard. Some of the lesser-known works that I describe may be found in *The Nineteenth-Century Piano Ballade: An Anthology* (Madison, Wisconsin: A-R Editions, 1990), a collection I recently edited that provides critical scores of ten *ballades*, very diverse in nature and long out of print, along with extensive commentary. Recordings of lesser-known *ballades* discussed here are listed in the Discography at the end. A glance through the Chronological List of Works Discussed, also at the end of this book, shows that a remarkable number of the works described are currently available either in modern editions (marked ME in the list) or on recordings (marked R) or both.

For Russian names that are well known in the United States, I have adopted the commonly used spelling (e.g., Tchaikovsky). Otherwise, I have transliterated Russian names and words according to the international scholarly system.

Acknowledgments

I owe thanks to the administration and music department of Bates College for supporting my work on this book, especially in granting me two leaves during which I completed the bulk of the research. A National Endowment for the Humanities Fellowship for College Teachers and Independent Scholars allowed me to research and write in Vienna and elsewhere in Europe. A Roger C. Schmutz Faculty Research Grant from Bates College allowed me to acquire copies of many scores.

The librarians at Bates College made it possible for me to do research there that I could have expected to accomplish only at a larger library. For that help I thank Laura Juraska, Janice Lee, Gilbert Marcotte, Paula Matthews, Sharon Saunders, LaVerne Winn, and above all Thomas Hayward.

I relied on the resources of the following additional libraries and institutions and the resourcefulness of their librarians: the libraries of Bowdoin College, Harvard University, Yale University, and the University of California at Berkeley; Boston Public Library; New York Public Library; Library of Congress; Nationalbibliothek, Vienna; the library of the Gesellschaft der Musikfreunde, Vienna; the library of the Musicological Institute at the University of Vienna; the music division of the Stadtbibliothek, Vienna; the library of the Conservatoire Royal de Musique, Brussels; Národní Muzeum, Prague; Association des Amis de Gabriel Fauré, Boulogne; Bibliothèque Nationale, Paris; Richard-Wagner-Museum, Bayreuth; Deutsche Staatsbibliothek, Berlin; Staatsbibliothek Preußischer Kulturbesitz, Berlin; Bayerische Staatsbibliothek, Munich; Széchényi National Library, Budapest; Muzeum Narodowe, Warsaw; and the British Library, London. In particular, I would like to express my gratitude to Gillian Anderson at the Library of Congress; Evžen Balaš of the B. Martinů Foundation, Prague; Mária Eckhardt of the Ferenc Liszt Memorial Museum, Budapest; Barbara Malinowska of the Muzeum Narodowe, Warsaw; Robert Murányi at the Széchényi National Library, Budapest; Andrea Raab of the Schott archive in Mainz; and M. Semrádová of the Národní Muzeum, Prague.

For help on linguistic and literary questions, I thank Karen Black, Jane

Costlow, David Das, Janina Hoskins, Gerda Neu-Sokol, Mary Rice-DeFosse, Benjamin Slay, and Lory Wallfisch. I especially thank Karen Black for translating Pushkin's "Voevoda" and allowing me to print her translation here. For help on musical questions, I thank David Brown, Mária Eckhardt, Jeffrey Kallberg, Katalin Komlós, and Imre Mező. William Austin and Mary Hunter read parts of this book at early stages, and I benefited from their responses.

I am grateful to Duncan Cumming, Dexter Edge, Andrea Johnson, Jill Lemon, and Linda Spugnardi for helping me prepare various parts of the book for the publisher.

I thank Neal Zaslaw for recommending my work to Reinhard Pauly, and I thank Reinhard Pauly and the staff of Amadeus Press for their encouragement and expert editorial work.

PLATE 1. Title-page of Saint-Saëns's "König Harald Harfagar" (1880).

PART I

The Chopin Ballades

CHAPTER 1

Introduction

In 1836, when Chopin's first Ballade appeared in various editions as either "Ballade" or "Ballade ohne Worte" ("Ballade Without Words"), his title was a novelty for an instrumental work.[1] Gottfried Wilhelm Fink (1783-1846), the editor of the *Allgemeine Musikalische Zeitung*, reviewing an edition that used the longer title, greeted the novelty with little surprise, but with no great enthusiasm either: "We have songs without words; why shouldn't we have ballads without words as well? Anyway, the newer music loves to compose stories in sound."[2]

Fink hardly needed to spell out for his readers the context in which Chopin's Ballade appeared. "Stories in sound," ranging from Mendelssohn's *Songs Without Words* (first published under that gracefully unspecific title in 1835) to the Berlioz symphonies (explicitly connected to programs and literary models), were everywhere in the 1830s. The same decade, as William Newman has demonstrated, saw a corresponding "slump" in the publication of sonatas.[3]

The novelty of Chopin's title, then, did not lie in proposing a new kind of piece, but simply in citing a genre that had not previously been chosen as a model for instrumental music. (It is traditional in English to use the French form of the title—"*ballade*"—for instrumental works, but the native form—"ballad"—for the songs and poems on which they are modeled. I follow that tradition, but with regret that in English the title "*ballade*" does not associate instrumental works so immediately with song and story as it does in Continental languages like French and German that have only one form of the term.)

The ballad genre itself needed no more introduction from Fink than the "stories in sound" did. Half a century earlier the ballad had seized the attention of the German public when it appeared simultaneously in several forms: texts of British and other folk ballads, translated by Herder; imitations of those texts by such poets as Bürger, Goethe, and Schiller; and musical settings of those new poems, usually as solo songs with piano accompaniment. In the succeeding decades the ballad continued to be at the forefront of developments in German folklore research, poetry, and song, while international borrowings made Germans aware that the enthusiasm for the genre was spreading across Europe.[4] The Polish poet Adam Mickiewicz (1798–1855), for example, influenced by German and English poetry as well as Slavic folk song, published ballads (in 1822) that were then translated into German and set as songs (published in 1835) by the leading ballad composer of his generation, Carl Loewe (1796–1869). Throughout Fink's lifetime the ballad had been the most important narrative genre in poetry and song. It cannot have seemed very surprising to him, then, that the title "Ballade" would appear on a piano piece by a composer of "the newer music," which, after all, "loved to compose stories in sound." He may even have wondered why it had taken so long for "ballads without words" to appear.

There was good reason, however, for composers not to choose ballads as models for instrumental music. The reason may not have been apparent to Fink and others at the time, precisely because no one before Chopin had tried the idea. Today, on the other hand, Chopin's choice seems inevitable precisely because his Ballades are so securely fixed in the piano repertory. But a comparison to the models that other composers of "the newer music" were taking for their "stories in sound" shows how remarkable a choice it was. In the years just before Chopin's first Ballade appeared, these composers had modeled some "stories in sound" on poems and others on programs connected to their own experience. Works modeled on poems include Mendelssohn's *Meeresstille und glückliche Fahrt* and Liszt's 1835 *Harmonies poétiques et religieuses*; those modeled on personal programs include Schumann's *Carnaval*, Mendelssohn's *Hebrides* overture, and Berlioz's *Symphonie fantastique*. Liszt's *Album d'un voyageur* and Berlioz's *Harold in Italy* use both kinds of models. In all these works, the model is an intimate portrait or history of a hero; its story consists of a series of episodes, each presenting an opportunity for the composer to describe something—a mood or an external phenomenon—in sound.

The ballad could hardly be more different. The description of the genre that has become classic among English-speaking scholars was offered by Gordon Gerould in 1932:

> A ballad is a folk-song that tells a story with stress on the crucial situation, tells it by letting the action unfold itself in event and speech, and tells it objectively with little comment or intrusion of personal bias.[5]

In contrast to the episodic models chosen by Chopin's contemporaries, as by earlier composers, for most "stories in sound," the ballad offered "action centred on a single situation."[6] Whereas most "stories in sound" depend on subjects rich in setting and characterization, the ballad, according to Albert Friedman, gives little attention to "setting," "circumstantial detail," "delineation of character," or "psychological motivation."[7] Instead, it is a story focused on the characters' words and on the actions accomplished through those words. Words themselves are the crucial deeds: in Bürger's "Lenore," Lenore's curse; in the British folk ballad "Edward," Edward's lies; in Goethe's "The Elf-King," the Elf-King's promises. The ballad, then, is not only different from other models for "stories in sound"; it is a far more problematic model. Chopin seems to have gone out of his way to choose the kind of story that would be hardest to illustrate in music without words. It is small wonder that no composer had made the attempt before him.

The circumstances of Chopin's career, however, may have made this undertaking peculiarly attractive to him. He wrote his first Ballade sometime in the early 1830s, the period when he faced what it meant to him as a composer to give up the bonds of shared culture that had linked him to his Polish public. Chopin had left Poland in November 1830, at the age of twenty, because his musical ambitions demanded an international audience; thereafter he had to discover how to draw that audience to a Polish musician. His letters home during his first year away leave no doubt as to how great a problem he found that to be. That year, most of which he spent in Vienna, coincided with the Polish Insurrection, which was crushed by the Russian army in September 1831, when Chopin was on his way to Paris. In Vienna, then, Chopin could never escape worry about his homeland and about the safety of his family and friends, while at the same time he was having little success promoting his career. His letters, describing again and again the indifference of the Viennese to the fate of Poland and indeed to everything Polish, show how sensitive he had become on the subject: "Just try to defend Polish music in Vienna after things like that; just express an opinion about it and they will take you for a madman."[8] The correspondence also reveals his concern about the effects of politics and national attitudes on his career. In one letter, he explains to Joseph Elsner, his principal teacher in Warsaw, why he has failed to give a recital in his first two months in Vienna:

> So I hope that, knowing me as you do, you will not think ill of me for having allowed my feelings for my people at home to take first place and for having so far done nothing about a concert. Today, in every respect, incomparably greater difficulties stand in my way. Not only does the continuous round of mediocre piano-recitals spoil this kind of music-making and frighten off the public, but in addition the events in Warsaw have changed my situation here for the worse, to the same extent as they might have improved my chances in Paris.[9]

One difficulty for an expatriate Polish composer was that audiences outside Poland had no interest in hearing music with Polish texts. Toward the end of Chopin's stay in Vienna, he had a letter from a friend in Warsaw, the poet Stefan Witwicki, eloquently urging him, as others in Poland had urged him before and would urge him later, to "become the creator of Polish opera."[10] No reply survives, but Witwicki's letter, tugging at Chopin through his passionate love of opera, of Slavic folk song, and of his country, can only have made more painful his awareness that his genius for the piano, on which his hopes for an illustrious career depended, was pulling him farther and farther from the one place where Polish opera could be performed. In the end his only vocal works were a dozen and a half Polish songs, which he did not publish. Still, there is plenty of evidence of Chopin's serious and sustained interest in opera, poetry, and song. He grew up surrounded by the leading poets and folklorists in a golden age of Polish letters;[11] in Paris he belonged to the Polish Literary Society. His letters from every period of his life are filled with observations about operas and singers he had heard, and in one letter he expresses pride in his gifts as an accompanist.[12]

Given these interests, it may seem surprising that in the two decades Chopin lived in France (from 1831 to his death in 1849), he never set a text in French, a language he had learned as a child and spoke fluently. In this respect he can be compared to another cosmopolitan and broadly educated Slavic composer, one who lived even longer in France and who shunned French texts almost as completely: Stravinsky. Each of these composers, when deprived of a public for music in his native language, chose not to address another national public in its own native language, but instead to address an international public by cosmopolitan means. Stravinsky's means, or rather, one of his means, was to set Latin texts. Chopin chose to restrict his output almost exclusively to the cosmopolitan medium of the piano, while devoting an important part of that output to works either openly or not so openly Polish in character.

Many of his earliest compositions had been piano pieces in traditional Polish dance forms: polonaises and mazurkas. As he grew older, he also began to compose potpourris on Polish themes. When he left Poland he tried pieces of both these kinds on foreign audiences, even though he could not have expected those audiences to hear them as Polish audiences had. He may have believed that what appealed to Polish audiences as their national music would appeal to other audiences by its exoticism. In fact, the Grand Fantasia on Polish Airs, Op. 13, which Chopin first performed in Warsaw in 1830, became, in 1834, the first of many works that he published simultaneously in French, German, and English editions.[13] He composed no more potpourris, however, after leaving Poland, though he continued to compose polonaises and mazurkas throughout his expatriate years. In these works he treated the national elements, such as the modal melodies in the mazurkas, ever more boldly (just as Bartók would do in the next century), so that the same elements he had once presented to his international public as exotically traditional came to belong to the avant-garde as well.

Even if he had known, when he left Poland, that he would one day challenge the thinking of the most sophisticated musicians in Europe with his Polish dances, Chopin might well have felt that dance music alone could not express all he wished to express as a Polish musician. Indeed, within a year of his departure from Poland, while he was still in Vienna, he began experimenting with new means of treating Polish subjects in piano music. The resulting compositions, by a composer who had suddenly grown defensive about his Polishness, were less openly Polish in character than polonaises and mazurkas. They were, in fact, "songs without words," "stories in sound" for the piano, works in which the cosmopolitan medium conceals a national "text."

The first such work was the B-minor Scherzo, Op. 20. Here the tune of the Polish Christmas song "Lulajże Jezuniu"[14] appears in the middle section, in the middle voice, very quietly, almost clandestinely, as if only Polish listeners were intended to understand its meaning. Later Chopin did not smuggle actual songs into his piano pieces, but he continued to write works— such as the Polonaise, Op. 44, the Fantasy, Op. 49, and the fourth Scherzo, Op. 54— in which a song-without-words is heard at the eye of a musical storm, where it seems to disclose a secret message.

The second of these works concealing a national "text" was the Ballade. The leading authorities have claimed that Chopin began it about the same time as the Scherzo, at the end of his stay in Vienna,[15] and though the little evidence supporting such an early date has recently been discredited,[16] the claim is still widely accepted. There appears to be no way to determine for sure how long before June 1835 (when it was ready for the printer) Chopin began the work. In any case the Ballade was another experimental work. Like the Scherzo, it was a freestanding instrumental work in a genre that had not previously been used for such works. But as a solution to the dilemma of a Polish nationalist seeking a European public for his music, the Ballade represented an improvement over the Scherzo. Its "text" was both national and cosmopolitan: Polish ballads, both folk and literary, belonged to larger European traditions; no matter what model Chopin had in mind as he composed, his title invited listeners in all countries to think of what ballads they knew. This time he was not offering his international public an exotic title like "mazurka," nor was he giving them exotic music.

Scholars who have sought connections between Polish folk music and Chopin's Ballades have come up with very little.[17] The Polish scholar Zofia Lissa, describing Chopin's "national style" through a discriminating, genre-by-genre survey of his compositions, has found that his Ballades, while lacking any direct connection with Polish folk traditions, are national in style by virtue of certain general qualities they share with Polish literary Romanticism.[18] It might seem that the nationalism of Chopin's first Ballade— audible only to those who know Polish poetry—is in its way just as secret in nature as that of his first Scherzo. But the remarkable thing about the Ballade is precisely that its nationalism is not secret; every nineteenth-century European would have understood it. In the twentieth century, though, it may be hard to understand how the ballad, common to every country of Europe, could have seemed like a nationalist genre, so much so that even a piano *ballade*, a ballad in no language, would be taken as nationalist. The explanation lies in the distinctive nature of nationalism in Chopin's Europe.

The nationalism that inspired the Polish Insurrection[19] and revolutions elsewhere in Europe around 1830 was not so successful at freeing nations as it was at redefining Europe. For centuries European political and spiritual authorities had been identified with, and legitimized by, the common high culture of Europe: the heritage of language, religion, and thought from the ancient world. This had been the culture that mattered in the politics of nations. As a result, the political role of culture, within Europe, had been to unite nations more than to distinguish them, to transcend boundaries more than to fix them.

The nationalism that emerged as a force around 1830, giving "special political significance" to the word "nationality" for the first time, as historian J. P. T. Bury writes,[20] was revolutionary in its rejection of the traditional cultural politics. The new nationalism made the culture of the common people the politically significant culture. Indeed, it made nationality an attribute of popular culture. Herder had declared that nationality could not come into existence without language;[21] throughout Europe, but especially in Central and Eastern Europe, where the Herder tradition was most influential, nations were now defined by the language of the common people.[22] To put this principle into effect entailed redrawing the map of Europe, uniting some groups of people and separating others. In the years around 1830, little of that sort was accomplished, except for the creation of Belgium and Greece as new nations. But the principle had already taken hold, inspiring some redrawing of the map later in the nineteenth century and much more at the end of World War I. Very late in the twentieth century the principle of defining nations by language is still fueling separatist movements in many parts of Europe.

Paradoxically, there was no conflict between nineteenth-century nationalism and the idea of Europe as a cultural entity. In fact, that nationalism was itself a product of European culture as a whole, not an idea developed differently in each nation. It was a uniform, international nationalism. Each nation needed the same things: its own language, folklore, and music, its own government and institutions, its own flag and anthem.[23] National movements proceeded by keeping in touch with and abreast of one another, as much as by turning inward. Giuseppe Mazzini's attempt to coordinate national movements under the banner of Young Europe failed as a revolutionary project but represented a truth about those movements: that they were European in consciousness.

Just as this nationalism was not itself national, so too it was not the idea of the common people, although it defined itself by reference to them. Resting on an ideal of traditional, national, vernacular cultures, it was actually part of a new European high culture. The paradox was not easy to sustain. How could a uniform nationalism be promoted in every European nation unless the traditional cultures of the many nations provided uniform material, unless, that is, the various traditional national cultures somehow constituted a unified European culture of their own? Nationalist Europe needed to define from below a previously unknown Europe in which it could see itself reflected.

The search for such a definition underlies a number of the great achievements of European scholarship in the first half of the nineteenth century. It is discernible in Franz Bopp's demonstration of the common Indo-European roots of apparently disparate European languages. It is discernible as well in the evolving study of folklore. Giuseppe Cocchiara, in his magisterial *History of Folklore in Europe*, sums up the achievement of this period, under the heading "The Romantic Lesson of Folklore," as follows:

> The open competition...to save the most intimate aspects of each people and each nation was certainly promoted by nationalistic sentiment; but wasn't this sentiment the product of a common national and European mission? The concept of Europe, the *new* concept of Europe, was empty and meaningless when not imbedded in the cultural and moral forces that folklore had helped to create. Folklore compelled scholars to think in German, English, Russian, or some other language, but at the same time it also compelled them, to use Madame de Staël's phrase, to "think in European."[24]

Folklorists "thinking in European" had made the ballad a European literary and musical genre by 1830. Herder had been thinking in European when he brought together folk poetry, including many ballads, from all over Europe in a single collection, published in 1778-79. And it was thinking in European that brought nationalist poet-scholars of many countries, inspired by the British ballads they read in Herder's translations or by the imitation folk poetry of Ossian (based on Gaelic traditions but written by James Macpherson [1736-1796]), to believe they would find songs of the same kind and value sung by peasants in remote regions of their own countries. Beginning with the publication of *Des Knaben Wunderhorn* by Arnim and Brentano in 1806-08, these folklorists had soon published texts of folk songs, many of which could be called ballads, from nearly every European country.[25]

By Chopin's time, then, ballad-collecting was providing material for an anthropology of Europe. That material had not yet been examined systematically. Not until the twentieth century would scholars divide the genre into regional and national categories,[26] argue about which songs could be called "ballads" and which could not,[27] or consider the tunes as well as the texts as evidence of a unified European culture.[28] But already by Chopin's time, some of the most celebrated ballad texts, along with the term "ballad" itself, had been made known throughout Europe, and the people of almost every European nation were discovering that they possessed a national repertory of ballads, a possession that distinctively expressed their national history and character at the same time that it bound them to a European culture too deep to be touched by political circumstance.

In the 1830s, then, when Chopin was trying in his music to embody his nationalist sentiments and yet to win the acclaim of a European public indifferent to the fate of Poland and to Polish culture, he would have been attracted to the ballad precisely because it had nationalist significance for nearly every European nation. His piano *ballade* could derive in some way from Polish tradition and still appeal to an international public ignorant of that tradition, so long as it somehow evoked the ballad as Europeans generally knew it. As Carl Dahlhaus writes of nineteenth-century composers in general, "nationalism was seen as a means, not a hindrance, to universality."[29]

But a ballad without words would not be easy to achieve. Since ballads offered composers little to depict but the characters' words, the usual methods of musical representation were not well suited to the genre. Nonetheless, music scholars long maintained that Chopin worked by exactly those usual methods in his Ballades, recreating in each one the moods, the setting, the episodes of a single story and then keeping his model secret, as Weber is supposed to have done with his *Konzertstück* for piano and orchestra. A number of writers even proposed what they considered the likely models—usually poems chosen from the ballads of Mickiewicz—for each of Chopin's four Ballades.[30] However, the only evidence ever cited in support of these proposals was Robert Schumann's review of the second Ballade, reporting a conversation in which Chopin told him that he had been "inspired to write his Ballades by some poems of Mickiewicz."[31] That much-cited sentence hardly sustains the meaning long derived from it. Nothing in it suggests a connection between any one poem and either of the Ballades Chopin had so far written, and it is hard to imagine that Schumann would have expressed himself so generally if his conversation with Chopin had convinced him of a more precise connection. Since World War II most scholars have rejected the idea that any Chopin Ballade is modeled on the particulars of any one poem. Zofia Lissa, for instance, writes: "In none of the four Chopin Ballades do we find detailed illustration, which in any case he notoriously and self-consciously opposed."[32]

As we have seen, Chopin's European ambitions would not have been served by modeling his first Ballade on the particulars of one little-known and unidentified Polish ballad. That is not to say that he could not have been thinking especially of one poem. But if he was to remind people throughout Europe of the ballads they knew, arousing in them some of the same feelings those ballads could arouse, he would have to draw on features that were common to many ballads. In effect, he would have to base his Ballade on an analysis of the ballad as a genre.

That approach would make his task doubly difficult. Already, in choosing to appeal to the nationalism of all Europeans through a piano work, Chopin had to discover how to evoke, without language, a nationalism defined by language. In choosing to make the work a ballad without words, he had to discover how to compose, without words, a story in which the main action was the speaking of words. Then, by making this work an instrumental version of the ballad as a genre, rather than a version of Mickiewicz's "Świtezianka" or Bürger's "Lenore" or the folk ballad "Edward," he was choosing to rely on the common features of many ballads to give his work the power and definition of a single ballad. The object of Part I in the present study is to discover the process by which Chopin accomplished this complicated task, first in one Ballade and then in three others.

His approach to the task, in the simplest terms, was to treat the ballad as both story and song. If he had treated the song as if it were not a story—if, in other words, his imitation had focused on the distinctive melodies of certain folk ballads—he would have evoked nationalism in its exotic rather than its broadly European sense. If he had treated the story as if it were not a song— if, that is, he had sought to represent the action of ballad stories without recalling the sound of ballad-telling—he would have denied himself the means to suggest in sound the crucial element of that action: the sounding of words. For it is in that element that the ballad unites song and story, telling and told. It is the sounding word, with its power to sing a song, to spin a tale, and to enact a complete drama, all in a short span of time, that defines the ballad. Accordingly, it is the various forms of the sounding word in ballads that constituted Chopin's analysis of the genre.

Even when a ballad appears as a printed text—as words abstracted from a song or as a poem composed for publication—the words have a distinctive sound, derived from their idiosyncratic diction and refrains as well as from their short lines and stanzas, that brings alive the idea that they might be sung. This sound, or tone, which can be embodied in a melody of a certain form, is the easiest thing to recognize—or to mock—about ballads. But equally characteristic is the narrative form that the sounding word takes. This form—a narrative carried by the voices of narrator and characters pressing often abruptly in on one another—gives the story its typically "precipitous" development.[33] At the same time, ballad plots characteristically follow a pattern determined, in a literal sense, by a particular form of the sounding word: a portentous voice, whether that of the narrator or that of a character, is answered in the end by a voice of retribution. This plot pattern, though it is the formal feature most clearly connected to the characteristic psychological power of ballads, is the feature that has been analyzed least by folklorists and literary scholars. No matter what ballads Chopin knew and analyzed, he would have found, in some version, all these formal features, which provided the material for a rich and vivid musical image of the ballad. Just what ballad repertories may have entered into Chopin's analysis and just what forms of the sounding word they presented to him are the subjects of Chapter 2 in Part I.

Chapter 3 in Part I treats the musical means by which Chopin embodied these forms in wordless music. His first Ballade, recognized at once by Fink as novel in genre, has long been celebrated for its originality in musical form and technique as well. What have not been clearly recognized are the equally original programmatic principles that gave rise to those musical innovations: the principle of modeling a programmatic composition on a genre of poems or songs rather than on a single work and the principle of imitating the forms of the sounding word in that genre. A curious result is that the musical innovations too have been relegated to a shadowy place in the history of music. Chopin's Ballades have been as much admired as any music of their period, but Chopin receives little credit for pioneering techniques of thematic transformation in those works. In contrast, Berlioz and Liszt, who were developing techniques akin to Chopin's during the same period, advertised their programmatic principles, in effect explaining the techniques, and their names are the ones consistently associated with those techniques.

Likewise, there have been many studies of musical form in the Chopin Ballades. These studies constitute a debate on whether the forms of most of the Ballades are adaptations of sonata form or whether each is a unique, unprecedented form. But until form is considered in the light of programmatic principles, that question, which continues to fascinate musical analysts more than half a century after it was posed, cannot be decided. When the Ballades are considered in that light—which has recently been brought to bear on the study of form in other nineteenth-century music[34]— not only can the sonata-form question be decided, but all four of Chopin's Ballades can be described, for the first time, in terms of a single formal model.

The legacy of Chopin's Ballades is, in part, the genre that he initiated, the *ballade*, or ballad without words. It was enormously popular with composers for the rest of the nineteenth century, and some of that appeal persists to this day. A substantial, if not definitive, catalog of piano *ballades* published in the nineteenth century lists about four hundred works.[35] Many *ballades* have also been written for orchestra and for various chamber groups, though not so many as for piano. Altogether this legacy, despite its bulk, seems at first glance incoherent, even irrelevant to Chopin's Ballades. Out of those hundreds of piano *ballades*, less than a dozen—works by Liszt, Brahms, Grieg, and Fauré—have stayed in the concert repertory, and not one of those proceeds from anything like the same conception of the genre as Chopin's. The orchestral *ballades*—of which only *The Sorcerer's Apprentice* by Dukas remains in the standard repertory—have even less connection to Chopin's Ballades. The Dukas, like most orchestral *ballades*, does exactly what Chopin's Ballades do not—it relates in music the story of a particular poetic ballad—and, like many of them, it does not use the term "*ballade*" even as a subtitle. The well-known piano and orchestral *ballades* present no common form, no common line of descent from Chopin's Ballades. Consequently, when Maurice Brown used essentially this small repertory to define the genre for *The New Grove Dictionary*, the diversity of the works permitted him to say no more than: "an instrumental (normally piano) piece in a narrative style."[36] It may seem that Chopin's ideas led to something of a dead end.

Actually, the opposite is true. The tremendous outpouring of instrumental *ballades* after Chopin can be credited in no small part to his Ballades, which gave an inspiring demonstration that the ballad would work as a model for instrumental music. His idea of creating narrative program music out of the structures of sounding words was taken up by other composers even outside the genre of the instrumental *ballade*. Later composers of *ballades* also used many of the specific techniques of representation and of musical process that he developed in his Ballades. If hardly any subsequent works embodied the same conjunction of narrative and musical ideas as his Ballades—an astonishingly powerful conjunction of original ideas that for his purposes demanded each other—nevertheless almost all of those ideas were developed separately, in the service of other purposes, by later composers of *ballades*. Chopin's Ballades inspired not imitation, but further exploration of ways to express the significance of the ballad in music without words.

Part II of the present study surveys piano *ballades* composed from the time of Chopin through World War I. While Chopin treated his model—the ballad—as both story and song, later composers of piano *ballades* concentrated on either the story or the song, creating several distinct traditions of piano *ballades* in the four decades up to 1880 (the period covered by Chapters 4 to 6). Chapter 4 deals with *ballades* that represent ballad narration in the abstract, as Chopin had done, or the story of a particular poetic ballad; Liszt's two major piano *ballades* are considered in this chapter. Chapters 5 and 6 deal with *ballades* inspired by the ballad as song: Chapter 5 covers lyrical or character-piece *ballades*, including the Brahms Ballades, Op. 10, and Chapter 6 covers *ballades* that are sets of variations on folk songs, including the Grieg Ballade, Op. 24. In the four decades after 1880 (the period covered by Chapter 7), new explorations were made both within the same traditions and—as in the case of Fauré's Ballade, Op. 19—outside them, and the genre was extended to the medium of chamber music.

Part III of the study covers orchestral *ballades* through World War I. In this medium there was only one leading tradition: narrative *ballades* that represent the story of a particular poetic model. The study of this tradition affords the pleasures of discovering the literary ballads of several countries, of studying little-known masterpieces by Franck, Tchaikovsky, Dvořák, and Janáček as well as the most popular work of Dukas, and of observing how the tradition of representing the sounding word in *ballades* could be combined with the Lisztian tradition of the symphonic poem. Part IV gives a brief survey of *ballades* since World War I, a time when, despite much hostility to program music among composers, the *ballade* has not only flourished in many forms, but has developed in an important new medium: the concerto *ballade*.

The inclusion of orchestral *ballades* and twentieth-century *ballades* in this study—two bodies of compositions that have not generally been considered as successors to the Chopin Ballades—make the genre initiated by Chopin seem, paradoxically, more coherent than when only nineteenth-century piano *ballades* are considered. In fact, when those parts of the repertory are included, it emerges for the first time that as a tradition of musical narration, the instrumental *ballade*, with its distinctive concept of representing the structures of the sounding word, has been the most important alternative to the program symphony and symphonic poem throughout the nineteenth and twentieth centuries.

CHAPTER 2

The Ballad as Narrative Model for Chopin

To deduce Chopin's idea of what ballads were like, given his reluctance to say which ballads he had in mind or what about them he imitated in his piano *ballades*,[1] means to take into account all the different kinds of things he knew or could have known as ballads—folk-song texts and their tunes as well as contemporary poems and their settings as accompanied songs. Such a procedure would emphasize universal and presumably essential features of the genre over incidental features of a single repertory or single example. To follow this procedure requires faith that ballads produced in utterly different ages, in different countries and languages, and in different media may nevertheless all reflect a coherent formative idea. But just such a faith can be presumed on the part of a composer who, at a time of awakening nationalist fervor throughout Europe, trusted the entire European musical public to comprehend four of his most ambitious piano compositions under the unprecedented and unexplained title of "Ballade."

Ballad scholarship, an enormous tradition to which poets, folklorists, literary scholars, musicologists, anthropologists, and others have contributed, has sought to establish the common elements among different kinds and traditions of ballads; but at the same time, it has revealed obstacles to considering ballads of all kinds as a single genre. It is not hard, for instance, to find resemblances between folk ballads, stripped of their melodies and printed as poems, and the literary ballads of eighteenth- and nineteenth-century poets; the literary ballads were, after all, imitations of those folk-ballad texts. But twentieth-century scholars have come more and more to perceive the effects of oral methods of composition in the structures of folk ballads; thus they leave it open to question how successfully poets in the modern era, composing with pen and paper, have imitated those structures, or whether they have changed the significance of those structures in imitating them.[2]

31

Scholars have found ballads to be united by a common narrative method, but when they consider the themes of ballad stories, they come up with no common thematic type, but rather several types.[3] In studies of ballad music, the main obstacle to defining the genre has been that whatever is found in ballad music can also be found elsewhere. The rhythms and modes and melody-types of folk ballads turn out to be common in other folk music.[4] Similarly, composers of German *Lieder* in the late eighteenth and early nineteenth centuries generally followed the same musical models—strophic, operatic, or a synthesis of the two—whether they were setting literary ballads or other kinds of texts.[5]

Some scholars have offered definitions of ballads in general terms, but without pretending to comprehend everything from the texts of thirteenth-century Danish *viser* to the music Carl Loewe set to poems by his contemporaries. Chopin did not have to cover such a wide field, either. The task he set himself was to compose wordless music which would somehow remind a varied audience of ballads. He did not have to set down his conception of the ballad in general terms, nor did he have to specify the limits of the repertory he was using as his model. But his task created its own difficulty. He had chosen to represent by music alone a genre in which everything depended on the words. Without its archaic tone of voice, without what Gerould called its "objective" narrative technique, above all without its story, a ballad was just another folk tune, and Chopin's Ballades are obviously no mere echoes of folk tunes. His task was to reconstruct the language of ballads as music, to find, that is, what verbal features of ballads he could make recognizable in equivalent musical forms. The purpose of the present chapter, then, is not simply to discover the essential features of the ballads that Chopin could have had in mind, but also to consider which of those features lent themselves best to representation by purely musical means.

The first step is to ask what ballads Chopin knew or could have known. The answer can be given only in terms of likelihoods. His correspondence and other biographical materials do not establish what particular ballads he read or heard. It can be taken for granted that he knew the Mickiewicz ballads (presumably the "certain poems of Mickiewicz" that Schumann reported as his inspiration): hardly any literary event during Chopin's youth caused a greater stir in Poland than the publication of Mickiewicz's *Ballads and Romances* in 1822.[6] At the same time, other Polish poets of Chopin's generation wrote ballads, and he is hardly less likely to have read those.[7] He could also have read ballads by foreign poets, including Bürger, Goethe, Schiller, Uhland, Heine, Hugo, and Scott, either in translation or in the original languages, before composing his first Ballade; by the time he composed his latter three Ballades, he knew Mickiewicz, Hugo, and Heine personally.

Poëme Symphonique

Musique de

Les Parties d'Orchestre net : 40 f
Transcription pour Piano à Quatre mains net : 4

Paris, LÉON GRUS, Editeur, Place Saint August...

PLATE 2. Title-page of Franck's *Le Chasseur maudit* (1882).

It is another question what ballads he knew as songs. He could have heard Polish folk ballads sung in Poland when he was young, and he might have seen transcriptions of folk-ballad melodies from Poland or elsewhere, though the collecting of folk-song melodies was just beginning in most countries. By 1847 he had seen and commented on transcriptions and arrangements by Oskar Kolberg (1814–1890), the great nineteenth-century collector of Polish folk music and folklore, but Kolberg had not begun his collecting and publishing projects by the time Chopin wrote his first Ballade. He surely knew the strophic settings of Polish literary ballads, for singer with piano accompaniment, by Polish composers including his teacher, Joseph Elsner (1769–1854), and the pianist Maria Szymanowska (1789–1831).[8] He may also have known some more complex musical settings of literary ballads by German composers like Schubert and Loewe, though it is doubtful that he could have seen Loewe's settings of the Mickiewicz ballads (1835) before composing his own first Ballade.

These repertories stretch from Scotland to Poland and from Chopin's day back through centuries, yet they have many interconnections. Modern scholars recognize, for instance, the influence of both Slavic folklore and modern Western European poets on Mickiewicz's ballads.[9] For that matter, Chopin, educated in lively literary surroundings, would have appreciated the international character of ballad-writing in his day, just as he would have understood that folk ballads in one way or another stood behind the literary ballads of his contemporaries.[10]

He could not, however, have understood the relationships among various repertories of folk ballads in the same way modern scholars do. Those scholars, drawing on more than a century of collecting and classifying in every corner of Europe, have divided European balladry into several regional traditions, of which the richest is the "Nordic," consisting of the ballads of Scandinavia, Britain, and Germany. William Entwistle, the scholar who has mapped these traditions most painstakingly, includes Poland and its neighbors in the Nordic tradition, though not all scholars agree.[11]

Thus, as it happens, this Nordic tradition comprehends precisely those repertories of folk ballads that Chopin could have known and that influenced the modern poets whose ballads he could have known. As a result, what today seem the peculiarities of one major branch of folk balladry, and of its literary offshoots, would have seemed to Chopin universal characteristics of the genre. For the purpose of considering what idea of ballads Chopin could have formed, it is fortunate that an accident of history allows us to limit our survey to one portion of the field of study, a portion that has already been defined and analyzed as a single tradition.

"The ballads of the north and center of Europe belong to one vast store of methods and themes,"[12] writes Entwistle. His definition of a Nordic tradition of ballads rests on analysis of themes and of prosody. From the themes and prosody of Nordic folk ballads came the themes and prosody of

Romantic literary ballads, and even the melodic rhythms of Romantic ballad *Lieder*. These two subjects, then, both lead to Chopin's doorstep.

BALLAD THEMES: THE BALLAD PROCESS

By "theme" Entwistle means a particular story that appears in many different versions throughout the Nordic region. Other scholars use the term to indicate something closer to a narrative motif that appears within a story.[13] Neither a list of stories nor a list of motifs seems useful for the study of Chopin's Ballades, since he never indicated that he had worked with a particular story in mind and since his method was not to illustrate the particulars of a story. More useful would be a single model of the theme or form of ballad stories in general, to see if anything in Chopin's Ballades conformed to that model. It is surprising that no such model has ever been published.

The one description of folk ballads that Chopin is sure to have known—the description given by Mickiewicz in the preface to his *Ballads and Romances* of 1822—hardly constitutes a narrative model, though it presents several ideas that might have interested Chopin:

> The British ballad is a tale based on the events of common life or on the annals of chivalry; it is usually enlivened by marvels from the romantic world; it is sung in a melancholy tone; it is dignified in style, simple and natural in expression.[14]

In the twentieth century it has been a central concern of literary scholars to propose general theories of narrative, along with narrative models of specific genres, ever since Vladimir Propp's *Morphology of the Folktale* (1928)[15] made its influence felt. Unfortunately, such a model has not been proposed about the ballad, and other models—such as A. J. Greimas's model of the myth[16]—or general theories that are nonetheless devised principally around the novel or other written genres—such as the theories of Gérard Genette or Paul Ricoeur[17]—are not particularly suited to the ballad. At the same time, the long and rich tradition of ballad study by folklorists has, as noted above, focused on specific narrative motifs rather than on general narrative structure.

It is possible, nevertheless, to propose—for the purpose of the present study—a general narrative model of the ballad, applicable to the genre as Chopin and his audiences knew it, by drawing to some extent on both the observations of generations of ballad scholars and the narratological methods of recent literary scholars and by defining a repertory that does not include all ballads, or even all Nordic ballads, but only those Nordic folk ballads that eighteenth- and nineteenth-century scholars and poets chose to anthologize and imitate,[18] along with their imitations of them.

This model might be described as the model of the *ballad process*, to choose a word associated with judicial forms of action, for a ballad typically tells the story of someone who provokes and receives justice. The process, in the first place, centers on one character, though that character interacts with others who are necessary to the process. In the terms proposed by Claude Bremond, whose *Logique du récit* is the recent theory of narrative most applicable to the ballad,[19] the process is marked by a single change in that principal character's role: from being an *agent*, an actor, she or he turns into a *patient*, someone passive or acted upon. The process, furthermore, is self-contained: it is initiated by an act of the principal character and completed by the response to that act. In ballads of our special repertory, the same kind of act and the same kind of response appear over and over again: the act is a defiance of the nature of things, and the response is a reckoning for that act of defiance. Though a ballad displays human, and sometimes supernatural, conflicts and cross-purposes, it also has about it the simple, irresistible force of a natural process, the process of nature absorbing a disturbance. The ballad process, as can be seen already, has something in common with the typical processes of tragedy and epic, two genres to which ballads have long been compared.[20]

The act of defiance that begins the process carries within itself the seed of its failure. It may be the denial of a truth that will inevitably assert itself: the refusal of the father in Goethe's "The Elf-King" ("Erlkönig") to admit to himself that his sick child is about to die; the refusal of the protagonist in "Edward" (a ballad from Percy's *Reliques of Ancient English Poetry*) to admit to his mother that he has killed his father. In Bürger's "Lenore" it is the protagonist's refusal to believe that her lover has been killed in battle. In other cases the act is a defiance of social relationships that have the force of nature. These cases include murders within families, such as the murder of the knight by his wife in Mickiewicz's "The Lilies" ("Lilije"); usurpations of power, as when the protagonist of Goethe's "The Sorcerer's Apprentice" ("Der Zauberlehrling") uses his master's powers before he has learned to control them; and the unnatural marriage of an old man and a young woman in Mickiewicz's "Czaty" ("Sentry," also translated as "Guards"). The act may also be the violation of a solemn word or taboo. Innumerable ballad lovers, like the protagonists of Mickiewicz's "Świtezianka" ("The Nymph of Lake Świteź") and "The Little Fish" ("Rybka"), pledge their fidelity to a woman (in both those cases a nymph of Lake Świteź) and then break their word. In the ballad "Chevy Chace" from Percy's *Reliques*, the battle is joined when Douglas vows to prevent Percy from doing what he has vowed to do. Taboos are violated in Mickiewicz's "Świteź" ("Lake Świteź") when the lake is dredged and in Coleridge's "The Rime of the Ancient Mariner" when the albatross is killed.

It is not necessary for the act of defiance actually to open the ballad; the ballad may open with activity consequent to an act of defiance that has already been committed. In "Czaty" the old soldier has already married his young wife when the ballad opens; the first event is his sudden arrival at home one night to discover that his wife is not in her bed. Sometimes the act of defiance, committed before the opening of the ballad, is held secret until the end, when it triggers the reckoning: at the end of Goethe's "Ballad [of the Banished and Returning Count]," the "children hear with delight" that the minstrel who has been entertaining them is their grandfather, the deposed ruler of the land. In the case of "Edward," the protagonist's withholding of the truth, which is the overarching act of defiance in the story, conceals two other acts of defiance: his murder of his father and his mother's instigating role in the murder. In fact, "Edward" is not exceptional in the complexity of its process. In "Chevy Chace" the role of protagonist is divided between the two enemies; in "Świteź" one ballad process is framed by another.

The acts of defiance are presented portentously in ballads, making it clear that a reckoning will ensue, if not always so clear what form it will take. It is obvious when Edward is first questioned about his sword dripping with blood that he will be discovered to have killed someone other than his hawk, but the double revelation nevertheless comes as a shock. "Edward" exemplifies two forms of reckoning found in ballads: revelation (by Edward of his own crime and his mother's part in it) and retribution (when he banishes himself from his home and family and curses his mother). Fatal retribution may seem to be the typical reckoning in ballads: the old soldier in "Czaty," about to kill his young wife for having a lover her own age, is himself killed by his would-be accomplice; characters who kill their lovers by spurning them (the protagonists in the Percy ballads "Barbara Allen" and "Fair Margaret and Sweet William") themselves die of broken hearts. But some return or restoration, often of a happy sort, is also common. The minstrel in Goethe's "Ballad" is restored to his family and his power. The master sorcerer in "The Sorcerer's Apprentice" restores his authority by restoring order. But returns, especially by the dead in ghostly form, do not always bring happy results: it spells doom for the protagonists of "Lenore" and "The Lilies" when their lovers reappear as ghosts.

There is no suggestion in these stories that the reckoning is unjust or simply unlucky. It is a given that whatever the protagonist defies—authority, truth, the laws of family and social life, the nature of things—is immutable and unyielding. The world is presented in ballads as an unchanging and unchangeable place, and that view of the world could be considered simply to reflect the beliefs of people living in the isolated, peasant "ballad society" where folk ballads developed.[21] But then why would Romantic poets, conscious of revolutions all around them and self-consciously revolutionary in their art, choose to cultivate a genre governed by a process that demonstrates the futility of all revolt?

Perhaps it is misleading to read ballads as a simple reflection of anyone's belief about the nature of the world. Instead, the ballad process can be understood as an artistic structure used by poets in very different times and places to articulate a psychological structure that is not peculiar to one kind of society: the structure of a guilty conscience. Then the unyielding world that is pictured in ballads, rather than being interpreted as someone's picture of the real world, can be interpreted as the image that a guilty conscience constructs to represent the forces defining its guilt. Guilt, in other words, is defined in ballads by a structure of powerlessness. In terms of the ballad process, the act of defiance is an image of human will; that human will is rendered powerless by forces implicit in the act of defiance and explicit in the act of reckoning. The guilty conscience that lies behind the story of a ballad does not belong to any character within the story; rather, the story as a whole is shaped as if it were the figment of a guilty conscience. In "The Elf-King," for example, the ballad process gives form to the feelings of inadequacy that trouble the consciences of parents. The father's refusal to acknowledge the presence of the Elf-King is the image of a parent's will to protect his or her child from harm, but the more he denies what he obviously sees—and he does so three times—the more undeniable he makes the danger seem, while at the same time he demonstrates that he has no power against it other than denial. A ballad story has the structure of a proof that a guilty conscience gives itself of its own guilt: the exercise of will is determined by the very forces that render the will powerless.

I have said that the guilty conscience does not belong to any character within a ballad story. In some ballads the protagonist develops a guilty conscience that mirrors the conscience that shapes the ballad, but the two are not the same. They do not even overlap. Barbara Allen and Sweet William and other protagonists who belatedly discover the depth of their lovers' devotion all develop guilty consciences, as does the sorcerer's apprentice. But in those cases the guilt structure of the ballad is already manifest in the act of defiance, which the protagonist commits before developing a guilty conscience. In "The Sorcerer's Apprentice," in fact, the character's guilty conscience has no effect at all on the ballad process: repentance achieves nothing for the apprentice, and the reckoning is entirely the work of the master sorcerer. Other ballad protagonists, meanwhile, show no signs of a guilty conscience. Some, including two Bürger characters—the wild huntsman (in the poem of that name) and Lenore—spurn repentance. Others, like the old soldier of "Czaty," meet their reckoning so abruptly that they have no chance to indicate the state of their conscience.

All in all, it can hardly be said that the working of the characters' consciences is a decisive factor in ballads. Once ballad protagonists commit their acts of defiance, they become powerless, passive (in Bremond's sense), and their fates are decided for them; they do not redeem themselves by repenting. It might even be imagined that Romantic poets turned to the ballad in part because it offered an alternative to sentimental genres in which the crucial action was the movement of characters' consciences toward repentance and redemption.

The guilty conscience that seems to shape a ballad is like the conscience that shapes a dream: it has no location or identity within the story it shapes, though it may at times project something of itself onto one character. But the conscience that shapes a dream belongs to the dreamer, while the conscience that shapes a ballad is a structure identified with no person or character. It does not belong to the narrator of the ballad, that figure whose impassivity and impersonality are taken as defining characteristics of the genre.[22] The narrator is a structure with a voice at least, especially since when a ballad is sung the narrator may seem identified with the performer. But the impersonal nature of the narration contributes to the ballad's immediate— that is, unmediated—effect on listeners. Likewise, the guilty-conscience structure also gives the story a direct, unmediated connection to its listeners. Invisible and inaudible, it preys on the listeners' feelings by shaping a story in such a way that it corresponds to their own potential for guilt.

It may be true of folklore generally, as Alan Dundes writes, that it "tends to cluster around times of anxiety be it in the individual life cycle or the calendrical cycle of the community."[23] In that case a particular genre of folklore may address a particular kind of anxiety. If fairy tales address the anxieties attendant on the transition from childhood to adulthood,[24] ballads address the anxieties of adults coming to realize the limits of their powers as adults. They are for the most part stories of young adults, and they play on many of the limitations that young adults come to feel: doubts about their worthiness as lovers ("Barbara Allen," "Fair Margaret and Sweet William," "The Elf-King's Daughter" [Herder's reworking of a Danish folk ballad], "Lenore," "The Lilies," "Świtezianka"), fear of being disloyal to one's family ("Edward" and the Percy ballad "Lord Thomas and Fair Annet"), men's doubts about their authority and strength ("Świteź," "Chevy Chace," and the Percy ballad "Sir Patrick Spence"), feelings of inadequacy by parents ("The Elf-King," Mickiewicz's "Father's Return" ["Powrót taty"]). Occasionally there are stories that play on the powerlessness of youth ("The Sorcerer's Apprentice") or old age ("Czaty"). In all these stories the protagonist's powerlessness must be established for the reckoning to be achieved, even if that reckoning is a happy one. Listeners are taught in effect to accept their own powerlessness in order to dispose of their anxieties, like dreamers who cannot be free of a dream until they accept some reality of their waking lives.

Thus, insofar as ballads express a widely held belief, it is a belief about the need to accept one's powerlessness rather than about the unchangeable nature of the world. The psychological nature of the message is emphasized in the Romantic literary ballads more than in the folk ballads because the literary ballads present their stories more explicitly in the guise of dreams. "Lenore," for instance, begins with the protagonist's dreams—

> Up leaped Lenore at break of day
> Out of oppressing dreams—

and concludes with her midnight ride. In fact, literary ballads are so consistently set at night that that detail alone becomes a signal that the reader or listener is entering a dream world. "The Elf-King" begins, "Who rides so late through night and wind?" The Mickiewicz ballads "Świteź" and "Świtezianka" are both set in moonlight by the same lake. In "Czaty" the old soldier discovers his wife in a nighttime tryst, while "The Lilies" begins with the wife murdering her husband and burying him by night—"All is dark and cold and foul"—and then rushing to a hermit's cottage, "like a vampire of the night," to confess.[25] It is as if these poets wanted to preclude any but a psychological interpretation of their ballads.

The ballad process, then, is a formal structure that is suited to a certain kind of theme. This connection of structure and theme had profound implications for the genesis of the instrumental *ballade*. It provided Chopin with a way to capture the thematic nature of ballads in notes, without resorting to the tone-painting of a single ballad story. Sensing the connection between structure and theme in the ballads he knew, he could, by creating a musical form equivalent to the formal structure of the ballad process, plot the typical theme of a ballad by musical means. He would thus be representing what was most universal in the ballad theme rather than what was peculiar, and perhaps incidental, to a single ballad story.

The structure of the ballad process could in fact be translated into the musical language of Chopin's day. It is the structure of a story told in one sweep; a structure in which the initial event contains the seed of the conclusion and the conclusion answers directly to the initial event; a structure in which a force that is defied or denied or suppressed at the beginning provides tension throughout and asserts itself at the end with more power than anything that has gone before; a structure that may be resolved by a return or restoration, but without things ending the way they began. Taken as a model for an instrumental *ballade*, this structure would influence the formation, reworking, and reappearance of musical material, the relationships of the principal sections, and the overall rhythm and resolution of the work. The structure of the ballad process, in other words, could have a decisive influence on the basic form and character of the instrumental *ballade*.

At the same time, this structure does not provide a particularly rich model. Taken alone it may suggest the thematic character of ballads, but it can hardly give a clear sense of the tone, the idiosyncrasies, the world of ballads. Toward that end, Chopin could consider some of the qualities that attach to the ballad process. Noticing the dreamlike quality of ballads, for instance, he could make his instrumental *ballade* dreamlike, either by imitating structural features of dreams or, following the lead of the Romantic ballad poets, by setting his music in a nocturnal mode. Beyond that, he would need to consider other features of the ballads he knew, features of language and melody, prosody and narration, matters of structure and tone, whether related to the ballad process or not.

BALLAD PROSODY AND MELODY

The structure of lines and stanzas in a ballad is unrelated to the ballad process. It is a song structure, not a narrative structure. But like the ballad process, it is an element of uniformity among all the kinds of ballads Chopin and his audience knew—songs and poems, folk and modern. Furthermore, imitating the line and stanza structure of ballads in the musical phrasing of his Ballades was a way for Chopin to remind listeners of the particular effect made by a story when it unfolds in a strophic song.

Nordic folk ballads, unlike those of certain other parts of Europe, are stanzaic, according to William Entwistle and other authorities; they have no standard stanza length or rhyme scheme, though four-line stanzas are common in several of the national traditions.[26] The lines of verse are measured by accent rather than syllable; ballad authorities describe it as typical for ballads to have four accents to a line, or lines of four accents alternating with lines of three accents. All of these common structures are illustrated by a stanza from one version of the British folk ballad "Barbara Allen":

It was in and about the Martinmas time,
When the green leaves were a-falling,
That Sir John Graeme in the west country
Fell in love with Barbara Allen.[27]

According to Bertrand Bronson, the prosody of folk ballads is bound up with their melodies. In the Nordic tradition, the melody repeats with each stanza of text. The phrases of the melody tend to have four beats each, even when the verse alternates lines of four and three accents, as in the example given above. There is no standard musical meter or mode or pattern of phrase repetition, though some favorite patterns occur within national repertories.[28] In view of Chopin's use of 6/4 or 6/8 meters in all four of his Ballades, it is worth noting that while rhythms with triple division are common throughout Polish folk song, there is no standard rhythm for Polish ballads or even for the melodies associated with a single text.[29]

Poetic imitations of Nordic ballads follow the prosody of their models in a general way. Poetic ballads are overwhelmingly stanzaic, with stanzas of various lengths. Mickiewicz favored a four-line stanza, while some German and Polish poets experimented with longer stanzas.[30] Some poets also experimented with accentual lines; others, without abandoning the literary habit of writing syllabic lines, experimented with complex meters that suggested the uneven rhythms of accentual verse. Mickiewicz did so in two ballads ("Czaty" and "The Three Brothers Budrys"), apparently following the example of Walter Scott.[31]

Composers who set literary ballads as accompanied songs took many different approaches to the line and stanza structures of their texts. Polish composers like Elsner and Szymanowska followed the model of folk song in writing strictly stanzaic settings—the same melody to each stanza of text. They also followed the example of Polish folk song in favoring no one meter for their ballad settings. These composers may have exerted a greater influence on Chopin's Ballades by the very act of setting Polish literary ballads (including a ballad of Mickiewicz, set by Szymanowska) to music than by any particular musical feature of their settings. Other composers, especially German ones, who set literary ballads in more complex musical structures may have suggested more to him about how to coordinate the representation of song structure with the representation of narrative progression in his wordless Ballades.

In the vocal ballads of Chopin's German contemporaries, such as Loewe and Schumann, stanzaic musical setting is blended with more dramatic structure, often in such a way that a repeating musical stanza is established and then gradually yields to contrasting music. An example of this technique is the opening of Loewe's setting of the Mickiewicz ballad "Świtezianka" ("Das Switesmädchen"), written and published in 1835, the same year that Chopin's first Ballade went to press. The example is not chosen to suggest that this particular ballad influenced Chopin in the conception and composition of his first Ballade—a virtual impossibility—or even of his three later ones, but to show how composers of ballad *Lieder* were modifying stanza structures into large, dramatic musical forms at exactly the time when Chopin was constructing themes of his wordless Ballades on the same principle. It seems to the present author that these ballad *Lieder* are closer in construction to the principal themes of Chopin's Ballades than any other contemporary music and that that similarity reflects a shared conception of how to represent sung narrative in musical form, whether Chopin knew any of those ballad *Lieder* or came to the conception independently.[32]

In Loewe's "Świtezianka" the first melodic stanza presents the first stanza of text, then it yields to a different melodic stanza (but in the same rhythm as the first) for the second stanza of text (see Example 2-1). For the next two stanzas of text, Loewe returns to the first melodic stanza, but gives it a different outcome each time (see Example 2-2). Then, with the following two stanzas of text, the motivic material and the keys of the first two musical stanzas converge (see Example 2-3).

Later the song changes abruptly in meter, tempo, key, and melodic material (see Example 2-4). In fact, the variety of musical meters Loewe puts to the same poetic meter in this song demonstrates that Chopin's choice of 6/4 or 6/8 meters in his Ballades was not required by the poetic meter of any particular poetic model. But the opening melodic stanza, with its alternatives, repetitions, and alterations, begins the song with at least a suggestion of the relentless stanzaic repetitions of Nordic folk ballads, at the same time allowing for some musical adaptation to the different words and voices of the successive stanzas of text, in preparation for still more dramatic adaptations to the text later in the song.

Example 2-1. Loewe, "Świtezianka," Op. 51, No. 6, mm. 1–21.

Example 2-2. Loewe, "Świtezianka," Op. 51, No. 6, mm. 25–46.

Example 2-3. Loewe, "Świtezianka," Op. 51, No. 6, mm. 50–66.

Example 2-4. Loewe, "Świtezianka," Op. 51, No. 6, mm. 126–30 (*above*) and mm. 197–201 (*below*).

It would have been difficult for Chopin to evoke ballads at all in wordless music without using some kind of repeating stanzalike structure. Because he was not setting words, it would have been unthinkable for him to repeat any musical "stanza" more than once without changing it. But a suggestion of stanzaic repetition, yielding now subtly, now dramatically to musical change, proved as suitable to the piano *ballade* as to the ballad *Lied*, as the next chapter will show.

NARRATIVE TECHNIQUES

The Nordic folk-ballad tradition, which as we have seen lies behind all the ballad repertories that Chopin is likely to have known, is defined by Entwistle (and to some extent by other scholars) on the basis of its uniformity of themes and prosody. But the Nordic ballad and its modern offshoots are unified in other ways as well, though these happen not to distinguish the Nordic from other traditions of European balladry. Chief among these unifying threads are a number of narrative techniques, long recognized as telltale marks of ballads, some of which, according to modern scholars, ballads owe to their musical nature and to the conditions of creation, performance, and transmission in an unlettered culture. Eighteenth- and nineteenth-century poets, though working in conditions very different from those of medieval balladeers, nevertheless noticed these narrative techniques as sources of the ballad's distinctive character (distinct, that is, from that of most poetry produced by lettered cultures) and adopted those techniques in their ballad imitations.

One of these techniques is a characteristic abruptness in the unfolding of events; ballads are, as Albert Friedman puts it, "precipitously developed." His description of folk-ballad openings—"characteristically a ballad breaks into its story at a moment when the train of action is decisively pointed toward the catastrophe"[33]—applies equally to the opening of Mickiewicz's "Czaty":

> From the bower of the garden, the Governor, breathless,
> Runs into the castle in anger and fear;
> In a hurry he pulls back his young wife's bed-curtain,
> He stares, and he trembles, for no one is there![34]

A special case of this technique, termed "leaping and lingering" by Francis Gummere at the turn of this century,[35] is described more recently by Alan Bold as a "tendency to initiate a sudden act and then to linger hypnotically after the event."[36] As early as 1821, Goethe described something of the same sort, and even as part of an oral process of re-creation, when he wrote of the ballad singer "changing the form at will, either to hurry to the end or to delay it considerably."[37]

Other narrative techniques characteristic of ballads have to do with patterning rather than with pacing. The patterns that have been most intensively studied in folk-ballad construction are two-part, three-part, and symmetrical patterns. Study of such patterns has relied from the start on the belief that folk narrative is composed by methods different from those of written narrative. (This belief is explicit in the classic essay "Epic Laws of Folk Narrative" [1909] by the Danish folklorist Axel Olrik.[38]) In *The Ballad and the Folk* (1972), an intensive study of these patterns within one singer's ballad repertory, David Buchan argues that facility with these patterns allowed ballad singers to create new versions of their songs at each performance.[39] Other scholars have rejected Buchan's claims that the patterns were used to create new versions, but they have disputed neither his descriptions of the structural patterns themselves nor the more general idea of associating those patterns with the exigencies of ballad performance and transmission.[40] Poets imitating ballads in the eighteenth and nineteenth centuries often seized on these patterns, not because they needed them as folk-ballad singers did, but because the patterns would help give their poems a tone reminiscent of medieval minstrelsy in general and of ballads in particular.

All these patterns, as Buchan describes them,[41] can be found at various levels, from lines and stanzas to the scenes and groups of scenes that make up an entire ballad. They can be the patterns by which characters or speeches are distributed in scenes, or by which the narrator's lines are distinguished from those of the characters. "The habit," as Buchan calls it, "of thinking in balances, antitheses, appositions and parallelisms" can produce two-part structures within a stanza—

> Lord John stood in his stable-door,
> Said he was bound to ride;
> Burd Ellen stood in her bowr-door,
> Said she'd rin by his side.[42]—

or it can produce the ballad process, the polar thematic structure of the whole ballad.[43]

If ballads present contrast usually in two-part structures, they make repetitions usually in three-part structures.[44] The repetition found in these three-part structures is seldom exact repetition; more often it is repetition with variation each time, or, as Gummere named it, "incremental repetition."[45] "In a number of ballads," Buchan writes, "the central action is developed in three steps."[46] Though he is writing about a repertory of Scottish folk ballads, there is no better example of this structure than the central dialogue of Goethe's "The Elf-King," which turns through a cycle of speeches—the boy calling on his father to notice the Elf-King, the father refusing, and the Elf-King appealing to the boy—three times, more alarmingly each time.

Finally, there are symmetrical structures. These may consist simply of "frames"—complementary stanzas that open and close a ballad or portion of a ballad—such as the opening and closing stanzas of "The Elf-King," the narrator's stanzas, both using the same image of the father riding with his child in his arms. But Buchan also points out cases of more elaborate symmetrical, or chiastic, structure, in which all the stanzas are paired around a crucial central point or stanza.[47] Equally elaborate symmetrical structures have been pointed out in modern ballad imitations, such as Keats's "La Belle Dame sans merci."[48]

Many such structures, of various sorts and sizes, can be found overlapping and in succession within a single ballad. The song or poem derives much of its overall narrative rhythm from the way these structures are coordinated. Earl Wasserman writes of "the intricate interlacing of the meaningfully balanced patterns" in "La Belle Dame sans merci."[49] Buchan writes of two sorts of coordination in folk ballads, the "concurrent," in which various structures "coincide to produce well-defined scenes," and the "contrapuntal," in which "the structures themselves weave through one another in a kind of counterpoint."[50] His use of the term "counterpoint" is a sign that the structural patterns he analyzes, like the techniques of "precipitous development," are in effect musical features of ballad narration. They are the techniques of narrative rhythm, of contrast, repetition, and variation, of development and return. Needless to say, composers of ballad *Lieder*, whenever they set a ballad in any form other than pure stanzaic repetition, seized on these narrative features of their texts and highlighted them with analogous musical techniques.[51]

For Chopin the whole enterprise of making the idea of the ballad recognizable in wordless music depended heavily on these "musical" techniques of ballad narration. The ballad process was crucial for the overall shape and tone of the work. The idea of the repeating stanza was necessary, but did not distinguish ballads from many other kinds of poems and songs. What most immediately identifies his works as *ballades* are his musical analogues to the narrative techniques and structures that poets of his day, without describing them quite as scholars do today, nevertheless seized on and imitated, precisely for their identifying power, for their contribution to what Albert Friedman calls the "distinctive otherness" of ballads.[52] In turn, as the next chapter shows, Chopin's analogues to these techniques largely determined the distinctive musical form he gave to his Ballades.

CHAPTER 3

Chopin's *Ballade* Form

Ballade: a name adopted by Chopin for four pieces of pianoforte music (op. 23, 38, 47, 52) which, however brilliant or beautiful, have no peculiar form or character of their own, beyond being written in triple time, and to which the name seems to be no more specially applicable than that of 'Sonnet' is to the pieces which Liszt and others have written under that name.

> —George Grove, *A Dictionary of Music and Musicians*, 1879

In order to make confusion worse confounded, the term Ballad has been employed in purely instrumental music, and now we have pianoforte, violin, and orchestral ballads, etc., which half belong to programme-music, inasmuch as composers in writing them would seem to have something definite in their mind. It would, however, be extremely difficult to show in what way Chopin's *Ballades* are entitled to that name.

> —Hugo Riemann, *Musik-Lexikon*, 1882; English translation by J. S. Shedlock, 1893

In previous studies of the Chopin Ballades, genre—that is, Chopin's narrative model—has generally been treated as separate from musical form. Some writers have concentrated on one subject and disregarded the other. Günther Wagner, addressing both, asserts that they are unrelated: "That Chopin resorts to sonata form in three of his four Ballades has absolutely nothing to do with the ballad element in these works."[1] Wagner's strong language places him in opposition to a few earlier writers who argued that a different Mickiewicz poem had dictated the form of each of the Chopin Ballades. One of these writers, James Huneker, suggested in 1900 that "the true narrative tone" was in Chopin's first Ballade,[2] and thereby provided a useful notion to the very writers who rejected his idea that Chopin worked from specific poetic models. By acknowledging the "true narrative tone" or "legendary atmosphere" in a Chopin Ballade, those writers could allow for

49

the work's title while regarding musical form as a separate matter. Hugo Leichtentritt adopted this strategy in a study (published in 1921-22) that is the earliest comprehensive analysis of Chopin's music: "With his four Ballades Chopin developed a new genre of piano music, characterized not so much by new formal ideas as by new moods, legendary in character."[3]

At the same time, he and later analysts have suggested that in one sense the musical form of Chopin's Ballades does correspond to the nature of ballad texts. Reaching back to Goethe's pronouncement that ballads succinctly unite the epic, lyric, and dramatic modes of poetry,[4] they have found an analogy to this union of poetic modes in Chopin's union of diverse musical styles or "tones" in his Ballades.[5] Wagner has painstakingly demonstrated the means by which Chopin evokes these poetic modes.[6] Carl Dahlhaus, in an account published in 1980, has gone so far as to identify the balancing of epic, lyric, and dramatic "tones" as the structural problem that Chopin set out to solve in his first Ballade—and the probable explanation for the title "Ballade."[7] While Dahlhaus, like Wagner, continues the tradition begun by Huneker of identifying a generic ballad "tone" in Chopin's Ballades, he breaks with the tradition by associating that generic tone with the musical form of the works and by suggesting that the musical form can be considered to be modeled on the ballad as a genre, rather than any single ballad text.[8]

This suggestion seems to me crucial for understanding Chopin's *ballade* form; I find more questionable the assertion by Dahlhaus that poetic tone is essential to Chopin's conception of the ballad and to his *ballade* form. That assertion seems reasonable while one is studying the first Ballade: an epic tone, for example, can surely be heard in its opening measures, which Dahlhaus calls "immediately recognizable as a musical rendering of a 'narrative posture.' "[9] But in the later Chopin Ballades that tone is never again sounded so strikingly, and it is far harder to discern a structure of epic, lyric, and dramatic tones. For that matter Goethe, in the passage that Dahlhaus relies on, describes Epic, Lyric, and Dramatic as modes characteristic of ballads, but he does not define the ballad by means of those modes.[10] In the literary ballads that he and his contemporaries wrote, no one feature or structure is definitive. Rather, as it is argued in the previous chapter, those literary ballads share with traditional Nordic ballads a particular network of narrative structures, and it is that common network that allowed the designation "ballad" to be applied to the two repertories. If, as Dahlhaus asserts, Chopin's Ballades owe their musical form in a serious way to the example of the ballad genre, it is reasonable to expect to find in those works a network of musical structures analogous to the narrative structures that Chopin's contemporaries identified with the ballad.

The purpose of the present chapter is to examine the musical structures that govern the Chopin Ballades and consider to what extent they correspond to the identifying narrative structures of the ballad genre. Because these musical structures are of different types, it is necessary to examine the

Ballades in different ways. One part of the chapter, consequently, is devoted to overall rhythms, a second to themes and transformations of themes, and a third to structures of overall organization. A final section is devoted to a question that has interested many analysts: how applicable sonata form is to the Chopin Ballades. Here that question will be considered both on its own terms and in relation to the question of how Chopin followed the narrative structures of his ballad model.

In the interest of clarity, this chapter will focus on a single Ballade: the first, in G minor, Op. 23. Besides being the work in which Chopin created this new genre of instrumental music, it is the Chopin Ballade that has inspired the largest and most interesting body of analytical literature. It may also be the most popular of Chopin's four Ballades with performers and audiences, though music scholars by no means universally rate it as the finest of the four. Even in the company of the later ones, the first Ballade deserves Schumann's description of it as one of Chopin's "wildest, most characteristic compositions."[11]

At every stage of this account, analysis of the first Ballade is supplemented by comparison to the other three, to show what features of the first Ballade were, or became, essential to his conception of the genre and to allow, in the end, a general appraisal of musical form in his Ballades. That is not to say that only the unvarying features of Chopin's Ballades (like their sextuple rhythms) can be considered essential to his conception. On the contrary, one can hardly measure the achievement and legacy of these works without first discovering what sorts of variety Chopin allowed himself in the genre.

OVERALL RHYTHMS

"The emphasis is on a single line of action precipitously developed," writes Albert Friedman about folk ballads.[12] It is significant that each of the Chopin Ballades is a single, uninterrupted work, not a suite of movements, not a set of variations or episodes or vignettes. This is significant because narrative instrumental music before Chopin had characteristically been episodic in form. Some of this music, such as the battle pieces for keyboard or Kuhnau's "Biblical Narratives," had consisted of many tiny, more or less independent episodes. In other cases, such as *The Four Seasons* of Vivaldi, composers had adapted a traditional sequence of movements to their stories. But even within traditional, multi-movement forms, a narrative program tended (as in Beethoven's *Pastoral Symphony* or Berlioz's *Symphonie fantastique*) to proliferate the movements.

Closer to Chopin's Ballades than any of these works is Weber's narrative *Konzertstück* for piano and orchestra (published in 1823), a work in several contrasting movements, but one in which "a single line of action" is suggested by the elaborate transitional passages that smooth the way from one movement to the next. Even the *Konzertstück*, however, is episodic in nature. By comparison to that work, one sees how remarkable the Chopin Ballades were among narrative instrumental works of their time, remarkable especially in their adherence to the "single line of action, precipitously developed" of their ballad model. Each of the Ballades unfolds in a single, unified musical form. Within that form, moreover, each develops a powerful rhythmic momentum of a sort that is almost unprecedented in earlier music. In that way these works answer to Bertrand Bronson's description of the ballad as a story "carried forward by its own momentum, leaping ahead or lingering over some details but never back-tracking."[13]

The momentum of the first Ballade carries through two striking changes of tempo, meter, and material, one at the end of a short introduction (m. 8)[14] and the other shortly before the end (m. 208). In a sense, Chopin maintains momentum through these changes by effecting the change during, rather than after, a cadence (see Example 3-1). In another sense, these changes themselves contribute to the momentum, to the increasingly "precipitous," or headlong, pace of action. They carry the musical action from an opening that is marked "slow" and "heavy," through a long section marked "moderate" in speed, to a "precipitous" ending in cut time, marked "fast and fiery."

Example 3-1. Chopin, first Ballade, Op. 23, mm. 6-9 (*above*) and mm. 206-08 (*below*).

Even within the long central section, Chopin uses rhythmic changes to increase the momentum. There are musical equivalents to what ballad scholars call the technique of "leaping and lingering," including passages marked as increasing in speed and others marked as held back. But these are arranged so that the tempo is generally faster in the second half of the section

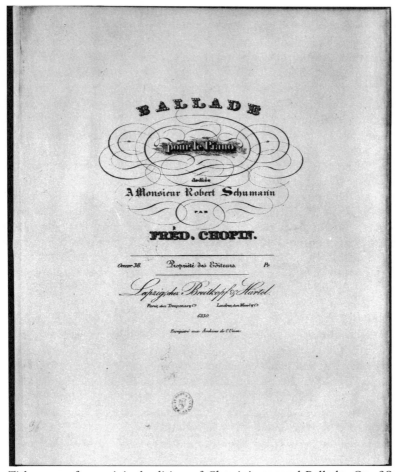

Title-page of an original edition of Chopin's second Ballade, Op. 38
(Leipzig: Breitkopf & Härtel, 1840). By permission of the Houghton
Library, Harvard University.

than in the first. At the same time, a steady flow of eighth notes is the rule in
the second half of the section, whereas in the first half the steadiest
movement is in quarter notes. The change is especially noticeable when the
most tranquil theme in the Ballade (*Meno mosso*, m. 68), accompanied in the
first half by long waves of quarter notes, returns in the second half on shorter
waves of eighth notes (m. 166). The two major rhythmic changes that begin
and end this section are thus absorbed into a general pattern of increasing
momentum from beginning to end of the Ballade.

All four of Chopin's Ballades are uninterrupted spans of music with
patterns of increasing momentum leading to a climax at the end. Only the
first has meter changes, but in the second (in F major, Op. 38) the two

alternating main themes are as highly contrasted in tempo and character as any two sections of the first Ballade. In fact, when the first theme cadences and dies away after its first hearing, the jolting entry of the second theme may suggest that the work has more than "a single line of action." But the continuous alternation of the two eventually binds them together, leaving room for Chopin to build power and momentum up to the end. The later two Chopin Ballades (in A-flat major, Op. 47, and F minor, Op. 52) have much less internal contrast of tempo or thematic character and rely more on a gradually increasing flow of notes per measure to build the momentum from beginning to end.

By different combinations of means, all four Ballades gain gradually in momentum from beginning to end. This effect of continuously increasing pace—which helps give the impression of a ballad story being carried irresistibly from its act of defiance to its reckoning—is a far rarer effect in music, whether by Chopin or anyone else, than that of a single, abrupt increase of momentum, as at a finale or coda or final variation. Ever-increasing momentum is a far more distinctive feature of Chopin's Ballades than that more obvious rhythmic feature, the sextuple meter that is common to all of them.

With the exception of the first seven measures and last three pages of the first Ballade, the four Ballades are all set in sextuple meter, each measure made of two large beats triply subdivided. Whether Chopin was drawn to that meter in the first place by ballads he knew (ballad tunes or ballad texts), it is impossible to say. In the folk-ballad tunes and ballad *Lieder* he could have known, sextuple rhythm is common, but it is not the only common rhythm. Furthermore, one poetic meter, as the previous chapter demonstrated, can be accommodated by melodies in several musical meters. For that matter, the different melodies within any one Chopin Ballade, though they have the same musical meter, would fit very different poetic lines.

In any case, the sextuple rhythm produces the same rhythmic character in all four Ballades. At or near the beginning of each Ballade, that rhythm is heard at a moderate speed and with a quiet lilt, giving the music the character—stronger at some times than at others—of a nocturne or a barcarolle. In each of the Ballades there are prominent accompaniments in the undulating arpeggiated rhythms typical of Chopin's nocturnes, as well as melodies in the barcarolle rhythm (|♪ᵧ♪♪ᵧ♪| mixed with |♫♫ ♩ ♪|) also typical of Chopin's nocturnes. In the first Ballade, both the "nocturne" accompaniment and the "barcarolle" melody are heard in one theme (see Example 3-2),[15] while in the third Ballade Chopin gives various sophisticated wrinkles to the "barcarolle" rhythm (see Example 3-3).

In none of Chopin's Ballades is this nocturne-barcarolle rhythm pervasive, the way it is in his Barcarolle, Op. 60, or in certain of his nocturnes, but it never yields to anything altogether different. Like the march

Example 3-2. Chopin, first Ballade, Op. 23, mm. 68–71.

Example 3-3. Chopin, third Ballade, Op. 47, mm. 9–12 (*above*) and mm. 52–55 (*below*).

rhythm in the Fantasy, Op. 49, or the polonaise rhythm in the Polonaise-Fantasy, Op. 61, this rhythm seems to have, in its absence as well as in its presence, a determining influence on the whole work. It brings to the Ballades the poetic associations of nocturnes and barcarolles: night, dream, love, and song. In other words, it gives Chopin's musical ballads the same nocturnal setting that Romantic poets gave their poetic ballads, with the same implication that the story has a dreamlike structure. In Chopin's Ballades the sextuple meter is consistently connected with nocturne-barcarolle rhythms and thus with the consistently dreamlike nature of ballad stories, rather than with ballad verse meters or musical meters, which are not consistent. In the course of writing his Ballades, Chopin came to rely entirely on sextuple meter, almost entirely at moderate tempo. To that extent he gave his new genre its own characteristic ballad rhythm. From the start he used that rhythm to characterize the ballad story as dreamlike; as he proceeded he accommodated to the same rhythm all the contrasts needed to unfold that story from beginning to end.

THEMES AND TRANSFORMATIONS

Chopin's method of unfolding his story was as new as his genre. He did not depict events or objects directly, as program music of the eighteenth century had often done, nor did he present them filtered through a single consciousness, as Berlioz had done in his *Symphonie fantastique* and *Harold in Italy*. But he did unfold a story; he did not abstract themes from a story and resolve them in his own musical synthesis, as Beethoven had done in overtures and as Liszt was to do in symphonic poems. He unfolded his story as a ballad unfolds it: through a complex of voices, the voice of a narrator and the voices of the characters. His method was to chart the unfolding rather than to depict what is unfolded; it was to represent the story as a structure of utterances. Writers who have commented on "the true narrative tone" in Chopin's Ballades have found the key to his method, but there is more to that method than tone.

In a Chopin Ballade a voice is always sounding. Almost always there is a melody, generally accompanied, but seldom in a way that diverts attention from the melody. Only occasionally do two simultaneous voices balance each other in importance. The melodies are generally plain enough that urgent sentences could be delivered in them. Rarely do they dissolve into the florid passages that are common in Chopin's nocturnes and concertos. Much more common than florid passages are virtuosic passages; in fact, virtuosic passages constitute a crucial structural element in the Ballades.[16] But those passages are almost all what Gerald Abraham has called "significant line"—"something between melody and passagework"[17]—rather than merely ornamental passages or filler. Even these passages have a restricted place in the Ballades. By far the largest part of each of the Ballades—a remarkable portion, given what dramatic works they are—is taken up by plain melodies, often in long, repetitive stretches, with the simplest of accompaniments. These are melodies that recall Mickiewicz's description of ballads as "dignified in style, simple and natural in expression." Paradoxically, it is through their plainness that one hears the play of voices in these melodies. They come to life when performers play them as ballad singers sing, not making each line expressive in a different way, but letting the song speak for itself. Thinking about the second Ballade, Schumann wrote that a poet could find words to put to Chopin's music.[18]

An unaccompanied voice is the first thing heard in each of the Ballades. In the first and fourth Ballades, which have discrete introductions, the melody is heard before the accompaniment both in the introduction and in the primary theme that follows. In the second Ballade, the melody takes a moment to find its voice, as it were, before beginning. The third Ballade begins with a single note from which both melody and accompaniment emerge.

The first Ballade is unique in being introduced by a voice that never reappears as such. That voice is also unique in all the Ballades for the ambiguity of its character. Its unaccompanied octaves give the purest possible pianistic representation of a human voice, but as the line rises through octave after octave, its range establishes that no ordinary singing voice is being represented (see Example 3-4). That point is made with particular force on pianos of the sort that Chopin played, since those pianos have a more distinctive timbre in each octave than modern pianos.

Example 3-4. Chopin, first Ballade, Op. 23, mm. 1–7.

The voice of this introduction seems in some respects not yet to have taken up its song: it finds its key only gradually (starting from what turns out to be a Neapolitan-sixth harmony in the tonic key), and it proceeds haltingly. The introduction is not, it turns out, in the meter and tempo of the song itself. It is plausible both for some writers to insist on the narrative tone of this introduction ("a musical rendering of a 'narrative posture,' " as Carl Dahlhaus calls it) and for others to describe it as separate from, prior to, the telling of the tale (Arthur Hedley writes: "It is as though the bard were collecting his thoughts and hesitating before beginning his tale").[19] On the other hand, something of the subject or matter of the story is present in the introduction. A number of writers have agreed with Frederick Niecks that the final chord of the introduction, the chord with the dissonant E-flat (m. 7), strikes "the emotional key-note of the whole poem."[20] In fact, not just that chord, but all the elements of the introduction reappear in the final section (*Presto con fuoco*), though reconstituted and rearranged, so that they assume a new voice.

Though Chopin did not use such an opening passage in his later Ballades, he carried over to them at least one idea from this introduction. The texture of unaccompanied octaves is important in them all, though it is not heard often and never for a stretch as long as the five measures at the beginning of the first Ballade. It is heard characteristically at beginnings or endings of a Ballade or section of a Ballade. The second and fourth Ballades begin, like the first, with unaccompanied octaves, but for only a couple of beats, repeating the same notes—not enough to establish a distinct voice. Elsewhere in the later Ballades unaccompanied octaves, in the bass register, make endings or connections (see Example 3-5).

Example 3-5. Chopin, third Ballade, Op. 47, mm. 47–50 (*above*), and fourth Ballade, Op. 52, mm. 37–38 (*below*).

These few, brief, bare-sounding utterances at pivotal moments suggest a voice that is always present in the narration but seldom needs to assert itself, exactly like the "impersonal" narrative voice that scholars identify as characteristic of the ballad, "letting the action unfold itself in event and speech... with little comment or intrusion of personal bias."[21] Later composers of piano *ballades* likewise evoked the narrative voice of a sung ballad with bare-octave textures and repeating-note melodies.

At the "emotional key-note" chord, the introduction to the first Ballade halts for the last time; that chord, a i$^6_4$ chord with an E-flat borrowed from the previous chord, is then resolved by the first phrase of a new theme (see Example 3-6).

Example 3-6. Chopin, first Ballade, Op. 23, mm. 6–9.

Title-page of an original edition of Chopin's third Ballade, Op. 47 (Paris: Schlesinger, 1841). By permission of the Houghton Library, Harvard University.

With this winding phrase the telling of the tale begins. The phrase acts as a cadence to the introduction, but its rhythm makes a complete break with the introduction. The new theme is as relentless and repetitive in its phrasing as the introduction is halting and changeable. The winding phrase is played seven times, in alternate measures, note-for-note the same almost every time. Each time, it is answered by a two-note phrase, which is less fixed. The pairing of these two phrases is relentlessly repeated, producing an extraordinary pattern of musical "lines," identical to each other in length and rhythm, like the lines of many ballads. From the structure of paired phrases Chopin produces a pattern of incremental repetition: the first (winding) phrase of each line repeats, while the second (two-note) phrase changes each time in pitch and harmonization.

After four lines, a larger-scale repetition begins: the fifth line (middle of m. 16 to middle of m. 18) is exactly the same as the first (mm. 8–10), the sixth (mm. 18–20) exactly the same as the second (mm. 10–12; see Example 3-7).

Example 3-7. Chopin, first Ballade, Op. 23, mm. 8–20.

Chopin is working not only with the idea of ballad lines, but also with that of ballad stanzas, in their most common, four-line form. He no sooner finishes the four bleakly repetitive lines of the first stanza (middle of m. 16) than he begins a second stanza exactly the way the first began. This extraordinary structure of unrelieved repetitions within unrelieved repetitions gives listeners no specific hint of the contents of a story;

instead, it powerfully focuses attention on the ballad as a structure or medium of telling; it perfectly represents the impersonal voice of a ballad narrator.

This theme would never be mistaken for an actual ballad tune. It is far too repetitive for a folk tune. Instead it schematically represents structures both of ballad tunes and of ballad texts. In its incremental repetition, for instance, it corresponds to a typical verbal, not musical, structure of ballads, a structure that can be observed in the following stanza from a British folk ballad:

> There's no room at my head, Margret,
> There's no room at my feet:
> There's no room at my side, Margret,
> My coffin's made so meet.
> —"Sweet William's Ghost"

The theme has a strong musical character, but not like that of any ballad tune. The relentlessly repeating phrases give the theme a portentous character that in a folk ballad would be imparted by the words, not the tune.

At the beginning of this theme, the structure of lines is clearly articulated. Already in the first stanza, though, the fourth line proceeds out of the third without the usual articulation (m. 14). In the middle of the next stanza the whole structure of two-measure lines and four-line stanzas yields to a more continuous structure. At an unexpected secondary dominant chord (m. 21; see Example 3-8), the theme changes to new material; only the rhythm of the accompaniment stays the same.

Short, regular, repetitious lines give way to an undivided, highly dramatic span of thirteen measures (mm. 21-34; see Example 3-8). The bass, no longer restricted to offbeats, assumes a voice of its own that complements the soprano voice. By using two voices, Chopin suggests a dialogue of characters, or at least a scene of interaction between two characters. He has switched, in other words, from the narrator's voice to the characters' voices and therefore from representing the structure of a narrative frame to representing a structure of words spoken within a particular scene.

The dialogue dissolves at a deceptive cadence (mm. 31-32), a joltingly deceptive cadence that steps backwards from its dominant chord. The melody stops, for the first time since the theme began, and then resumes in a coloratura mode that is completely alien to the melodies heard so far. With melodic and harmonic abruptness—one of the "leaps" of ballad "leaping and lingering"—the two-character scene that was barely sketched suddenly dissolves. The measure of coloratura leads smoothly to two measures (mm. 34-35) again in the tone of the main theme, providing the G-minor cadence that was postponed just before by the deceptive

Example 3-8. Chopin, first Ballade, Op. 23, mm. 20-35.

cadence. With this cadence the thirteen measures of short, regular "lines" (mm. 8-21) and the thirteen measures of continuous phrasing (mm. 21-34) become bound together as a single theme. The narrative stanzas that gave way to a dramatic, two-character scene seem to return momentarily, to be completed. Even the "emotional key-note" chord is heard again here (beginning of m. 35), this time resolved more smoothly, its previously threatening tone suppressed for now.

This primary theme, now completed, can be compared in its form to the first section of Loewe's "Świtezianka" (or other contemporaneous ballad *Lieder*): it establishes a repeating musical stanza, then slips away from that structure—now subtly, now completely—but then returns to it. Chopin's theme, however, is both more compact and more complex than the comparable passage of Loewe. Because he has no words to work with, Chopin has to represent the opening of both song and story by means of musical structure. The first part of the theme, with its line-and-stanza structure, emphasizes the song and its singer; it gives sounding form to the role of the narrator. The second part of the theme, by breaking the structure of lines and stanzas and then restoring it, emphasizes the action that emerges from the narrative, the story within the song. At this point Chopin substitutes a dialogue structure for the line-and-stanza structure, suggesting one of those moments in ballads when the narrator lets the characters speak for themselves. The first part of the theme, then, presents what belongs to the ballad as a whole—the verse structure and the narrator's voice; the second part presents what is particular to the first scene of the action. Later in this Ballade the first part of the theme keeps returning, while the second part never does.

Before going on to discover how the entire Ballade unfolds from this theme, we might turn briefly to Chopin's other Ballades and consider the comparable themes as successors to the one just examined. The primary themes of the four Ballades form an extraordinary family, all clearly related, though each goes its own way. The line-and-stanza structure of the theme in the first Ballade is also found in the themes of the second and fourth, but with differences.

In the second Ballade the stanza structure never gives way; instead, the initial eight-measure stanza is heard twice, it is followed by a different eight-measure stanza, which modulates to the dominant, and that is followed by the initial stanza again. This time the stanza is diverted, as the theme of the first Ballade was, just at its cadence (m. 33; see Example 3-9). But in this case the melody is extended, not dissolved. The theme is not uneventful, but its narrative structure is simple: it unfolds in a single voice.[22]

Example 3-9. Chopin, second Ballade, Op. 38, mm. 31-33.

On the other hand, the theme of the fourth Ballade (beginning at m. 8) is like that of the first but even more complex. The lines are longer (four measures instead of two), and the stanza is subtler in construction: its third line (mm. 17-18) is a half-line, and the breaths between lines vary in length. When the stanza is repeated (at m. 23), it is slightly ornamented. This second stanza gives way, as does the second stanza in the first Ballade, to a two-voice structure that stands apart from the narrating stanza structure (mm. 37-45). Also as in the first Ballade, the stanza structure returns, but here it is not simply to round things out: after the rounding-out, the initial stanza begins again (m. 58). This time (in fact, beginning in the rounding-out, at m. 50) a counterpoint in sixteenth notes, largely in the alto register, is heard against the eighth notes of the melody. The two-voice texture, which earlier in this theme—as in the theme of the first Ballade—stood apart from the stanza structure of the narrative voice, has now been combined with that structure. With this stanza the theme ends, without being rounded off by a cadence; instead, it veers out of its stanza structure and breaks off (m. 71).[23] But by then it has already gone on twice as long as the theme of the first Ballade and suggested a ballad opening of unusually complex narrative structure.

Family resemblance is weakest in the primary theme of the third Ballade. In fact, that Ballade is in general the one least like the other three. Its primary theme does not have the same kind of line-and-stanza structure. It does have four-measure lines, but they come in couplets, not quatrains. To be sure, there are some folk and literary ballads in couplets: Herder's "The Elf-King's Daughter," an adaptation of a Danish folk ballad, is an example. But Chopin does not establish his couplet structure here the way he establishes the stanza structure in his other Ballades: by immediate repetition of the music. He does, however, maintain a structure of couplets—paired, four-measure lines—for a page, then breaks out of that structure into more continuous material (mm. 25–36), and then returns to his initial couplet, which, as in the second Ballade, he extends before allowing it to settle into a cadence. In the sense that this theme uses a stanza structure not only to suggest the verse form and musical form of a ballad, but also to suggest the narration of a scene in a ballad, it has a strong relation to the primary themes of the other Chopin Ballades.

The relationships among themes are amazingly uniform from one Chopin Ballade to another. The primary theme of each Ballade is the only one to embody the stanza structure of a ballad; that theme is primary not only in its position, but in its controlling presence, like that of a narrator who is always present even when speaking through the characters of the story. The primary theme always returns, though at nothing like its original length (except in the second Ballade, where the return, mm. 82–139, is longer and more dramatic than the original theme). At its first appearance it sets up the ballad process, establishing itself by insistent repetition as an irrepressible subject that needs to be reckoned with. Later in the work the theme reasserts itself, sometimes creeping in as in a dream (first Ballade, mm. 93–94 and again at mm. 193–94; fourth Ballade, m. 121 and mm. 134–35). In the third Ballade (mm. 189–92) and the fourth (m. 91) it even creeps into another theme. In the first Ballade (mm. 194*ff.*), the second (mm. 156*ff.*), and the third (mm. 189*ff.*), a reassertion of the primary theme ushers in the finale, in effect the reckoning of the ballad process.

The Ballades are rich in other themes; the sounding word takes many forms as it sings its tale. But the theme types are few, and the same few appear in all the Ballades. There is always a secondary theme, a second theme that returns (in the third Ballade there is also a tertiary theme, at m. 116, that returns at m. 231). Like the primary themes, these themes have second parts or extensions when they first appear (in the first Ballade, mm. 82-90). Those extensions, like the comparable parts of the primary themes, give the thematic complex the particularity of a scene in the story; they are omitted when the secondary theme returns (except in the first Ballade, where the secondary theme returns once without its extension, at m. 106, and once with it, at m. 166).

The secondary theme is always presented in a secondary key. In fact, the presentation of two important themes in different keys provides crucial evidence in any argument for sonata-form analysis of the Ballades. In its thematic contrast of primary and secondary themes, the first Ballade, as Carl Dahlhaus nicely puts it, "distantly recalls" a sonata movement.[24] But the degree of contrast between the themes varies considerably from one Ballade to another, and only in the third Ballade is a secondary theme "recapitulated" in the tonic key (at m. 146; the tertiary theme is heard only in the tonic key, at mm. 116 and 231). In any case, the secondary theme constitutes a counterpoise to the primary theme: if the primary theme principally represents the narrating function, the secondary theme serves more of a characterizing function, suggesting one of the forces at conflict in a story (in the first Ballade it could be a love relationship, in the second Ballade some destructive force).

In addition to the primary and secondary themes are themes that never return. These are generally short themes, often more dancelike than songlike, sometimes sequential in construction, and usually leading without a break into passagework (in the first Ballade, mm. 36-44 and mm. 138-154). Such themes are like passages in ballad texts that have little to do with the forces at conflict and everything to do with advancing the action, passages that give the action its "precipitous development," passages in which each stanza "finds the action one step farther on."[25] These musical themes suggest a quickening of action by their active rhythms, their rising sequences, their increasing volume or speed. They can be called "precipitating" themes.

All that remains is passagework. The passagework is most "significant"—to use Gerald Abraham's term—in the finales of the Ballades, where it responds to earlier themes, often by transforming their material almost beyond recognition. But there is passagework throughout the Ballades; except in the finales, its importance lies primarily in its transitional function, for the types of transition in the Chopin Ballades are as distinctive as the types of theme.

The types of transition are suggested in the ballad scholar's phrase "leaping and lingering." In the Chopin Ballades there are "leaping" transitions, where one theme simply breaks off and the next leaps in (see Example 3-10). "Lingering" transitions come either in the form of long dominant preparations (in the first Ballade the second "precipitating" theme is introduced by twelve measures of passagework in dominant harmony, mm. 126-37) or in passages of rest after a cadence (third Ballade, mm. 50-52; fourth Ballade, m. 134).

Example 3-10. Chopin, second Ballade, Op. 38, mm. 138-40.

Some of Chopin's most wonderful transitions—and the ones that come closest to what Gerould calls the "startling effects"[26] of ballad narration—are those that leap after lingering. In the first Ballade, for instance, the passagework after the first "precipitating" theme creates a flurry of activity without moving away from the G-minor cadence with which it began (mm. 44-56). At this point the music becomes mysterious (see Example 3-11).

Example 3-11. Chopin, first Ballade, Op. 23, mm. 56-69.

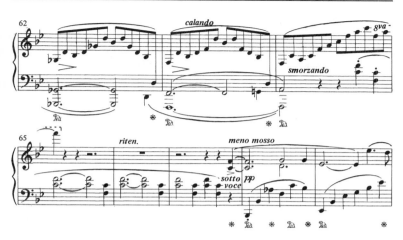

Chord changes slow down, but the harmony, hesitantly, begins to move. An augmented triad (m. 59) that at first slips back smoothly to G minor (m. 60) is heard again (m. 62); this time it slips just as smoothly to the dominant of B-flat, effecting the first modulation of the piece. The eighth notes that have given this whole passage its feeling of activity clear away, and the music lingers, for three measures of quiet horn call, on its dominant harmony. The "leap" occurs in the resolution of that harmony: a B-flat, entering in the bass on the downbeat (m. 68) while the F and C are still sounding above, is itself turned into a dominant by the A-flat two notes later. This B-flat leaps ahead, then, not only by superimposing itself on its own dominant, but by changing the outcome of the modulation that has been so lingeringly prepared. André Gide praises this "stroke" that "alters the landscape," comparing it to "a surprising foreshortening by [Baudelaire]."[27] The transition in effect produces the theme that it introduces, since the new theme continues to be pushed forward by the same "foreshortening": the same "lingering" of the right hand produces the same dissonances against the "leaping ahead" of the bass (see Example 3-12).

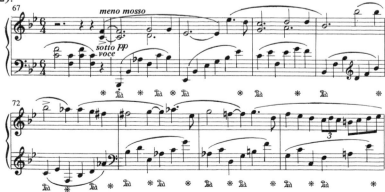

Example 3-12. Chopin, first Ballade, Op. 23, mm. 67-75.

Transitions in the Chopin Ballades, as this example illustrates, may consist largely of passagework. The voice heard at these times seems therefore to be extending and elaborating, controlling the intensity of the narration, rather than relating the pith of the story. But this same example also illustrates how deeply transitions may be connected to themes in the Chopin Ballades.

It is in the next transitional passage of the first Ballade, in fact, that we first meet thematic transformation. Thematic transformations have been pointed out many times in the Chopin Ballades, whether or not that term has been used to characterize them. But no one has taken stock of the kinds and functions of thematic transformations in these works. The term can in fact be used to describe a whole repertory of practices in the Ballades. These practices are logically considered together because they serve a common narrative function in the Ballades. They also deserve to be called thematic transformations because as recastings of previously stated material they correspond more or less closely to the classic examples of thematic transformation in symphonies of Berlioz and large instrumental works of Liszt. But Chopin's practices are in several ways very different from those of Berlioz and Liszt. Whereas Berlioz, for instance, in the *Symphonie fantastique* concentrates on transforming one theme, the *idée fixe*, Chopin in the Ballades often uses thematic transformation to connect one theme to another. The first example that we find in the first Ballade does just that.

In this example the second part, or extension, of the secondary theme (mm. 82–90) is transformed into the primary theme. The transformation occurs in stages, gradually revealing a relationship that would not otherwise be obvious between the two themes. The triplets of the concluding phrase of the extension (see Example 3-13) are straightened out into eighth notes, still forming a five-note upbeat (see Example 3-14), which repeats in various shapes and harmonies until it falls suddenly into the "winding phrase" of the primary theme (see Example 3-15).

Example 3-13. Chopin, first Ballade, Op. 23, m. 89.

Example 3-14. Chopin, first Ballade, Op. 23, m. 90.

Example 3-15. Chopin, first Ballade, Op. 23, mm. 93–95.

This process might be called "thematic convergence" to distinguish it from other kinds of thematic transformation. Chopin used it again in the fourth Ballade (mm. 121*ff.*), where music that recalls the primary theme gradually (by m. 129) turns into the introductory theme. A somewhat different convergence occurs in the third Ballade, where the descending motive of the second theme (m. 186) is answered by the ascending motive of the primary theme (m. 189) until they join to form a single phrase (mm. 201–04; see Example 3-16), which in turn ushers in the return of the primary theme, transformed (m. 213).

Example 3-16. Chopin, third Ballade, Op. 47, mm. 201–04.

All three of these convergences occur in sequential passages that modulate to remote keys; the convergence in the first Ballade, for instance, takes place during a modulation from E-flat major to A minor. In all three cases the theme that returns comes from the beginning of the Ballade and has been absent, out of mind, for some time. The process of modulation makes it seem like a remote memory being recalled, at the same time that the process of convergence makes it seem to have been present, unrecognized, all along. The combination of modulation and thematic convergence gives these three moments the structure of a guilty conscience suddenly recognizing, in an unguarded moment (all three of these passages are quiet and ruminative), the memory that it had repressed. By means of thematic convergence Chopin shows the inescapable presence of an initial musical theme through all its withdrawals and returns, the inescapable force of a narrator's portentous opening lines, the inescapable consequences of an initial act of defiance in the ballad process.

In the first Ballade, once the primary theme returns, on a dominant pedal of A minor, it too is transformed (mm. 94–105). This time it is the character of the music, rather than the identity of the theme, that is transformed, and it is transformed gradually, in what might be called "progressive transformation." Even as it begins, the theme has a more ominous character than it had before, thanks to the unresolving pedal point. But in itself this subtle change is not the classic thematic transformation of Berlioz and Liszt: a theme that is completely changed in musical character from the moment it returns. This progressive transformation is not completed until the end of the thematic statement. The theme develops more and more tension, which expresses itself in an abrupt crescendo that breaks off and then returns (mm. 99 and 101). Finally, the yearning two-note phrase that answered the winding phrase works itself into an impassioned three-note phrase that pushes aside the winding phrase (see Example 3-17). This phrase yields to another theme, in still another sort of transformation (at m. 106); progressive transformation, like thematic convergence, is a device of transition.

Example 3-17. Chopin, first Ballade, Op. 23, mm. 100–03.

Each of the later Ballades has a comparable passage of progressive transformation, progressing to a state of heightened volume and tension (second Ballade, mm. 156–67; third Ballade, after the thematic convergence described earlier, at mm. 205–212; fourth Ballade, in the last stanza of the primary theme, mm. 58–71). In the first Ballade there is even a second passage of progressive transformation, a transposition of the first passage to G minor (mm. 194–205), leading to the finale, the reckoning, of the work. In all these cases, it is the primary theme of the Ballade that is transformed. It makes sense that the theme connected to the initial act in the ballad process would be the theme to rise up in this irrepressible way, sometimes to have its force diverted, sometimes to bring on the reckoning.

The first progressive transformation in the first Ballade is one that has its force diverted: the tension of its dominant pedal resolves finally into A major as the primary theme is answered by the secondary theme, itself now transformed (at m. 106). This is a thematic transformation of a third kind, but a kind that hardly needs a term of its own since it is very much the kind made famous by Berlioz and Liszt. The theme is transformed altogether from the character it had before. In this case, and in others like it in the Chopin Ballades, there is also a transformation in another sense: the ominous tension that built up in the previous passage is here transformed into exuberant energy. In this Ballade the working-out of the ballad process can be especially identified with the primary theme, and the will to escape that process can be especially identified with the secondary theme; the transformation of the secondary theme at this point in the Ballade seems to represent the scene or moment when that will is expressed most confidently. Subtle reminders of the primary theme do not undermine this confidence,[28] nor is the energy of this passage dissipated when the theme strays from its original course and breaks off at the strongest climax in the work so far (the widely spaced tritone at m. 124). Instead the energy, now channeled into continuous eighth-note movement, persists through two more scenes, the second of which is yet another transformation of the secondary theme.

In that new transformation (mm. 166-87) the theme is heard in its original length, including the second part, or extension. It is more characteristic of Chopin, however, when he is writing thematic transformations of this Berlioz-Liszt type, to turn the theme from its original course once he has established its new character. The clearest examples of this practice in the later Ballades are the final appearance of the primary theme in the third Ballade (mm. 213-25) and of the secondary theme in the fourth Ballade (mm. 169-91).[29]

Thematic transformation in the Chopin Ballades takes various forms, none of them in itself unique to the Ballades or to Chopin. Chopin is highly unusual, however, in the function he makes thematic transformation serve in these works. It does not, for instance, have the generative function here that it has in many works of Liszt, creating new episodes, new movements, out of a given theme. Chopin's transformations stay very much within the single, overriding movement, or rhythm, of the work. They do serve a unifying function, but not by bringing a single "fixed idea" to diverse musical episodes, as in the *Symphonie fantastique*. Rather, they allow Chopin to develop "a single line of action" in his Ballades. They allow him to keep the action moving forward without resorting to much new material. They unify the work in the special sense that they bring together the themes already presented. This they do by making evident the connections among themes and by giving the themes new characters in which they can respond to each other. Because they bring together narrating themes and characterizing themes, they mediate between the two planes of representation in the

Ballades—the representation of telling and of the thing told.

The various transformations work together. In the first Ballade, for instance, three transformations—each of a different kind—come in close succession (mm. 89–124). Within the works as a whole, the transformations tend to cluster in the middle. That placement is explained by their function in the narrative: by bringing together forces, or themes, that seemed separate, they force the action to an issue. They propel the ballad process from the initial act of defiance to the brink of the final reckoning. In only one case is thematic transformation heard during the reckoning itself: the third Ballade—exceptional in its happy outcome[30] as in other ways—has at its close a thematic transformation of the kind that Edward Cone calls an "apotheosis."[31] Even this transformation serves a function specific to the ballad process: it is the first and only return of a primary theme that has been suppressed for almost the entire length of the piece.

STRUCTURES OF OVERALL ORGANIZATION

Chopin's *ballade* structure seems to require three musical events: statement of themes, transformation of themes, and resolution. He may or may not use those three events to organize the *ballade* into three-part musical form. Folk and literary ballads known to him certainly presented three-part forms as one possible model. "Many ballads," writes David Buchan about a Scottish repertory in particular, "have a trinary conceptual organization dominating the entire story."[32]

Chopin's first Ballade, considered without its "pre-narrative" introduction, in fact has a three-part musical form. That form is manifested by the structure of the narrative voice in the work. The three utterances of the primary theme—each issuing arrestingly at a moment when the piece has lost momentum—announce the start of the three parts, or stages, of the musical form (see Diagram 3-1).

The first stage gets under way in a full utterance of the theme, which establishes the narrative voice and expresses the tension of the tale at the same time that it presents the first scene of the action. The later two stages, by contrast, do not get under way until they have been ushered in by that theme, briefly reasserting its voice and tension over a dominant pedal. Each of the first two stages consists of thematic "scenes" marked off from each other by passagework; the third is a single scene dominated by passagework. The first two stages are nearly equal in length (mm. 8–93 and 106–93), the third considerably shorter (mm. 208–64, at a faster speed). The musical progression from statement to transformation to resolution of themes is set out in these three stages, as is the progression in the ballad process from the act of defiance to the movement toward reckoning to the reckoning itself.

The second and fourth Ballades have similar three-stage forms. In the

Diagram 3-1. Three-stage form of Chopin's first Ballade, Op. 23.

STAGE 1					STAGE 2					STAGE 3	
Scene 1			Scene 2		Scene 1		Scene 2		Scene 3		
m. 1	8	36	44	68	94	106	124	138	154	166	194	208–64
Intro.	Primary Theme	1st Precipitating Theme	Passagework	Secondary Theme	Primary Theme	Secondary Theme	Passagework	2nd Precipitating Theme	Passagework	Secondary Theme	Primary Theme	Reckoning (Passagework)

Diagram 3-2. Three-stage form of Chopin's third Ballade, Op. 47.

STAGE 1 (Scene 1)		STAGE 2 (Central Action)				STAGE 3 (Reckoning)	
		1st Step	2nd Step	3rd Step			
m. 1	52	103	116	144	183	213	231
Primary Theme	Secondary Theme, with extensions	Secondary Theme	Tertiary Theme, with extensions	Secondary Theme	Convergence of Primary and Secondary Themes	Primary Theme	Tertiary Theme

second Ballade two stages (mm. 1–81 and 82–155) are begun by large statements of the primary theme, and the third (mm. 168–203) is ushered in by a brief transformation of that theme (mm. 156–67). In the fourth Ballade the introduction returns (at m. 129), followed by the primary theme (at m. 135), to begin the second stage, and something like a skeleton of the introduction (at m. 203) ushers in the third stage. The third Ballade, too, has a three-stage form, but the central stage is defined by the absence of the primary theme. That central stage is itself, in Buchan's words, "a central action...developed in three steps"[33] (see Diagram 3-2). Each step is introduced by the secondary theme (mm. 52, 103, and 144), and the third step—the step in which the primary theme finally begins to reemerge—leads right into the reckoning, announced by the "apotheosis" of that primary theme (m. 213). The central stage, like a series of three tests through which a character passes, gives the third Ballade the most ritualistic form of the four Ballades.

By itself, three-stage form does not completely account for the organization of any of the Ballades. Other structures organize the same span of music in other ways. In the first Ballade, for instance, one of the great climaxes of the work comes in the middle of the second stage: the widely spaced, triple-*forte* tritone (m. 124), noted earlier, at which the transformed secondary theme breaks off. This blast divides the Ballade at essentially its midpoint; at the end of the work a comparable blast—also a widely spaced, triple-*forte* tritone—breaks in (m. 258), leading without pause to the final chord. The two halves into which the Ballade is divided by this striking gesture (or pair of gestures) contrast with each other in two respects: rhythm and volume (see Diagram 3-3). The second half of the work proceeds mostly at faster speeds than the first (two measures after the division, the score is marked *Sempre più animato*) and mostly with a steady flow of eighth notes, rather than quarter notes. The music of the first half is predominantly quiet, though it reaches *fortissimo* shortly before the division (m. 106); it stays at something like that level, with only a few respites, for the rest of the piece.

A two-part structure, according to students of ballads and other oral narrative, may present a balance or opposition of elements,[34] as it does here with the elements of rhythm and volume. At the same time, a two-part structure allows for symmetrical or framing organization.[35] Symmetrical organization has in fact been observed in the first Ballade. Analysts interested in the question of how close the work comes to sonata form point out that the primary and secondary themes are recapitulated in reverse order;[36] one of these analysts, Gerald Abraham, notices that this reversal contributes to the work's "'arch'-like outline."[37] But his simple outline does not reveal the extent of the symmetrical relationships in the work. Like most analysts, he labels as a coda the final stage of the Ballade m.1 Tritone — m.124 Tritone — m.258 Tritone

TWO-PART STRUCTURES

RHYTHM

m.1	8	45	68	82	94	126	194	208
Largo C ¼ notes	Moderato 6/4 ¼ notes	(Sempre più mosso) ⅛ notes	Meno mosso ¼ (⅛) notes		A tempo ¼ notes	Sempre più animato ⅛ notes	(Meno mosso) ¼ notes	Presto con fuoco ¢

VOLUME

m.1	8	48	68	106	124	154	194	208
(f) p	p	(f — dim.)	pp	ff	fff — (dim.)	ff	(pp)	ff

SYMMETRICAL KEY STRUCTURE

m.1	68	94	106	126	194
G minor	E-flat major	A minor	A major	E-flat major	G minor

THREE-STAGE THEMATIC STRUCTURE

STAGE 1

Scene 1				Scene 2	
m.1 Intro. Primary Theme	8 Primary Theme	36 1st Precipitating Theme	44 Passagework	68 Secondary Theme	94 Primary Theme

STAGE 2

Scene 1		Scene 2		Scene 3	
106 Secondary Theme	124 Passagework	138 2nd Precipitating Theme	154 Passagework	166 Secondary Theme	194 Primary Theme

STAGE 3

208-64 Reckoning (Passagework)

Diagram 3-3. "Counterpoint" of structures in Chopin's first Ballade, Op. 23. Parentheses in the rhythm line indicate passages that are exceptions to the overall pattern of steadily quickening note-values. Likewise, parentheses in the volume line mark passages that are exceptions to the overall pattern of a quiet first half followed by a loud second half.

(the *Presto con fuoco* ["Fast, with fire"] section that I have identified with the reckoning of the ballad process), and he says nothing about what happens in it. Franz Eibner, the one analyst who examines that section, is a strong opponent of analyzing the Ballade in sonata form; he labels as coda only the last fifteen measures of the Ballade.[38] He considers the whole *Presto con fuoco* section a new thought and finds only one reference in it to previous thematic material.[39] Much about this section is of course new, but as the reckoning of the work, it responds in various ways to the opening—the initial act—thereby giving a frame to the whole work. The section hardly makes sense, in fact, except as a reckoning with the material with which the Ballade begins. An analysis of that thematic process of reckoning—in this and the other Chopin Ballades—is therefore crucial for understanding Chopin's *ballade* form.

In the first Ballade, this reckoning does not come as a new, transformed statement of the opening theme. It comes as a furious energy—Chopin calls for "fire"—that has been building up steadily throughout the Ballade and that now consumes the earlier themes, leaving only scattered signs of those themes. The section is brought on, for instance, as the main movement of the Ballade was, by a cadencing phrase (i$^6_4$-V^7-i in G minor) that changes to a new rhythm and faster tempo as it concludes (see Example 3-18). There is even (on the downbeat of m. 207) a passing version of the "emotional key-note" chord (of m. 7) in the course of this cadence. But in the first phrase of the new section, all that remains of the primary theme are the chord progression (i-ii^7-V^7-i) of its first phrase (mm. 9-11) and the rhythmic trait of starting melodic phrases just after the beat.

Example 3-18. Chopin, first Ballade, Op. 23, mm. 206-12.

The next new chord heard (in m. 216)—and insistently repeated over the course of a dozen measures—is not from the primary theme, but from the introduction: the Neapolitan-sixth chord with which the Ballade began. But now the inconclusive ending of the opening phrase (the A-flat to G to F-sharp of m. 3) is resolved (see Example 3-19). The music goes on in this way, reworking elements of the opening material, until it descends to a bare, low D octave (m. 242), when a new stage of reckoning begins (see Example 3-20).

Example 3-19. Chopin, first Ballade, Op. 23, mm. 216–17.

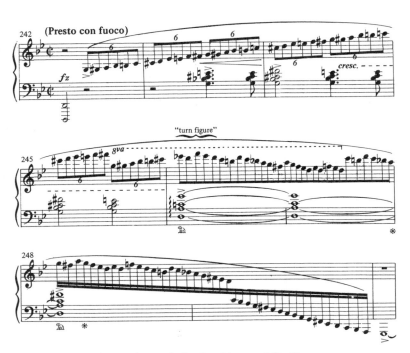

Example 3-20. Chopin, first Ballade, Op. 23, mm. 242–50.

This low D begins a long cadence, the final cadence of the work, ending on the low G eight measures later. The two notes are connected by an enormous scale that sweeps up and down, a reminder of the passagework that has swept the narration forward all through the Ballade. At the peak of this passage (the beginning of m. 246), the chromatic scale gives way to a five-note turn figure derived from the second phrase of the introduction (see Example 3-21). Just before, the motive derived from the transformation of the primary theme (in mm. 201–04) is heard in the left-hand part (mm. 243–45). That motive ends, and the turn figure from the introduction begins, on a chord that is, like the "emotional key-note" chord, a multiple-appoggiatura chord on the dominant. This is the moment of truth in the musical narrative, when motives from the introduction and the primary theme converge to produce a transformation of the chord that once separated them.

Example 3-21. Chopin, first Ballade, Op. 23, m. 5.

This version of the chord resolves more smoothly than the first, but the process of reckoning continues. The fire of this process now throws off fragments of music, in each of which some element from the introduction is fused with an element from the main movement of the Ballade (see Example 3-22). First comes a rising scale, an element heard most often in the middle of the work, but now in unaccompanied octaves, a "voice" not heard since the introduction. Next, a soft chord is played three times, in the rhythm heard most recently in the motive from the transformed primary theme (mm. 243–45; see Example 3-20), but first heard in the introduction (see Example 3-23). Third comes another phrase in unaccompanied octaves, this one transforming the "winding phrase" from the primary theme.

Example 3-22. Chopin, first Ballade, Op. 23, mm. 250–64.

[3-22 continued]

Example 3-23. Chopin, first Ballade, Op. 23, mm. 6–7.

The next three fragments are expansions of the previous three; the third of this group (m. 257) not only fuses the unaccompanied octaves of the introduction with the "winding phrase" of the primary theme, but does it with the notes of the "emotional key-note" chord. In the final fragment (mm. 258–62), the tritone adapted from the midpoint of the Ballade (m. 124) sets off scales in contrary motion (fusing the rising and falling scales of mm. 242–250), scales that converge into the most powerful of all the utterances in bare octaves. The voice that emerges at the very end of the Ballade is, despite the transformation it has undergone as the tale unfolds, the same voice heard at the very beginning: it sings in the same disconnected phrases, in the same human timbre extended beyond human range. Chopin has framed the whole Ballade with two short passages that reflect and reckon with each other intensely.

Within this frame the first Ballade has a general symmetrical, or arching, organization. This organization is not so much thematic as tonal. The piece has, after all, three parts that all begin with the same theme. The key structure, however, follows Abraham's "'arch'-like outline." The music modulates from G minor to E-flat major, then to A minor and A major, turning at the midpoint back to E-flat and then to G minor (see Diagram 3-3, p. 75). This key structure, though unconventional, is simple and restrained, perhaps surprisingly so, given how striking the modulations in the Ballade are. Two of them, including the modulation from E-flat to A minor (mm. 90–94), described earlier, are striking because they occur with a thematic convergence. All of them are striking because they are effected by means that can be called "leaping and lingering" (or, in the first modulation to E-flat, also described earlier, "lingering and leaping"). In the modulations with thematic convergence, Chopin simply takes a small leap, or series of small leaps, from the tonic chord in one key to the tonic chord in the other, and then "lingers" on a dominant pedal for many measures, letting the new key take hold. By contrast, the longest transitional passage of a conventional sort in the work (mm. 146–66) makes no modulation at all.[40]

The "arch" of the key structure helps to make the ballad process vivid in this Ballade. The initial act in G minor is answered by the reckoning in G minor. In between, all the while that the reckoning is being evaded, the music stays in other keys, principally E-flat; in the very center of the work, the reckoning seems to be most remote when the secondary theme is heard, at its most exuberant, in the key that is (and is made to seem) most remote from the others: the key of A.

The themes are coordinated very simply with the keys (again, see Diagram 3-3, p. 75): the primary theme is heard twice in G minor and once in A minor, the secondary theme twice in E-flat major and once in A major. But the three-stage thematic structure does not fit in a simple way with the symmetrical key structure, the frame structure, or the two-part dynamic and rhythmic structure of the Ballade. Modulations occur at the turning points between stages, but also within stages. The key of E-flat is heard at the ends of the first and second stages only; the key of A, at the beginning of the second stage only. The introduction stands outside the stage structure, the response to the introduction inside it. The climactic turning point in the two-part structure comes within, but well before the middle of, the second stage. The three-part and two-part structures of the Ballade, it seems, work somewhat independently of each other, not always giving emphasis, by their different means, to the same moments or events in the music.[41]

The various structural organizations, then, do not always reinforce one another. Instead, they create a complicated progression with a rather large number of climactic moments or turning points of various sorts. It is a progression of the kind that David Buchan calls a "contrapuntal" rather than a "concurrent" architectonic. In the contrapuntal architectonic, he writes, "the units of the various structures do not always coincide and the structures themselves weave through one another in a kind of counterpoint." Ballads of this sort, he says, tend to be the long narrative ones (the ones that rely more on narration and less on dialogue) and "tend to be in three Acts with some Acts incorporating a number of scenes, and to maintain a general balancing relationship among these scenes and Acts."[42] The description seems apt in every way for Chopin's first Ballade. But Chopin, like Mrs. Brown of Falkland, the singer whose repertory Buchan is describing, did not confine himself to *ballades* organized in a single way.

Each of the later Ballades has overall structures in addition to its three-stage thematic structure, but each Ballade is different from the others in its structures and in the way those structures are coordinated. The second Ballade is unique in its ending. Its final stage, like that of the first Ballade, reckons with two thematic sections from the beginning, but in this case the two do not converge. Instead, they are reckoned with in reverse order (the secondary theme in mm. 168–96 and the primary theme in mm. 196–203), giving the whole work a double frame. Other symmetrical structures are lacking in this Ballade: the work does not even end in the same key in which it began. The unmistakable two-part structure is a division, not of the whole Ballade, but of each of its three stages—an opposition of theme, rhythm, key, volume, and character all at once. Just as the first Ballade fits Buchan's definition of "contrapuntal" architectonic, the second fits his definition of the "concurrent": "The units of the structures all consistently coincide to produce well-defined scenes."

In the third Ballade the final stage completes both a frame and a two-part thematic structure (see Diagram 3-2, p. 73). The frame is completed by the only return of the primary theme (m. 213); the two-part structure, by the only return of the tertiary theme (m. 231), which marked the midpoint of the Ballade (m. 116). These two themes, like the two in the final stage of the second Ballade, do not converge; here the primary theme has already converged with the secondary. Rhythmic and dynamic structures do not coincide with thematic and tonal ones. As in the first Ballade, the coordination of structures is more "contrapuntal" than "concurrent," but here the effect is smoother: whereas in the first Ballade the counterpoint of structures seems to multiply the moments of extreme contrast, in the third Ballade change of one sort always seems softened by continuity of other sorts.

The fourth Ballade is in many respects the one that follows the pattern of the first most closely, with more sophistication, but with hardly any less of the wildness that Schumann admired in the first. The sophistication can be heard in the modulations: not only is the structure of modulations richer than in the first Ballade, but almost every modulation is achieved by a subtle new

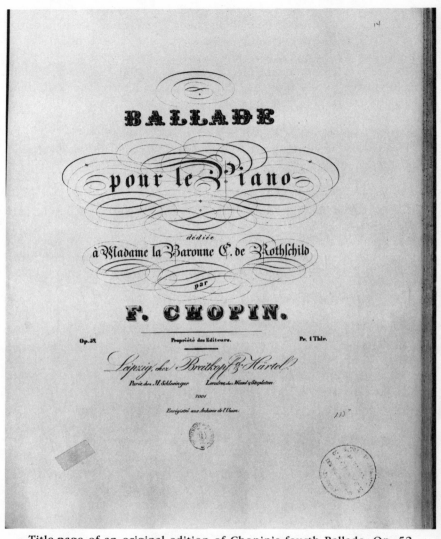

Title-page of an original edition of Chopin's fourth Ballade, Op. 52
(Leipzig: Breitkopf & Härtel, 1843). By permission of the Houghton
Library, Harvard University.

wrinkle on the idea of "leaping and lingering." Chopin moves, for instance,
from his primary theme in F minor to B-flat major, the key of his secondary
theme, without modulating at all. He simply breaks off from the primary
theme in the middle of a phrase in B-flat minor. Then he makes his way to a
dominant chord in B-flat, on which he lingers for six measures (mm. 74–79)
before reaching the tonic, B-flat major. But just before beginning the new
theme, he slides quickly from B-flat to A major and back to B-flat

(mm. 81–84), creating the sensation that the new theme leaps out of the blue, while at the same time showing that it steps directly out of the primary theme. In the first Ballade, by means of thematic convergence, themes were shown to be paradoxically both close to and remote from each other; here that paradox is extended to harmonic relationships as well.

Two-part structures are less developed in the fourth Ballade than in the first. Once again there is a returning introduction, but this time its structural function is to define the beginning of each stage in the three-stage structure, rather than to create a frame. In fact, this Ballade has no frame, because the final section reckons with the primary and secondary themes, not with the introduction. What is more, there is no overall symmetry, in the key structure or any other structure. The midpoint is emphasized, to be sure, but as a moment of repose—in the cadenza (m. 134) just after the introduction returns in D—rather than as a climax and breaking point, as in the first Ballade. Because of the proportions of the three stages of this Ballade, this moment of repose comes just after the beginning of the second stage: it seems hardly independent of the three-stage structure. The change to a more active rhythm in the second half of the Ballade likewise comes at no climactic moment: the triplet sixteenth notes that dominate the second half insinuate themselves gradually (by m. 157) into the ornamented melody of the returning primary theme. There are, then, structures independent of the three-stage structure in this Ballade, but they do not pose "points" that "counter" those of the three-stage structure. Rather, they impart a fluid momentum to an orderly sequence of musical scenes.

The four Chopin Ballades have some overall structures in common; but aside from the three-stage structure, there is no common structure by which to define a characteristic musical form (and even that structure is not always identified in the same way). Is it possible, then, to say that Chopin gave his new genre its own musical form? The answer is no if a musical form must have a fixed sequence or a fixed correspondence of thematic and harmonic events. The most that earlier writers have allowed is that each of Chopin's Ballades represents a different adaptation, or distortion, of sonata form; others have denied even that much.

It might be imagined that Chopin, finding in poetic and song ballads no uniform poetic model except at the level of the stanza, felt free to devise a different musical form for each of his Ballades. Certain of Chopin's contemporaries viewed folk-ballad singing as a fluid and improvisatory art. Goethe, for instance, wrote in 1821:

> The singer... has his pregnant subject—his figures, their actions and emotions—so deep in his mind that he does not know how he will bring it to light... He can begin lyrically, epically, dramatically and proceed, changing the form at will, either to hurry to the end or to delay it considerably.[43]

But in the same essay Goethe also wrote of a larger sense in which the ballads of all peoples "always proceed the same way in the same matters."
The most recent ballad scholars provide a mechanism for reconciling these two observations. David Buchan compares two versions of the same ballad, performed "some months apart" by the same singer, as follows:

> The a version has two Acts each with three scenes, and the b version three Acts each with two scenes. Though the individual organizations are different, the method of organization, by binary and trinary patterns, remains constant; and though the structures may differ, the story itself is not altered in any essential.[44]

Even re-creations of a single ballad by a single singer, then,—or, as Buchan's critics might say, different versions that one singer knows of the same ballad—have different formal organizations, but they all result from the same distinctive "method of organization."
Chopin follows something like that method of organization in his four Ballades. All his musical material and processes in these works—themes that enclose eventful episodes within narrating stanzas, thematic transformations that demonstrate the closeness of the apparently remote, fiery new reckonings with the initial themes and motives—approximate by musical means the features of ballad narration. It is hardly surprising, then, that he also turned to the ballad model for his method of organizing that material. The result in both cases was new to instrumental music. His adaptation of the ballad's "method of organization" produces an unusual kind of musical form. It is neither a three-part form nor a two-part form nor even a particular way of combining three-part and two-part structures. The Chopin Ballades have a common musical form in the sense that ballads have a common narrative form: whatever the rhythm of overall structures in a given Ballade, the musical form always corresponds to the form of the ballad process.

THE ISSUE OF SONATA FORM

The tradition of analyzing Chopin's Ballades in terms of sonata form stems largely from Hugo Leichtentritt's *Analyse der Chopin'schen Klavierwerke*, published in 1921-22.[45] At a time when published accounts of Chopin's music were mostly impressionistic, his use of the sonata model provided a means of comparing the Ballades to the works of the Viennese classical composers, and it must thereby have helped secure Chopin's position among the greatest masters. Leichtentritt's analysis recognizes that Chopin departs from sonata form somewhat even in the first Ballade and more in the later three. Yet even his qualified use of the sonata model has aroused as much opposition as assent. His separation of the programmatic element from the formal, on the other hand, carried the day, at least until very recently.

At nearly the same time, Heinrich Schenker devised a bold alternative analysis of the first Ballade. In the section on "song forms" in *Der freie Satz (Free Composition)*, published just after his death in 1935, Schenker describes that Ballade as "a very extended three-part form, boldly derived from a neighboring note, yet unfolding in a single broad sweep"[46] (see Diagram 3-4). However peculiar it may seem, especially under the title of "song forms," to describe as the third part (A_2) of a ternary form a passage (mm. 208-64) that does not bring back the theme of the first part, Schenker's analysis has several advantages over Leichtentritt's. In particular, Schenker's third part—the part I have identified with the reckoning in the ballad process—is given its due as the part that answers to the opening theme; Leichtentritt had reduced it to a coda.

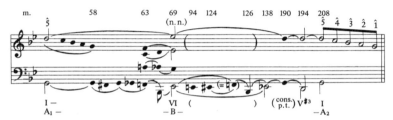

Diagram 3-4. Heinrich Schenker's graph of Chopin's first Ballade (1935).

Within the next few decades something like a debate arose, more or less within the lines drawn by Leichtentritt and Schenker, about the form of the first Ballade (the other three Ballades were only occasionally brought into the debate). On the Schenkerian side Franz Eibner, in the 1958 article discussed earlier,[47] contributed as much by enumerating the weaknesses of Leichtentritt's analysis as by his own refinement of Schenker's analysis. But even before Eibner's article appeared, analysts more sympathetic to the sonata model were adapting it to deal with the difficulties posed by the first Ballade. Gerald Abraham, in 1939, proposed his "'arch'-like outline" to deal with the "recapitulation" of the secondary theme, still in its secondary key, before the primary theme. But in 1965 Douglass Green pointed out that the "arch" design, though it copes with the problem of the returning secondary theme, does not cope with that of the returning primary theme: the version that returns on the dominant of G minor (at m. 194) resembles the original primary theme less than it resembles the version on the dominant of A minor (at m. 94), "both standing in opposition to the original statement."[48] Green's own analysis, while describing the Ballade as "unique" in design and tonal structure, has much in common with Schenker's three-part analysis, especially in its emphasis on the "lengthy chord succession which prolongs VI" through the middle of the work.

It is perhaps surprising to discover that after the debate had progressed this far, Günther Wagner, while revealing even more difficulties in applying sonata form than Eibner or Green had, still relied on that model to analyze the first Ballade.[49] What is more interesting than the mere persistence of sonata-form analysis is that those, like Wagner, who separate the narrative, or ballad, element from their formal analysis salvage the most from the sonata model, while a writer like Carl Dahlhaus, who considers the ballad model to have posed Chopin a "structural problem," finds in the first Ballade only a "distant reminder" of sonata form.[50] In fact, a useful comparison between sonata form and Chopin's *ballade* form can be made only when the narrative element of his Ballades is considered. In the first place, the narrative model of the *ballade* has more natural affinity with the rhetorical model of the sonata than with most other musical models, such as lyric song forms or dance forms: both are models of a continuous verbal progression with a single "argument." But to look beyond this general affinity is to find that Chopin's narrating themes are modeled on song themes (such as those of Loewe's ballads) rather than on the rhetorical themes of sonatas and that the nature of the primary themes determines the overall nature of the work, particularly the nature of thematic returns.

It is at the point of thematic returns that analysts, beginning with Leichtentritt, have had the most trouble applying the sonata model to the first Ballade (and, for that matter, to the other three), just as it is at this point that the very terminology of sonata form sits most uncomfortably with the ballad as a narrative model. George Bernard Shaw puts the matter with wry bluntness: "It is impossible to tell a story in sonata form, because the end of a story is not a recapitulation of the beginning, and the end of a movement in sonata form is."[51] Perhaps he is too blunt. In each of the Chopin Ballades the principal themes are reasserted or recalled at the end, with no harm to the narrative force of the whole. But then, not every reassertion of a theme can fairly be called a "recapitulation," summoning not only the musical but also the original rhetorical associations of that term. The reassertions or recollections of themes in the Chopin Ballades take the forms they do because of the kinds of themes they are.

Primary themes in the Ballades, constructed so that they suggest both the incessantly repeating stanza structure of the song and one episode of the story, return with a difference, suggesting the ever-repeating tune of a ballad now bearing different words, relating a later episode. The return is thus both a resumption and a continuation, but far from a recapitulation. Resumption is suggested at the moment of return, when the theme is reiterated or transposed very exactly; the new stage of narrative is suggested just afterward, in the first Ballade by progressive transformation, in the second and in the third (where it is the secondary theme that plays this role) by a changed continuation of the theme, and in the fourth by variation. In fact, this resort to the technique of variation, which unfolds changes through strophic repetition, has implications for later instrumental *ballades*, notably Grieg's *Ballade in the Form of Variations on a Norwegian Melody*.

In the comparison of Chopin's *ballade* form to sonata form there is, besides the general similarity of a narrative and a rhetorical musical model, the similarity noticed by Dahlhaus, that Chopin's first Ballade "distantly recalls sonata form, being based on an underlying contrast of themes." Again a closer look reveals an essential difference, or at least reveals what a special case a Chopin Ballade is. In sonata form the reworking of thematic material in the middle (development) leads to a new relationship—especially a new resolution of the tonal "contrast"—between themes at the end (recapitulation), while in a Chopin Ballade the creation of new relationships between themes (especially new dissolutions of the apparent "contrasts" between themes) is concentrated in the middle, leading to the crucial reworking of—reckoning with—thematic material at the end. A Chopin Ballade is like many other nineteenth-century works in its end-directed form—that is, in sustaining unresolved tensions until the very end; but it is distinctive (even, as it turns out, from most *ballades* by other composers) in both the way it sustains tension (through continuously increasing rhythmic momentum and through long suppression of themes) and the way it resolves it (by bringing back long-suppressed material from the opening, usually in a fiery reckoning that transforms that material almost beyond recognition).

What makes the Chopin Ballades similar in form to each other and distinct from other music is not a shared relationship to sonata form, but a shared analogy to another model, the narrative model that Chopin advertised in their title. Not only is this model needed to reveal the narrative significance of Chopin's musical procedures, but without it one can hardly discover the originality of his musical material and of his ways of organizing that material. Without it, for that matter, one can hardly discover what later composers of instrumental *ballades* might have learned from Chopin's Ballades.

PART II

The Piano *Ballade* Through World War I

CHAPTER 4

Liszt and the Narrative Tradition to 1880

INTRODUCTION

In 1842, when the first three of Chopin's Ballades had appeared, an album of miscellaneous compositions in honor of Mozart was published, including a Ballade by the pianist and composer Ignaz Moscheles. Schumann, in his review of this Ballade, wrote: "Chopin no doubt was the first to transfer the word *ballad* into music. Only the word, however, seems new to us; the thing can already be found in Beethoven and Schubert."[1] Schumann's grudging tone suggests that the Chopin Ballades were making a great impression in the musical world, as his comments elsewhere reveal they had made on him. But his invocation of Beethoven and Schubert suggests that the Chopin Ballades had by no means defined the genre for him. In what works of Beethoven or Schubert, after all, could he have found Chopin's conception of the *ballade* anticipated?

The ambiguity in Schumann's thought is matched in the practice of composers ever since Chopin. That Chopin's Ballades have always been the main inspiration for the genre can be deduced from the outpouring of piano *ballades* in the wake of his, including many by his friends and students and by virtuosos who knew him; from certain important piano *ballades*, written within a decade of Chopin's death, which in various ways come to terms with his narrative conception and methods; and from other piano *ballades*, written later, which pay tribute to Chopin's piano style more than to the

91

formal or conceptual nature of his Ballades. At the same time, the piano *ballade* flourished in types barely if at all related to the Chopin type. Beginning with Clara Wieck's Ballade, Op. 6, No. 2, published in the same year as Chopin's first Ballade, a great many piano *ballades*—probably the majority—have had little if any resemblance to the Chopin Ballades. Furthermore, some of the most distinctive features of the Chopin Ballades— notably the complex structure of their primary themes—have never been imitated very closely in later piano *ballades*. So, while the term *"ballade"* in piano music has always evoked Chopin above all, as it did already for Schumann in 1842, the development of the genre has never been confined by Chopin's example.

The history of the *ballade* in fact provides a typical case of Chopin's pervasive but elusive influence on genres of piano music in the nineteenth century and beyond. Most of his works bear generic titles that were new or almost new to piano music then (Ballade, Nocturne, Barcarolle, Berceuse) or that had been used for piano music largely of an unpretentious sort (Etude, Waltz, Polonaise, Mazurka). Within these genres he created a type of single-movement piano piece that was poetic, often more dramatic and complex than a simple character piece, yet not tied to the colors or details of a specific program. Such pieces had been written by earlier composers, under such titles as Impromptu, Romanze, or Rhapsody; other comparable generic titles were invented by Chopin's contemporaries: Schumann's "Novelletten," Liszt's "Consolations."

Still, Chopin's contributions to the genres of serious piano music make a remarkable group, rich in variety and uniformly successful: each was taken up by countless later piano composers. For all their variety, these genres are unified in derivation: except for the étude, they all come from genres of song or dance, none from purely literary sources, and none from other instrumental media. Because these sources are musical, Chopin could give each of his genres a strongly defined musical character, by rhythmic and other means. Because the sources had little prior association with other instrumental media—and thanks to Chopin's own work—these genres (except for the waltz) have remained principally associated with the piano ever since. It is this strong association of genre with instrument that defines Chopin's importance in the field of musical genres, even though later works in all his new genres—as in the *ballade* genre—sometimes have only the slightest resemblance to his. Chopin's sense of genre, like his pedal-based innovations in texture and harmony, helped piano music to go its own way in the ensuing decades.[2]

The piano *ballade*, for instance, is connected to the orchestral *ballade* in the years up to World War I only by their common poetic source of inspiration. The repertory of orchestral *ballades* is made up largely of orchestral pieces based on specified poetic ballads; some of these pieces do not use the term *"ballade"* even in a subtitle, and in many cases it is hard to imagine that the composer was conscious of working in a musical tradition specific to the orchestral *ballade*, let alone a tradition that included Chopin's Ballades for piano. In this study, consequently, treatment of the nineteenth- and early twentieth-century orchestral *ballade* is reserved for a separate part. Concerto *ballades* were so few in this period that they are not treated separately here. Later in the twentieth century, however, they became a most important part of the genre. A small, but distinctive repertory of *ballades* for chamber duos or other small ensembles developed late in the nineteenth century; that repertory is treated here alongside the piano *ballades*, in Chapter 7.

In Part II of the present study, three chapters deal with the three main types or traditions of piano *ballades*[3] from the time of Chopin's first Ballade (published in 1836) to 1880, and one chapter treats all types of piano *ballades* from 1880 to the end of World War I. Chapter 4 deals with the works that responded most directly to Chopin's example, works—like the two Ballades of Liszt—that evoke the narrative structure of a ballad. *Ballades* in this tradition characteristically take complex musical forms—forms in which themes in different keys become integrated, rather than simply being juxtaposed. A few *ballades* that narrate a particular story, however, take multi-movement additive, or compound, forms. Chapter 5 considers the enormous repertory of lyrical *ballades*—*ballades* based on the idea of a ballad as a song. These *ballades* are character pieces; though they are not all short, as a rule they take simpler forms than the narrative *ballades*: ternary, rondo, variation, or some mixture of those forms. This tradition begins with the Wieck Ballade and includes the Ballades for piano of Brahms.

Chapter 6 is a study of folk ballads turned into piano pieces. Though these are mostly small and unpretentious pieces, they reveal an important musical evolution in the course of the nineteenth century. They also include one of the greatest and most ambitious of all piano *ballades*, Grieg's *Ballade in the Form of Variations on a Norwegian Melody*. The final chapter in this part, Chapter 7, treats piano and chamber *ballades* in the last two decades of the nineteenth century and the first two decades of the twentieth. In this period all the earlier traditions were continued, but they began to merge more than before. Fauré's Ballade for piano (or piano with orchestra) is the masterpiece of this period.

MOSCHELES

The background that Schumann's review gave to the Moscheles Ballade[4] still seems an excellent starting point for a study of that work: on the one hand, he mentions Beethoven and Schubert, and on the other, Chopin. Ignaz Moscheles (1794–1870) was a close contemporary of Schubert and a devoted early follower of Beethoven. He seems to have had more difficulty coming to appreciate the music of Chopin, who was sixteen years his junior. In 1835 he wrote: "Personally, I dislike his artificial and forced modulation. My fingers struggle and tumble over such passages; practice them as I will, I never can do them smoothly."[5] Nevertheless, he and François-Joseph Fétis commissioned Chopin's "Trois Nouvelles Etudes" for their *Méthode des méthodes* (1837), and in 1839 he and Chopin performed together. There is no evidence to show what he knew or thought of Chopin's Ballades by 1842. At that time he was living in London, and a couple of his most famous pieces were fantasies on Scottish popular melodies, written after travels to Scotland.[6] His Ballade, though it contains nothing like a Scottish folk melody, could be in some sense another reminiscence of Scotland; Schumann, who knew Moscheles and followed his career, wrote that the piece makes a "gloomy, misty" impression that "reminds us of the coast of Scotland."[7] Though the piece was published in a fund-raising anthology for a Mozart memorial, there is nothing in it that can be heard as a reference to Mozart.

The differences between this work and the Chopin Ballades that Moscheles might have known are more evident from the start than any similarities. In the first two measures, before the theme begins, Moscheles announces a dotted march rhythm, in contrast to the sextuplet rhythm that is the most obvious common feature of the Chopin Ballades. The theme, which embodies the dotted rhythmic motive, evolves and grows dramatic without any of the stanzaic repetitions of Chopin's Ballade themes. The accompaniment to this theme, very low and with a rhythm of its own, gives the theme a more distinctive mood and color than any Chopin Ballade theme has. The whole work, in fact, consists of themes of orchestrally differentiated coloring. There is no suggestion of a recurring narrative voice, as there is in Chopin. It is not surprising that Schumann, who never managed to pin a specific story or setting on a Chopin Ballade, had no trouble identifying the Moscheles with the mist and gloom of the Scottish coast.

The form of the work connects it with Beethoven and even more with Schubert, rather than with Chopin. The first half of the Ballade makes a fluid exposition, moving from the main theme in A-flat minor to themes in C-flat major (m. 29), B-flat major (m. 46), and G-flat major (m. 65) without any clear demarcation between exposition and development. The second half recapitulates the first two themes, in A-flat minor and major, respectively, and the third theme in a coda (beginning at m. 123). The most effective part of the work is also the most Schubertian: the retransition (mm. 73–88), full of stormy climaxes and breakings off, after which the main theme returns (mm. 89*ff.*), changed in texture and even more subdued than before, but soon rising to greater outbursts than ever. The dynamic of recapitulation, in other words, is like that in many Schubert sonata-allegro and slow movements.

In a way, the Moscheles Ballade is what some analysts have believed one or more of the Chopin Ballades to be: a Romantic adaptation of sonata form.

But it could just as well be said that Moscheles shared Chopin's premise that a piano *ballade* required a complex musical form. Sonata form, of course, is the classic case of such a complex form, and Moscheles—closer in several ways to the Viennese classical tradition than Chopin was—perhaps naturally came closer to classical sonata form in his Ballade than Chopin did in any of his. In any case, it is complex form, rather than sonata form specifically, that defines the narrative type within the history of the piano *ballade*. Among later piano *ballades* in the narrative tradition, few pay as much respect to sonata form as the Moscheles does. At the same time, the forms of the Chopin Ballades themselves were hardly ever taken as models for direct imitation; each *ballade* in the narrative tradition has a unique form, but, except for some of those that illustrate particular poems, each has a complex form.

In other matters besides form, Moscheles's Ballade is not so far from Chopin's example as it may at first seem. His sometimes march-like duple rhythm is different from Chopin's sometimes barcarolle-like sextuple rhythm, but he shares Chopin's concept—that is, the concept that Chopin was then arriving at—of evoking the changes and contrasts of a ballad narration within a single meter. The sometimes wild modulations, the sudden stops and starts, and the web of connected themes all contribute to the impression that Moscheles was keeping up with Romantic trends, if not aping Chopin.

This Ballade is a lovely piece to discover: through a variety of moods the music is always expressive, and its tight construction makes the highly dramatic gestures effective. Its contribution to the genre lies in its special combination of mood and drama. Each of its themes, colored by a distinctive accompaniment, takes the listener into a distinct mood. Whereas the themes in Chopin Ballades suggest episodes within a tale, these seem more like visions within a dream. The narrative structure of a ballad may, of course, have something dreamlike about it, but here the story is dissolved in dreaming. The gloomy opening theme returns with great drama, but that does not end the work. Other themes, with other moods, return later; and the resolution is no reckoning, but a dreamy drifting away, ended by a sudden reawakening (as Moscheles himself marked the last few measures). It is a shame that Moscheles's conception of the genre seems to have inspired no subsequent composers of piano *ballades*.

LISZT

Liszt began his D-flat Ballade in 1845, in the midst of a concert tour of France; the final version was done in 1848 and published in 1849. The Second Ballade, in B minor, he finished in 1853, though he revised the ending as the work was being engraved in 1854.[8] The two works span almost ten years. The first was begun when Chopin's Ballades were all published and known to Liszt, though the two composers were no longer friendly, as they had been in the 1830s. Starting with this Ballade, which he published in the year of Chopin's death, Liszt produced a series of piano works in genres associated with Chopin: the *Mazurka brillante* of 1850, the Two Polonaises of 1851, the Second Ballade of 1853, and the Berceuse (first version) of 1854. In 1852 he also brought out his book on Chopin.

From these facts and others, and from his analysis of the music, Günther Wagner has argued that Liszt's first Ballade should be taken as his tribute to the Chopin he knew in the 1830s, while the second, written toward the end of this period of reflection on Chopin, is Liszt's own contribution to the genre, a work that strikes out in a direction very different from Chopin's.[9] The two works certainly stand in very different relationships to Chopin's Ballades. If length is counted by number of measures, Liszt's first Ballade is shorter than the shortest of Chopin's, while his second is longer than the longest. The first begins with a *Preludio* that bears comparison on several counts with the *Largo* opening of Chopin's first Ballade, while Liszt's second begins with a chromatic rumble that has no clear equivalent in Chopin's Ballades. Wagner, after comparing the introductions of the two first Ballades, goes on to argue that other themes in Liszt's first Ballade are modeled on themes from a Chopin waltz, sonata, and polonaise from the 1830s; but by the same token, models for the themes of Liszt's Second Ballade could be found in Chopin's works.

Liszt published his Second Ballade, as Chopin had published all of his, without a hint of a poetic model or program, though later writers have proposed models, just as they have for Chopin's Ballades. Liszt's first Ballade appeared simply as "Ballade" in one of its original editions, but as "The Song of the Crusader: Ballade" ("Le Chant du croisé: Ballade") in the other. That title may not have been Liszt's idea; publishers of the time often took liberties with titles. But if the title did come from Liszt, it could indicate something about the origin of the work.[10] A number of Liszt's medium-sized piano works, including several in the *Années de pèlerinage*, are formed around a preexisting or imagined song, and the first Ballade resembles those pieces, especially in its main theme. The interrupting march theme is the only clue that the transcribed song is by or about a crusader, the only hint of a story in the song. Still, it is ironic that of all the Chopin and Liszt Ballades, the one that was published with a programmatic title is the only one that later writers have not been interested in interpreting programmatically.

In musical form, the two Liszt Ballades are very different, yet neither has a clear connection to the Chopin Ballades. Each seems to belong to a different group of piano works within Liszt's output: the D-flat Ballade to the group of medium-sized works based on a song or the idea of a song, and the Second Ballade to a group including the Sonata and the *Grosses Konzertsolo*, his largest, most complex, and most dramatic piano works. The two Ballades are united, though, in a formal feature that distinguishes them both from the

Z CYKLU ILLUSTRACYI „BALLADY MICKIEWICZA")   KONSTANTY GORSKI

PLATE 3. A 1904 illustration of Mickiewicz's ballad "Czaty." This ballad, in Pushkin's translation, inspired Tchaikovsky's *Voevoda*.

Chopin Ballades: their thematic contrasts are underlined by changes of meter. It is as characteristic of Liszt to make metrical contrasts central to the process of a work as it is characteristic of Chopin to use a secondary meter as a means of stepping outside the main process.

The question of how Liszt's two Ballades are related to Chopin's Ballades is inextricable from the question of how Liszt's two are related to each other. Can the two works be considered together, in terms of Liszt's own concept of the genre, or only separately, as Wagner argues, in terms of Liszt's changing response to Chopin's concept? The two Ballades are examined separately here, but with these questions in mind.

Ballade in D-flat

The interaction of two metrically opposed themes is already hinted at in the *Preludio* of the first Ballade. Since the main body of the work is itself rhythmically diverse, and since the *Preludio* to some extent reflects that diversity, the *Preludio* cannot be analyzed like a classical symphonic introduction (or, for that matter, like the *Largo* of Chopin's first Ballade), that is, as an introduction in one rhythm that is set against a movement in another rhythm. This *Preludio* has a different function. Though it is all written in common time, its first phrase—a single, upward-winding line—is set across the bars in a way that obscures the downbeats. The third appearance of that phrase, consequently, brings on the new 3/4 rhythm of the main theme with hardly any effect of contrast (see Example 4-1).

Rhythmic contrast is much clearer within the *Preludio*, between the alternating first and second phrases. The rhythm of the second phrase, which anticipates the march rhythm of the second theme (*Tempo di marcia*, m. 63), is as clear as the rhythm of the first phrase is ambiguous. Liszt did not specify how great a contrast in speed or volume the performer should make between these first and second phrases: though the second phrase is marked *pp vivo*, the first has no tempo or dynamic indication at all.[11] But within a single meter he manages to suggest the opposition of rhythmic characters in the main body of the Ballade.

Günther Wagner writes sensitively about the question-and-answer structure of the *Preludio*, its "short-winded, heterogeneous, cut-up" character, which gives an "impression of memory, of reminiscence, of looking back."[12] The cut-up phrases and the harmonic progression—moving from what turns out to be a Neapolitan harmony to a tonic that is reached only in the main theme—follow the example of Chopin's first Ballade, as several writers have pointed out. But because Chopin's introduction arches along a single, purposeful line, all the breaks in that line, as well as the key-note chord, sound foreboding, and the introduction as a whole draws the listener into the Ballade with the authority of a well-practiced storyteller. The Liszt *Preludio*, by contrast, makes three different starts, not even in sequence, but twice from the same note. Wagner's idea of memory at play fits the music

Example 4-1. Liszt, Ballade in D-flat, mm. 1–17.

perfectly: from disconnected flashes the storyteller seems to be groping to remember how the adventure began.

The tentativeness hangs over into the main theme. But Peter Raabe misses the point when he deprecates this Ballade for its "weak themes."[13] Each of the two main themes has a strongly realized character, in fact a more identifiable character than the impersonal main themes of the Chopin Ballades have. If Chopin's themes are narrating stanzas from which some hints of content eventually emerge, Liszt's are all content, all character, from the start—a love theme (*Andantino, con sentimento*) and a march theme (*Tempo di marcia, animato*). The love theme is "sung" in thirds from the start; the voices suggested are those of the characters in the story, not that of a narrator. But if a narrator's voice can never be distinguished after the *Preludio*, a narrator's presence can be detected in the way both themes begin tentatively and grow ardent as they proceed, like memories that come alive as the narrator dwells on them. Raabe complains that Liszt elaborated these themes "in the virtuoso manner" and less attractively than in other works, but the effect of a memory coming back to life derives precisely from the method that Liszt employs: embellishing his themes as he states and repeats them, giving them new harmonic turns, placing them in higher and higher registers, but keeping the form of the theme intact.

The *Andantino* section of the Ballade consists of nothing but theme and embellishment, interrupted by a cadenza after the full theme is first completed (m. 45) and trailing off in the middle of its repetition. The *Tempo di marcia* section is more complicated. The march theme arrives abruptly (on an enharmonic switch from D-flat to A major), is shorter than the first theme, and grows bold more quickly. It soon reaches a climactic third statement in the dominant and cadences (m. 86). But for the rest of the section the march theme has to contend with interruptions by the second phrase of the *Preludio*. This phrase, though it shares the dotted rhythm of the march theme, always stays distinct from it. What is more, it has just as much character as the two main themes, an irrepressible, puckish spirit that steals the show from the march theme. Whenever the march theme rises to a new height of grandeur (mm. 83–86 and 115–19), this phrase, brought in by what seems like a wave of the narrator's wand, pushes it aside (see Example 4-2).

Example 4-2. Liszt, Ballade in D-flat, mm. 83–87.

The phrase rises to grandeur of its own (at mm. 96–100 and 129–38), but even then it is engaged in a playful choice between cadencing in A major (the key of the march theme) and cadencing in C-sharp major (D-flat, the key of the love theme). The second time this happens, the music reaches such a pitch of indecision that it seems to be a prank that ushers the love theme, rather than the march theme, back in. The *Tempo di marcia* section, then, is a contrasting middle section with a new theme, new rhythm, and new key, but it is not simply that. It is both exposition and development for the new theme, which is no sooner presented than it is challenged and undermined by other material.

The forcefulness, if not the playfulness, of that section carries over into the return of the love theme. Liszt marked this section *Tempo I*, but also *Animato*. As in the Chopin Ballades, the momentum is increased here by faster figuration, and later by faster beats. The faster figuration (sixteenth notes) becomes faster still (sextuplet sixteenth notes) in the course of this variation, but then settles back to its original form at the very end (mm. 159–60, 163–64). From then on, however, only the second half of the theme appears, and the momentum is increased relentlessly by means of accelerando. The sensation of rushing to the end is increased by the cascading of the figuration on every beat and by the wonderful cascading of melody and harmony in a single downward sweep six measures long (mm. 177–82). The final rush, marked by no cadence, comes so forcefully that the return of the march theme, in its own meter, fails to break the pace (m. 185), and it takes the puckish phrase from the *Preludio* (m. 188), not surprisingly, to bring things to an end.

This Ballade, as Günther Wagner writes,[14] has to be considered ternary in form, with allowance for the role of the *Preludio* in the main body of the work. The ternary division of the work is as clear as it could be, the inner section contrasted with the outer ones in theme, meter, character, and—for the most part—key. But it is not just the reappearance of a phrase from the *Preludio* in the middle section that complicates the analysis; the third section, too, changes in function as it proceeds. Starting simply as a varied return of the first section, it is carried away by an accelerando that eventually draws in the themes from the *Preludio* and the middle section. In a modest way, Liszt may have been following Chopin's model of how to end a *ballade*; if that was the case, it was the third of Chopin's Ballades that Liszt followed most closely. The very speed of his ending is his means of resolving the opposition of rhythms that has occupied the piece since the *Preludio*. Earlier, the rhythmic opposition of the love and march themes was a matter of tempo as well as meter; now the love theme has reached such a fast tempo that only the metrical difference is left, and at a whirlwind tempo, still increasing (*Più animato*), the change of meter has little effect.

Not much is resolved, perhaps, in this resolution. Liszt has smoothed over the change in meters, but he had already done that, much more subtly, at the beginning, in moving from the *Preludio* to the love theme. The opposition of two rhythms has produced no real accommodation between them (like the accommodation achieved in Liszt's Second Ballade), nor does the march theme really reestablish itself in the key of the love theme. That theme and the *Preludio* phrase, as they rush past at the end, do not wrap up the story so much as recall its elements to mind. The Ballade ends, as it began, with scattered flashes of memory. At the close, as elsewhere in the piece, Liszt did not fully follow Chopin's model of a highly dramatized musical narration, nor did he fully follow the lyric model of a *ballade* in ternary form; he did not seriously rework his themes, nor did he simply elaborate them. Instead he managed to achieve a thorough if uneasy balance between those two seemingly incompatible models.

Second Ballade, in B minor

No such balance or ambiguity characterizes Liszt's Second Ballade: it is one of his largest, most powerful piano works, fully narrative, or programmatic, in nature. In this work Liszt gives no nod to the lyrical tradition of piano *ballades*, but embraces a conception of the genre as ambitious as Chopin's. That is not to say that he necessarily derived this conception from his study of Chopin. In the five years between completing his first and second Ballades (1848 and 1853, respectively), Liszt wrote not only several other piano works in Chopin genres—mazurka and polonaise— but also some of the works now regarded as his most original in conception: the first few symphonic poems for orchestra and, for piano, the *Grosses Konzertsolo*, the Scherzo and March, and the Sonata. The Second Ballade belongs with these works in its heroic character and in the rhythmic complexity of its thematic interactions and transformations. It is a real question, then, how much this work has to do with Chopin's Ballades or Liszt's own earlier Ballade, how much it really belongs to the *ballade* genre at all.

Differences from previous *ballades* are apparent from the start. The Second Ballade opens not with a voice, but with an accompaniment, and not so much an accompaniment as a presence in the bass, starting before the melody and lasting throughout it (see Example 4-3). Like the similar opening bass line of Wagner's *Die Walküre*, written a year later, this line sets a natural scene and a human mood. The monotonous repetition of the line, without break and with no crescendo until the very end,[15] makes the mood immediate: the situation, the characters here are gloomy, not—as in the opening of Chopin's first Ballade—doomed. The slow-moving melody has less presence of its own; rather, it converts the rise and fall of the bass line to a singable range and pace, without altogether stealing attention away from that continuing line. But this melody is not chromatic; rather, like the main theme of the Moscheles Ballade, it follows a descending melodic minor scale when it rises as well as when it falls. The practically unchanging bass, the melody

Example 4-3. Liszt, Second Ballade, mm. 1–8.

with no leading tone, and the monotonous filler between bass and melody together create a remarkably static harmony, slow to move away from the tonic and never sounding the dominant.

The melody ends without finality (m. 17), and so, after assuming the singing role for three measures, does the bass (m. 20). Resolution comes in the succeeding phrases (*Lento assai* and *Allegretto*), but in a new rhythm and in the key of the dominant, F-sharp. The *Lento assai* phrase smooths the way to the *Allegretto* phrase in harmony, rhythm, and range. The *Allegretto* phrase, with its double and triple appoggiaturas, is in the same sentimental vein as the main theme of Liszt's first Ballade. This phrase (mm. 24–34) finally brings a cadence; in fact it is nothing but a single, long cadence. Contrasting in every way with the original melody, it is the resolution of that melody.

What happens next is the strangest event in the work: Liszt repeats everything that has been heard so far, almost note for note, a half-tone lower. The repetition has sometimes been explained as analogous to the repetition of a sonata-form exposition, and the tonal change has been described as "not a very happy innovation," designed to bring "extra variety" to that traditional repetition.[16] This explanation presumes that the opening passage (the first thirty-four measures) of the Ballade constitutes an exposition, in something like the sonata-form sense.

Before investigating the implications of that term for the rest of the work, we might consider other ways of analyzing this opening passage. Louis Kentner writes of the entire passage as "making an unusually long first subject in which the germs of the coming conflict are presented as in a prologue."[17] Models of unusually long and eventful first subjects were certainly available to Liszt in the Chopin Ballades, though nothing in the Liszt distinguishes the telling from the subject of the tale in Chopin's way. Kentner's language suggests a closer analogy with the *Preludio* of Liszt's first Ballade. The "germs of the coming conflict" are certainly presented in the form of two systematically contrasted statements, just as they are in the opening five measures of the first Ballade. What is more, both openings proceed with the same stops and starts. Of course, there is a great difference between a contrast made within five measures and one that takes thirty-four, but the two works themselves are vastly different in scale. Allowing for that difference, the opening of the Second Ballade, with its transposed repetition, can be compared in the first Ballade to the whole *Preludio*, the second half of which is, if not an exactly transposed repetition of the first, a revision that pulls the music down by a half-step.

Kentner is right to compare the opening section of the Second Ballade in one respect to a Prologue, but his description of it as a "first subject" is less satisfactory. Unlike the long first themes of the Chopin Ballades, this section contains both principal components of the work, contrasted in key. In that sense it is like a sonata-form exposition. But it is unlike sonata expositions in the peculiar relationship of its two components.

The *Allegro moderato* music and the *Allegretto* music are not separate themes, but theme and co-theme, opposites that can be presented, or imagined, only by reference to each other. In the terms of Márta Grabócz's illuminating structural-semiotic analysis, the two together constitute a "thematic complex."[18] Between the two components of this "thematic complex" there is not so much a conflict as a perpetual engagement, a fixed progression. The progression has no continuation; it breaks off and starts again. The abrupt chromatic transposition at the first of these moments of discontinuity dramatizes the structure: it shows how fixed the progression is. This progression goes on being repeated throughout the Ballade, but at each further repetition—each new episode—the relationship between theme and co-theme shifts, until in the end a new stability is established between them. Chopin's Ballades, especially the second, may have influenced Liszt's idea of two opposed musical components in a recurring interaction, but it is characteristic of Liszt, and not of Chopin, to move systematically within a work from a most unsettled to a most stable and definitive statement of the musical material.[19]

In these terms the long *Allegro deciso* section at the middle of the work (mm. 70–253), described by Günther Wagner as the development section,[20] can be heard instead as the third and fourth episodes in the Ballade. This section begins in a march rhythm, the third rhythmic character to appear in the work. Gradually the elements are assembled for a new version of the theme in this march rhythm. A tremolo scale figure (beginning at m. 96), recalling the chromatic bass line of the opening, is accompanied by melodic fragments recalling the melody of the theme. Finally that melody itself is heard (at m. 113), transformed into the character and meter of a heroic march and accompanied by a combination of chromatic scales from the opening and dotted march rhythms from the beginning of the *Allegro deciso*. Though the melody is formed from the same scale as before, its harmonization is now more decisive. As before, it breaks off without cadencing; and as before, a largely solo transitional passage (mm. 129–34) smooths the way for the co-theme to appear, in a new key and character.

In this transition, however, Liszt detours harmonically and then delays the co-theme further by introducing a new melody (*A piacere*, at m. 135). This melody, the most tentative, the most incomplete in the Ballade, takes a course typical of the work: it breaks off after four measures and starts in again, chromatically transposed (in this case, a half-tone higher). In view of the unusual structure of the work, it is misleading to call this new melody the "second theme," as Kentner and Grabócz call it. It is rather a new part of the thematic progression already established. So far it serves to introduce and, in Grabócz's word, "underline" the character of the co-theme; later it takes on more life of its own.

The co-theme now returns. Its new form can hardly be called a thematic transformation, but everything new about it is significant (see Example 4-4). Whereas the theme has just been transformed from its original triplet rhythm (6/4) to the 4/4 rhythm of the co-theme, the co-theme keeps its overall rhythm. But its eighth-note motion is now played off against a triplet-eighth-note accompaniment. In other words, Liszt has made each component of his main progression yield, in some measure, to the rhythm of the other. The co-theme is also changed, stabilized, by being played over a tonic, rather than a dominant, pedal. Starting in the fourth measure, though, C-naturals convert that tonic D into a new dominant, while hardly disturbing the course of the melody. The cadence, with a turn (m. 150) that now seems to derive from the *A piacere* melody, takes the music to G major, where the co-theme and the modulatory process repeat themselves.

Example 4-4. Liszt, Second Ballade, mm. 143–50.

This time there is no cadence; the bass drops out and the melody drifts dreamily down, making a dominant-seventh harmony in C major, until a mysterious intrusion in E-flat, with the accompaniment and melody of the co-theme now inverted (m. 159), leads quickly back to the theme, now in G-sharp (A-flat) minor. The narrative idea here is straight out of Chopin's Ballades: just when reckoning seems most remote, when the lyrical, major-key theme is losing itself in a dreamy haze, an unexpected harmonic turn brings the stern or gloomy theme abruptly back. Liszt made the idea his own with his wonderful modulation over the unmoving bass. If anything, this moment looks ahead to Debussy rather than back to Chopin.

Within the Second Ballade, this passage ends the third episode and begins the fourth. The arresting modulation marks the fresh start, just as the switch to B-flat minor marked the start of the second episode. But this time there is no pause between episodes. In fact, this passage is the first transition in the work to be made without an elaborate halt and pause. After this point all transitions are made with no halt or only a brief one. The story is being swept toward its crisis, and Liszt, like Chopin but by somewhat different means, is increasing the momentum.

The theme returns (at m. 162) in its new (4/4) rhythm, but with something very close to its original chromatic bass line. This bass line, transforming itself into a longer-waved tremolo form, rises in force as it leads through modulation (from G-sharp minor to C minor) and reiteration of the theme to the climax of the Ballade (mm. 207-15). At the same time that it is the climax of the whole work, this passage serves as the transition from the theme to the co-theme in the fourth episode, and its principal element—the movement between G and C-sharp in the bass—derives from bass lines in the previous versions of this same transition (see Example 4-5). Following the

Example 4-5. Liszt, Second Ballade, mm. 21–22 (*above*), mm. 129–31 (*center*), and mm. 207–08 (*below*).

method of Chopin's reckonings, Liszt here forges together motives from various earlier moments: the G-to-C-sharp interval from the transitions, the chromatic scale from the very opening, and the triplet repeated chords from the beginning of the *Allegro deciso* section. But though Liszt advances his narrative by some of the same musical techniques that Chopin had developed in his Ballades, his tale follows a very different course. It reaches its climax, or reckoning, in a transitional passage, when the work is barely two-thirds done.

The return of the *A piacere* melody and then of the co-theme is for Kentner the beginning of the recapitulation, unusual in that it begins with the "second subject." But the co-theme is less settled than ever, drifting dreamily again, this time on a variety of dominant pedals, the last of which, F-sharp (mm. 250–53), leads finally to a stable return, a new transformation of the theme, in B major (m. 254). Liszt creates a strong sensation of reconciliation in this transformation by making the theme flow naturally out of the co-theme, by putting the theme in the major mode for the first time, and by changing its rhythm again. Though its meter is once more the 6/4 of the opening, the melody now moves twice as quickly through the 6/4 measures, the harmony now changes once or even twice per measure, and the feeling of strain that has previously characterized this theme is marvelously alleviated. The theme is repeated (mm. 262–68) with growing confidence, moving to the dominant. In the autograph score this second statement of the theme stands alone; Liszt added the first statement in front of it just before the score was printed. The expansion makes a great difference. Not only is the moment underscored, but the theme in this periodic form now stands complete in itself for the first time.

Liszt's late revisions extend from this passage to the end of the work. Study of these revisions shows Liszt choosing among several models of ending and therefore among several different narrative ideas. The revisions are described by Sulyok and Mező in their critical notes to the Second Ballade in the New Liszt Edition. Among other revisions, Liszt wrote three different versions of the coda, the passage after the final transformation of the theme (roughly, from m. 298 of the final version to the end).[21] Of these endings, the first appears in print in the present volume for the first time, while the second has been printed several times; it is most accessible in the appendices to the Vianna da Motta (Breitkopf & Härtel) and Sauer (Peters) editions. We will note the revisions as we continue tracing the course of the final version.

The theme, transformed and doubled in length (mm. 254-68), leads directly into a new version of the *A piacere* melody (at m. 269). The lack of transition, the increase in tempo (*Un poco più mosso*), and a more active accompaniment than before all contribute to the impression that the Second Ballade, like Liszt's first, is ending in a jumble of memories. At the same time, this melody, which before always yielded after two indecisive phrases to the co-theme, now comes into its own. Rising to a climax and dissolving into a virtuosic cascade, it leads not to the co-theme this time, but to a second B-major transformation of the theme. Given that the theme and co-theme have succeeded each other relentlessly in the same order throughout this long Ballade, the breaking of the pattern here has great force, especially in signaling the close.

The new transformation itself (mm. 284-97, *Grandioso*), picking up where the previous transformation left off, sounds final in the sense that more grandeur could hardly be expected of a single person sitting at a piano. Liszt expanded this transformation, like the previous one, at the last moment by adding what is now its first statement (mm. 284-91). He also offered the performer a choice between two versions of the second phrase (mm. 292-97). As these two versions have exactly the same range, it is not a matter here—as it is with the alternative passages in Liszt's first Ballade—of accommodating pianos of different compass. Here the version with scales (preferred by most present-day performers) expands on the wavelike scales of the previous statement, while the version with the dotted rhythms (given by Liszt as the primary version) recalls the *Allegro deciso* episode. Maybe Liszt was secretly wishing for a second piano at this point, so that he could present both versions simultaneously and bring back the whole history of the theme at its final appearance.

This transformation is interrupted by a galloping scalar passage, at first chromatic and then diatonic (mm. 298–301), another rush of memory. In the final version, however, the rush is soon braked, and the Ballade is closed by the co-theme, played at least as slowly and quietly as ever before. Though it is not easy for a performer to bring the Ballade so suddenly to so calm a close, this ending is satisfactory on several counts. First, the co-theme was displaced just before (m. 284), when the *A piacere* melody was followed by the *Grandioso* transformation of the theme; the restoration of the co-theme is now all that is needed to complete the final episode and resolve the work. It is also satisfying that the co-theme is restored in its original form, with its original accompaniment. After a long process of engagement between the theme and co-theme—an engagement in which each accommodated to the rhythm of the other—the Ballade ends by restoring their original rhythmic distinctness. The interdependence remains: the theme still breaks off, to be completed by the co-theme; but now the completion is made in the same key, the tonic major. Still incomplete without each other, theme and co-theme end, in effect, at peace with themselves.

In coming to this final version of the ending, Liszt evidently reconsidered the nature of the work. His first version (or at least the earliest extant version), here transcribed from the autograph (see Example 4-6), brought the co-theme back instead in a new series of motivic reworkings, leading to an excited and triumphant conclusion.[22] At the beginning of this section (m. 302a) Liszt reworked the melodic motive of the co-theme in the dotted rhythm of the *Allegro deciso* episode, a rhythm previously associated with the theme. By so doing he prolonged the central process of the work, the

Example 4-6. Liszt, Second Ballade, Ending (first version, crossed out in the autograph). Reproduced by permission of B. Schott's Söhne, Mainz.

process of rhythmic engagement between the theme and co-theme. That engagement takes a new form in a later passage (m. 318a) in which the triple rhythm of the theme and the duple rhythm of the co-theme join to produce a cross-rhythm in the right-hand passagework. Liszt, in writing passagework of this sort over a repeating harmonic progression, could well have been inspired by similar passagework in the Chopin Ballades. This ending as a whole, giving the work a last burst of virtuoso excitement and leaving the themes transformed by contact with each other, is much more like the ending of a Chopin Ballade than Liszt's final version is.

In his next version of the ending (transcribed in the Breitkopf and the Peters editions) he went even further in the same direction. There Liszt specifies the new meter and tempo for the ending, and, as at the ending of a Chopin Ballade, they signal the fastest speed in the entire work; in fact, they are precisely the same meter and tempo as in the ending of Chopin's first Ballade, ¢ and *Presto* (the ¢ in the autograph is mistranscribed as C in all the printed editions of this version). In this version Liszt introduces a two-against-three cross-rhythm right away (see Example 4-7); otherwise this version follows substantially the same course as the earlier one. Liszt extends this version, however, with a triumphant climax (*Allegro non troppo*) that recapitulates the climax heard earlier, in the fourth episode. Though recapitulation as such is not an idea borrowed from the Chopin Ballades, this passage, a fiery last interaction of diverse motives, is composed like a Chopin Ballade reckoning.

Example 4-7. Liszt, Second Ballade, first two measures of the Ending (second version in the autograph).

Whatever his motives in replacing that ending with the final version, Liszt certainly turned from an ending that recalls Chopin's practice to one completely different in nature. In the process, he threw into relief the difference between Chopin's conception of the *ballade* and his own. A Chopin Ballade is a narrative of avoidance; when the crucial musical issue is finally joined, the work is finished. In this Liszt Ballade, by contrast, the issue is joined all along. In a series of episodes that all enact nearly the same thematic progression, this issue evolves. Unlike a ballad process, which naturally presses to a resolution, an evolutionary process continues more naturally than it ends. Even the fourth episode of Liszt's Second Ballade, rising to a climax and then resolving into the tonic key, does not end the work, but leads on to a fifth episode (see Diagram 4-1). Liszt's difficulty finding a satisfactory form for that last episode can be understood as a consequence of the work's overall process, which left both too much and too little to be accomplished in that episode.

In other terms—David Buchan's terms of ballad construction—Liszt's Second Ballade begins, like Chopin's second Ballade, with a "concurrent"

1st EPISODE

m. 1	24
Allegro moderato 6/4	Allegretto 4/4
B minor	F-sharp major
Theme	Co-theme

2nd EPISODE

36	59
Allegro moderato 6/4	Allegretto 4/4
B-flat minor	F major
Theme	Co-theme

3rd EPISODE

70	113	135	143
Allegro deciso 4/4	—	A piacere —	Allegretto —
V/D minor: F-sharp minor	F-sharp minor	D major	D major: G major
Introduction to Theme	Theme (Transformed)	A piacere Melody	Co-theme

4th EPISODE

162	207	225	234
—	—	Rubato —	Allegretto —
G-sharp minor: C minor	(vii°7/b)	B major	B major: E-flat major: V/B major ⟶
Theme (Transformed)	Climax	A piacere Melody	Co-theme

5th EPISODE

254	269	284	305
Allegro moderato 6/4	Un poco più mosso 4/4	Allegro moderato 6/4	Andantino 4/4
B major	V/B major ⟶	B major	B major
Theme (Transformed)	A piacere Melody	Theme (Transformed: Grandioso)	Co-theme

Diagram 4-1. Episodic form of Liszt's Second Ballade.

architectonic: "The units of the structures all consistently coincide to produce well-defined scenes." Each new episode is marked off from the last by a combination of thematic, harmonic, and rhythmic changes (see, again, Diagram 4-1). But at the climax of the piece in the middle of the fourth episode, Liszt changes to a more "contrapuntal" architectonic principle, like that of Chopin's first Ballade. He reaches B major, the closing key, not at a juncture of episodes, but in the middle of the fourth episode, right after the climax. From then on, the lack of harmonic change (as every theme is presented in B major) and the frequency of rhythmic change obscure the structure of episodes. There is nothing more characteristically evolutionary about this work, nothing that more clearly distinguishes it from the Chopin Ballades, than this change of architectonic principles at the climax.

To bring the work to a close in the fifth episode, Liszt resorted to one of his favorite devices of closure: he transformed the theme into an apotheosis. Here the apotheosis adds to the already considerable difficulty of associating the work with any ballad story or any model of the ballad. A number of pianists have claimed, without citing any evidence, that Liszt modeled the work on the story of Hero and Leander.[23] The idea is particularly attractive if the model is specified as Schiller's "Hero und Leander," which the poet called a ballad, but which stretches any definition of that genre. Even Schiller's poem can scarcely accommodate the apotheosis of Liszt's Ballade. If the association serves any purpose, it is not so much in identifying the theme with the stormy waters of the Hellespont and the co-theme with the protagonists' love, but in drawing attention to what is remarkable even within Liszt's output, a musical narration consisting of essentially the same action—the same thematic progression—repeated five times.

If there is no sign of the ballad process in this Ballade, there is also hardly anything suggesting the structure of sounding voices in a ballad, the interplay of narration and dialogue. Melodies sound in a great many textures and ranges, but none can easily be singled out as a narrator's or a character's voice. The theme and co-theme, interacting rhythmically with each other, seem to represent two forces within the story rather than two voices or characters. In this interaction of two themes, negotiated, as it were, by a third (the *A piacere* melody), Liszt was continuing the practice of his own first Ballade, while ignoring Chopin's practice.

The difference between this work and the Chopin Ballades goes even further. In the Liszt Second Ballade the narrative method rests on a principle of rhythmic flexibility: if the themes, which are presented initially in different meters, represent different forces or ideas in a story, the progress of the narration is marked largely by rhythmic accommodations in those themes. This association of narrative progression with the rhythmic adaptation of themes connects the work not only with other programmatic works of Liszt—notably his symphonies and symphonic poems—but also with the Wagnerian leitmotif system and with subsequent developments in narrative

PLATE 4. Illustration of the opening episode of Erben's "The Water Goblin." This 1890 illustration is nearly contemporary with Dvořák's symphonic poem on the subject.

methods for opera, ballet music, incidental music, and film music. In other words, the rhythmic adaptation of themes, which allowed each new episode of a story its own distinctive musical rhythms, was of particular importance wherever musical narration had to accommodate sung or spoken words or mimed action. By contrast, the narrative method of the Chopin Ballades, in which themes embody voices and song structures, depends precisely upon the rhythmic stability of themes to represent the unchanging constituents of a sung narrative. It is hardly surprising that Chopin's method was virtually never adapted to dramatic music and proved influential only in narrative instrumental music, especially within the *ballade* genre, while Liszt's method proved equally influential in programmatic and dramatic music.

In certain respects, though, Liszt was imitating Chopin's Ballades and imitating them more deeply in his Second Ballade than in his first, for all the resemblance between the introductions of the two composers' first Ballades. The idea of a climax made by bringing together tiny motives from several earlier moments, rather than by recapitulating a single theme, seems to come from Chopin's *ballade* endings. The progression from one moment to another, sometimes after a wandering transition and sometimes with no transition at all, is close to Chopin's "leaping and lingering" *ballade* technique. Most significant of all is the concentration on a single action, as a ballad concentrates on a single situation. Liszt's Second Ballade (in the final version), with its fastest tempos in the middle, does not have the irresistible momentum of Chopin's Ballades, but it has an even more remarkable concentration on a fixed thematic progression over a longer span. Liszt's knowledge of folk and poetic ballads may of course have mixed with his study of Chopin as he produced these features in his Ballade. But his bringing all these features together in a Ballade indicates that he studied the musical structures of Chopin's Ballades, rather than simply borrowing the title for a big, programmatic piano piece or, on the other hand, imitating one or another of the Chopin Ballades in key or in telltale motives or rhythms. In that sense, his Second Ballade can be considered a true contribution to the genre, not just another major Liszt piano piece, incidentally titled in tribute to Chopin.

Within the repertory of piano *ballades*, the Second Ballade has hardly any imitators. A number of later piano *ballades* are indebted to Liszt in one way or another, but rarely in ways that specifically derive from this work. The form and scale of the Ballade may have daunted any would-be imitators. At the same time, this Ballade can be seen to have had an influence on the genre, and especially on a number of large-scale and serious piano *ballades* composed in its wake by students and disciples of Liszt. For the composers of these *ballades* (which are considered in the following pages), Liszt's Second Ballade seems to have opened up the genre to musical forms other than Chopin's and narrative types other than that of the ballad. While Liszt's work is in its way profoundly indebted to Chopin, its importance in the history of the *ballade* lies precisely in its distance from Chopin: it freed the genre from any particular tie to ballads, making the title "*ballade*" available for narrative piano pieces on many different models and, by the end of the nineteenth century, making "*ballade*" the preeminent name for programmatic piano pieces, as "symphonic poem" was for programmatic orchestral works.

OTHER *BALLADES* IN THE NARRATIVE TRADITION

Bülow

Liszt's example may have spurred a few younger composers in the 1850s to take up Chopin's challenge. It seems significant, at any rate, that the two most impressive piano *ballades* in the narrative tradition to come in the wake of Liszt's Ballades were both written by followers of Liszt: the Ballade, Op. 11,[24] by Hans von Bülow (1830–1894) and the incomplete Ballade in E minor by Bedřich Smetana (1824–1884). Both bring fresh narrative and formal ideas to the genre.

Bülow had studied piano with Liszt (beginning in 1851) and had promoted Liszt's music as a performer and as a critic by the time his own Ballade appeared in 1856; he would marry Liszt's daughter Cosima a year later. He had also performed Chopin's music, including the G-minor Ballade.[25] Later one of the most important pianists, conductors, and editors of his period, he was at this early stage in his career a productive composer of piano, orchestral, and vocal music. At the publication of the Ballade he was twenty-six, the same age at which Chopin had published his first Ballade. Bülow himself described his Ballade as his "most passable work to date."[26]

The work is huge and earnest, even longer (in measures) than Liszt's Second Ballade, and strenuous for both performer and listener throughout. The length comes not so much from thematic repetitions (no theme is repeated as such more than once) as from the spinning-out of motives. The music is strenuous in part because Bülow relentlessly combines motives and themes in counterpoint with one another and with themselves. In his phrase-rhythms and textures, then, he breaks—even more decisively than Liszt— with Chopin's method of presenting voices in succession and largely within songlike phrase structures. At the same time, Bülow uses certain of Chopin's formal techniques. His contribution to the genre can be seen as an accommodation—not easily achieved—between the narrative methods of Chopin's Ballades and the musical processes of older instrumental traditions, notably those of Classical sonata style.

The Ballade opens, in C-sharp minor, with a theme in one phrase (*Sostenuto*; see Example 4-8). The hollow first chord, the monotonous accompaniment, and the sequential progression of the melody all contribute to the gloomy tone and the suggestion of folk song. The idea of beginning with the narrating voice comes from Chopin. But once Bülow gets to the end

Example 4-8. Bülow, Ballade, Op. 11, mm. 1-6.

of that introductory theme, his way of proceeding is unlike Chopin's. Some form of this theme, or some motive from it, or some sign of it is almost always present in the rest of the piece. From the introductory theme, for instance, Bülow works his way by means of a generating passage on the opening rhythmic motive (*Quasi recitando*, mm. 7-13; see Example 4-9) to the main theme (*Moderato*, m. 14), which itself begins as an inversion of the introductory theme. There are other, independent themes—a second theme beginning in the tonic (*Appassionato vivace*, m. 49) and a lovely, lyrical theme in F- sharp major (*Cantabile quasi andante*, m. 114)—but even they are accompanied by triplet-eighth-note rhythms derived from the melody of the introductory theme. Later, the *Appassionato vivace* theme is twice heard in contrapuntal combination with the introductory theme (mm. 73-78 and 176-83). Bülow's narrative idea for the Ballade, in other words, is that the subject disclosed at the beginning should remain obsessively, oppressively present as the story works itself out.

Example 4-9. Bülow, Ballade, Op. 11, mm. 7-13.

That is not to say that the working-out is all combination and recombination, without differentiation. Bülow makes a clear distinction between reworking and recapitulating. It is the recapitulating that marks new stages in the musical form. Oddly enough, the main theme is never recapitulated—never reappears as itself—while the generating passage (*Quasi recitando*, Example 4-9) that produced it returns twice. The first time (m. 103) it leads on to the lyrical theme, the second time (m. 279; see Example 4-10) back to the introductory theme.

Example 4-10. Bülow, Ballade, Op. 11, mm. 274–80.

That second return is especially worth noticing. Just before, the lyrical F-sharp major theme has been recapitulated, in a grand apotheosis (*Maestoso moderato*, m. 243). Both the grandeur and the sonata-like formal function (recapitulating in the tonic key the theme that originally came in a secondary key) connect this moment with Liszt's Second Ballade, rather than with Chopin's Ballades. It is also the moment that provides the greatest relief from triplet figuration. All in all, it signals the beginning of the work's resolution. To move from this theme back to the main material of the Ballade, Bülow creates a thematic convergence, modeled on those in Chopin's Ballades (see, again, Example 4-10). In this convergence the generating passage now emerges out of the lyrical theme (mm. 279–80), with its rhythm accommodated to that of the phrase from which it emerges.

The most dramatic stroke in the entire work is that this generating passage now leads, not to the main theme, as it originally did, but to the introductory theme, its original gloomy tone intensified by canonic imitation (m. 283). The effect of a symmetrical rounding-off, of an unexpected and ironic reminder of the opening, recalls many ballad texts, as well as the ending of Chopin's second Ballade. But Chopin had given his Ballade a furious reckoning by that point, and Bülow now gives his Ballade one—a spectacular virtuoso passage (*Presto*, m. 288) modeled on Chopin's reckonings in spirit and in some stylistic details.

Like Liszt, Bülow faced the problem of too many resolutions: once a work had achieved an apotheosis, a grandiose thematic transformation, how could it go on to end, as Chopin's example suggested a piano *ballade* should end, with a furious reckoning? Bülow accepted the challenge that Liszt had at first taken up and then declined: by means of a complicated and problematic transition, Bülow yoked together both kinds of resolution. In its own way, the ending of his Ballade is no easier to bring off in performance than the ending of Liszt's Second Ballade.

Bülow's role in the history of the *ballade* does not end with this work. His second *ballade*, however, is an orchestral work and takes its title and form from a poetic ballad of Uhland. Though in some way it perhaps builds on Bülow's experience with his piano *ballade*, in this study it is taken up separately (Chapter 8).

Smetana

Smetana's E-minor Ballade exists today only as a fragment, though the 209 existing measures constitute a major part of a substantial work.[27] Hana Séquardtová, the editor of the fragment, cites evidence to suggest that Smetana finished the work, but that the finished version is lost.[28] No matter what became of the work, the surviving fragment is a tantalizing indication of what could have been an important contribution to the nineteenth-century piano repertory, as well as a worthy successor to the Chopin and Liszt Ballades. Not having brought the work out as a piano piece, Smetana reused its main theme, virtually unaltered, in an opera aria years later. This change of medium, not an isolated occurrence in the history of the *ballade*, is of interest in itself: if the *ballade* as a genre is derived from song, or at least from the idea of a certain kind of song, it is hardly surprising to find a *ballade* that turns back into song.

In 1858, when Smetana wrote the Ballade, he was nearing the end of several years of residence in Göteborg, Sweden, where he made his career largely as a pianist and piano teacher. The year 1858 was one of experimentation for him as a composer, when he wrote, under the influence of Liszt, several programmatic works (not all brought to completion), among the most daring in concept and musical style that he would ever write. He had fallen under the spell of Liszt's playing years before, had been helped by Liszt toward his first publication, and kept abreast of Liszt's latest work. He was also an admired performer of Chopin's music and indicated several times that Chopin was an inspiration to him as a composer.[29]

Among his earlier piano works—mostly character pieces and polkas—one is worth mentioning here for its connection to a poetic ballad. The "Album Leaf" in C-sharp minor, which Smetana intended to be the third piece in his Opus 3, appears to have been linked by him to a verse from Schiller's ballad, "Der Taucher."[30] This "Album Leaf" is no narrative *ballade*, but a short character piece that may depict the swirling waves into which the diver of Schiller's ballad sinks. It is noteworthy that the apparent literary inspiration for this piece is a German poem: even years later, in 1858 when he wrote the Ballade, Smetana was still not at home in the Czech language.

If the Ballade had a specific model in poetry or song, no evidence of it has been found. The work belongs to the narrative tradition of piano *ballades*. Its piano style owes little either to Chopin or Liszt, but several crucial elements of its form connect it to Chopin's Ballades. Study of the work is hampered by two kinds of incompleteness: the principal surviving score not only breaks off before the end, but also contains no dynamic, expressive, or articulation markings. Another source, however, gives at least the main theme of the Ballade fully marked.[31] It is helpful to have Smetana's indication that the theme should be played "not fast, in a grand tone," as well as other, more local markings.

In an introduction (mm. 1–22) before the main theme, Smetana presents a twisting line that will turn into two separate but paired middle voices accompanying the main theme (see Example 4-11). In fact, given the modest accompaniments that Chopin put to his Ballade themes, Smetana's main theme has to be counted most remarkable, not for the beauty of its melody— though that too is remarkable—but for its complex of accompanying voices. The writing throughout the theme is generally in five parts: the melody is heard on top, and the two paired voices derived from the introduction are heard in the next-to-highest and next-to-lowest parts. By means of bold counterpoint Smetana keeps any of these parts from getting submerged. He is especially bold in keeping the two paired middle voices distinct from each other. In the third measure of the theme, for instance, the higher of those voices has B–C–D against B–C-double-sharp–D-sharp in the lower voice (see Example 4-11, m. 25). Other such dissonances arise between the theme itself and the middle voices (see m. 37, for instance), though less frequently.

Example 4-11. Smetana, Ballade in E minor, mm. 23–48.

What kind of melody can hold its own in these surroundings? Not the impersonal narrating melody of a Chopin Ballade or the slow, somber motive that opens Liszt's Second Ballade, but a passionate utterance that, pulled this way and that by turbulent inner voices, suggests the conflicting emotions of a single character. Naturally enough, it was precisely for a character suffering from conflicting emotions that Smetana turned this theme into an aria.

Even if this theme is dramatic rather than narrative in character, it does not just express a character's feelings; it unfolds its own story out of those feelings, and does so by the same means that Chopin had developed in his narrating themes: by a process of interrupting and resuming the theme.

Smetana's theme is heard for twenty-five measures before it is interrupted in the middle of a phrase (m. 48). The melody breaks off while the accompaniment continues, and even that soon dissolves into a cadenza. The theme returns (m. 68), not where it left off and not with its earlier accompaniment, but from the beginning and in a new, monumental version. After one phrase, however, it returns (m. 76) to exactly the form it had before, so that it seems in effect to have resumed in the middle. It proceeds as before and breaks off again at precisely the same point as before (m. 92). This time, though, the theme is not so much interrupted as developed: a sequence (mm. 92–104) is built on a motive from the first phrase of the theme. Treating the last phrase of the sequence as if it were a new beginning of the theme, Smetana resumes the theme from that point (m. 105), again in the monumental version. This time, however, the theme does not continue as before, but is rounded off by a cadential phrase that it had never reached before (mm. 109–22). In effect, three stanzas or statements of the theme have been heard, though none of them runs a full course. Overall, the theme seems to carry a message of such urgency that its speaker is repeatedly overcome in the process of delivering it and finally reaches the end only by dint of enormous effort.

That theme closes in the tonic key, E minor, and the second theme, abruptly moving toward C major, begins immediately (m. 122; see Example 4-12). This theme, almost as long and just as complex as the first, is completely different in style and form. It presents a simple, five- or six-note motive in a variety of versions, eventually evolving into a definitive statement in E major. This process of evolution is perhaps the most Lisztian feature of the work. The motive is heard in C major, first in a tentative form (mm. 122–32) and then in a stately form (mm. 133–36). The third form is in modal style without counterpoint and with only the simplest chords, sometimes simply thirds (mm. 137–44). This modal style, which may owe

Example 4-12. Smetana, Ballade in E minor, mm. 122–44.

something to Chopin,[32] was later developed by Smetana into one element of his nationalist Czech style; it has been adopted as such by Czech composers well into this century. Here, though, it is soon dissolved into a strongly tonal sequence reminiscent of Schumann (mm. 145-52). Then, after a passage that is as restless motivically as it is harmonically, Smetana arrives at the definitive form of his motive, an expansive line sustained by a graceful and consonant middle voice (mm. 159-77). This passage, which lingers dreamily, cadencing again and again, represents, like passages in the Chopin Ballades, the moment in the story when reckoning seems remote, but is about to creep in.

Chopin is also the model for the transition that follows. After the second theme cadences and stops (m. 177), its motive begins again, with something like the same rocking accompaniment as before, but now forming a mysterious augmented-triad harmony. As this motive ends, however (see Example 4-13, motive *a*), it is already turning into the opening motive of the main theme (see motive *b*) by a process of thematic convergence identical to the one that brings back the main theme in Chopin's third Ballade (see Example 3-16, p. 69). Here, too, the new composite phrase is repeated in a sequence (mm. 178-91). This sequence resembles the earlier sequence in the same work (mm. 92-104), built on the same motive from the main theme. In both cases the sequence, embodying at least a motive from the first phrase of the main theme, leads into a later phrase of that theme. Here, though, the main theme is not being interrupted, but is returning after a long absence, and even so, it resumes in the middle, as if it were already under way. This extraordinary structural effect, like the thematic convergence, has its precedent in a Chopin Ballade: the reemergence of the main theme of the fourth Ballade likewise proceeds out of a sequential treatment of the first phrase, but gets under way only at a later phrase.

Example 4-13. Smetana, Ballade in E minor, mm. 178-82.

Smetana's theme, from this point, takes the same course as before, except that the twisting lines of its accompaniment are now smoothed into rolling waves. Just at the point when the theme broke off before (mm. 48 and 92), it does so again (m. 208), but then the manuscript itself breaks off, giving no clue how the work would end. Brian Large speculates that "it is likely Smetana had a ternary structure in mind";[33] but the interaction, or convergence, between the two main themes in the surviving fragment makes that description seem inadequate. It is hard to believe, given the dramatic development of material so far, that Smetana was done with his second theme at this point or that he would simply round things off with the reprise of the main theme. It is also hard to believe so, given that there is evidence of more profound and fruitful study of Chopin's Ballades in this fragment than in any other *ballade* of the nineteenth century.

Almost ten years later Smetana reused the main theme of the Ballade for Milada's aria "Jaká to bouře ňadra mi plní" in his opera *Dalibor* (Act 1, Scene 6).[34] The adaptation is remarkably straightforward. Smetana gives the melody from the Ballade to both the singer and the first violins, and where the preexisting notes do not fit the given words, he lets the singer pause and rejoin the violins a few notes later (see Example 4-14). He keeps his original strong bass line and simplifies the original pair of middle voices into a single line, thereby sacrificing some of the original dissonant counterpoint.

Example 4-14. Smetana, *Dalibor*, Act 1, Scene 6, mm. 991–1003.

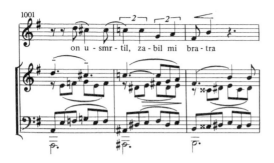

on u - smr - til, za - bil mi bra - tra

The aria sheds light on the Ballade, especially when one considers the dramatic situation to which Smetana was adapting the music and the formal correspondence between the aria and the Ballade. The story of *Dalibor*, drawn by Josef Wenzig from Czech legend, would make a perfect ballad subject: the knight Dalibor, tried and imprisoned for committing a revenge-murder, inspires love in the murdered man's sister, Milada, who dies trying to rescue him. This aria represents, in terms of the ballad process, the act of defiance—Milada's admission to herself that she loves Dalibor, in defiance of her family loyalty. The second couplet of the aria puts the matter concisely: "It's true that he killed, that he murdered my brother / and yet I'm attracted to him!"[35]

Here is a conflict of feelings such as Smetana had already expressed in musical form years earlier, in the theme of his Ballade. But while the Ballade, in its completed form, would have represented an entire ballad story—a completed ballad process—the aria represents only the crucial first action in its story. One theme from the Ballade, not an interplay of themes, serves to represent that first action, and even that theme, with its interruptions and resumptions, is longer and more complicated than Milada's aria. But Smetana retained a simplified version of that structure, which so powerfully suggests a speaker overcome by her own thoughts. After one quatrain and the first phrase of the next line ("Oh, do not blame me, brother!"), Milada breaks off, just before the violins reach what in the Ballade was the first interruption of the main theme. After an orchestral interruption, a resumption of the theme, and a second interruption (in which the singer participates), the aria closes on a sudden and tremendous climax, without any further resumption of the theme as such.

It may be that Smetana succeeded in converting his piano *ballade* so straightforwardly into an opera aria in part because his piano style in the first place was more orchestral in conception than Chopin's.[36] But the nature of this conversion also confirms the evidence in the Ballade fragment itself that Smetana, very much in the tradition of Chopin though in his own style, was grappling with the problem of how to make a piano work represent the narrative course that a ballad takes in sung words.

After Smetana, after the 1850s, composers defined the challenge of the piano *ballade* to themselves less and less in narrative terms. There were still piano *ballades* written in a somewhat dramatic vein, taking complex musical form, but these works seldom suggest the voices and narrative process of a ballad. Most of them respond to Chopin's example in other ways.

In 1873, for instance, the great Polish pianist Xaver Scharwenka (1850–1924) published his Ballade, Op. 8,[37] a work in sonata form, adopting Chopin's 6/4 *ballade* meter, but exploiting the ambiguity of that meter far more than Chopin had. His metrical ambiguities in fact owe more to Schumann than to Chopin (see Example 4-15), as does much else about the piece.[38] For him, as for a number of composers at the end of the nineteenth century (to be considered in Chapter 7), the piano *ballade* seems to have meant a serious work in complex form, a work for which Chopin's Ballades might suggest certain musical details, but hardly any narrative ideal.

Example 4-15. Xaver Scharwenka, Ballade, Op. 8, mm. 59–65.

BALLADES MODELED ON PARTICULAR STORIES

For composers with a narrative bent, there was always another possibility: to write a work tracing the story of a particular ballad. In some respects ballads may not have lent themselves well to that kind of treatment: they tend, as we have seen, to be vague in setting and to concentrate on actions accomplished through words. But composers found ways of dealing with the difficulties: the nineteenth-century repertory of orchestral *ballades* consists almost entirely of works tracing particular ballad stories. Composers of piano *ballades* in the same period, however, seldom took this approach.

Among the hundreds of nineteenth-century piano *ballades* in the list compiled by Günther Wagner, barely a dozen bear the title of a particular ballad model. Others, of course, may reveal their model in other ways—in an epigraph, for instance—or may keep it entirely hidden.

The extent of this sub-repertory, then, is hard to ascertain. It is striking, though, that it is a sub-repertory of piano *ballades*, while it is the main repertory of orchestral *ballades* of the same period. The influence of Chopin's abstractly narrative Ballades over the piano *ballade* repertory must have been responsible to some extent for this difference, for, notwithstanding Schumann's attempt to draw Chopin out, his Ballades seem to have been largely accepted through the nineteenth century as works needing no particular poetic explanation. If anything, as the epigraphs to Chapter 3 of the present study attest, the title "*ballade*" itself was considered too specific, at least by dictionary writers. Only at the turn of the century was serious consideration given to the idea that Chopin followed a particular poem in each of his Ballades.

Fontana

It is ironic, then, that one of the earliest piano *ballades* that openly refers to a poetic model was written by Julian Fontana (1810-1865), Chopin's friend from conservatory days in Warsaw, later his valued copyist in Paris, and finally the posthumous editor of his music. Fontana's Ballade, Op. 17, was published in 1849,[39] during the years (1842-51) when he was making his career in North America.

The work is titled simply "Ballade," but it has as an epigraph a couple of lines from a French version of Bürger's "Die Entführung" ("The Abduction"), a ballad first published in 1778. The epigraph comes from the description of the horseback abduction that is both the central action of the poem and the focus of Fontana's musical illustration: "*Il soutient la jeune fille, et de l'éperon excite l'ardeur de son coursier*" ("He supports the girl, and with his spur excites the spirit of his charger"). Fontana chose, in other words, a ballad centered on a scene of galloping, a movement that lent itself easily to illustration on the piano. It is probably no coincidence that the most popular single model for piano *ballades* was another Bürger ballad with even more galloping in it, "Lenore." Fontana's Ballade is so dominated by galloping rhythms that it can hardly be said to follow the episodes of Bürger's poem in any clear sense. The first theme is already more gallop than melody; several subsequent themes are more melodic, but keep a galloping rhythm in their accompaniment. Somewhere along the way, we may imagine the scene in which the lover, Ritter Karl, overcomes the resistance of the beloved, Fräulein Gertrude, and persuades her to ride into the night with him to escape the marriage her father has arranged for her. Aside from the galloping, the only clear detail of Fontana's program is the moment when the galloping stops and a tiny recitative leads to a new theme (see Example 4-16).

Example 4-16. Fontana, Ballade, Op. 17, mm. 176–82.

Here the recitative evidently represents the relenting father's decision to let his daughter marry the man she loves, and the new theme, *Allegro grandioso*, represents the couple's joy at this news. This theme is reminiscent of a theme in Chopin's Polonaise-Fantasy, Op. 61, published in 1846. The passage is exceptional in its explicitness; the piece as a whole has only the simplest narrative or dramatic progression, from minor to major, from anxiety to joy.

Kullak and Rubinstein

By contrast, explicitness is the rule in "Lénore: Ballade," Op. 81, by Theodor Kullak (1818–1882).[40] Kullak, already established in Berlin as a piano teacher by 1853, when "Lénore" was published, later taught some of the greatest pianists of the nineteenth century, including Xaver Scharwenka. "Lénore" stands apart from the piano studies and salon pieces that make up the greatest part of his compositions and even from his earlier Ballade, Op. 54,[41] a work in a lighter vein, though in sonata form and with some rhythmic reminiscences of Chopin's third Ballade. The interesting thing about "Lénore" is how little it has to do with the Chopin Ballades and other narrative piano *ballades* of its day. In a sense it belongs to a tradition of programmatic keyboard pieces stretching back to the eighteenth century and earlier: Kullak has taken an action-filled story and depicted its episodes one by one in a series of linked, but separate movements. The form of the work, then, has nothing to do with the complex forms of the Chopin or Liszt Ballades.

In fact, it may seem to have made little difference to Kullak that the story he was illustrating was a ballad. But his episodic treatment of the "Lenore" story may also be connected to the late eighteenth-century German tradition of ballad setting. Composers in this tradition, from André to Zumsteeg,[42] grouped stanzas of the poems they were setting into episodes and set each group as a discrete movement, some in strophic, folklike style, others in operatic styles. Kullak's procedure is like theirs, but with a couple of differences: his range of styles is all operatic, never folklike, and, because he was not setting the poetic text, he could adjust the lengths of the different episodes at will. Accordingly, he made the love scene—which takes just a few stanzas of Bürger's long poem—into the longest and most important part of his work, while the famous midnight ride he held to a few quick pages of pianistic galloping.

The appeal of an instrumental composition that follows a story in detail—whether it is Kullak's "Lénore" of 1853 or one of Kuhnau's "Biblical Narratives" of 1700—must always have been in large part the pleasure of recognizing in a musical form the episodes of a story one already knows in literary form. It is hardly surprising, then, that for a work of this sort Kullak chose the best-known of all ballads, a story that in his day was as familiar as a Bible story, and not just in German-speaking lands. Beyond that, Kullak's "Lénore" appealed to the popular taste for virtuoso piano music, offering both a pianistic equivalent of the florid operatic love-duet and, in the concluding gallop, a whirlwind of tremolos and scales. Kullak could afford to be old-fashioned in his programmatic conception since his piano-writing was stylishly virtuosic.

Twenty years later, at the hundredth anniversary of Bürger's poem (1873), the Russian pianist and composer Anton Rubinstein used exactly the same formula for his own "Lénore."[43] Rubinstein (1829–1894), a more famous virtuoso than Kullak and a more prolific composer, makes much less of the love scene and much more of the galloping. Otherwise he goes through the story in much the same way as Kullak, using musical styles that are only slightly, if at all, more modern than Kullak's.

The two works taken together suggest some of the continuities of nineteenth-century middle-class tastes. Evidently composers could count on Bürger's ballads to interest audiences throughout the nineteenth century, even though those ballads had been ridiculed already by Schiller in 1791 and had exhausted their influence on poets from Scotland to Russia by the first quarter of the nineteenth century.[44] Moreover, the continuing taste for an old-fashioned kind of narrative keyboard music relied on the continuity in literary culture: Kullak and Rubinstein could count on their listeners to enjoy following an episodic musical structure because the structure illustrated a ballad that those listeners had probably known since childhood.

Tausig

A composer who chose a less well-known poetic model had to engage his listeners by different means. When one opens the original published score of the piano *ballade* "The Ghost Ship: Symphonic Ballade After a Poem by Strachwitz"[45] by Carl Tausig (1841–1871), it is no surprise to find the poem by Strachwitz printed in the front. For Kullak, as for Fontana, it was enough to remind listeners and performers of the poem by printing a couple of lines from it as an epigraph. But if the poem Tausig chose was less than a classic, it was also a very different sort of poem from a Bürger ballad, and the nature of this poem led Tausig to a kind of musical illustration totally unlike Kullak's, making a very different appeal to listeners.

Moritz von Strachwitz (1822–1847) was a late participant in the ballad revival, and "Das Geisterschiff" ("The Ghost Ship"), published in his collection *Neue Gedichte* (1847), is connected to balladry by its Nordic setting and ghostly subject. But it is not clear that Strachwitz himself called the poem a ballad, and the poem differs from earlier ballads, both folk and literary, in essential ways. It is spoken in the first person; it is a narrative within a lyric frame. Its story consists entirely of an encounter with a ghost Viking ship during a storm on the North Sea, and even that encounter turns out to be a kind of visionary metaphor for the speaker's sea-weary longings. There is nothing approaching a ballad process in the poem. It is possible that Strachwitz's vision of ghost Vikings, yearning for "Viking pleasure and Viking pain" and appearing in their ghost ship before storm-weary sailors, was inspired by the balladlike Flying Dutchman legend, through either Heine's story or Wagner's opera. But if Tausig in turn was thinking of Wagner's *Flying Dutchman* in his "Symphonic Ballade," he was remembering, not the narrative ballad sung by the heroine Senta, but the sea music.

The Polish pianist Carl Tausig was one of Liszt's greatest pupils; his virtuosic bent is obvious in "The Ghost Ship." His interest in transferring orchestral effects to the piano is as obvious here as in his piano transcriptions of Berlioz and Wagner scores. He composed "The Ghost Ship," in fact, in both an orchestral and a piano version. In the piano version, the longer first part of the work, describing the storm at sea and the appearance of the ghost ship, taxes both performer and instrument to their limits, and the strain gives the music excitement. Only in the slow concluding section (*Langsam*) does the piano's lack of orchestral color and power leave the music flat.

The earlier section is also the more interesting musically. A single, breathless stretch of music almost five hundred measures long, it is if anything less narrative, less episodic than the section of the poem it illustrates. It represents the storm at sea not only by a conventional depictive vocabulary—tremolos, chromatic scales, driving rhythms—but by an intense restlessness in its harmony and phrase structure. The music unfolds through a series of short motives, each one clear enough in form and key, but each one repeated in a rising sequence (rising by constant intervals, whether half-step, minor third, tritone, or fifth), so that no one statement of the motive seems tonally definitive. Whole-tone passages marking the appearance of the ghost ship (one of these passages is labeled "ghostly") fit in with the general tonal restlessness. Altogether, this stretch of music offers the listener the speaker's vision as the speaker himself experiences it: unmediated, seamless, unpredictable, apparently chaotic. For the listener who is prepared to be engaged by such a musical vision, a quick glance through the poem is enough to explain what Tausig is up to.

The concluding section (*Langsam*), harder to play persuasively on the piano, also has a subtler relationship to the poem. After a long passage on the dominant of D minor, this section begins in D major, with a new theme in a new rhythm. Dawn has come, the storm has passed, and the ghostly vision is gone. But the new theme, by a process of thematic convergence, becomes a thematic transformation of one of the ghost-ship motives (m. 518), just as the speaker realizes that the vision is a sign of his own sea-weariness: "My heart turns into the Viking ship / and sails straight to the South." The final section of the music, in other words, calls on the listener to hear a process of musical transformation in the light of the metaphorical process of the poem.

In the end, Tausig's music requires just as much attention to its poetic model as Kullak's or Rubinstein's does, but Tausig asks his listener to follow the poem in a very different way. In fact, the whole of "The Ghost Ship" is highly unusual for an instrumental *ballade* in its relationship of music to language: the first part in that it represents a wordless vision, and the second part in that it uses thematic transformation to suggest a poetic metaphor.

Piano *ballades* modeled on particular stories make an extremely diverse group. Even the four just described show no unity in their poetic models, their programmatic principles, or their musical forms. Almost the only thing that unites them as a group and distinguishes them from other piano *ballades* is a negative characteristic: they do not treat the ballad as song, as narrating voice, as sounding word. In this respect they constitute an extreme case within the whole *ballade* repertory: even orchestral *ballades*—and this group of piano *ballades* seems otherwise like crossover orchestral *ballades*—usually focus on an important voice or utterance from the ballad story they are illustrating. These few piano *ballades* concentrate on an action that, whether it is a ride on horseback or a spiritual progression, is wordless.

CHAPTER 5

Brahms and the Lyrical Tradition to 1880

WIECK AND SCHUMANN

Most of the piano *ballades* written in the mid-nineteenth century are fairly short works in simple musical forms. Though they may set a tone appropriate to a ballad story, they do not pretend to suggest a narrative progression, and though they may have a songlike character, they do not pretend to suggest the complex of voices heard in the course of a ballad. The largest part of the mid-nineteenth-century piano *ballade* repertory, in other words, belongs to a tradition that owes little to Chopin's Ballades. That tradition begins, in fact, with a work published in the same year (1836) as the first Chopin Ballade, the Ballade in the *Soirées musicales*, Op. 6, by Clara Wieck (1819–1896).[1]

This Ballade, without resembling Chopin's first Ballade, has some connection with Chopin. Wieck had first heard Chopin play his music (the Variations on "Là ci darem la mano") in Paris in 1832; from about that time she, along with her father and Schumann (who was then attached to their household), followed Chopin's publications with enthusiasm. In 1835 the twenty-five-year-old Chopin, already a famous composer, and the sixteen-year-old Wieck, already a famous performer, met in Leipzig and admired each other's playing. In 1836, when Chopin came again to Leipzig, Wieck was thrilled that he praised her newest compositions, including the *Soirées musicales*. Whether she heard his just-published first Ballade at that time is uncertain; Schumann heard Chopin play it then, but in that period Schumann was banished from Wieck's company by her father.

The six pieces of the *Soirées musicales* seem to acknowledge Chopin's influence in their titles—Toccatina, Ballade, Nocturne, Polonaise, and two Mazurkas—and commentators have considered the Ballade one of the pieces most clearly under Chopin's "guiding star."[2] But it is Chopin's Nocturnes, rather than his Ballades, that are recalled in this piece. They are recalled particularly in the opening section, with its floridly operatic melody, sometimes in duet texture, over a march bass (see Example 5-1).

Example 5-1. Wieck, Ballade, Op. 6, No. 2, mm. 1–23.

At the opening, in a few remarkable lines, Wieck captures in her own style almost everything that is distinctive about Chopin's Nocturnes: the atmosphere of hushed excitement, the impulsive, passionate outbursts, and the delicate effects of piano color. The form of the piece, too, connects it to Chopin's Nocturnes: ternary form with a shortened reprise of the first section and a coda based on the middle section. The opening section is in D minor, the middle section (which is stylistically independent of Chopin) in D major, but with subtle reminders of D minor throughout. In the reprise Wieck compresses the opening section by a process of harmonic elision. The opening section moved in five long phrases from D minor through F major to A-flat major and back through F major to D minor. In the reprise Wieck makes the same progression, omitting the intermediary steps, in a single, bold, arching phrase (see Example 5-2). The coda brings back not only the material of the middle section, but also the interplay of major and minor mode, and ends on a note of perfect modal ambiguity.

Example 5-2. Wieck, Ballade, Op. 6, No. 2, mm. 110–16.

Why might Wieck have called this nocturne-like piece a *ballade*? Among the pieces in her *Soirées musicales*, the title "Ballade" would mark it as a song-inspired piece, connecting it to the Nocturne and distinguishing it from the étude-like Toccatina and the dance-inspired Polonaise and Mazurkas. *Soirées musicales* was a collection of character pieces, and the title "Ballade" added to the stock of songlike titles for piano character pieces. It is a little hard to see what else the title specifies—what qualities of ballads it exemplifies—when it is applied to such an operatic, nocturne-like piece. The piece has no stylistic ties to folk ballads, to the dramatic settings of poetic ballads by composers like Loewe, or for that matter to English drawing-room ballads of the period.

If anything, its character of an operatic love scene suggests one episode in a ballad—one kind of episode, though a kind crucial for the immense popularity of the genre in the eighteenth and nineteenth centuries. In that case the volatile character of the opening section and the disquieting mixture of modes in the middle section and coda help to tie this music specifically to ballads, since love relationships in ballads are characteristically threatened, if not doomed. Capturing the poetic nature of the ballad in a musical character piece was not a simple undertaking. Critics since Goethe had considered the ballad to have no single poetic character, but a composite of several. Wieck, concentrating on a single kind of ballad episode, not only chose a kind that was typical of the genre—the love scene—but also colored the music to suggest the larger narrative context—the threat of reckoning—in which a ballad love scene unfolds.

Schumann took over the idea of the piano *ballade* as character piece in his *Davidsbündlertänze*, Op. 6, of which the tenth is marked "Balladenmässig" ("balladlike").[3] The publication of Wieck's *Soirées musicales* in 1836 allowed him to see that work even though he was prevented from seeing her. He wrote his review praising it in September 1837,[4] just after she had secretly pledged herself to him. At the same time he composed the *Davidsbündlertänze*, in which, he wrote to her, there were "many wedding thoughts."[5] The work even opens with what he marks as "Motto von C. W.," a motive from the G Major Mazurka of the *Soirées musicales*. For all that, his "Balladenmässig" character piece is no more like Wieck's Ballade than it is like the only other piano *ballade* Schumann knew, Chopin's first Ballade.

Schumann attributed each of the *Davidsbündlertänze* to one or both of his imaginary friends, Eusebius and Florestan. The "balladlike" piece, marked "very rapid," is given the initial of the impetuous Florestan. The most distinctive feature of the piece, though—the cross-rhythm between a soprano line in 6/8 and a bass in 3/4—connects it with the second piece of the set ("Innig"), a piece of pensive character, attributed to Eusebius. The *Davidsbündlertänze* are, of course, dances, and two-thirds of them have a 3/4 meter, though not all those have the character of a waltz or other dance. The persistently jagged cross-rhythm in the "balladlike" piece, for instance, keeps that piece from falling into a danceable swing.

At the same time, the cross-rhythm makes it difficult to speak of the piece as songlike, or even at moments to find its leading voice. In the opening line, for example, the melody (each note of which is marked *sf*) moves from the lowest register to the highest, and each phrase begins, in the bass, with an upbeat that is out of rhythm with the rest (see Example 5-3). Later on, the cross-rhythm helps keep two simultaneous melodies distinct, one in the soprano and another in the bass, so that neither sounds subordinate to the other.

Example 5-3. Schumann, *Davidsbündlertänze,* Op. 6, No. 10, mm. 1-9.

If, then, Schumann meant to suggest a singing voice when he called this piece "balladlike," he was working from a complicated model of a singing voice. Even in the opening line, where there is clearly just one melody, that melody is unsettled in rhythm. It is no representation of the calm, impersonal narrative voice of the folk ballad. For Schumann's version of such a voice, we need to turn to the solemn theme (marked "in legendary tone") in the middle of the first movement of his Fantasy, Op. 17, a work written—in its first version—a year earlier. If the opening line of the "balladlike" piece does not suggest a narrator's voice, neither do the subsequent passages with simultaneous melodies suggest a dialogue of characters: they are more like diverse thoughts crowding into one person's mind.

Despite these complications of texture, the piece speaks, as it were, in a single voice: its message is undivided in tone, unrelieved in mood. Its opening line is never gone for long, and all the other lines are continuations of it. Though they go to other keys, they stay in the same mode: only the Picardy-third ending takes the music out of the minor mode. Whereas Wieck's Ballade has the character of a single, typical ballad episode, Schumann's "balladlike" piece expresses a relentlessly unsettled mood that can be associated with ballads in general.

The two pieces offered two very different examples of how a piano character piece could be modeled on the ballad. But though a great many short, lyrical piano *ballades* were written in the years just after these two pieces, they did not follow the Wieck or Schumann model. Those *ballades* were salon pieces, not character pieces. When, after almost twenty years, composers again turned to the *ballade* as character piece, their interests in ballads and their conceptions of *ballades* were almost always different from Wieck's or Schumann's, and their music differed correspondingly. These two pieces, then, represent an isolated dialogue of the 1830s about the piano *ballade*, shedding little light on the important tradition of piano *ballades* that they initiated.

SALON *BALLADES*

"Salon music" is not so much the term of performers and patrons to describe the music they actually played and heard in salons as it is the term of outsiders like Schumann (or like everyone in the twentieth century) to describe published music that seems to belong in the salons of their imagination.[6] The term, while it appears to define a body of music according to its provenance, actually defines it according to musical characteristics, though these characteristics are determined by the conditions of the imagined provenance. Salon pianists were the great virtuosos of the day, playing in exclusive and intimate settings. The music they could be imagined playing in salons was the intimate side of their repertory, music of a cultivated simplicity, sentimental music with a touch of brilliance—not so much brilliance as to suggest the virtuoso astounding thousands in a great concert hall or to frighten away all non-virtuoso buyers (this was, after all, music published for a mass market), but just enough to remind everyone that the composer—and imagined performer—was a virtuoso and to give amateur pianists the pleasure of imagining themselves as dazzling performers.

"Ballade" was a popular title for such pieces. The attraction of the title evidently lay in its suggestion of cultivated simplicity. The themes of these ballades have the melodic simplicity of contemporary sentimental or operatic ballads, not that of folk ballads. The salon ballade may in fact have developed partly out of the tradition of published piano arrangements of the musical numbers from operas: English operas, full of ballads, were popular all over Europe in these arrangements, and those ballads appeared in the piano arrangements as simple musical stanzas, repeated several times without embellishment.[7]

The themes of salon *ballades* generally have plain accompaniments, in keeping with the melodies, so that the themes look more like the main theme of a Chopin Ballade than like that of Wieck's Ballade, with its florid melody, or Schumann's "balladlike" piece, with its elaborate texture. There the resemblance to Chopin's Ballades ends, however. In a salon *ballade* everything depends on the attractive melody; there is scarcely a hint of a story. The theme alone in a Chopin Ballade is more eventful, more dramatic than a whole *ballade* by Herz or Gottschalk or Thalberg. The theme of a salon *ballade* may alternate with another theme or two; it may be repeated with embellishments. Ternary and variation forms are the most common patterns in the repertory. The whole repertory is characterized by simplicity of form: themes in salon *ballades* are not worked over, developed, transposed, or transformed, as they would be in complex musical forms.

The ternary model of the salon *ballade* appears at its simplest in the Ballade "La Romantique," by Henry Cramer (1818-1877).[8] The melody of the first section gives way to a short middle section that is all throbbing chords, in the relative minor key, rising to a climax. The first section returns, embellished and diverted by reminders of the middle section, but soon settles to a peaceful version of its original close. Somewhat larger and more elaborate ternary forms—sometimes with introductions and cadenzas and interrupted themes—are found in other *ballades* of the 1840s and 1850s by Henri Herz, Theodor Döhler, Edouard Wolff, Adolf Gutmann, and Julius Schulhoff.[9] Gutmann was Chopin's pupil, as was Carol Mikuli, composer of another such *ballade*, which appeared as late as 1871.[10] But though the *ballades* of those two composers owe much to Chopin in piano figuration, they show no particular debt to his Ballades.

Variation form in the salon *ballade* is represented by the Ballade, Op. 76, of Sigismond Thalberg (1812-1871).[11] The piece, not published until 1862, was probably composed much earlier, since it was published as Thalberg's "Famous Ballade... Executed at His Concerts in Paris and London." Thalberg seems to have kept the piece for his own use while he was performing to enormous acclaim in Europe and the Americas, publishing it only when he was practically retired from concert life. The first French edition was embellished with an engraved scene of a noble young man meeting a ghost in the shadow of a crumbling medieval castle,[12] but that image tells more about the associations of the word "*ballade*" at the time than about the piece of music Thalberg wrote. That piece offers a long, sentimental theme in the minor mode, with a middle section in the tonic major, during which Thalberg already begins to embellish the melody with his characteristic "three-handed" texture (melody in the middle). The rest of the piece consists simply of the theme repeated with even more elaborate embellishments. The term "variation," though it is the only word available to describe this musical form, seems too grand for the musical process. Embellishment of the theme in a salon *ballade*—whether the piece is in variation form or ternary form or another form—hardly ever touches the theme itself, but usually consists simply of an added voice moving in faster notes.

Among other variation-form salon *ballades* is a piece that brought fame to Louis Moreau Gottschalk (1829-1869) before he was twenty: "La Savane: Ballade créole."[13] Gottschalk deserves separate mention as a composer of salon *ballades* because he wrote more than half a dozen, each one different from the others in form and nature. "La Savane," three variations on a folk song that Gottschalk brought to Paris with him from Louisiana, had charm perhaps because it seemed more exotic than it actually sounded.[14] From the same early period in his career comes "Ossian: Two Ballades,"[15] two tiny, symmetrical pieces that draw the listener into a nostalgic mood, befitting the verses of Ossian that adorn the score. A few years later (1853) Gottschalk wrote, but never published, a Ballade in A-flat[16] with a stately dance character like "La Savane," but also with some of the nostalgic quality of "Ossian," now derived from passing chromaticism.

In 1877, eight years after Gottschalk's death in 1869, three more of his piano *ballades* were published, entitled Sixth Ballade, Seventh Ballade, and Eighth Ballade.[17] The composition dates of these pieces have not been determined, though Gottschalk scholars speculate that they were written in the 1860s, the last decade of Gottschalk's life.[18] In any case, these are longer works than his early *ballades*, both more songful and more dancing. The three together seem to be Gottschalk's tribute to Chopin, who had admired his playing in Paris: all three use mazurka rhythms, and the Eighth Ballade has a waltzing main theme that derives from the funeral-march theme of Chopin's C-minor Prelude, Op. 28, No. 20 (see Example 5-4).

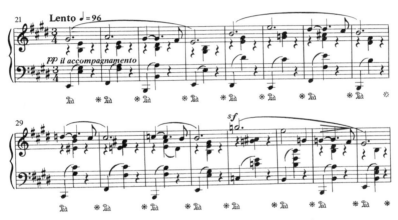

Example 5-4. Gottschalk, Eighth Ballade, Op. 90, mm. 21–36.

In the Sixth and Seventh Ballades, formal characteristics that would not mar a short salon piece take their toll: repetition of themes and (despite two far-ranging modulatory passages in the Seventh Ballade) tonal sameness. The Eighth, however, makes a strong progression among related themes and keys, and the long-prepared return to the main theme creates a beautiful effect. It is moving to hear this piece grow, as it progresses, from the tone and form of a salon piece into something more serious and self-conscious.

Other composers wrote *ballades* that can be compared to Gottschalk's Eighth Ballade: salon *ballades* grown into something bigger and more ambitious. One is the Ballade, Op. 9, composed in 1844 by the twenty-two-year-old César Franck (1822–1890).[19] This work, like many salon *ballades*, is in ternary form, with an innocently melodious main section, a stormier, modulating middle section, and an embellished return. The scale of the piece, however, is unusual (it is twenty-eight pages long), the demands on the performer are considerable, and the middle section is interrupted twice by reminiscences of the main theme heard over rumbling dominant pedals.

More unusual still is the hesitant opening of the work: an introduction in which each small phrase ends in a pause, followed by a main theme in which, despite a new pulsing accompaniment, the pauses after each phrase continue. The phrases are simplicity itself: there is not a single accidental in the whole of the introduction and theme. The pauses seem to promise something more dramatic than a salon *ballade*, but that promise is unfulfilled: all that overtakes the simple phrases is virtuosic display. In the 1840s Franck was a young piano virtuoso struggling to establish himself in a crowded field of more experienced virtuosos; his compositions of this period can hardly be considered forerunners of the music—including an orchestral *ballade*—that he wrote forty years later.

A more successful virtuoso who likewise withdrew from concert life and continued to compose was Adolf Henselt (1814-1889). After 1838 Henselt lived in isolation in St. Petersburg, and his musical style—unlike Franck's—did not develop further. His Ballade,[20] published in the 1850s, is as long and ambitious a salon *ballade* as the Gottschalk Eighth or the Franck and more skillfully written than either of them. It is full of long, songful, Mendelssohnian themes, several of them worked out with inventive figuration, but as in any salon *ballade*, the themes or groups of themes succeed each other without development or integration.

Yet another long salon *ballade*[21] was written, apparently in the 1860s, by the precocious Venezuelan pianist and composer Teresa Carreño (1853-1917), a pupil of Gottschalk. In this work exuberant embellishment fills out a straightforward ternary form.

The attraction of salon music must always have been that it brought together sweet melody and virtuosity without demanding attention to complex musical processes. Franck, Henselt, and Carreño, by writing lengthy pieces while accepting that condition, were forcing the limits of salon music. At the same time that they were writing, other composers, including Brahms, were reviving the character-piece *ballade* as a vehicle for serious musical expression, and they were doing it, paradoxically, by keeping to the small scale, to simple forms, and to the barest thematic material yet heard in piano *ballades*.

BRAHMS

In 1856, when Brahms, at the age of twenty-three, published his *Four Ballades*, Op. 10,[22] it was unprecedented for more than a pair of piano pieces to appear under the common title "Ballade." Brahms could have been using the title—as others had used titles like "Nocturne" and "Waltz"—to describe the common character of the pieces or—as others had used "Impromptu" and "Bagatelle"—as a catch-all title for pieces varied in character. He did not clarify his meaning with respect to the whole collection when he wrote over the first Ballade: "after the Scottish ballad 'Edward' in Herder's *Stimmen der Völker*," and when he gave the third Ballade its own title, "Intermezzo." If the first Ballade is based on a poetic text, could the other three be as well? Max Kalbeck, the early Brahms biographer, felt entitled to suppose so,[23] and others have at least entertained the possibility. On the other hand, Brahms may have been using the title that properly belonged to the first piece as a solution to the problem of what to call the whole set, even at the price of mislabeling the others to a greater or lesser extent.

For that matter, in what sense does the first Ballade take after the ballad "Edward"? In a programmatic sense, says Kalbeck, who describes the piece as if it belonged to the narrative tradition of piano *ballades*. But Paul Mies, arguing that Brahms started to set "Edward" as a song and then converted his material into a piano piece, denies that the resulting piano piece can be called programmatic.[24] Brahms, by publishing the pieces as he did, gives some credence to each of these contradictory interpretations.

The four pieces have enough in common to cohere as a set. Together they created a new type of piano *ballade*: considerably shorter than a Chopin Ballade, though not tiny like a *Davidsbündler* dance; ternary in form, with great flexibility in the relationships of the sections; more serious in character than a salon *ballade*, but unadorned in melody—unlike the Wieck Ballade— and austere in accompaniment. For three of the four Ballades, Brahms marks the tempo of the main section as *Andante*. If Brahms's conception of the piano *ballade* is difficult to apprehend, it is not because the four pieces are too varied; to performers, in fact, the very lack of variety among them presents a challenge. The confusing thing about the type of *ballade* that Brahms created is rather that it seems more like a Schubert impromptu or Mendelssohn "song without words" than like any piano *ballade* that came before.

Brahms's use of a poetic model in the first of these Ballades was also new, new in that the words of the poem he cited—Herder's translation of "Edward"—can be sung to his music.[25] In a rough way, one can sing a whole stanza of the poem to the opening lines of the music (see Example 5-5); one merely has to drop a word here and a line there, as well as transposing the melody at times if one is not comfortable in a range of more than two octaves. Herder's opening stanza is as follows:

Dein Schwert, wie ists von Blut so roth?
Edward, Edward!
Dein Schwert, wie ists von Blut so roth,
Und gehst so traurig her?—O!
O ich hab geschlagen meinen Geyer todt,
Mutter, Mutter!
O ich hab geschlagen meinen Geyer todt,
Und keinen hab ich wie Er—O!

The stanza in the original English is:

"Why dois your brand sae drap wi' bluid,
Edward, Edward?
Why dois your brand sae drip wi' bluid?
And why sae sad gang yee, O?"
"O, I hae killed my hauke sae guid,
Mither, mither,
O, I hae killed my hauke sae guid,
And I had nae mair bot hee, O."[26]

Example 5-5. Brahms, Ballade, Op. 10, No. 1, mm. 1–13.

Not only does the melody fit the words, but the stark, homophonic texture helps one to hear that melody as a vehicle for words. The archaic touches in the melody—phrases stated and then transposed down a fifth— and in the harmony—Brahms twice avoids the dominant by omitting the third in a cadential chord on A—seem fitting for a text taken from a folk ballad. Mies's hypothesis that this piano *ballade* began life as a song is appealing not so much because of the details of his careful argument as because the hypothesis rests on a simple truth about the nature of the music.

Even more striking than the way the melody fits the words, however, is the way the structure of that melody fits the structure of voices in the poem. "Edward" is among the few ballads—folk or literary—with a text that is all dialogue. Each of its stanzas consists of a mother's question and her son's reply; under this relentless questioning the son reveals first (stanza 3) that he has killed his father and at the very end (stanza 7) that his mother urged him to it ("Sic conseils ye gave to me, O"). In the Brahms Ballade the D-minor opening section represents two stanzas of this structure, each *Andante* "couplet" and *Poco più moto* "couplet" of music representing the question couplet and answer couplet that make up a stanza of the poem. The second "stanza" of music is a continuation, rather than a variation or embellishment, of the first: the same lines come to new cadences, and in the second *Poco più moto* couplet the original bass becomes the melody.

The structure of this theme, then, is surprisingly like that of a Chopin Ballade: a songlike stanza that changes in the course of literal repetition. That is not to say that Brahms was imitating Chopin here. It is not even clear that Brahms knew Chopin's Ballades at the time that he wrote this piece. But Günther Wagner goes too far in asserting that he would not have known the Chopin until several years later; if, as Wagner himself notes, Brahms had the run of the Schumanns' library at the very time that he wrote these Ballades, he could certainly have discovered the Chopin Ballades then.[27] But he would not have needed them as a model. "Edward" served as his model, just as other ballads had served as Chopin's model: the peculiar, two-part structure of his musical stanza is modeled on the two-part stanza structure that is the distinguishing feature of "Edward."

In the poem, this monotonous stanza structure controls an irresistible rhythm of withholding and revealing. In a piano *ballade* an equivalent structure neither withholds nor reveals anything; the composer has to move beyond it. Brahms moves to a new section, in the major mode and a faster tempo (*Allegro*), using the motive that was first the bass and then the melody of the *Poco più moto* couplet, but abandoning the stanza structure of the first section altogether. It is in dealing with this section that Kalbeck's programmatic interpretation of the work is most attractive: the motive, rising in strength throughout the section, "is revealed as the threatening voice of the evil knowledge that trembles in the anxious questions of the mother and the evasive answers of the son."[28] Brahms moves, in other words, from representing the structure of voices and verses to representing the ballad process in the poem, the process by which the son is forced, by admitting first his own guilt and then his mother's, to reckon with everything he has tried to deny.

This middle section leads right back to the *Poco più moto* couplet (not the opening *Andante* couplet) without cadence or break and without returning to the original tempo or volume. In Kalbeck's terms, this is the point at which the son, unable to withstand his rising guilt, confesses his deed and curses his mother for her role. But to bring those two utterances, one from the middle of the poem and the other from the very end, together at one moment in the music is to admit—as all commentators do—that a programmatic interpretation of the music breaks down at this point. Whereas the poem ends with the son's sensational last answer, revealing the mother's role only in the very last line, Brahms ends his Ballade with the mother's voice, the *Andante* couplet, returning in the most subdued tone yet heard in the piece. Kalbeck deals with the discrepancy by taking his programmatic explanation beyond the poem; but an explanation that does not take the poem as Brahms's program is scarcely a programmatic explanation at all. Instead of making up a new program for Brahms, it would be reasonable to conclude that since the sensational revelation at the end of the poem is an inescapable part of the poem's narrative structure, Brahms, in ending his Ballade as he did, was not taking the poem primarily as a narrative, or programmatic, model.

At the beginning of the piece Brahms took the poem as a structural model—a structure of voices within stanzas. What he does for the rest of the piece is best heard not as abandoning that structure, but as recasting it. The resolution of the Ballade can only in a very partial sense be called a return of the original theme or section. Brahms brings back the two couplets of that section not only in reverse order, but extended and separated from each other, so that they no longer form a stanza or have a question-and-answer relationship. The son's couplet—its original, internal transposition now extended into a sequence—is more a continuation of the middle section than a reprise. The reprise consists solely of the mother's couplet (*Tempo I*), which reestablishes the tonic key, but is in its own way also tonally unsettled: the incomplete dominant chord that originally characterized it is now completed once by a major chord (m. 61) and once by a minor chord (m. 64), and even the tonic chord at the cadence is heard first as major, then as minor.

The form of this Ballade is not determined by any vocal setting that Brahms may have made first, nor by the progression of the story, but by an idea of "Edward" as a dialogue in song. By fashioning a dialogue structure that is more fluid than that of the poem, Brahms suggested a progression within his wordless dialogue: a progression of utterances that at first respond to each other, but then lose themselves in self-absorption. Although this progression is very different from the narrative progression of "Edward," the music has a concentrated dramatic power that is clearly inspired by the narrative power of "Edward."

Two things set this Ballade apart from the other three of Opus 10: the unusual phrase relationships (the couplet and stanza structure) of the theme, and the highly dramatic course of the work. But in a more general way this Ballade serves as a model for its companions: as a work in which a theme of unadorned (perhaps balladlike) songfulness undergoes considerable alteration, even within a simple ternary process of departure and return. This model in fact applies not only to these four Ballades of Brahms, but also to a number of lyrical piano *ballades* written by other composers in the following decades.

The second Ballade of Opus 10 is about twice as long as the first and more diverse in themes and sections. The soothing main theme, with its long-breathed phrases floating over a scarcely changing accompaniment, could hardly stand in greater contrast to the clipped, tense phrases of the "Edward" theme. After an opening line of exceptional tonal stillness (mm. 1-9), the sudden moves from D major to B minor and then to B major make an especially arresting effect; but even these small disturbances are soon absorbed as the ending of the first line returns to close out the theme. This small tonal excursion within the theme, however, predicts the overall tonal course of the Ballade.

The middle section (*Allegro non troppo [doppio movimento]*) is itself ternary in form, but united by a common tempo and a common tonal center (the outer parts in B minor, the central part in B major). The thematic material of the central part is anticipated at the very end of the first part (mm. 46-48), but that anticipation hardly justifies Günther Wagner's assertion that the two parts have the "same thematic material."[29] More apt is his observation that the middle section as a whole has an instrumental character, contrasting with the vocal character of the opening section.[30] Wagner is not the first to worry about the relation of the middle section to the opening section of this Ballade. Robert Schumann, when he had first seen the four Ballades, wrote to his wife: "Only the *doppio movimento* of the second do I not understand; isn't it too fast?"[31] Evidently he understood the previous tempo (*Andante*) literally, so that the indication to double that tempo (*doppio movimento*) would have made the music of the middle section faster than the indicated tempo, *Allegro non troppo*.

Wagner and Schumann together suggest a larger question: what is this long section of instrumental character—a scherzo complete with trio—doing in the middle of a lyrical piano *ballade*? If it provides eventfulness to the work, it would be of an episodic kind, not at all the concentrated eventfulness of the "Edward" Ballade. But narrative explanations seem even less satisfactory for the second Ballade than for the first. The connection between the opening and middle sections is primarily tonal, and the influence of the middle section on the return of the opening section is also tonal: that return begins still in B, though the piece ends, as it began, in D. In this irregular tonal design there is no implication of a narrative reconciliation between the two contrasting sections of the Ballade.

It seems rather as if the new key, B, becomes so firmly established in the long middle section that it does not yield readily to the original key, D, at the return of the opening section, or as if Brahms, having devised within the middle section a transitional passage that feints at modulation without modulating (mm. 72-79), could not resist devising an even more extravagant version of the same passage to bring back the opening section (mm. 108-17). Furthermore, the return in the wrong key sets up a new and wonderful effect when the theme turns again to B minor (m. 127), as well as a lovely coda in D (m. 139 to the end) that brings the opening of the main theme—or at least a reminder of it—finally back to its original key.

In the third Ballade there is again a mixture of lyrical and instrumental material, but here the arrangement is reversed: the Ballade is like a scherzo with a lyrical trio. Brahms has now moved so far from the song model that it seems natural for him to have dissociated this piece from the *ballade* genre by giving it its own title: "Intermezzo." It is distinct from the others of the set in ways other than its general character. The first section, for instance, is more complex than that of the other Ballades, it cadences in the dominant, and it is immediately repeated whole. Though the middle section contrasts in many ways with the first section, it stays, according to Brahms's indications, in the same tempo; this is the only one of the four Ballades to remain in one tempo throughout.

At the same time, the Intermezzo has much in common with the other pieces in the set. The texture of the middle section, a homophonic texture of root-position triads, recalls the *Poco più moto* couplet of the "Edward" Ballade. In both cases the simple chords and the movement of all parts in rhythm with the melody suggest choral singing in some archaic style—not a style in which ballads are likely to have been sung, but perhaps one evoking the same lost world that the name "ballad" evokes. This style in piano music is credited to Chopin; the modal progressions and the opposition of three upper voices to one lower one in the Intermezzo invite comparison to the *Religioso* section of Chopin's Nocturne, Op. 15, No. 3, of 1833.[32] But Brahms's use of predominantly high registers gives his passage a distinctive ring (Schumann describes the section as "transfigured"), and the distinctiveness grows as the passage proceeds. When the bass falls out of rhythm with the upper parts (mm. 71*ff.*) and when a single chord is divided between two alternating sonorities (mm. 79-92), Brahms seems to be imitating a distant pealing of bells.

In the return of the first section there are still more connections to the other Ballades. As in the second Ballade, there is a tonal lingering from the middle section at the return; in this case it is the dominant pedal (a series of low F-sharps) from the retransitional passage, replacing the original changing bass harmonies for the first few measures of the return. The very quiet dynamic of the middle section also lingers for the entire return (*sempre pianissimo*, whereas the opening had been *forte*). The Picardy-third ending (from m. 113) recalls the major-minor ending of the "Edward" Ballade, and the very last phrase (mm. 121-24; see Example 5-6) recalls not only the first notes of the middle section (m. 43), but also the first notes—the introduction, in effect—of the second Ballade.

Example 5-6. Brahms, Ballade, Op. 10, No. 3, mm. 121-24 (*above*) and mm. 43-44 (*center*); Ballade, Op. 10, No. 2, m. 1 (*below*).

The fourth Ballade is both the most obviously derivative of the set and the one that most clearly foreshadows Brahms's later music. The opening section (*Andante con moto*) could almost be from a Mendelssohn "song without words,"[33] while the middle section (*Più lento*), with its alto-tenor duet and in the general contour and rhythm of its melody, seems to be modeled on Schumann's Romance in F-sharp Major, Op. 28, No. 2. But correspondences to the other Ballades of the set are also evident—evident, in fact, from the first two notes of the melody. The D-natural that is transformed from a member of a B-minor chord into an appoggiatura to a B-major chord recalls the major-minor ambiguities in the earlier Ballades, but the boldness with which Brahms places it at the beginning of the piece, and so disconcertingly in a sweetly lyrical texture, is new to the set. Even more beautifully' disconcerting is the way the melody later slips back in (mm. 27–30), with a different opening and at an unguarded moment after a wayward five-phrase excursion. The middle section, which Brahms asks the performer to play with "most intimate sentiment," is just as masterfully bold, especially in mixing thickly clustered dissonances with open fifths and bare octaves. Open fifths and octaves also characterized the theme of the "Edward" Ballade, but here, instead of giving the music an archaic sound, they clear the air at moments of cadence in newly established keys.

The return of the opening section (*Tempo I*) seems at first to be the most straightforward return in any of the four Ballades; only a new rhythmic figure and articulation in the accompaniment distinguish the return from the original. At the next double bar, though, in place of a repetition Brahms puts new music that follows the contours of the old, in a chordal texture, with a new harmonic rhythm, and at greater length. Whereas some earlier chordal passages in the Ballades sounded archaic, here the tone is more Mendelssohnian.

There is nothing derivative, however, in the freedom with which Brahms varies the material he is repeating. After the double bar is reached again (m. 114), he follows his original melody for a while—as if to allow listeners to check their bearings—before finishing off with the freest departures yet from the original progression. In the end this return, far from being more straightforward than the returns of the other three Ballades, is the most markedly altered of them all. The alterations here, moreover, are different from those in the returns of the other Ballades: here there is nothing held over from the middle section. Instead, the middle section makes its own, coda-like return (*Più lento*) and reaches a different kind of accommodation with the opening section, an overlapping of phrases from the end of the middle section and the beginning of the opening section (mm. 141–44). Since both of these phrases play on the minor and major versions of a chord, the overlapping of the two phrases foreshadows the thematic reconciliations in later Brahms works more than it resembles the thematic convergences in the Chopin Ballades.

Schumann, in his letter to his wife, gave particular praise to this ending. "In the fourth Ballade," he wrote, "how beautiful that the strange first note of the melody wavers between minor and major at the end and is left in melancholy major." But if this ending has a beauty all its own, it is not simply the wavering between minor and major that makes it distinctive: modal ambiguity is as characteristic of the whole set of Ballades as are bare fifths and octaves or passages in chordal style. This group of stylistic features binds the four Ballades together.

In another way key relationships do the same. Schumann pointed out that the bass F-sharp at the close of the second (D-major) Ballade seems to introduce the third (B-minor) Ballade, which begins with the same note in the new tonal context. Kalbeck extended Schumann's observation to describe the relationship between those two Ballades as like that between "the Adagio and Scherzo of a cyclical work."[34] But the tonal relationships among all the Ballades are as close as among movements of a sonata, and it is not only between the second and third that Brahms reinforces that closeness. The "strange first note" of the fourth Ballade, for instance, is anticipated by exactly the same configuration—a D that becomes a D-sharp over a constant B in the bass—just before the end of the previous Ballade (m. 113), where it introduces the Picardy third (see Example 5-7).

Example 5-7. Brahms, Ballade, Op. 10, No. 4, mm. 1-2 (*above*), and Ballade, Op. 10, No. 3, m. 113 (*below*).

Besides creating a new type of piano *ballade*, Brahms created the piano *ballade* cycle in his Ballades, Op. 10. It is a cycle formed by musical relationships: the four pieces are stylistically and tonally connected, as well as related in musical character and form. They do not all have the same relationship to the title "Ballade," and there would be no point in comparing them to a ballad cycle that tells different episodes of a single story or single life. They are like a set of songs to poems by one poet, or on one theme, but without a narrative sequence. The common title "Ballade" makes sense, then, as a description not so much of the nature of each piece as of the relationships among them: it suggests that they belong together, and should be performed together, like a purposefully constructed set of songs.

OTHER LYRICAL *BALLADES*

Lyrical piano *ballades* of the type Brahms introduced in the four Ballades of 1856 flourished in the following decade and beyond. But it is not strictly true to say that Brahms invented the type, and there is no reason to believe that his Ballades exerted much influence on the lyrical *ballades* written later. Credit for invention of the type seems to belong to Joachim Raff (1822–1882), for a Ballade that he evidently composed in 1849, but did not publish until 1874.[35] Brahms could hardly have known the piece when he wrote his four Ballades. His Ballades, in turn, seem not to have made much impact when they were new. Though they were published by Breitkopf & Härtel in 1856, they were not performed in public until years later, the second and third by Clara Schumann in 1860 and the other two by Brahms himself in 1867.[36] It seems unlikely that the older and better-established composers who wrote lyrical piano *ballades* in the 1860s—composers like Ferdinand Hiller (1811–1885) and Stephen Heller (1813–1888)—paid much attention to the Ballades written and published by Brahms in his early twenties. In any case, the similarities among all of these *ballades* are not such that they need to be explained by a chain of influence.

The Raff Ballade introduced not only the new type of lyrical *ballade*, but also a texture that would become a hallmark of piano *ballades* for the rest of the nineteenth century. It opens with an unharmonized melody in octaves, and the first chord is not heard until the cadence in the eighth measure. Afterwards chords are heard more regularly, but generally on off-beats, and the entire theme, twenty-six measures long, is presented in octaves, sometimes with chords and sometimes without. The texture of bare octaves, which appeared only fleetingly in the Chopin Ballades, as it was to do in the Brahms Ballades, is established by Raff as a prime element of his Ballade. The texture suits the melody, which for the most part spells out its own harmony, as the opening theme of the Brahms "Edward" Ballade was to do but the themes of the Chopin Ballades did not. In that sense, Raff's melody is reminiscent of a folk song, though it could not be confused with the folk songs he knew from his native Switzerland or from elsewhere. Like the themes of the Chopin Ballades or Loewe ballads, this theme is shaped to suggest the tension of a ballad story; it is not, like the melodies of folk ballads, an impartial vehicle for the words of the tale. All the same, the melody and texture together evoke the singing of a folk song, unaccompanied or sporadically accompanied by an instrument, more strongly than any earlier piano *ballade* did.

At the end of the theme, Raff moves on to another theme and other textures. Though the thematic material is all plain and singable, nothing else evokes folk song as the opening does. Instead, separate and contrasting sections seem to suggest the episodes of a story. Even the return of the opening theme continues the dramatic progression: the tone of triumph in which the theme first returns (in the wrong key and major mode) quickly gives way—like an illusory happy outcome in a ballad—to a full return in the original key and mode and in a new whirlwind of motion that nevertheless recalls the original bare octaves. Just as Brahms was to do in his "Edward" Ballade, Raff suggested the tautness of ballad narration by confining highly charged musical developments within a short piece in simple form built on a songlike theme.

Raff did not follow up on his own innovations; his next piano *ballade*, written three years later,[37] makes no reference at all to folk song, even though it too opens in bare octaves. The Ballade, Op. 74, is hard to categorize: its sentimental opening and closing sections fit oddly with a middle section that is not only stormy in character but dramatic in its processes of thematic transformation and convergence.

Other composers of lyrical piano *ballades* in the 1850s and 1860s used the bare-octave texture, often in new ways. In 1860 the Norwegian composer Thomas Tellefsen (1823–1874), a pupil of Chopin, published a Ballade[38] that begins, in bare octaves, with a theme very much like that of Raff's Ballade from Opus 17. But as Tellefsen enriches the accompanying textures, he demonstrates the resemblance of his theme to the barcarolle-like themes of Chopin's Ballades.

Stephen Heller, one of the most accomplished composers of Chopin's own generation, wrote—as Chopin did—almost exclusively for the piano. Born in Budapest, he moved to Paris at the age of twenty-five and remained there for fifty years, cultivating the art of the piano character piece. Among his works are the *Three Ballades*, Op. 115, and the Ballade in his *Three Pieces*, Op. 121, all published in the 1860s.[39]

These are lyrical pieces, constantly changing in texture. While Brahms and Raff usually maintain a constant texture for the length of a theme or section, Heller's themes consist of tiny phrases in contrasting textures. He constructs themes, in other words, on late eighteenth-century principles, though the textures and styles he uses are of the nineteenth century. In the second Ballade of Opus 115, for instance, he uses four textures, including two different bare-octave textures, within the first eight measures (see Example 5-8). The third of these textures (*piano, calmato*) has a narrative tone appropriate to a *ballade*, a suddenly calm, impassive tone after the fiery opening; there is nothing folklike, however, in the leaping intervals with which this phrase begins.

Later another octave texture appears, this time punctuated by chords (see Example 5-9). This dancelike theme could have been inspired by the passage of similar texture in one of Chopin's Mazurkas.[40] The wealth of unharmonized or partly harmonized textures unites this Ballade the way the voice of a singing narrator unites the episodes of a ballad, and it is not surprising that the piece ends with an extension of the *calmato* phrase at the opening.

Example 5-8. Heller, Ballade, Op. 115, No. 2, mm. 1-8.

Example 5-9. Heller, Ballade, Op. 115, No. 2, mm. 44-51.

Formally Heller contributed something new to the piano *ballade*. Each of his Ballades consists of a recurring complex of themes. Usually the complex recurs once with changes—more or less like a recapitulation—and again in a considerably shortened version—like a coda. Perhaps an idea of stanzaic repetition in ballads underlies this form. The most elaborate version of it appears in the Ballade of Opus 121, where there are three recurrences and where the changes in the recurrences include a new theme. In the *Three Ballades* of Opus 115 the similarity of form, along with closeness in keys (D major-B minor-D minor), gives a unity to the set very much like the unity in Brahms's *Four Ballades*.

Heller's contemporary Ferdinand Hiller wrote two piano *ballades*, of which the second, which appeared in his *Six Piano Pieces* of 1867,[41] uses the same form as Heller's Ballades and also favors unharmonized and partly harmonized textures. Another contemporary, Robert Volkmann (1815-1883), published a Ballade[42] in 1866, the same year as Heller's *Three Ballades*. This simple piece consists of contrasting melodies in alternation. One of the melodies sounds like a folk song, thanks to the setting as much as to the melody itself: it is harmonized almost entirely over a dominant pedal. In 1867 a younger composer, Josef Rheinberger (1839–1901), later an important teacher of composition, published a Ballade in a set of *Three Character Pieces*, Op. 7.[43] Here it is rhythmic ambiguity that suggests folk song: in the middle section of this piece a simple melody in 3/4 rhythm is set against a 6/8 accompaniment.

By 1870, then, a number of composers, most of them German at least in training, had developed a type of piano *ballade* that was very different from Chopin's. This type was lyrical in both material and form; its material was sometimes cast so as to suggest folk song; at the same time it allowed for some dramatic effects, some reminder that ballads are eventful stories. In the remaining three decades of the nineteenth century this type of piano *ballade* was turned increasingly toward folk-song imitation, often at the expense of any reference to story, by composers in virtually every part of Europe. The way for this trend had been prepared by an art that developed all through the nineteenth century: the art of transcribing and arranging the melodies of folk songs for the piano.

CHAPTER 6

Grieg and the Folk-Song *Ballade* to 1880

FOLK BALLADS ARRANGED FOR THE PIANO

When the melody of a folk ballad is turned into a piano piece, it scarcely remains a ballad in any sense. As melodies, ballads are "only hypothetically separable from the mass of lyric folksong," writes Bertrand Bronson.[1] It is the words that make them ballads, and the words are left out when the melody is turned into a piano piece. The history of folk ballads arranged for the piano, then, is part of—not even a distinct chapter in—the history of folk songs arranged for the piano. That larger history—in fact, the whole history of folk-song arrangement—remains to be written.

Even a preliminary look through nineteenth-century publishers' catalogs or research-library catalogs, however, makes it clear that the arrangement of folk songs for the piano was a large and varied enterprise throughout the nineteenth century, changing gradually in nature over the course of the century. In the first half of the century, folk songs—or "national airs," as they were more often called—were used along with popular opera melodies and dance tunes as subjects for piano potpourris, variations, fantasies, and rondos. The "national airs" were chosen not so much for their nationalist appeal as for their tourist appeal. They were often contemporary sentimental songs with local associations or a little local color; if they happened to be older in origin, they had shed any awkward musical features. The composers of these arrangements had little thought of discovering, preserving, or propagating folk music: the titles of the arrangements show that the songs were often "beloved" already. Hardly any of these songs appear to be ballads.

The "Finnish Song" ("Finskaja pesnja"; see Example 6-1)[2] published in 1830 by Mikhail Glinka (1804–1857) is exceptional in this context, besides having its own peculiar connection to the ballad. Glinka discovered and transcribed the tune himself on a visit to Finland. He seems not to have

Example 6-1. Glinka, "Finnish Song" (complete).

recorded the words and may not have understood them. His arrangement of the song for piano, and especially his harmonization of the second half with scales, is skillful in such a modern way that it is hard now to imagine how it may have sounded to anyone in 1830. The song is not rounded off with an ending on the apparent tonic, or rounded off in a larger sense by an introduction, variations, or other extensions. By comparison to other "national air" arrangements of the day, this arrangement seems less like a piano piece made from the melody than like a device for repeating the melody at the piano and imagining it as a stanzaic song. Glinka himself is said to have played the tune with variations at the piano.[3] His published arrangement, which appeared in a literary journal, seems designed for home use.

In 1838 Glinka turned the melody from the simplest of piano pieces into one of the major numbers in his opera *Ruslan and Lyudmila*, Finn's Ballad. This number is a ballad in that its text is narrative: the Finnish wizard is recounting his past to Ruslan. There is nothing to suggest that Glinka thought of the original "Finnish Song" as a ballad. He thought enough of his earlier piano arrangement, though, to use it quite literally as the basis for the first stanza of Finn's Ballad. In a sense he was anticipating what Smetana would later do in turning a Ballade for piano into an aria in *Dalibor*. But Smetana's

Ballade was already more opera aria than folk song. The revealing thing about Glinka's adaptation of his own piano piece is that it shows how two apparently opposed kinds of folk-song arrangement—the simple harmonization of a folk melody for home use and the construction of grand-scale professional music on folk-song themes—can belong to the same process of transformation.

The most famous composer to arrange national airs for the piano in the 1830s and 1840s was Liszt. His arrangements include one that he called a *ballade*, the "Ballade d'Ukraine" in his *Glanes de Woronince*, published in 1849.[4] It has been argued that his persistent arranging of songs from countries that he visited in the course of his concert tours was a matter of political conviction, a sympathetic response to the nationalist yearnings of Italians, Hungarians, Czechs, and others.[5] At the same time, it is hard to see how his arrangements differ in kind from hundreds of other contemporary arrangements, about which no such argument is likely to be made. Like other composers, he chose songs from varied sources: the material for his "Canzone napolitana," his "Deux Mélodies russes," his "Faribolo pastour," and similar pieces ranges from contemporary songs to traditional songs that he himself transcribed in fairly remote spots. His arrangements also followed the common pattern of the day: a brief introduction on motives from the song, the song itself in a simple setting, a florid variation or two, and perhaps a short coda. There was not even anything unusual in the variety of nations he saluted in this way. For that matter, Liszt's national-air arrangements suffered the same fate as those by other composers when the taste for such arrangements waned: when the New Liszt Edition issues these pieces, most will be appearing in print for the first time since their original editions.

Glanes de Woronince stands somewhat apart from these other national-air arrangements, yet there is nothing unusual about either the kinds of songs Liszt chose to include or the forms of his arrangements. Liszt reported hearing musicians, some of them Gypsies, play and sing at a country celebration near Woronince, in the Ukrainian region of Podolia, in 1847, and this experience apparently provided most of the melodies for the *Glanes*, including that of the "Ballade d'Ukraine." But the set also includes a transcription of Chopin's Polish song "The Maiden's Wish."[6]

The "Ballade d'Ukraine" is based, according to Alan Walker, on a folk ballad with the text "Hryts, do not go to the party tonight." Liszt shaped the melody of the song into a tonally well-rounded theme for variations. This theme has two phrases in the tonic, B minor (see Example 6-2), a transposition into the relative major, and a return of the first two phrases, now varied and extended with a cadenza, ending on the dominant. Apart from new modulations in the second variation, the most interesting feature of this piece is the embellishment reminiscent of Chopin in the first variation, *Grazioso con malinconia* (see Example 6-3).

Example 6-2. Liszt, *Glanes de Woronince*: "Ballade d'Ukraine," mm. 36–43.

Example 6-3. Liszt, *Glanes de Woronince*: "Ballade d'Ukraine," mm. 86–89.

This reminiscence is reinforced by the other two pieces in the *Glanes*. The second, "Mélodies polonaises," uses the Chopin song, and the third, "Complainte," though it begins with the most folklike of the melodies in the most austere of piano settings, ends, in its second variation, as a Chopinian polonaise (*Andante quasi in tempo della polacca*). In this set of small national-air arrangements, then, Liszt paid tribute to Chopin by means of quotation and stylistic imitation, very different means from those he would choose soon afterward in his two Ballades.

In a curious way, and despite Liszt's conflation of Gypsy, Ukrainian, and Polish sources, this tribute gives *Glanes de Woronince* a more strongly nationalist emphasis than his earlier national-air arrangements had. In fact, it is characteristic of Liszt to embody nationalist spirit in music by combining national airs with tributes to national heroes: Guillaume Tell in *Album d'un voyageur*, Chopin here, and seven Hungarian contemporaries in *Historical Hungarian Portraits*. When Liszt, like many of his contemporaries, published arrangements of one or two national airs from a place he had visited, he was hardly making a serious contribution to the nationalist movement of that place, though the variety of his arrangements taken together may recall the internationalist nationalism of Herder. He was more clearly paying tribute to a national culture when he brought several Slavic folk songs together with references to Chopin in *Glanes de Woronince*. But the very terms of that tribute—the identification of the national hero with the folk—mark Liszt's nationalist spirit apart from Herder's.

The years between 1847, when Liszt visited Woronince, and 1849, when *Glanes de Woronince* was published, were eventful in several respects. In 1848 revolution broke out in many parts of Europe. In 1849 Chopin died. The 1848 revolutions, which in Paris, Vienna, and Berlin were motivated for the most part by social politics, in other places were largely revolutions of national liberation, and the general suppression of the revolutions left nationalists throughout Europe with new determination to develop national consciousness among their people. In this situation the collecting of folk songs took on greater importance than ever, and new forms of folk-song arrangement became prominent.

In the decades after 1848, folk songs began to be published in national collections, arranged for the piano, in many parts of Europe. One of the first of these collections was created by Carol Mikuli (1819–1897), once Chopin's pupil and later his editor. In his forty-eight *National Rumanian Airs*, published between 1852 and 1857, he took credit for collecting as well as arranging the melodies.[7] To a remarkable extent, compared to earlier arrangers, Mikuli preserved the distinctiveness, and especially the modal variety, of the melodies, even when that created awkwardness for his harmonization. His arrangements are settings of a single strophe of melody, much more like Glinka's "Finnish Song" than like the rondos and variation sets of Liszt and others. His title pages promise "ballads" as well as other kinds of songs and dances, but because each song is presented with at most the first few words of text and because Rumanian folk singers freely exchange texts and melodies, it is difficult to isolate ballads within this collection.

Other collections appeared, presenting folk songs in simple piano arrangements, explicitly for the use of piano students. Though the arrangers were not always as scrupulous as Mikuli in preserving the distinctive features of the folk songs, they believed in teaching children their national heritage of melodies as they taught them to play an instrument. As István Bartalus

(1821–1899), one of the most prolific Hungarian folk-song arrangers of the nineteenth century, wrote in the introduction to his collection *Children's Lyre* (1860): "There are things that a child learns more easily from his wet-nurse than, at a more advanced age, from his learned master; such is the correct pronunciation of his mother tongue, and likewise the interpretation of our national music in the Magyar spirit."[8]

Children's Lyre is a collection of six Hungarian songs in arrangements for a piano student at a fairly early stage of study. Other collections presented folk songs in piano-duet arrangements, the folk melody in octaves or even in single notes for the student to play and a more complicated accompaniment for the teacher. Among these collections are the *Czech National Songs, for Elementary Instruction in Piano Playing* published in the early 1860s by the Czech piano composer Vojtech Preisler (1806–1877) and the *Twenty Good Old German Folk Songs for Piano, Four Hands, for Use in Teaching* (1878) by the Swiss piano pedagogue Johann Karl Eschmann (1826–1882).[9] Most of these collections give the titles or first lines of each song, but no more text than that. The idea was evidently to teach children to play, rather than to sing, their national songs.

In other kinds of collections, by contrast, even though the folk songs are arranged for the piano, the piano is treated almost as an incidental means of transmission. This is the case in the monumental *Older and Newer Norwegian Mountain Melodies, Collected and Arranged for Pianoforte*[10] published between 1853 and 1867 by the Oslo church musician and field collector Ludvig Lindeman (1812–1887). Lindeman's work fit into an active folklore movement in a Norway that was not yet linguistically and culturally independent of Denmark and would not be politically independent of Sweden until 1905. The folk-song melodies that he collected complemented the Norwegian folk-song texts that had already been collected and published in great numbers. In his collection he printed the words of the songs under their melodies, and he indicated text collections in which further verses could be found. Some of his song arrangements seem designed for one person to sing and play: the right-hand part has just the melody, while the left-hand part has a simple harmonization. In other cases Lindeman put the melody on a separate staff and created a somewhat independent piano accompaniment. All his arrangements, however, seem more suited to performance at home than in a concert hall.

Other Norwegian composers soon went to work making their own arrangements of the same melodies.[11] The ballad "Sjugurd og trollbrura" ("Sjugurd and the Troll-Bride"),[12] for instance, was arranged at least four times as an instrumental piece by the leading Norwegian composers of the day. Halfdan Kjerulf (1815–1868) published a piano arrangement of it, as unpretentious as Lindeman's, in his *Norwegian Folk Ballads*,[13] published in 1867. Edvard Grieg (1843–1907) discovered the Lindeman collection in 1868 and used its melodies for the first time in his *Twenty-five Norwegian Folk*

Ballads and Dances, Op. 17,[14] published in 1870. His "Sjugurd og trollbrura" is the fourth of the *Six Norwegian Mountain Melodies*[15] that he arranged for piano in 1869, but did not publish until 1886. In the meantime, Johan Svendsen (1840–1911) used the same melody in his second *Norwegian Rhapsody* for orchestra,[16] published in 1877. Grieg returned to his own arrangement of the melody later, using it virtually unchanged as the theme of his *Old Norwegian Romance with Variations*,[17] Op. 51, for two pianos, published in 1891.

Grieg's arrangement of the melody, in the *Six Norwegian Mountain Melodies* (see Example 6-4), invites comparison to Glinka's "Finnish Song" (Example 6-1). Aside from transposing the melody down a whole-step and altering the upbeat note with which it begins, Grieg took the melody over exactly as he found it in Lindeman's collection: two complementary couplets, followed by a short refrain in a different meter. Grieg's arrangement is just as spare as Lindeman's or Kjerulf's, but harmonically both sturdier and more sophisticated. His bass line has a deliberate motion: in the first couplet it moves from a surprising F, which begins the song on a second-inversion chord and creates strong dissonances already in the first measure, to C, and in the second couplet back from C to F. He takes advantage of this strong bass motion to find unexpected harmonies for the A-flats that are the most interesting notes of the melody. He gives the refrain a static effect by harmonizing it with repeating dominant notes, ornamented by grace-notes.[18]

Example 6-4. Grieg, *Six Norwegian Mountain Melodies*: "Sjugurd og trollbrura" (complete).

Grieg presents the whole song as a single rounded phrase, and it seems only natural that he would later feel moved to extend this tiny, strong progression into a longer work by writing variations on it. In the meanwhile, though, he wrote another set of piano variations on another melody from Lindeman's collection. This work, the *Ballade in the Form of Variations on a Norwegian Melody*, Op. 24,[19] written in 1875 and published the following year, is universally described as his most important work for solo piano.

THE GRIEG BALLADE

The work that Grieg named "Romance" is a set of variations on the melody of a ballad; the work that he named "Ballade" is a set of variations on a song that is not a ballad. Grieg may have settled on the title "Ballade"[20] partly to connect this work with the tradition of piano *ballades* begun by Chopin. But a work in the form of variations on a folk melody does not fit readily into that tradition, except in the general sense of a large, serious, single-movement composition that refers to folk song. The largeness and seriousness of the Ballade separate it from earlier small national-air settings, even from those—like Liszt's "Ballade d'Ukraine"—that consist of variations.

For Grieg, as for Liszt and others, the variation form may have been tied to the idea of strophic repetitions in a folk song. But in Grieg's Ballade the variations make such a dramatic progression that one wonders whether to understand the work as a new venture—within the piano *ballade* tradition— in suggesting both the form of the song and the progression of the story. Grieg's idea of a *ballade* in the form of variations on a folk song was imitated in his friend Julius Röntgen's 1896 *Ballade for Orchestra on a Norwegian Folk Melody* (discussed in Chapter 8), and a similar idea can be found in two small Bartók piano *ballades* (discussed in Chapter 7), but the Grieg Ballade is unique in the kind of musical "story" it tells.

The theme of the Ballade is the song "Den nordlandske bondestand" ("The Northland Peasantry"), Number 337 in Lindeman's collection. Lindeman indicates that he transcribed the song from the singing of Anders Nilsen Perlesteinbakken in Valdres. The words come from a poem written by Kristine Aas and published in 1832; the melody is said to be virtually identical to that of a drinking song from Lista.[21] The song as a whole, in other words, derived not from any pure, ancient folk source, but from a recent folk processing of a literary product. Moreover, the words do not imitate folk-song verse so much as they comment on folk-song:

> I know so many a lovely song
> Of beautiful lands elsewhere,
> But ne'er have I heard a single song
> Of my home in the north so fair.

So now I'm going to try my skill
To write a song so that people will
See that life up north can be happy and gay—
No matter what folks down south might say.[22]

These words do not tell a story, let alone a ballad story. Their proud message may have had a significance for Grieg—who was struggling to establish Norwegian music on the European scene—that it had lacked for Kristine Aas or Anders Nilsen Perlesteinbakken. The whole character of his *Ballade*, musically one of the most ambitious works he would ever write, could have been formed by a determination to "write a song so that people will see." Grieg wrote the work at a time of great personal stress, and it remained a stressful undertaking for him to play it for anyone; indeed, he never played it in public.[23] His strong feelings about the work could only have been increased by a sense that it represented the project of proving himself in the wide world as a composer. Instead of a story within the music, then, there may be a story behind the music: the story of the composer's confrontation with his own historical position.

Lindeman's field transcription of the song, which has been preserved and reprinted in facsimile, shows that he adjusted details of the melody in his published arrangement.[24] In particular, he changed rhythmic values in the first line of the second half ("O derfor vil e no prøvø paa"), making it rhythmically identical to the succeeding line (see Example 6-5).

Example 6-5. Lindeman: "Den nordlandske bondestand" (complete) from *Older and Newer Norwegian Mountain Melodies*.

Grieg took the process one step further. The opening motive of the melody (B-flat–G–F-sharp) is heard six times in all, and Grieg eliminated variant details from the repetitions (see Example 6-6). When the melody is sung, these variants accommodate the variable feet of the verse; Grieg, turning the melody into a piano theme, chose to emphasize the identity of the motive in all its repetitions. At the same time, however, he introduced subtle rhythmic variety into the B-flat–C–D motive, which Lindeman had given the same way each time. The cadential B-flat–A–G motive, which makes its own rhythmic contrast with the other motives, is treated alike in all versions. The three versions of the melody do not differ much in principle; in all three versions—and especially the two published ones—the rhythm of closely related, three-beat motives, all starting on the upbeat, is relentless and powerful.

Example 6-6. Grieg, Ballade, Op. 24, mm. 1–16.

Grieg's harmonization, however, is very different from Lindeman's. Grieg uses a much greater variety of chords (without moving further from G minor than Lindeman does) and connects those chords with chromatically rich movement of the parts. The most remarkable feature of Grieg's arrangement is the long, descending chromatic bass line, which binds the whole first half of the melody into a single phrase, justifying the single slur that Grieg extends over that entire half. In connecting the little phrases of a folk song into one long phrase by means of a firm bass line, he was following the same principle as in his arrangement of "Sjugurd og trollbrura" (Example 6-4); in using a descending scale for this purpose, he was anticipating the folk-song arrangements of Bartók.

Grieg took pains to carry the momentum of the music past internal cadential points in the melody. At the end of the first couplet of the melody (m. 4), where Lindeman makes a perfect cadence in G minor, Grieg chooses a weaker "modal" cadence (F major to G minor) and denies even that cadence a cadential effect by holding the bass on F while the other parts settle on the G-minor chord. In the second half of the theme a different technique prevents a strong effect of cadencing: when the first two phrases of that half (mm. 9–12) reach their cadence-point, the bass drops out, replaced by a descant voice, or overtone effect, above the melody. These two phrases also stand apart from the rest of the theme in tempo and volume.

All in all Grieg, rather than arranging his folk song as if he wanted to foster enjoyment of it as a folk song, has reshaped it, as he had reshaped the shorter "Sjugurd" melody, into a single, clearly defined progression. In doing so, he has introduced such strong new elements—notably the chromatic bass line—as to raise from the start the question of whether the subject of his variations is to be simply the Norwegian melody or the whole theme that he has created around that melody.

A blunt answer is given by the first variation (*Poco meno andante, ma molto tranquillo*). Grieg's chromatic bass line is heard from the start, and his chord progression from the third measure, but only tiny fragments of the melody ever appear. Actually, the pulsing chords in the right-hand part follow the contour of the melody in a rough sense, even as they counter the bass with long chromatic lines of their own. With this first variation Grieg not only makes clear that the whole theme is to be the subject of the work, but also rules out any systematic division of function between melody and setting: the melody will not serve in this work, as it does in the Chopin Ballades, as a symbol of stanzaic repetition.

The first nine of the fourteen variations are, as Nils Grinde writes, "distinct character variations, which illuminate various aspects of the folksong while retaining its formal structure."[25] The second variation (*Allegro agitato*), accordingly, sets a faster tempo and étude-like energy against the tranquillity of the first. But it also differs from the theme in some of the same ways as the first variation: it has the same 9/8 meter (though Grieg did not notate it as such in the first variation) and many of the same new chords and pungent dissonances. To say that this is a "character variation" does not mean that it is all of one character or that the only contrast is between one variation and the next. In fact, there is an enormous dynamic range within this variation, and the rigors of the étude give way after the double bar to a playfulness reminiscent of "The Prophet-Bird" in Schumann's *Waldscenen*, Op. 82. In the theme, Grieg has already emphasized the distinctiveness of the couplet after the double bar; in this variation and some later ones he exaggerates the distinctiveness, in effect defining the "character" of the variation as a dynamic relationship between two opposed characters.

The third variation (*Adagio*) brings the melody of the folk song back for the first time, as the tenor voice in a duet texture very much like that of Schumann's F-sharp major Romance, Op. 28. At the same time the rich chords and chromatic bass line of the theme are gone, replaced by the simplest harmonies over pedal points. For the first time Grieg introduces a transposition: the second couplet of the melody (mm. 5–8) is heard in B-flat minor instead of G minor. Because of this transposition Grieg can simply repeat the second phrase of the couplet, changing only the mode, as the first phrase of the following couplet (B-flat major, mm. 9–10). No such lovely effect could be made by coming back to this B-flat major phrase from G minor, and Grieg, for the only time in the nine "structural" variations, leaves the second half of the variation unrepeated.

By the time he wrote this Ballade, Grieg was already experienced at arranging (or rearranging) Hardanger-fiddle dances for the piano, and the next variation (*Allegro capriccioso*), with its sometimes offbeat, sometimes droning accompaniment, imitates the style of that music. If Grieg was consciously proving himself as a Norwegian composer in this work, a variation in Norwegian folk-dance style, along with a nationalist Norwegian song as his theme, would make its point within a generally traditional and cosmopolitan variation scheme. In this dance variation the interaction of melody and bass line takes a new step: the melody is hinted at in the course of a sixteenth-note melody that begins as a falling chromatic scale.

The following variation (*Più lento*) combines the melody and chromatic bass line in yet another fresh way. A rhapsodic line climbing up from the bass and embodying, paradoxically, short stretches of descending chromatic scales is answered at two-measure intervals by a phrase embodying the cadential motive (B-flat–A–G) of the melody. The rhapsodic line, which Grieg labels *recitando* and marks to be played with rhythmic freedom, seems to imitate a parlando-rubato style of folk music, but Grieg's inspiration for this passage may not have come directly or solely from Norwegian folk music.

His idea of representing folk-music recitation in this style may have come from a very different source. The introduction to Chopin's first Ballade (also in G minor) has the same structure of a slowly rising line that lingers near its peak (ending on F–E-flat–D–D instead of Grieg's chromatic F–E–E-flat–D–D), answered by a cadence phrase. The resemblance to this Chopin model becomes even stronger when Grieg repeats the first half of the theme (for the only time in the Ballade). In this written-out repeat, the rising line, like Chopin's, is played in octaves, and the first chord of the cadence phrase is precisely the "emotional key-note" chord of Chopin's introduction (m. 7). In this variation the title "Ballade" comes alive as a modern tradition of evoking the age-old narrating voice of the ballad singer. After the double bar this variation, like the second, shows the opposite side of its character: enclosed within the passages of gloomy ballad recitation is a peaceful passage of nature painting that could come from the slow movement of Grieg's Piano Concerto, a passage in which the rhapsodic rising line and the cadence phrase are blended together.

In the sixth variation (*Allegro scherzando*) the pianist's hands take turns imitating each other in pairs of chords. Grieg follows neither the melody nor the bass line of his theme, but only the harmonic progression, and that only loosely. One of the delightful touches in this variation is that the F major–G minor progression that Grieg used at an internal cadence in the theme, where it helped carry the momentum of the lines past the cadence, he uses here (adding an E-flat to the F chord) as the final cadence. Perhaps his purpose is the same here, since for the first time in the Ballade he marks no pause at the end of the variation and since the following variation is the mate of this one. Not only is the new variation the only one in the set without its own tempo indication, but its notes (at least to the double bar) are exactly the same as those of the previous variation, now spread out in two continuous individual lines, so that they form a canon. The canon may be a light-handed gesture toward the tradition of imitative counterpoint in variation sets. Grieg may even have been thinking of the occasional canonic setting in Lindeman's folk song collection.[26] There is something irreverent in the way he ends this canon, spinning out both lines to the final sixteenth-note of the final measure and then cutting them both off, on the dominant instead of the tonic.

The next two variations are both slow in tempo, but they are utterly different from each other in character and in their relation to the theme. The eighth (*Lento*) is a whispered funeral march in triple time. Here the Norwegian melody is presented in its original form, in as many as five registers at once. So far in the Ballade, the melody is heard as itself in only the most somber and subdued of settings. The chords in this variation make more forceful progressions than the chords in the theme did, while an inner voice provides a strong, simple counterpoint (E-natural–F-sharp–G) to the cadencing motive (B-flat–A–G).

The following variation (*Un poco andante*) is the dreamiest of the set, the most changeable in texture, speed, and volume. Grieg takes, on the whole, twice as many measures as usual for each phrase of the theme, but even that rate is not fixed. In contrast to the theme, this variation has a chromatic melody and a more diatonic bass. In the cadential phrase, though, a chromatic alteration in the bass line (A-flat instead of A) produces a new sonority, a ninth chord, which suspends movement toward the cadence for two measures, and later for six. In this variation, by interrupting the progress of the theme for increasingly long stretches, Grieg creates a dreamy sensation of breaking free from the constraints of time.

Actually he is breaking free from the structures of his theme for the rest of the Ballade. Elements of key, mode, rhythm, and phrase-structure that until now have been taken for granted—through all the alterations in style and character, through all the novel interactions of melody and bass lines—now in turn become subject to alteration. The next variation (*Un poco allegro e alla burla*) is the first that is not in triple meter. Its material is derived from the opening motive of the melody, and not so much from the pitches as from the ♫♪ rhythm of that motive. The phrases of the theme are given radically new proportions: the two halves of the theme, which are equal in length (not counting the repeat of the second half), take four and eleven measures respectively in this variation. The chromatic bass line of the theme does not figure at all in the variation until well into the repeat of the second half, when it appears as the music begins to modulate for the first time. Whereas in the theme a sequence of chords sliding chromatically downward led to a cadence in the tonic key, here a similar sequence, sliding upward, makes an open-ended modulatory progression that breaks off instead of cadencing (see Example 6-7).

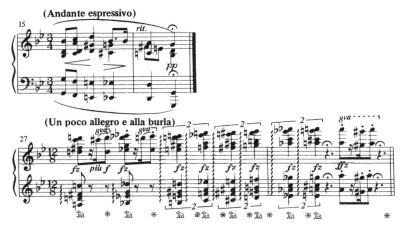

Example 6-7. Grieg, Ballade, Op. 24: Theme, mm. 15–16 (*above*), and Variation 10 (*Un poco allegro e alla burla*), mm. 27–28 (*below*).

The next variation (*Più animato*) begins abruptly, on the dominant of D-flat rather than of D, several octaves below the register where the previous one broke off, and at a whisper after a thundering crescendo. It continues the dotted rhythmic motive of the previous variation, but now that motive, which derived from the melody of the theme, is separated from the melody and turned into a drum-roll accompaniment. This variation is the first that is not based on the whole theme. Instead it is a modulating sequence (in that sense a continuation of the previous variation) based on the first phrase of the theme. As the sequence proceeds, the phrase is reshaped and shortened, the pulse quickens, the volume increases, and all the elements are put in place for the next variation, which follows without a break. A process very much like the progressive transformations in the Chopin Ballades has taken place.

The new variation (*Meno allegro e maestoso*) makes a triumphant climax to the whole Ballade. The melody of the theme is heard once again at its full length, though now broadened (each beat of the theme gets a measure here), simplified (by the elimination of repeated notes), and in the major mode. The major mode has been prepared in the previous variation, but this is the only time in the Ballade that the melody appears whole and undisguised in the major mode; all its other appearances are not only in the minor mode, but utterly untriumphant in character. The triumph here is a matter of undivided spirit. The variation is entirely of one character; there is no change of mood in the second half of the theme. Everything in the variation derives from the melody, rather than from its original chromatic accompaniment. The melody is accompanied here by the dotted rhythm (continuing from the previous two variations) of the original melody and by chords that are generally more consonant with their melody notes than those of the theme were. In a sense Grieg is glorifying the folk melody by displaying both the whole melody and the elements that comprise it.

The melody as a whole has now been heard for the last time, but the Ballade does not end on this triumphant note. A new variation (*Allegro furioso*) brings back the minor mode, the original meter, and above all the interaction—now presented as a struggle—between the diatonic melody and the chromatic bass. A diatonic version of the first phrase is answered by a sequencing phrase rich in the augmented-sixth chords that characterized the original harmonization of the melody. Then a new diatonic version of the opening phrase is completed by a sequence of third-related chords, which present a new form of chromaticism. The last two of these chords, F major and D major, become locked in a struggle so fierce that it displaces the downbeat of the music. In the theme, both these chords led to the tonic chord at different cadences. The alternation of the two chords here seems like a struggle not only over a cadence, but over the whole issue of how to arrange a folk melody. At this moment—the most Lisztian in the work—Grieg has reduced the dramatic issue of the Ballade to a confrontation between two functionally unrelated chords.

The confrontation has the character of a psychological deadlock, and what happens when the theme resumes (*Prestissimo*) can be adequately described only in psychological terms. Grieg himself called this moment "that mighty passage that increases in intensity until it breaks out in sheer fury."[27] The repetition, fragmentation, and dissolution of motives from the theme portray a mental obsession, a cycle of hysteria that ends in blackout. At the moment of blackout, a terrifying, low E-flat octave brings back the chromatic bass line of the theme, followed by the theme itself in its original form, though only the first half of it, to end the Ballade. By this stroke Grieg restores a kind of equilibrium to the work. But it is only half the theme, and returning after a complete breakdown in the variation process. There is no effect of rounding off here, as there is in Bach's Goldberg variations or the finale of Beethoven's piano sonata, Op. 109.

Despite its dramatic ending, Grieg's Ballade cannot fairly be called a narrative work. It is a variation set in which some of the later variations no longer adhere to the structure of the theme. In that sense Grieg can be said to be following, or perhaps proving himself against, classic variation models, notably Beethoven's. To analyze the departure from the structure of the theme as a narrative event would be to portray the earlier part of the work—the larger part and much of the subtlest music—as relatively inert. It is preferable instead to consider the whole work as a single, consistent progression. The progression responds to the challenge of a theme that is neither the composer's own nor someone else's, but something of both: his own arrangement of a preexisting melody. By choosing a simple folk melody and giving it the richest, most modern accompaniment imaginable, Grieg succinctly formulated the dilemma of a composer from a country on the outskirts of modern European culture, trying to win recognition from that European culture on contemporary terms while remaining faithful to the tradition of his own country. In that sense Grieg was responding to the same dilemma that Chopin had responded to in his Ballades, although the musical means Grieg chose for his response are completely different from Chopin's.

The Ballade unfolds as an exploration of the dilemma; the only story it tells is of possible relationships between the two opposed elements that make up the theme. If the last part of the work comes across as especially dramatic, especially personal, Grieg has made it so by breaking away from the structure of the theme to prepare for the triumph of the melody over the arrangement (in the *Maestoso* twelfth variation). Though this triumph may appear to twentieth-century listeners as the proposal of a new concept of folk-song arrangement—conjuring the accompaniment out of the substance of the melody—in the dialectic of this Ballade it represents a rejection of the composer's own part in the theme, his own style, his place in modern European music. The return to the theme at the end marks a retreat from this extreme solution, a truce in a confrontation that has grown too harrowing. In Nils Grinde's words, the return "gives the whole work a feeling of unresolved struggle."[28]

In later works Grieg would test new ways of arranging Norwegian folk music. The Ballade, however, is not so much an essay in folk-song arrangement as it is Grieg's eloquent testament to the effort it cost to find an honorable place for folk-song arrangement within European concert music.

CHAPTER 7

Fauré and the *Ballade* from 1880 to 1918

THE FAURÉ BALLADE

Gabriel Fauré (1845–1924), Grieg's contemporary, published his Ballade for piano[1] in 1880, only a few years after Grieg's. Fauré's Ballade, like Grieg's, was the composer's biggest and finest early work for solo piano and the only one to which he ever gave the title "Ballade." In Fauré's case, the Ballade marked an important step in the development of the composer's musical language, and it is possible to trace this step in part to the influence of the first master of the piano *ballade*, Chopin. At the same time, Fauré's Ballade, unlike Grieg's, introduced ideas that were to become increasingly prevalent in *ballades* in the following decades; the most important of these was the idea of the *ballade* as a nature piece. Finally, by rearranging the work for piano and orchestra (this version was first performed in 1881 and first published in 1901),[2] Fauré began a tradition of concerto *ballades*, which would become an especially vital part of the *ballade* genre in the twentieth century.

For all that, the work was not begun as a *ballade*. Though the early versions have disappeared, a letter by Fauré, published and judiciously appraised by Jean-Michel Nectoux, tells us something about the evolution of the work:

> . . . I can tell you, dear Madame, that my piano pieces nos. 2 and 3 have assumed considerably greater importance thanks to a no. 5, which is a link passage between 2 and 3. That is to say, by using *new* but at the same time *old* methods I have found a way of developing the phrases of no. 2 in a sort of interlude and at the same time stating the premises of no. 3 in such a way that the three pieces become one. It has thus turned into a Fantasy rather out of the usual run, at least I very much hope so.[3]

Writing to a friend who evidently knew the pieces in their earlier version, Fauré is simply reporting the gist of the change he has made. For later readers, who cannot know the earlier version, this report, naturally enough, raises more questions than it answers. Why, for example, does he write only of the link passage and interlude as unifying devices, when the interplay of themes is virtually continuous throughout the published version of the Ballade? Nevertheless, by the language of this letter, even more than by the information it divulges, Fauré imparts precious insight into his compositional thinking in this work.

The title he uses in the letter, "Fantasy," makes perfect sense for describing a work in several continuous movements, each having its own theme, but with links between the movements. The Ballade as he eventually published it begins with an *Andante cantabile* movement (4/4, F-sharp major) that simply presents its theme (theme A; see Example 7-1), then comes to a full close (*Lento*). This movement presumably derives from the original piece "number 1."

Example 7-1. Fauré, Ballade, Op. 19, mm. 1–5 (theme A).

An enharmonic key-signature change introduces the second movement, *Allegro moderato*, in E-flat minor, the relative minor. This movement, presumably derived from piece "number 2," has its own theme (theme B; see Example 7-2), but that theme alternates frequently with theme A.

Example 7-2. Fauré, Ballade, Op. 19, mm. 36–39 (theme B).

The movement flows without cadence into the passage that Fauré seems to be calling the "link passage" (*"trait d'alliance"*) between pieces numbers 2 and 3 (*Andante; Un poco più mosso*). This passage, in a new meter (6/8), begins with a first version of the theme that dominates the rest of the work (theme C; see Example 7-3). This version of the theme soon gives way to another (theme C'; see Example 7-4) in a new movement (*Allegro*, 4/4).

Example 7-3. Fauré, Ballade, Op. 19, mm. 85–86 (theme C).

Example 7-4. Fauré, Ballade, Op. 19, mm. 103–04 (theme C').

This movement, which leads from B major back to F-sharp major, is presumably Fauré's "sort of interlude" (*"une sorte d'intermède"*). Here, true to his description, the phrases of themes B and C' are developed together so that the pieces become as one. This movement leads, after a cadenza, to a second "link passage" (*Andante*, 6/8), which Fauré does not mention, and then to the final movement (*Allegro moderato*, 6/8), which presumably derived from Fauré's piece "number 3." Here the final version of theme C (theme C''; see Example 7-5) appears, in 6/8 meter and F-sharp major, and alternates with a new 6/8 version of theme B right up to the end of the Ballade.

Example 7-5. Fauré, Ballade, Op. 19, mm. 172–75 (theme C'').

One wonders why Fauré, after hitting upon such a perfect title as "Fantasy," published it as "Ballade" a year later. All one can do is speculate, since no explanation by Fauré survives. Certain possibilities can be excluded with confidence, however. There is no suggestion of folk song in the music and hardly anything that could be associated with a narrative process.[4] Formally, moreover, the work was clearly not modeled on any of the earlier piano *ballades* Fauré could have known. Only in the most general way could he have been imitating earlier *ballades*. He himself raised the issue of models when he asserted that he had turned the three pieces into one by using "*new* but at the same time *old* methods" ("*des procédés nouveaux quoique anciens*"). The question of what Fauré meant by "Ballade" thus fits within the larger question of what is new and what is old in this work. To answer this question requires a closer examination of the work.

The first two movements of the Ballade seem to be modeled on Chopin's Barcarolle (also in F-sharp major) more than on any *ballade*. In the first movement the resemblance can be heard at the first cadence, when the cadential chord (C-sharp major) suddenly turns to the minor as a preparation for further abrupt modulation; at the cadenza, which takes the music just as abruptly back to the tonic (via a chromatic passage of eighth-note chords that has precedents elsewhere in Chopin); at the varied return of the theme (here, a canon); and at the close in the tonic, followed by a transitional unison phrase (*Lento*) that is the only "narrative" stroke in the Ballade (as it is in the Barcarolle).

In the second movement (*Allegro moderato*) the resemblance lies mainly in the answering of the new theme (theme B) by the theme of the previous movement (theme A). Fauré has adapted theme A so that there is an easy discourse between the two themes, as there is in the second movement of the Chopin Barcarolle, rather than a dramatic thematic convergence, as is typical of the Chopin Ballades. At the climax of the movement (eight measures before the *Andante*) the two themes are pressed together dramatically, but there the influence of Chopin takes a new form. Theme A is reshaped and reharmonized until it becomes practically a quotation from Chopin's B-minor Sonata (see Example 7-6).

This literal reliance on an earlier model at a moment of climax stands out in the Ballade, which in general shows Fauré's stylistic originality fully developed. In particular, it shows what Florent Schmitt describes as Fauré's trait of ending a phrase, after the most audacious harmonic (and, he could have added, melodic and contrapuntal) turns, on firm ground—"as if it were nothing."[5]

The first "link passage" (*Andante*) is at first as much of a pause as a link. It begins with a two-measure phrase (theme C) that introduces the main melodic motives for the remainder of the Ballade while dwelling on a single dominant-seventh chord. The following passagework plays that chord against a second chord, a tritone apart from the first. The phrase and the passagework alternate in new arrangements, and gradually the "link passage" gathers momentum, as a dominant pedal point gives the passagework a goal.

Example 7-6. Fauré, Ballade, Op. 19, mm. 79–80 (*above*), and Chopin, Sonata, Op. 58, first movement, mm. 84–85 (*below*).

The momentum carries into the next movement (*Allegro*), Fauré's "sort of interlude," which is the fastest and most exuberant part of the Ballade. The exuberance results, in part, from Fauré's reworking of his themes. The theme of the "link passage" (theme C) is reworked (into theme C') as a restless alternation of two melody notes, C-sharp and D-sharp, as well as of two chords, neither one a tonic chord. Then the theme of the *Allegro moderato* movement (theme B) is compressed into one measure (m. 7 of the *Allegro*) and formed into a canon (which was only suggested before), the two voices of the canon together making a sequence that rises by step twice in every measure. Further sequencing and further alternation of the two themes— both developing continuously into new versions—lead to the second "link passage."

In the *Allegro* movement, then, as in the earlier *Allegro moderato*, a new theme and an old alternate with each other so that the different movements seem, as Fauré suggested, to become one. What he called his "*new* but at the same time *old* methods" may have been in part the transforming procedures he used to adapt the old theme (theme B) to the tempo and spirit of the new. Those procedures were certainly not altogether new; in fact, they are too universal to be traced to any one source. More novel is the continuous evolution of both themes—a more subtle process of change than "thematic transformation"—throughout the movement. Fauré touches on this process when he writes of "stating the premises of no. 3": in this movement he states "the premises of no. 3" in many forms (theme C' and its further evolutions), but a definitive version awaits the last movement, and even that version (theme C") may be definitive only in the sense that Fauré wrote it first and then developed the earlier versions to "link" with it.

The last movement (*Allegro moderato*) begins, then, with a theme that has been developing through the preceding three sections. It also begins with hardly any change of rhythm: whereas earlier in the Ballade every new section has a new tempo (and almost every one brings a change of meter), the last movement has the same 6/8 meter and virtually the same relaxed tempo as the preceding link passage.

Both harmonically and melodically the new version of the theme represents a principle carried, or evolved, to extremes. If the harmonic principle of the earlier versions is a principle of alternating chords, here an anchoring F-sharp major chord alternates with one chord after another, each sounding less connected to it than the last. For all its dissonant juxtapositions, the passage, lacking any real harmonic motion away from the F-sharp major chord, amounts to a radical distillation of Fauré's characteristic technique of making audacious turns within a stable phrase. Melodically, meanwhile, the first phrase of the theme is reduced to an alternation of two adjoining notes, a slow warble. This phrase is succeeded by two measures that are even more birdlike: a double trill over an unchanging tonic chord.

The theme as a whole, with its relaxed rhythm, its unprogressing harmony, its equally unprogressing melody, and no independent rhythm in its accompaniment, produces a remarkable effect of stillness. It is an effect like that of the "link passages," which are similar in musical means, but here the means are refined and the effect is intensified. This is the pathbreaking moment in the Ballade. Tone-painting with bird calls was not new to music, but the sensuous stillness of this passage was. That effect was soon to be developed, by Debussy even more than by Fauré, using precisely the musical means that Fauré combined here, especially the alternating unrelated chords and the melody that warbles on two adjacent notes. Nectoux's assertion that Fauré "anticipated impressionism" in the Ballade[6] is warranted above all by this theme, along with the close of the work.

The theme is repeated with a wavelike accompaniment and then gives way to the theme of the earlier *Allegro moderato* (theme B; see Example 7-2), adapted to the new movement by being fitted to the 6/8 meter and by exchanging its canonic accompaniment for a twittering descant (see Example 7-7).

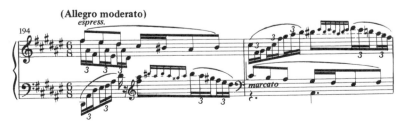

Example 7-7. Fauré, Ballade, Op. 19, mm. 194–95.

Two versions of this theme alternate, the first quiet, stable, and repetitive, the second loud and restless over a rising bass line, so that the alternation both builds and defuses tension. Even though the restless version somewhat resembles a passage leading toward the climax in Chopin's fourth Ballade (mm. 185–91 of that work), the rhythm of alternation here gives assurance that there is no balladlike reckoning to come. After a cadence on D-flat, new versions of theme C" are heard, including two sequentially climbing versions (marked *espressivo*), wonderfully restless transformations of a theme that was previously so still. Theme B returns for one more alternation, leading into a cadenza.

After the cadenza the tension is gone from the music, and reconciliations of several kinds are reached. First, a new version of theme C" unites its alternating unrelated chords over a tonic pedal. Then the wavelike accompaniment that has been heard for most of the *Allegro moderato* movement drops away, and the theme is heard in its original still rhythm, but with more ambiguous chords—the F-sharp major chord is not such a reliable anchor. Next, themes B and C" (represented by its trill) are combined, superimposed, for the first time in the work. In the final few measures Fauré moves beyond themes and chord progressions altogether, bringing the wavelike accompaniment back by itself to dissolve any remaining tensions: in this passage he discovered a closing formula that he would rework inventively in many later works, especially his Barcarolles.

In the quiet timbres and peaceful rocking of the final page and a half, he distills the themes and harmonies, the distinctive sonorities and rhythms of the whole Ballade. Instead of coming to a balladlike reckoning of his material, he achieves, as Nectoux writes, a "spiritualization" of material that issued from the realm of "sensation."[7]

The Ballade presents on the one hand a succession of separate movements, showing its origins in three separate pieces, and on the other hand a continuous process of thematic interaction and evolution. Evidently Fauré not only linked his three original pieces, but also rewrote them so that each "piece" shares its material with another "piece" (and not just with the "link passage"). When Nectoux writes of a "convergent structure" in which "all the forces of the work appear to be oriented towards the central *allegro*,"[8] he is taking Fauré's account of his modifications too literally as a description of the finished work. In fact, the themes alternate with each other, in pairs, throughout the work. They never converge and, except at the end of the second movement and the last page of the work, they do not overlap. Rather, they evolve side by side, each under the influence of the other. Nectoux's language is more felicitous when he is drawing attention to the thematic evolution: he calls the Ballade "a work inventing its form."[9]

The partnership of themes gives this work a stronger connection to the Chopin Barcarolle than to more dramatic or narrative works (like the Chopin and Liszt Ballades) in which themes are contrasted with and opposed to each other. The evolution of each theme is gradual—unlike the dramatic transformation of themes in the Chopin Ballades—and impartial—unlike the evolution of themes toward an apotheosis in the Liszt Second Ballade. This cooperative, gradual, and impartial thematic evolution not only distinguishes the Fauré Ballade from the earlier *ballade* tradition, but seems to make a wholly original contribution to musical form.

The coincidence of an impartial process of thematic evolution with naturalistic tone-painting allows one to consider the Ballade a musical discourse on the subject of nature or of natural process. A remark by Fauré himself, reported by Alfred Cortot, supports this conception: "[The Ballade] is an impression of nature, analogous to the one that suggested to R. Wagner his musical evocation of the "Forest Murmurs.""[10] As evidence of how Fauré regarded his own composition, this remark is especially valuable since there is no similarity of musical means between his Ballade and the "Forest Murmurs" passage of *Siegfried*.[11] As a nature piece the Ballade can be found to make a progression from the human—represented by the songlike phrases and strolling accompaniment of the first movement—to the natural world— represented by the bird calls, leaf-fluttering, and wavelike accompaniments of the last movement. With the title "Ballade" Fauré made a connection that was to become increasingly important in instrumental *ballades* of the next few decades, a connection between song and the countryside, where the most natural form of song—folk song—originated.

Despite the novel associations and the novel form Fauré brought to the piano *ballade*, it would be a mistake to dissociate the work entirely from the piano *ballade* tradition that he knew. In a general sense—as a large solo-piano work on several themes, each of them songful in a simple way—it can be placed in that tradition. If in more specific ways it relies on works of Chopin in other genres—the B-minor Sonata and above all the Barcarolle— Fauré was by no means exceptional among composers of the late nineteenth century in using Chopin's genre title "Ballade" to acknowledge a debt to Chopin that was not confined to a single genre. His use of this title in fact fits with his lifelong practice in naming piano pieces. Without ever quite adopting Chopin's conception of a genre, he confined himself almost entirely to Chopin's generic titles, especially in those titles that he used for more than one work: Nocturne, Barcarolle, Impromptu, Valse, and Prélude. For him as for Chopin, each of these titles evoked a particular musical character: "Ballade" evidently had a character of "natural" lyricism. It might have been possible to specify more about the character if he had written more than one work in the genre.

Within a year of the publication of the Ballade, Fauré recast the work for piano with orchestra, and it is in this form that it has been best known ever since. Stories told by Fauré about his meetings with Liszt at about the time he was working on the Ballade have led writers to the conclusion that Liszt "found the writing of the work too dense to be entrusted to two hands" and consequently advised Fauré to redo the piece with orchestral accompaniment.[12] Nectoux's sifting of the evidence about these meetings raises questions as to when Liszt might have tried or heard the work and what version he might have encountered. It remains to be added that whatever Liszt may have advised Fauré, Fauré's orchestral version scarcely alters the denseness of the piano part. Many of the most complicated passages are left exactly as they were, for the piano.

In any case, the difficulty of the piano version—like that of all Fauré's piano music—lies not so much in playing all the notes as in giving all the voices their due, and this difficulty is not diminished in the few cases where Fauré took a voice out of the piano version and gave it to an instrument of the orchestra. For the most part, his version with orchestra divides the score in a different way: piano and orchestra answer each other's phrases. In this way the alternation of themes—the characteristic feature of the work—is often thrown into relief. The effect of nature-painting is increased as well. But it would not be right to exaggerate the difference between the two versions; even in the orchestral version, the Ballade belongs largely to the piano. Fauré opened the door to the concerto *ballade,* but left it to others to consider how the relationship of solo and concerted instruments could be used in evoking the ballad as song or as story.

OTHER *BALLADES,* 1880–1918

Four and a half decades passed between the publication of Chopin's first Ballade in 1836 and that of Fauré's Ballade in 1880; the period from the publication of the Fauré to the end of World War I (1918) was almost as long again. In this second period the *ballade* became far less restricted to the solo piano. Fauré's arrangement of his Ballade for piano with orchestra heralds the change. A survey of lyrical *ballades* in the later period needs to take account of works for piano duet and for piano with another instrument, and narrative *ballades* for orchestra far outweigh narrative piano *ballades* in importance.

Although the genre was expanding into new media, its types and forms stayed largely the same. Hybrids of the *ballade* with other genres were proposed, but without much success. The Sonata-Ballade, Op. 27[13] (perhaps 1912–14), by the Russian composer Nikolai Metner (1880–1951) is readily comprehended as a sonata, readily connected to the piano sonatas of Prokofiev, but not easily connected to ballads or to piano *ballades,* and the title was not taken up by other composers. All the existing types and forms of piano *ballades,* however, were given new life in this period. New subjects and models inspired both lyric and narrative *ballades,* and the imitation and arrangement of folk ballads took on new purposes and new prominence. There were also blendings of these existing types in *ballades* of the period. Finally, a new generation of composers came to the piano *ballade* not only

Vodník.

...a topole nad jezerem
seděl Vodník pod večerem:
„Sviť, měsíčku, sviť,
ať mi šije niť."

„Šiju, šiju si botičky
do sucha i do vodičky:
sviť, měsíčku, sviť,
ať mi šije niť."

„Dnes je čtvrtek, zejtra pátek —
šiju, šiju si kabátek:
sviť, měsíčku, sviť,
ať mi šije niť."

„Zelené šaty, botky rudé,
zejtra moje svatba bude:
sviť, měsíčku, sviť,
ať mi šije niť."

— 55 —

PLATE 5. Illustrated first page of "The Water Goblin," from an 1890 edition of Erben's *Kytice*.

with new musical styles, but also in a new relationship to Chopin and his contemporaries.

The *ballade* continued to be, as it had been since the time of Chopin, a field for nationalist sentiment addressed to a cosmopolitan audience. In a period when nationalism was becoming an increasingly competitive and racist force in European political life, cosmopolitanism still had the upper hand in this musical genre. Up to 1900, few composers referred to the styles of their national folk music in piano *ballades*; many more wrote in the latest international styles or colored their piano *ballades* with exotic styles, styles from the music of other lands. A number of composers cultivated an exoticism of time rather than of place, exploiting the stylistic antiquity of the European folk ballad in much the way that contemporary poets like Detlev von Liliencron (1844-1909) and Charles Algernon Swinburne (1837-1909) exploited the diction of medieval balladry. Only in a few pieces written just before and during World War I is the *ballade* made a vehicle for assertions of national identity.

Lyrical Piano *Ballades*

In the period after 1880, the largest number of piano *ballades* were short pieces that played in one way or another on the exoticism of ballads. Some of these pieces were called simply "Ballade," while others had titles associating the music with a particular country or subject. Camille Saint-Saëns (1835-1921) published his "King Harald Harfagar (after H. Heine): Ballade"[14] for piano, four hands, in 1880, the same year that the Ballade by his former pupil Fauré appeared. A French work on a German poem about a medieval Norwegian king, this piece has nothing Norwegian or medieval about it. Instead, it evokes the watery setting of Heine's ballad. (The original title-page, reproduced as Plate 1 of the present study, perfectly suits the music.) Like the Fauré, then, it is a nature *ballade*, though of a more conventionally descriptive sort.

The resources of two performers at the piano enrich the tone-painting in this *ballade*, as they do also in the Ballade from the set of *Drei Poesien* (*Three Poems*)[15] for piano, four hands (1886), by the American composer Edward MacDowell (1860-1908). The dreamy atmosphere of this work evokes not an exotic setting, but a distant memory. The title "Ballade" here stands for fairy tales as an adult might remember hearing them, frightening at times, but comforting in the end. In the Ballade[16] of 1895 by Grieg's Norwegian contemporary Agathe Backer-Grøndahl (1847-1907), olden times and a courtly setting are suggested by a theme in a stiff eighteenth-century dance style, reminiscent of Grieg's suite *From Holberg's Time* (1885).

Two years later Grieg himself published his final contribution to the genre, the fifth number of his *Lyrical Pieces*, Op. 65, called "In Ballad-Tone."[17] The "tone" is extremely plain: the unchanging choral texture and the partly modal, partly chromatic harmonies—typical of Grieg's folk-song settings—

suggest a deep-rooted singing tradition without making it possible to identify that tradition precisely. The two mournful melodic periods, alternating with each other but not ornamented or varied, are not especially folklike. In this piece Grieg arrives at the same heavy-hearted conclusion as in his earlier Ballade, but by much simpler, more direct means.

Similar in form, with its alternation of two related melodies, is the "Petite Ballade" of the *Twenty-four Characteristic Pieces*[18] (1895) by the Russian composer Anton Arensky (1861–1906). In tone, however, this piece is utterly different from Grieg's. If there are references in this *ballade*, as in the Backer-Grøndahl, to eighteenth-century dance music, it is the elegance of that music, not its remoteness, that Arensky cherished. A third work in the same alternating form is the Ballade in the *Five Bagatelles*[19] (1905) by the German composer and pianist Eugen d'Albert (1864–1932).

A few piano *ballades* of this period derive their color from folk song. In most cases the reference to folk song is not very specific, though it is clearer than in the *ballades* of Raff, Brahms, and Heller at mid-century. The "Peasant Ballade" ("Selská balada") from *Poetic Tone-Pictures (Poetické nálady)*[20] (1889) by Antonín Dvořák (1841–1904) shows how a few folklike details, none of them especially exotic in itself, could be brought together to produce a composite "tone-picture" of peasant musical life. The main theme of the piece is a short singing phrase, unaccompanied, in the minor mode, answered by a dancing phrase, with chords, in the major mode (see Example 7-8).

Example 7-8. Dvořák, "Peasant Ballade," Op. 85, No. 5, mm. 1–8.

These two contrasting phrases together suggest two sides of peasant music, though either taken alone is only vaguely folklike and neither is recognizably Czech. The other themes are in the same vein, and the whole Ballade progresses rather like a Schubert scherzo, through colorful juxtapositions rather than dramatic development. Peasant music, as Dvořák presented it in this piece, was nothing new to the urban European musical public; it was exotic only in the very limited sense that as a well-established style within the cosmopolitan musical language, it retained a distinct identity.

Even a piano *ballade* with more local color, with a more specific folk style, could still adhere to the premise of Dvořák's "Peasant Ballade." The "Ballade: From Olden Times"[21] (1890) by Anatol Liadov (1855–1914) uses distinctly Russian material: the melody takes its 5/4 rhythm from Russian folk song,[22] and the pealing bass derives from Russian operatic and orchestral music of the period (see Example 7-9).

Example 7-9. Liadov, Ballade, Op. 21, mm. 42-47.

The folk rhythm was a common enough feature in Russian art music of the time, barely more than a flag of Russian identity within the cosmopolitan musical style. But the pealing bass, evoking the distant Russian past, has a more unusual and genuinely exotic effect. Gerald Abraham calls the epic tone of the piece unique in Russian piano music,[23] and that tone owes much to an orchestral device not often transferred to the piano. The transfer is awkward, but that very awkwardness gives the music its exotic effect by reminding listeners of the musical distance between the heroic age evoked and their own age, represented by the medium of evocation, the piano.

The following year, 1891, Claude Debussy (1865-1918) published his "Slavic Ballade" ("Ballade slave"),[24] which he later republished simply as "Ballade." His Slavic flavoring is of a very different sort from Liadov's. The main theme of Debussy's Ballade has no folklike rhythm, though it may be generically folklike in its tonal ambiguity and in its repetition of a tiny melodic motive (see Example 7-10).

Example 7-10. Debussy, Ballade, mm. 6-9.

Even so, Debussy has no difficulty turning to another realm of exoticism—an antique courtliness in parallel chords—as he draws the theme to its first cadence. He then repeats his theme, changing its form at each repetition, as if following in the narrative *ballade* tradition of Chopin. The work as a whole is poised between lyric and narrative conceptions of the genre: its form is ternary, but the final section is like a ballad reckoning, at least in the sense that the main theme returns like an unbidden, unexpected memory. This return introduces new elements: the main theme unharmonized, a distant tolling of bells (unlike Liadov's noisy pealing), and a recollection of the second theme that is probably what reminded Léon Vallas of Borodin or Balakirev.[25] For a French composer writing "Slavic" music, the stylistic model offered by contemporary Russian composers could be just as exotic, just as apt for evoking a ballad atmosphere, as that offered by Russian folk music.

The title "Nordic Ballade" ("Nordische Ballade") given by Max Reger (1873–1916) to the fourth piece in his *Watercolors: Little Tone-Pictures (Aquarellen: Kleine Tonbilder)*,[26] composed in 1897–98, refers to a folk-song tradition larger than one nation, and the piece evokes folk song in an unspecific way. The melody avoids the confines of its sextuplet meter and of the minor mode without exemplifying any particular folk-song rhythm or mode (see Example 7-11).

Example 7-11. Reger, "Nordic Ballade," Op. 25, No. 4, mm. 1–6.

The melody in octaves, accompanied by offbeat chords, belongs to a tradition of folk-song evocation that includes the Raff Ballade, Op. 17 (discussed in Chapter 5). The unusual thing about Reger's use of this texture is that he does not abandon it at the completion of the theme, but adapts it, through a series of excursions and variations, up to the end of the piece. As flowing middle voices are added to the melody and offbeat bass-notes, the music comes to resemble a chorale prelude for organ in texture. Reger's transferral of an unaccustomed idiom to the piano, unlike Liadov's, is extremely smooth. But there is no suggestion of a link between folk song and hymn in the "Nordic Ballade," not even in its mysterious ending.

The same combination of folk song and organ music is at work in the "Finnish Ballade" ("Finnische Ballade") from the *Six Pieces (Sechs Stücke)*[27] (1896) by Ferruccio Busoni (1866–1924). This title, too, refers to a Northern European ballad tradition, while the music imitates organ music—this time more specifically Bach's organ music. However, the theme of Busoni's Ballade (see Example 7-12) is an actual Finnish folk song; at least he described it as such when he used the same theme, in almost identical form, in a work for cello and piano of a few years earlier.[28] Evidently he learned the theme

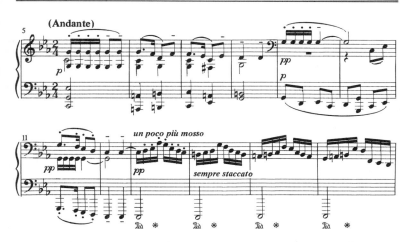

Example 7-12. Busoni, "Finnish Ballade," Op. 33b, No. 5, mm. 5-16.

during the period (1888–90) when he taught at the Helsinki Institute of Music.

This theme immediately gives way to a toccata passage (the last four measures of Example 7-12), which is followed in due course by a fugal passage. Bachian contrapuntal manipulations occupy the piece from then until the very end. The difference between this Ballade and Reger's is not that Busoni was even more obsessed with Bach than Reger was, but that Busoni was more boldly twisting the idea of musical exoticism. The character of the "Finnish Ballade," which could have been suggested to Busoni by his readings in the *Kalevala*, the Finnish epic, is darkly, moodily heroic. That character of the music, however, comes much more from the persistent and unmistakable Bachian processes than from the two short, rather neutral phrases of the folk theme. By deriving a folk-narrative character from a Bachian musical language, Busoni in effect asserts that an exotic, legendary world can be evoked by means that are the opposite of exotic.

A comparable assertion is made by Alexander Scriabin (1872–1915) in his Etude "Alla ballata" (Number 9 of the *Twelve Etudes*, Op. 8; 1895),[29] another unlikely hybrid of styles. It opens with a repeating-note motive much like that of Busoni's "Finnish Ballade." The "study" for the performer is to put the element of musical continuity that makes the work an étude—the running octaves of the left-hand part—at the service of the abrupt and dramatic discontinuities of mood that make it a *ballade*.

A decade and a half later (1911), a conventional idea of exoticism in piano music reached its geographical limit when the Czech composer Vítězslav Novák (1870–1949) used folk music from all over Eurasia in a suite of small piano pieces called *Exotikon*, including a Ballade on a Lapp motive.[30]

In the face of this trend to suggest settings or atmospheres, a few composers persisted in older conceptions of the lyrical piano *ballade*. One of these was Julius Röntgen (1855-1932), a German composer who played an important role in Dutch musical life. He wrote one Ballade[31] (1875) largely in the form of variations on a folklike theme and a second Ballade[32] (1884) that is more a character piece, Brahmsian in its harmonic and rhythmic play. Theodor Kirchner (1823-1903), a follower of Schumann, was an important German composer of piano character pieces. The number entitled "Balladenmässig" in his *Romantic Stories (Romantische Geschichten)*[33] (1884) recalls Schumann's piece of the same title in its restless rhythms. Kirchner's, however, is a longer, more episodic piece and comes at times to sound more like Brahms than Schumann. Brahms, however, was not everyone's model for lyrical piano *ballades* in this period. The French composer and pianist Cécile Chaminade (1857-1944) wrote a Ballade[34] (1896) that belongs to a barcarolle tradition going back through Fauré to Chopin.

Brahms himself published one more piano *ballade* almost forty years after the four Ballades of his Opus 10. This Ballade is the third number of his *Piano Pieces (Klavierstücke)*, Op. 118.[35] Here the typical ternary form of the lyrical *ballade* permits a novel kind of narrative progression. As Brahms substituted the title "Ballade" for "Rhapsody" after the piece was completed,[36] there would be no point in seeking possible models for this piece in the traditions of ballads or piano *ballades* or in his own earlier Ballades for piano. Both "rhapsody" and "ballad," of course, refer to ancient traditions of narrative song, and this Ballade, like many of Brahms's other piano character pieces, can be imagined almost measure by measure as a song. But there is less suggestion of folk song here than in the Intermezzos of Opus 117 or other Brahms piano pieces of the same period, and there is not even the vague tint of musical antiquity that Brahms gave to the "Edward" Ballade of Opus 10 with an occasional open-fifth sonority. In this case the title "Ballade" that he eventually settled on is justified by the suggestion of a narrative song such as Brahms himself might have written, free of exoticism.

The narrative progression of this later Brahms Ballade is not like the impersonal narration of a folk ballad, but more like the personal narration of much late nineteenth-century fiction, with shifts of consciousness between present and remembered events. Within the constant tempo of the work, each theme occupies an isolated realm, distinct in key, in volume, and in sonority. Differentiation by pedaling—which Brahms indicates more by articulation signs and lengths of bass notes than by pedal marks—is especially important in distinguishing the bright "presence" of the main theme from the haze of memory in which the other two themes appear. A performance true to Brahms's markings would give each theme its own sonority, articulation, and volume, making clear the kind of consciousness represented by each theme and giving each shift to a new theme—to a new state of consciousness—a different and arresting effect.

The first shift, from the main theme in G minor to the closely related theme in E-flat, comes without warning: the key and volume change abruptly, while the bass, which has moved energetically, suddenly gets stuck on one note (see Example 7-13). The second shift, back to the main theme, is entirely different: a gradual and effortful reemergence. The original volume returns, the damper pedal is lifted, and the upbeat to the theme is drawn out, as if overcoming some resistance, before the theme gets going again (see Example 7-14). Two later and more elaborate shifts of theme in the Ballade are more complicated: at the beginning and end of the B-major middle section, Brahms changes the volume gradually and gives hints of the coming theme, but still shifts abruptly to the new key.

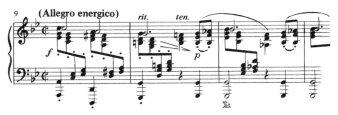

Example 7-13. Brahms, Ballade, Op. 118, No. 3, mm. 9–11.

Example 7-14. Brahms, Ballade, Op. 118, No. 3, mm. 18–23.

At only two moments are the themes not isolated from one another. One comes in the middle section, when the theme of that section, in B major, is briefly displaced by the main theme, now in D-sharp minor, transformed to match the character of the B-major theme. This mingling of themes suggests a hidden affinity among states of consciousness that seem otherwise to exclude each other. The other moment of thematic interaction comes at the end, after a reprise that is identical to the opening section. The final cadence, however, ends in the minor this time and is immediately followed by what Max Kalbeck calls a "stroke of the guillotine."[37] After this the B-major theme, transposed to G minor, starts again; just enough of it is heard to leave a feeling of emptiness in its wake. Here there is no mingling of themes; rather, the prevailing state of consciousness—that of the main theme—is shattered, and a memory—a thought from another state—takes its place. For the kind of narration that Brahms is evoking in this Ballade, it is appropriate that memory, rather than event, has the last word.

Lyrical *Ballades* for Chamber Groups

In the 1880s, as composers like Saint-Saëns and MacDowell were writing *ballades* for piano duo, other composers were developing the *ballade* for chamber duo, usually violin and piano. *Ballades* in this medium are almost all lyrical pieces, but they follow a path of their own. They have less exotic coloring than most lyrical piano *ballades* of the same period. They follow a simple formula, perhaps even an obvious formula for instrumental *ballades*, though it was never used very much in piano *ballades*: they present sad melodies. These are not melodies that could have come from folk ballads—those in any case are not necessarily sad—but melodies of a sadness appropriate to the sad story told in a ballad. The melody is usually carried almost uninterruptedly by the singing instrument, while the piano plays a supporting role.

The *ballades* of the 1880s were not quite the first of this type. A Ballade for violin and piano was written by the Hungarian composer Mihály Mosonyi (1815–1870) in 1841 (when he was still named Michael Brand), only five years after Chopin's first Ballade was published.[38] The same year a Ballade for violin and piano by Heinrich Panofka (1807–1887) was reviewed.[39] The *Ballade and Polonaise* that the great Belgian violinist Henri Vieuxtemps (1820–1881) wrote in versions for violin and piano and for violin and orchestra was published around 1860.[40] This piece, with its refrain in bare octaves, was popular into the twentieth century. The Ballade, in G minor, serves as a slow introduction to the lively Polonaise in G major. About a decade later the Belgian cellist Jules de Swert (1843–1891) published several Ballades for cello and piano.[41]

It was in the 1880s, however, that the sad-song *ballade* became fixed as a type. This type is found at its most beautiful in the well-known Ballade for violin and piano (1884) by Dvořák.[42] The dignified melody of this piece is embellished with ornaments in the late nineteenth-century Gypsy style, but as those ornaments are never merely violinistic, they give the impression of a rhapsodic vocal delivery.

Many other violin (or cello) *ballades* of the same type, usually in ternary form, were written in the 1880s and following decades. In *ballades* by Franz

Neruda (1843-1915), Anton Arensky (1861-1906), Jenő Hubay (1858-1937), and Christian Sinding (1856-1941),[43] the melodies are unadorned, while others by George Henschel (1850-1934), Moritz Moszkowski (1854-1925), Alexander Mackenzie (1847-1935), and Josef Suk (1874-1935)[44] have a rhapsodic side. The highly rhapsodic Ballade[45] by the violin virtuoso Pablo de Sarasate (1844-1908) owes its style to flamenco singing. The Ballade[46] (1903) for cello and piano by Reinhold Glière (1875-1956) is distinguished by an unusual sharing of melody between the two instruments.

After the turn of the century, new sorts of chamber *ballades*, some of them for new instrumental combinations, began to appear. The "balladlike" piano trio[47] by Vítězslav Novák (1870-1949) uses melodic material inspired by Moravian folk song.[48] The word "ballata" (ballad) in the title evidently pertains to the overall course of the four movements. The Ballade[49] (1912) for clarinet and piano by the Hungarian composer Leó Weiner (1885-1960) has one movement, but is a longer, more complex work than the nineteenth-century chamber *ballades*. It is rhapsodic without the expressive intensity of Dvořák's violin Ballade, emphasizing instead the instrumental colors of the clarinet. Joseph Marx (1882-1964) wrote a Ballade[50] for piano quartet (1912) that is mainly fugal in texture. Philipp Jarnach (1892-1982) wrote a Ballade[51] for violin and piano (1913), linking folk song and church music—as Reger had not done—in an austerely modal melodic line, richly harmonized. The Ballade[52] for violin and orchestra (or for violin and piano) published in 1917 by Joseph Bohuslav Foerster (1859-1951) is an extreme case of the songfulness of chamber *ballades*. It is an outpouring of melodies, each one new, with only the briefest reprise to shape its ending.

The Ballade[53] for violoncello and piano, Op. 15 (1912), by Sergei Prokofiev (1891-1953) begins as if it belonged to the tradition of simple *ballades* on sad melodies (see Example 7-15). It begins, in fact, with a sad theme he had written for a violin sonata at the age of eleven, but, as he himself described it: "From that point on, in the Ballade, I went in for great complexity."[54] The complexity is a matter both of form—one episode succeeds another, all in greatly contrasting moods, keys, and rhythms—and of texture—the cello and piano often play different themes simultaneously,

Example 7-15. Prokofiev, Ballade, Op. 15, mm. 1-13.

[7-15 continued]

while clashing with each other harmonically. The return of the opening theme is a beautifully complex moment: the theme enters quietly on the cello while the piano is in the middle of playing the opening chordal accompaniment, but with a different theme.

Narrative Piano *Ballades*

Many composers of this period wrote long narrative piano *ballades*, but without creating new modes of musical narration. Instead they drew attention to the sensationalism of ballad narration—the "precipitous" and shocking way ballads have of bringing on catastrophes—by writing in a new style of musical sensationalism—the late nineteenth-century style most familiar now in operatic *verismo*. The title "Ballade" for these works is justified not only by their sensationalism, but in some cases also by their musical reference to Chopin. That reference is not to the forms of Chopin's Ballades, except insofar as his four Ballades authorized later composers to think of a piano *ballade* as a unique musical story requiring a unique musical form. Their *ballades* refer to Chopin more clearly by echoing phrases or traits of his music. The Ballade[55] (1894) by Philipp Scharwenka (1847–1917), brother of Xaver Scharwenka, opens with a theme that at first recalls the main theme of Chopin's first Ballade; only as chords join in does the theme turn to the sensational style that dominates the work as a whole (see Example 7-16).

For the purpose of recalling Chopin as the creator of the piano *ballade*, a composer could refer—as Fauré did in his Ballade—to any of Chopin's music,

Example 7-16. Philipp Scharwenka, Ballade, Op. 94a, mm. 1-8.

not necessarily to his Ballades. Echoes of various Chopin works—subtler, more complex, and more pervasive references than in Scharwenka's Ballade—can be heard in the Ballade[56] (1884) by another Polish composer, Józef Wieniawski (1837-1912), brother of the violinist Henryk Wieniawski. Polish composers in the late nineteenth century found themselves in a political situation essentially unchanged since Chopin's day, but they had the advantage of the prestige he had given to Polish music. Wieniawski and Scharwenka drew on that prestige by writing, under titles associated with Chopin, piano music in which echoes of Chopin's music could be heard.[57] Their Ballades, though connected in this superficial way to a Polish tradition, were nevertheless works in a cosmopolitan and contemporary style.

More explicit reference to Chopin, incidentally, is found in the titles of two later piano *ballades* by Czech composers: the unpublished "Ballade: Before the Picture of the Cross: Chopin's Last Chords,"[58] written in 1912 by Bohuslav Martinů (1890-1959), and the "Ballade in Memory of the Great Master Fr. Chopin: Drama of Passion,"[59] Op. 130 (1924), by Anatol Provazník (1887-1950). In these works Chopin—a Romanticized picture of Chopin—is the subject of musical narrative, rather than the musical model for it. Both works are in sensational styles far removed from Chopin's own style, though in the middle of the Martinů is a hymnlike passage derived from Chopin Nocturnes.

Polish composers of the generation after the Scharwenkas and Wieniawskis, formed into a group called Young Poland, of which Karol Szymanowski (1882-1937) was the most important member, devoted themselves more openly to the cause of Polish nationalism. Of this group, it was Ludomir Różycki (1884-1953) who contributed to the piano *ballade*, not only in his Ballade for piano and orchestra[60] (1904), but also in his "Poem for Piano," "Balladyna"[61] (1909), in which many layers of Polish musical and literary history meet. The title of the work evidently comes from the tragic drama (named for its main character) by Chopin's great literary contemporary, Juliusz Słowacki (1809-1849), and the story of the drama itself comes in part from a Polish folk ballad.

In his musical "poem" Różycki, like Wieniawski and Scharwenka, borrows from several genres of Chopin's music; but his borrowings from other genres, instead of making a generalized tribute to Chopin, serve to expand and renew the narrative model he found in the Chopin Ballades. In one passage, for example, Różycki suggests a Chopin Polonaise in 3/4 rhythm while maintaining the 6/8 meter of a Chopin Ballade; this becomes a passage of "progressive transformation" from one principal theme of the work to another (see Example 7-17). In making rhythmic change a primary element of his "progressive transformation," Różycki moves beyond the model provided for this procedure in the Chopin Ballades.

Example 7-17. Różycki, "Balladyna," Op. 25, mm. 91–104.

Composers of other nationalities also wrote narrative piano *ballades* in free forms and sensational styles. The Ballade of the *Four Piano Pieces* (*Vier Klavierstücke*)[62] (1898) by the German Eugen d'Albert has effective contrasts of character, as might be expected of a successful opera composer, and effective contrasts of piano sonority, as might be expected of a great piano virtuoso, though it fails to develop any dramatic momentum until near the end. The form is sprawling and the style eclectic in the two Ballades[63] by George Templeton Strong (1856–1948), an American composer who spent even more of his career in Europe than his friend MacDowell.

A more disciplined and interesting American work is the Ballad[64] (1894) by Amy Beach (1867–1944). By calling the work "Ballad" rather than "Ballade," she perhaps drew attention away from the Chopin tradition and toward English-language traditions of songs and poems, but there is no specifically British or American character or reference in the music. At most, there may be a reference to drawing-room ballads in the first half of the work, with its sentimental tone and free adaptation of variation form. Later the music grows more sensational in tone, but the sentimental opening allows Beach to move more gracefully than Wieniawski or Scharwenka from a sensational climax to a peaceful close.

It was precisely on such cosmopolitan—that is to say, European—terms that Beach, like MacDowell, Strong, and other American contemporaries, sought to prove herself. It is typical of her generation that in writing a Ballad for piano she did not refer to American folk ballads or poetic ballads. She had perhaps never heard much American folk singing, though she undoubtedly knew American poetic ballads like "The Wreck of the Hesperus" (1840) by Henry Wadsworth Longfellow, who had been a family friend as she was growing up. But she would not have sought out American models for her Ballad, any more than Longfellow had sought out American models for his poetic ballads, any more than the American literary scholar Francis Child was seeking out American versions of British ballads as he compiled his standard collection, *English and Scottish Popular Ballads* (1882-98).[65] Composers in the Americas differed from their European counterparts in that they could look for the sources of both their national culture and their cosmopolitan culture in foreign lands, across the sea.

Europeans in some lands, however, found themselves in a comparable situation: their cosmopolitan culture came almost entirely from foreign sources, while the roots and materials of their national culture were just being discovered. Vítězslav Novák was barely aware of the folk music of his own land in 1893, when his studies with Dvořák at the Prague Conservatory were concluded and he wrote his first piano *ballade*. Later, before he wrote his *Trio quasi una ballata*, his "balladlike" piano trio of 1903, he was to discover Czechoslovak folk music at first hand. Later still he would write the Ballade on Lapp folk music, mentioned above. But in the earlier piano *ballade*, the "Ballada, dle Byronova *Manfreda*" ("Ballade after Byron's *Manfred*),[66] Novák treated the most cosmopolitan of subjects in the most cosmopolitan of musical styles. Byron's *Manfred* (1817) was part of the Western literary heritage by the time Novák came to it; it had already inspired several other musical works, most recently Tchaikovsky's *Manfred Symphony*, first performed in 1886. Novák's title "Ballade" seems odd, given that Byron's *Manfred* is a dramatic rather than a narrative poem and, besides, a monumental display of a character's self-consciousness, exactly what ballad characters notoriously do not display. But the poem springs from the same kind of psychological impulse as a ballad: it is a story of guilt, self-accusation, and suicide. That story allowed Novák to write a work as sensational in tone as any other piano *ballade* of the period.

He does not concern himself with the various scenes and settings of the drama, even to the degree that Tchaikovsky did in plotting the movements of his symphony. Instead, he represents the evolution of the protagonist's thoughts and moods in a single, unified, almost monothematic movement. The first stages of this evolution—from gloomy to stormy thoughts—he fits into a sonata-like progression from exposition to development (mm. 1–79). Thereafter the music works on a very different principle: four different thematic transformations of the main theme, connected to each other by further developmental passages, represent four further stages in the evolution of the character's thought. As the first of these transformations (*Grandioso*, m. 80) has all the hallmarks of a Lisztian apotheosis, the remainder of the work in a sense represents Novák's solution to a problem addressed earlier in Ballades of Liszt and Bülow and more recently by Wieniawski and Beach: how to move past an apotheosis to an ending in a very different tone.

Novák's solution begins in the apotheosis itself: like the vision of salvation that fades from Manfred's eyes even as he speaks to it, this *Grandioso* thematic transformation turns to the minor mode, decreases abruptly in volume, and breaks off (at m. 96). Each succeeding transformation then brings the music a step closer to a musically and poetically satisfying conclusion. The second transformation (*Allegro assai passionato*, m. 120) brings the music back to its tonic key, E minor, but is agitated in tone; the third (*Andante*, m. 149) begins calmly where the first broke off and leads directly into the last, which is really no transformation at all, but the theme itself heard again, for the first time since the beginning, with its distinctive gloomy accompaniment. With this stroke Novák not only completes the musical evolution away from the false hope of the *Grandioso* transformation, but also resolves the formal difference between the two halves of the work. Better than any earlier composer of a piano *ballade* based on a cited literary model, Novák matched the progression of his model in the form of his music.

In the company of Różycki's "Balladyna" and Novák's "Manfred" should be mentioned another drama turned into piano music, the suite *Goyescas*[67] (1911) by the Spanish composer Enrique Granados (1867–1916). In this case, the drama was an idea in the composer's mind when he wrote the piano music, but realized years later (1916) as an opera of the same name, using the same music. Granados gave the subtitle "Balada" ("Ballad") not to the whole suite, but to the movement that represents the tragic dénouement in this balladlike story of jealous lovers, "El Amor y la Muerte" ("Love and Death")—a musical reckoning with the themes of all the previous movements.

These narrative *ballades*, most of them little known, are nevertheless important for what they contribute to a balanced history of piano music: they show that programmatic or narrative piano music did not die out after the death of Liszt (1886), but continued to flourish in the decades up to the outbreak of World War I, a period remembered now as the heyday of piano tone pictures.

Nationalist *Ballades*, 1900–1918

A few piano and chamber *ballades* of the prewar and wartime period—mostly works using folk music of a composer's own land—reflect the political passions of the time and make new links between nationalism and ballad traditions. Among the works of this period by American composers who were trying to create a national American music based on songs of American Indians is the Ballad[68] (1906) by Noble W. Kreider (1874–1959). The work was published by the leader of that group of composers, Arthur Farwell (1872–1951). Great numbers of Indian songs were available by then in transcriptions by American and German ethnomusicologists, above all by Frances Densmore (1867–1957). In this form Indian songs interested not only American composers, but also Europeans such as Busoni, who used them in several works.[69] But to American composers looking for a way to deal with the foreignness of their cultural roots, this indisputably native material had special significance. The title "Ballad" incongruously applied to a piece based on American Indian melody—like Robert Louis Stevenson's inclusion of poems on Samoan subjects in a volume entitled *Ballads* (1890)—can be taken as a sign of ethnocentrism, but also as a recognition that storytelling in song is a universal human activity.

Kreider's Ballad, however, is not successful either as a piece of musical exoticism or as an exercise in musical naturalization. The music is competently written, and the idea of leading a folk (or folklike) melody from a bare texture (see Example 7-18) to a complex development has many precedents, even in the tradition of piano *ballades*. But the project was hopeless in political terms. The idea of making nationalist art music out of folk music was a European idea that depended on historical continuity between the folk and the nation—a relationship that no amount of hope could create between Native Americans and the nation of immigrants that had all but destroyed their culture.

Example 7-18. Kreider, Ballad, Op. 3, mm. 1–4.

In Europe, at the same time, a long-established tradition of folk-song arrangement was kept alive in such works as the "Ballade on Two Portuguese Melodies,"[70] Op. 16, by the Portuguese pianist and composer José Vianna da Motta (1868–1948), a pupil of Liszt and later an editor of Liszt's music. The heritage of Liszt shows in Vianna da Motta's arrangement of his folk songs into a potpourri with variations.

The first decade of the twentieth century also brought important new ideas about folk-song arrangement, notably from Béla Bartók (1881–1945), who was then making his first field trips to record Hungarian and other Central European folk music. His interest in recording, transcribing, and arranging folk music—an interest at first inspired by nationalist feeling—soon developed into a much broader and deeper interest in folk cultures, sustained by principles still recognizably originating in nationalism. Without his experience of collecting most of the folk songs that he later arranged as pedagogical and concert pieces, he could not have learned to naturalize the material in such an alien new medium with so little effect of exoticism. Even under circumstances more favorable than those of American composers like Kreider, Bartók did not escape the contradictions inherent in folk-song arrangement. His self-consciousness about those contradictions, however, yielded musical richness in the simplest of piano pieces. Among those simple piano pieces are two that Bartók called "Ballads," settings of the melodies of folk ballads. In these pieces he does not isolate the melodies from their original contexts, but makes use of the whole sung story, bringing into a new combination the traditions of folk-song arrangement, lyric piano *ballades*, and narrative piano *ballades*.

The earlier of these two pieces was published in the fourth and final volume (1911) of Bartók's collection *For Children*[71] (two volumes based on Hungarian folk songs and two volumes on Slovak folk songs). The Ballad, Number 39 of the Slovak set, is based on the song "Pásou Janko dva voli." The collection was commissioned by the publisher Károly Rozsnyai. Bartók himself, as he later explained, felt as a piano teacher that good material was lacking for beginning students and that the best way to write pieces easy enough for beginners and at the same time valuable as music would be to use folk melodies.[72]

It was more than a lucky coincidence, however, that Bartók the folk-song collector knew of melodies that would make good pedagogical piano pieces; his presentation of the material testifies to a more complex motivation. In the original editions, the texts of the songs are given in an appendix, the texts of the Hungarian songs in Hungarian and those of the Slovak songs in Slovak, Hungarian, and French. Evidently Bartók hoped that students would learn to sing the songs while they learned to play them; the experience of singing the songs would nourish the students' performance at the piano. But teaching folk songs to students also had an importance of its own. Teaching these songs to Hungarian or Slovak students meant introducing those students to their national heritage, their national musical identity. Teaching them to students elsewhere (and the French texts were presumably designed for the widest possible use) meant acquainting those students with the achievements of Hungarian and Slovak musical culture.

Each number of *For Children* consists of a folk melody, usually presented several times, like a song in several verses, each time in a different setting.

Přišel večer. Muž zelený
  chodí venku po dvoře;
dvéře klínem zastrčeny,
  matka s dcerou v komoře.

Když klekání odzvonili,
  buch buch! venku na dvéře:
,Pojď již domů, ženo moje!
  nemám ještě večeře.' —

„„Neboj se, má drahá duše!
nic ti neuškodí v suše,
vrah jezerní nemá k tobě
žádné moci nahoře."" —

„„Vari od našeho prahu,
vari pryč, ty lstivý vrahu!
a co dřív jsi večeříval,
  večeř zase v jezeře."" —

— 59 —

PLATE 6. Illustration of the final episode of "The Water Goblin," from an 1890 edition
of Erben's *Kytice*.

Bartók's musical technique, in other words, is closer to what scholars of nineteenth-century Russian music call the "changing-background method"[73] than to variation technique. The Ballad is among the longer pieces, for more advanced students. It has five verses, a fairly high number for a piece in *For Children*, but not quite the same as the six verses of text that Bartók printed. There is no question, then, of the piano piece corresponding to the song text verse for verse, though there may be a more general correspondence.

The story told in the text is a very simple one: the herdsman Janko is stopped by highwaymen, and when he refuses to give them his cape, they kill him. In the final verse he is lying dead, covered with rosemary.[74] In Bartók's piano piece the melody is played in different registers, but without transposition, and with short transitional phrases between verses, but without rearrangement of phrases within a verse. Compared to other pieces in *For Children*, the Ballad makes a straightforward progression through its melodic verses. In the course of the first four verses, several things change progressively: the tempo gets faster, the accompaniment becomes more active (the first verse is in bare octaves, a rare texture for this collection), and the melody and accompaniment are raised to higher registers. In the last line of the fourth verse, these changes are abruptly reversed: the melody is marked *tranquillo*, and the accompaniment drops out, but then returns with a harsh, emphatic chord, which is held while the last three notes of the line are repeated (see Example 7-19). New versions of this chord and phrase provide the accompaniment for the subdued last verse of the piece.

Example 7-19. Bartók, Ballad, *For Children*, Slovak set, No. 39, mm. 43–48.

The steadily growing excitement of Bartók's first four verses corresponds to the growing tension in the first five verses of the ballad text, ending with the murder of Janko. In the text, that murder is announced in the last line of the fifth verse, the word "killed"—*zabili*—coming on the last three notes, the very notes that Bartók treats so dramatically in his fourth verse. The echo of those notes—of that word—are heard in Bartók's last verse, as Janko lies dead.

The general premises of *For Children* dictated that Bartók would illustrate the story of Janko by extremely confined means, repeating the given melody in changing settings that all stayed within the grasp of a third- or fourth-year piano student. Within those confines he created a remarkably dramatic setting of the folk song, though it is by no means the only such dramatic setting in *For Children*.[75] It is worth remembering that Bartók was not the first to compose folk-song settings as pedagogical piano pieces. What was new about *For Children* was the way Bartók drew his settings out of the nature of the songs. In his writings about folk-song setting, he emphasized the modal nature of the songs, which suggested new possibilities of harmonization to him.[76] But evidently he was also interested in the progression of words and story through the repeating melody, suggesting new possibilities of musical narration. The Janko Ballad challenges piano students to sustain a musical story at the piano by the simplest means. The same simplicity of means defines the unique position of this piece within the genre of the piano *ballade*. By studying what narrative-shaping resources were left to him once he was committed to remaining within his melodic verse-structure (rather than to breaking out of it, as Chopin had done), Bartók created a new narrative technique.

Seven years later, on the eve of Hungarian independence, Bartók wrote another piano *ballade*, based on a Hungarian folk ballad ("Angoli Borbála") that he had just collected, and published it in his collection of *Fifteen Hungarian Peasant Songs* for piano (1920).[77] This Ballad is more complex and harder to play than the one in *For Children*, but it is still, at least in part, a pedagogical piece. Bartók included it among the pieces about which he wrote: "I wanted to place at the disposal of more progressed pupils transcriptions of folk music; transcriptions of simple structure, not too difficult to grasp and to play."[78] All the same, when he orchestrated the Ballad, along with other numbers of the *Fifteen Hungarian Peasant Songs*, years later,[79] he showed he could also imagine it as concert music.

This Ballad is about twice as long as the one in *For Children* (ten verses instead of five) and very different in progression: most of its verses are set by the changing-background method, but in the middle comes a quiet interlude of three verses in which the melody itself assumes new forms. The Ballad has the subtitle "Theme with Variations," which does not so much describe the technique of the piece as it points out the continuing presence of the theme. Incidentally, the title draws attention to the similar progression in a later work, the "Free Variations" in Book 6 of Bartók's *Mikrokosmos*.

Bartók was evidently working again with the narrative structure of the folk song, but this text did not lend itself to the same direct treatment he had given to the ballad of Janko: the ballad of Angoli Borbála is twenty-three verses long. Bartók was not able to print the whole text in the appendix of the *Fifteen Hungarian Peasant Songs*, but only the first five verses. He later published the entire text, along with his transcription of the melody, in his ethnomusicological treatise and collection, *Hungarian Folk Music*.[80]

The Angoli Borbála text—colorful, artfully constructed, funny as well as tragic—has little in common with the simple tale of Janko. It opens with the heroine, Angoli Borbála, resisting her mother's questions about why her hips are growing broader, just as Edward in the Scottish ballad resists his mother's questions about the blood on his sword; finally she confesses she is pregnant by Squire Gyöngyvári. The mother sends her to prison without food or drink, and after thirteen days Angoli Borbála writes to the Squire. When he goes to her mother to ask for her, the mother at first lies, as her daughter had lied to her; but finally, using the same lines of confession the daughter earlier spoke to her, the mother reveals that her daughter is dead. The Squire goes to her coffin and drives a knife into his heart.

Bartók's Ballad opens *forte* and *pesante*, the folk melody in bare octaves, every note emphasized by a tenuto mark. If the rhythms and phrasing of this melody can be awkward for piano students, the verses of text that Bartók printed in the appendix made it possible for Hungarian students at least to master the difficulties in the most natural way (see Example 7-20).

1. An-go-li Bor-bá-la Kis szok-nyát va-ra-tott.   E-lül kur-táb-bo-dott, Há-tul hos-szab-bo-dott.

Example 7-20. Bartók, transcription of "Angoli Borbála" from *Hungarian Folk Music*.

Bartók's opening verse is heavy with Angoli Borbála's guilt; only in the succeeding verses does he suggest the bantering tone with which the folk ballad begins. These three verses (*Più andante*) have more continuity than any succession of verses in the Janko Ballad; in that, they resemble the dialogue of the mother and daughter. The music is spun out with an unbroken eighth-note accompaniment, a bass line that descends steadily throughout the three verses, and inconclusive harmonies at the end of each verse. At the same time, the volume increases steadily through these verses, returning to the opening level by the beginning of the fifth verse. In this verse, with its cold triads—the first chords in the Ballad—fitted heavily to the melody, the story seems to reach Angoli Borbála's confession and condemnation.

The next three verses, in which the melody itself is changed, work together as an interlude. Nevertheless, each presents a different form of the melody, with a different rhythm, in a different texture, at a different tonal level. This sudden lack of continuity, along with the disguising of the theme, suggests the lull in the action while Angoli Borbála sits in prison; in terms of the ballad process, this is a postponement of consequences that nevertheless brings on the final reckoning. Of these three verses, the second (*Più andante*, 6/8), with its contrapuntal accompaniment, best suggests the passage of the thirteen days. Tension builds toward the reckoning, especially at the end of the next verse (*Più andante*, 7/8), when the melody is obsessively extended by reworkings of its last four notes, while the accompaniment dwells on clashing notes of the same scale.

The reckoning itself is short, just two verses, but it responds very precisely to the opening group of five verses, just as the ending of the folk-ballad text responds to its opening, especially in the lines of confession that the mother takes over from her daughter. Here the melody is restored to its original form, and the accompaniment consists of strong punctuating chords, like those in the fifth verse. But now the chords rise step by step through both verses, just as the bass in the second through fourth verses descended step by step. This time, though, the accompaniment, clashing with the melody along the way, drives toward a final tone in common with that melody. For this Ballad Bartók chose a narrative model that ends as violently as the ballad of Janko, but here his musical means are less confined and more intense, connecting the art of the folk songs he was then collecting to that of the expressionist music he was writing at the same time for the ballet *The Miraculous Mandarin*.

Both Bartók *ballades* come from collections that survey a nation's folk music. Within those collections they represent the ballad alongside pieces representing other song and dance genres. In compiling such national surveys Bartók was creating a national music out of repertories that were local by nature. He himself, more than most folk-song arrangers, insisted on the local and individual identity of a song or song variant. But arranging folk songs was inescapably a nationalizing act. It nationalized in that it transferred local songs to a national audience, but also in that it transferred homespun songs to instruments of modern technology, such as the piano. Nothing so clearly distinguished a national culture from a local one as the technological footing of the national culture. A national culture, in nineteenth-century terms, needed not only its own language and flag and folk songs, as other national cultures had, but also its own share in the technology of the most advanced nations. Among the clearest signs of a developing national musical culture in Hungary was the founding of a modern piano factory in Budapest by Lajos Beregszászy (1817–1891) just at the time of the 1848 revolution. Bartók's folk-song arrangements for piano belonged to the same development: what he had found as local songs he turned into national piano music embodying national songs.

Between national and international culture there was no such sharp distinction. Bartók and his publishers were right to suppose that pedagogical piano pieces based on Hungarian or Slovak folk songs might interest teachers and students in more than one country. As a folk-song collector, Bartók himself specialized in the musical relations of the Hungarians and their neighbors. He was right to believe that peoples like the Hungarians and Slovaks, though they had less access than the Germans and French to the cosmopolitan musical culture of Europe, were at no disadvantage in their heritage of folk songs. He had no way of knowing that the pedagogical pieces he produced from those folk songs would eventually be used on an enormous, international scale, with the result that piano students in many countries could grow up knowing some Hungarian and Slovak folk melodies better than folk songs of their own countries and thus thinking of those melodies less as Hungarian or Slovak than simply as folk.

Even before this ironic posthumous triumph, Bartók had stood on its head the nationalist dilemma that Chopin faced before him. If it was a disadvantage to be from a peripheral country when addressing the international musical audience, he made it an advantage by drawing on the resource of folk music that persisted more vigorously in the peripheral countries, relatively isolated as they were from technological development, than in the central ones. If Bartók's treatment of folk music met with great resistance throughout his career, nevertheless cosmopolitan culture was making more room for folk music even at the beginning of Bartók's career than it had made in Chopin's day, thanks to new prevailing political and educational ideologies as well as to the work of folk-song collectors and arrangers and even of those composers who borrowed only an exotic coloring from folk music. One small result of this change was that Bartók could conceive of the piano *ballade* in a way that would have been unthinkable for Chopin or any of his contemporaries: as a narrative piano work built entirely on an authentic folk-song melody.

The second movement of the Sonata for violin and piano (1922)[81] by Leoš Janáček (1854–1928) is titled "Ballade." Janáček wrote the original version of the Sonata at the beginning of World War I, and his own later testimony connects the music to his expectations of national liberation as the Russian army seemed about to enter Moravia.[82] Students of his music have considered the sonata to be among his most Russian-influenced works.[83] The evidence connecting the work to the war and to Russia, however, pertains less directly to the Ballade than to other movements. In fact, Janáček, in the course of revising the Sonata, published the Ballade separately (1915),[84] and the movement as he eventually published it within the Sonata can be discussed on its own as a self-contained work, embodying its own kind of musical nationalism. The Ballade is nationalist in the general sense that it refers to the ballad as a genre of folk song, not of cosmopolitan poetry. But whereas Bartók constructed a *ballade* on a particular song of a particular folk, Janáček used his own folklike melodic material to make a balladlike narrative progression. Like Bartók, Janáček made the *ballade* what it had not been before: a wordless rendering of the ballad as both folk song and story. His musical means, though just as original as Bartók's, are completely different.

His title "Ballade" could derive in part from the glowing songfulness of the movement and also in part from the refrain structure of its opening pages. It has three themes, all about the same length and all strongly related, following each other without break in a succession reminiscent of a ballad with a refrain stanza: A–B–C–B. The first theme is made out of a folklike six-note motive (see Example 7-21), spun out in an un-folklike sequence of phrases; the motive evolves in the course of seven repetitions, which are

shared between the violin and the bass of the piano. In fact, all the voices
share in the melody-making: as Jaroslav Vogel has pointed out, the fluttering
figure that accompanies the entire theme is itself a diminution of the theme.[85]
The various voices, all working over the same melodic motive, but not in an
imitative way, produce an effect that is both excited and static. In such a
context, any new element—such as the high G-natural (m. 11) that is the first
note outside the established scale—can be hair-raising. The movement as a
whole has the same dynamic: the static energy of the first half is released by
simple, abrupt changes in the second half. In principle at least, Janáček is
close to Chopin in the way he makes a dramatic narrative out of his structure
of themes.

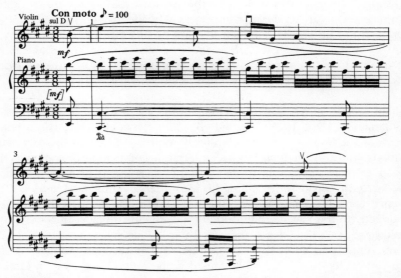

Example 7-21. Janáček, Sonata for Violin and Piano, second movement
(Ballade), mm. 1–4.

The second theme (*Meno mosso*, *ppp*) is both a refrain and a further
stage in the evolution of the opening motive, without the fluttering figure.
The third theme (*A tempo*, *p dolce*), according to Vogel, is "one of the rare
occasions when Janáček develops a melody to any great length."[86] Janáček
distinguishes it from the earlier themes by giving it to both instruments to
play together. Though the theme is new in its motives, it is accompanied by
the same fluttering figure as the first theme. Then, after the recurrence of the
refrain theme, the story becomes dramatic. The third theme is heard again
(*Poco mosso*) in a version that is harmonically static at first, but then slips
ominously downward with a sliding series of chords. Meanwhile the
fluttering figure is heard for the first time from the violin, a less likely medium
for it than the piano, and in a disturbingly sporadic form.

From then on everything fixed in the piece becomes unfixed. The strophic structure of the themes has already been abandoned. Now even the steady beats give way during a rhapsodic passage partly in free rhythm, based on the motive of the first theme. The orderly separation of themes also gives way: as the rhapsodic passage based on the first theme reaches a climactic dominant chord, the motive of the third theme is heard in its most powerful transformation. At this moment a tranquil resolution seems to be reached: the opening of the Ballade returns, quieter and in higher registers than originally, introduced by the only perfect cadence in the movement. But if the story has passed its crisis by this point, there is still uncertainty at the end of the Ballade. The tranquil resolution is not completed, its key—E major—is not heard again, reminders of various earlier passages alternate with each other, the fluttering figure starts and stops, and the final sonority is not a choice made among possible chords, but a blur of two choices.

The last work to be considered in this chapter is not a *ballade* at all. But it rounds out a survey of piano and chamber *ballades* at the time of World War I because it points the way to new relationships between nationalist concerns and musical narration and because it takes its epigraph from a *ballade*—a *ballade*, however, of a kind that has never inspired piano *ballades*. The second movement of Debussy's *En blanc et noir*[87] for two pianos, written in 1915, is in every sense a war piece; its epigraph is the envoi of the "Ballade Against the Enemies of France" (*"Ballade contre les ennemis de la France"*) by the fifteenth-century poet François Villon:

> *Prince, porté soit des serfs Eolus*
> *En la forest ou domine Glaucus.*
> *Ou privé soit de paix et d'espérance*
> *Car digne n'est de posséder vertus*
> *Qui mal vouldroit au royaulme de France.*

> Prince let Aeolus' lackeys bear him
> Far out in that forest where Glaucus rules
> Or let peace and hope be taken from him
> For he isn't worthy to possess virtues
> He who wishes ill on the kingdom of France.
> —translation by Galway Kinnell[88]

"Ballade" in this case names the medieval French genre of lyric poetry, not the narrative genre of folk song or Romantic poetry. The music belongs more to the tradition of battle pieces than to that of piano *ballades*. Like Tchaikovsky's *1812 Overture* and other battle pieces, it presents a progression from pre-battle quiet to noisy fighting. This is not so much a narrative of characters as Debussy's earlier battle piece, in *La Boîte à joujoux* (1913). It is a more atmospheric work, "a rather mysterious picture of war," according to Léon Vallas.[89] The mystery is connected to a realist technique: a texture of musical events unrelated to each other in their timing or tonal orientation evokes the unpredictability, the anxiety of waiting, in trench warfare.

At the height of the battle, Debussy identifies the Germans by the Lutheran hymn "Ein feste Burg," and in the aftermath, as he wrote in a letter, "a modest carillon sounds a pre-Marseillaise."[90] This typical battle-piece device has an unusually complex significance here. "Ein feste Burg," notorious as Meyerbeer had used it in *Les Huguenots* (1836), perfectly represented the susceptibility of French music in the nineteenth century to German influences. Debussy wrote of clearing the atmosphere, in this piece, "of the poisoned vapors that Luther's hymn has momentarily spread, or rather that it represents, for it is beautiful all the same."[91] Out of his nationalist reading of music history Debussy fashioned a musical exorcism. It is as exorcism that this music comes closest to Villon's *ballade*, which is an elaborate and learned curse.

PART III

The Orchestral *Ballade* Through World War I

CHAPTER 8

Orchestral *Ballades* in Western Europe

INTRODUCTION

The history of the piano *ballade* begins with its greatest works; the genre was created by Chopin in one stroke. The history of the orchestral *ballade*, by contrast, has an uncertain beginning. A few forerunners from the time of Chopin's Ballades—overtures to operas that take their plots from ballads—are considered in this chapter. But not until the 1860s—when the major types of piano *ballade* were already well established—did a few autonomous orchestral *ballades* appear. And not until the 1870s—when the centenary of Bürger's "Lenore" was celebrated with several orchestral works on the subject—did orchestral *ballades* begin to be produced steadily, in several countries. No one composition or composer launched the genre. It is all the more striking, then, that orchestral *ballades*—unlike piano *ballades*—almost all belong to a single type.

This type is narrative and specific: the orchestral *ballade* follows the story of a particular ballad. While the great majority of piano *ballades* are called simply "Ballade," only a handful of orchestral *ballades* written through World War I have that title. The rest take the title of a poetic model; sometimes, but by no means generally, the word *"ballade"* appears in a subtitle. Literary ballads far outnumber folk ballads among the models, and even when the models are folk ballads, they are folk ballads transcribed or reworked into literary form. The difference between the orchestral and piano repertories of *ballades* corresponds to a general difference between orchestral and piano music in the nineteenth and early twentieth centuries: the orchestral music of the period often follows specific literary models, while the piano music is more often modeled on genres, and usually musical—song and dance—genres.

On the whole, then, orchestral *ballades* are simply those symphonic

203

poems that happen to have ballads for their poems. Do the *ballades* constitute a distinct type of symphonic poem? For that to be the case, the *ballades* would have to translate into musical form some significant literary trait or traits that distinguish ballads from the other types of poems on which composers modeled symphonic poems. One such trait might be the distinctive narrative structure of ballads—the mixture of narrative and dialogue—but as it happens, composers almost never gave that structure the prominence in orchestral *ballades* that Chopin gave it in his piano *ballades*.

A more significant trait for orchestral *ballades* is that ballads are preeminently poems of action. While narrative action might be barely suggested in other symphonic poems, it is the shaping force in most orchestral *ballades*. Furthermore, ballad stories depend on two highly characteristic kinds of action: actions accomplished through words, and endings that are reckonings, often tragic reckonings, for earlier actions. Largely because composers found distinctive means of representation and distinctive musical forms to accommodate these two kinds of action, orchestral *ballades* make a distinct and coherent group within the repertory of symphonic poems. That is not to say that composers agreed on a single musical form or a single scheme of musical representation for orchestral *ballades*. But it is striking how much they agreed on the nature of the problem when it came to making a symphonic poem out of a ballad.

The repertory of orchestral *ballades* cannot naturally be divided into types, as piano *ballades* of the period through World War I are divided in the previous chapters, since the orchestral *ballades* of the period almost all correspond to a single type of piano *ballade*: the narrative *ballade* based on a particular ballad. Instead, orchestral *ballades* can be divided as poetic ballads themselves most naturally divide: by nation of origin. In the nineteenth century almost every European nation (or language area) developed its own tradition of literary ballads, founded more or less on a native tradition of folk ballads, and in half a dozen of those nations small groups of composers drew on their national ballad traditions to create orchestral *ballades*. (The French *ballades* are an exceptional case in that they are all based on German ballads.)

The present part of this study, accordingly, presents a half-dozen national repertories of orchestral *ballades*. This plan of organization reveals a number of connections among works, since in each national group there were composers who knew and influenced one another, affecting musical methods as well as choices of poetic models. These connections are strongest in the Czech repertory, which, with its masterpieces by Dvořák and Janáček, is also the most impressive collection of orchestral *ballades* from any nation.

GERMAN-SPEAKING COUNTRIES

German-speaking composers created the most diverse and most diffuse of the national repertories. They invented the narrative type of orchestral *ballade* that eventually prevailed throughout Europe, but they also wrote several of the exceptional works not of that type. Within the German repertory, even works based on the same poem usually belong to entirely different musical worlds. An overture of 1835 to an opera on Bürger's "Lenore," for instance, has no musical relation at all to a couple of symphonies on the same subject written four decades later. The creation of the opera *Lenore* by the Austrian composer Anselm Hüttenbrenner (1794–1868), at the time that Chopin and Wieck were publishing the first piano *ballades*, testifies to the spread of the ballad into musical realms far from folk song. But Hüttenbrenner's overture to *Lenore*[1] can hardly be considered a step toward the orchestral *ballade*: it gives little hint of the character, let alone the plot, of the ballad.

Orchestral works based on ballads and independent of any stage work seem to have come later. The earliest I have found, from any country, are two *ballades* from around 1860 by students of Liszt: Carl Tausig and Hans von Bülow. The Tausig is the orchestral version of the piano *ballade* "The Ghost Ship" ("Das Geisterschiff")(1860), discussed in Chapter 4 (see pp. 127-29). This work is subtitled "Symphonic Ballade" even in its piano version, but I can add nothing here about the orchestral version since I have found only indirect evidence of its existence.[2] The Bülow *ballade*, unrelated to his piano *ballade* of 1856 (discussed in Chapter 4, pp. 114-17), is his *Ballade for Large Orchestra, After Uhland's Poem "The Minstrel's Curse"* (1863).[3]

Bülow wrote the work for an Uhland commemoration in Berlin held on January 30, 1863,[4] a few months after the poet's death. Bülow was not only a leading figure in Berlin musical life at the time, but also a politically appropriate one—known for his democratic-nationalist articles on art and politics—to take part in honoring the memory of Uhland. Uhland's ballad "The Minstrel's Curse" ("Des Sängers Fluch"), first published in 1814, was by 1863 a famous allegory of the artist confronting tyranny.[5] The poem had already been set more than once as a song,[6] and Schumann had set the text, as expanded for him by Richard Pohl, partly with interpolations from other Uhland poems, as a cantata for solo singers, chorus, and orchestra. That work, published in 1858, may have suggested to Bülow at least one narrative detail that is not in Uhland's poem.

The poem tells of a lofty castle ruled in olden times by a stony-hearted king and of a pair of minstrels, one old and the other young, who dare to visit the castle and perform before the king. The young man sings, accompanied by the old man's harp and voice:

They sing of love and springtime, of happy golden days—
Of manly worth and freedom, of truth and holy ways;
They sing of all things lovely, that human hearts delight,
They sing of all things lofty, that human souls excite.[7]

The king, enraged by the powerful effect of the song on his people and his wife, strikes the young minstrel dead with his sword. The old minstrel bears the body away, smashes his harp, and curses the place and the king. The terms of the curse are fulfilled: the castle falls into decay, the surrounding lands turn to desert, and the king's name, ignored in songs and books, is forgotten. "The Minstrel's Curse," even if it ends in a lesson about the power of silence, is true to the ballad tradition in that its action advances mainly through utterances: the song and the curse. If a symphonic poem on a ballad text was still quite a novel project in 1863, Bülow may have been spurred not only by the occasion of the Uhland commemoration, but also by the challenge of transforming the described song embedded in Uhland's narrative poem into an orchestral song embedded in a symphonic narrative.

Bülow's Ballade unfolds in three sections, and each can be fitted to a section of the poem. The first, in B-flat major and lively common-time rhythm, seems to represent the life of the royal court; the second, in the same key and meter, but for the most part at more measured speed, represents the minstrels' song and the responses it evokes; the third, in B-flat minor and solemn triple time, represents the aftermath of the young minstrel's murder, including the old minstrel's curse. The opening section is processional music, evoking medieval pageantry in a style like that of *Die Meistersinger*, which Wagner was composing at the same time. If Bülow's opening music seems surprisingly festive for Uhland's poem, it may have been right in tone for a public celebration of Uhland's life. At the same time, this section introduces several themes of contrasting characters, representing the king, queen, and courtiers. These themes are easier to identify later, when they reappear as responses to the minstrels' song.

Bülow not only allotted the song half the length of his Ballade, but also took pains to give it a distinct identity as a song within his symphonic narration. Initially this identity is established largely by means of orchestration: the melody is played by solo cello—a distinctive timbre suggesting the voice of the young minstrel—accompanied principally by pizzicato strings, suggesting the older minstrel's harp (see Example 8-1). As the melody proceeds, other timbres take over the accompaniment, and other instruments double the solo cello. When a second verse is heard, the melody is carried by altogether different instruments. But by the time these changes take hold, the distinctiveness of the song has been established by its melodic structure: a structure of four continuous phrases, all but the last of them eight measures long, standing out in a work otherwise characterized by short answering or contrasting phrases.

Example 8-1. Bülow, *The Minstrel's Curse,* Op. 16, rehearsal-letter H, mm. 1–16.

Though this theme stands apart from the rest of the work as a representation of song, it is not a particularly warm melody, not even the warmest in the Ballade. But then, the song that Uhland describes (in the stanza quoted above) is a call to civic idealism, and Bülow's melodic rhetoric fits Uhland's description. Bülow also suggests, by a system of motivic correspondences, the receptivity of the people and the queen to the themes

of the minstrels' song: he incorporates into the "song" several motives that
have been heard in the opening section and are to be heard again in the
response to the song. One of these motives (marked *a* in Example 8-1)
reappears in the warmest of the responses to the song (Example 8-2), where
it evidently represents the feelings of the queen, who "throws down to the
singers the rose from her breast."

Example 8-2. Bülow, *The Minstrel's Curse*, Op. 16, rehearsal-letter P,
mm. 1–6.

By giving the minstrels two verses to sing, each followed by responses,
Bülow showed both the growing acclaim of the people and the growing
hostility of the king. The idea of showing this progression may have come
from Pohl and Schumann, who gave their minstrels four different songs to
sing, each followed by a different response. In Bülow's version, the response
to the second verse of the song brings on the calamity: the queen's theme
leads into, or provokes, a brief passage showing the king's rising wrath, and
that passage ends in a tremendous crash that marks the slaying of the young
minstrel.

The third and final section of the Ballade follows immediately. The music
of this section evolves from one solemn phrase to another, with no special
device—comparable to the orchestration and phrase structure of the middle
section—to mark any phrases apart as sounding words, as the curse of the old
minstrel. In other words, Bülow does not distinguish musically between the
uttering of the curse and its fulfillment. Instead he calls up many of the
motives of the earlier sections, ending with a forceful transformation of the
minstrels' song, in a new rhythm and the minor mode (see Example 8-3). The
function of this phrase is exegetical rather than narrative: Bülow is asserting
by musical means that the desolation wrought by the minstrel's curse is
simply the other side of the joy promised by the minstrels' song.

Bülow's Ballade received some enthusiastic publicity,[8] but had no more

Example 8-3. Bülow, *The Minstrel's Curse,* Op. 16, rehearsal-letter V, mm. 1-10.

lasting success than his other compositions and little apparent influence. Perhaps it was partly in response to Bülow's example that his Hungarian friend and former piano student Ödön de Mihalovich (1842–1929) wrote four orchestral *ballades* in the 1870s. But Mihalovich chose poetic models that are very different from Bülow's, and his musical conception of the genre owes nothing to Bülow. Mihalovich later became a central figure in Hungarian musical life; in 1887 he succeeded Liszt as head of the Academy of Music in Budapest, a position he held for more than three decades. But his training, in the 1860s, was with German composers, and his orchestral *ballades* are as cosmopolitan in style as they are in their poetic models: two are based on German poems, one on a French poem, and one on a Hungarian poem. Mihalovich is treated here alongside composers of German-speaking countries because the sources of his musical cosmopolitanism were largely German.

Mihalovich began his series of orchestral *ballades* (all published in 1879) with the *Ballade, after Strachwitz' Poem "The Ghost Ship"* ("Das Geisterschiff").[9] He could well have known Tausig's "Symphonic Ballade" on the same poem, but his version is not indebted to Tausig's in any obvious way. Any composer of the day writing music on that subject would have used the same combination of material: storm music, a sailor's song, and a yearning theme. In form Mihalovich's Ballade is more conventional than Tausig's. What distinguishes the work—and, for that matter, all Mihalovich's *ballades*—is his imaginative orchestral writing.

His second *ballade*[10] is based on Paul Gyulai's ballad "The Water Nymph" ("A sellő"), a Hungarian poem that, like many Central European ballads, tells of a young man lured by a seductive nymph to a watery death. In this work even more than in *The Ghost Ship,* Mihalovich concentrates on evoking the atmosphere of the poem, leaving room for only the barest suggestion of narrative progression. With its almost seamless shifts in harmonies and orchestral colors, this is the most forward-looking, the most impressionistic of Mihalovich's *ballades*. *Hero and Leander, after Schiller's Ballad*[11] comes closer to a Liszt symphonic poem in tone and means, in its contrasts and reconciliations, in its varieties of thematic material, chromatic harmony, and rhythmic manipulation. The fourth *ballade, La Ronde du sabbat (The Witches' Sabbath, after the Ballad by Victor Hugo)*,[12] is an orchestral scherzo, with an enchantingly light ending. Mihalovich evidently chose his ballad models more as scenic tableaux than as narrative structures. But in composing the music he followed no single pictorial formula: each of his four *ballades* is different in musical conception as well as in scenic character.

In 1873 two German-speaking composers—August Klughardt and Joachim Raff—produced programmatic symphonies for the centenary of Bürger's "Lenore." A centenary is not ordinarily an occasion for artistic adventure, and these two works both follow the story of the famous ballad in a traditional episodic way, just as Kullak had done and as Rubinstein was just then doing, both in piano *ballades*. But it was novel to equate episodes of a ballad with the traditional movements of a symphony. Klughardt (1847–1902), then a young conductor and Wagner enthusiast, called his *Lenore* a "Symphonic Poem,"[13] while Raff (1822–1882), then one of the most famous and experienced composers in Germany, gave the title *Lenore* to his fifth symphony.[14] Among the eight symphonies that Raff eventually published with programmatic titles, this is the only one naming a story, let alone a ballad; most of the others are pictures of nature.

Klughardt had verses of the poem printed at the beginnings of movements and other points in his score, showing how the music fits the poem. He varied the nature of the fit from movement to movement, making the work as a whole conform to a conventional symphonic plan. The long first movement in sonata form, for instance, does not follow any part of the story. But it is headed by the scene-setting first stanza of the poem, and it presents portentous themes that return to close each of the succeeding movements. The fourth and final movement, by contrast, is highly episodic, following many details of the visit from the ghostly lover and Lenore's fatal ride.

Raff's overall progression of movements is not very different from Klughardt's, but his use of the poem is much freer. The first two movements of his symphony give in effect a prehistory of the poem: the first (really two symphonic movements combined) is called "Happiness in Love," and the second, a march, is called "Separation." In the third and last movement— "Reunion in Death," subtitled "Introduction and Ballad (After G. Bürger's 'Lenore')"—Raff then follows the course of the entire poem. When he reaches the episode of the ride, he recapitulates the mysterious opening of the movement and then introduces a galloping motive. His relentless repetition of that motive through the next forty or more pages of the score obliterates whatever impression the earlier parts of the symphony made. In dissolving the story and its meaning into a single, drawn-out, nightmarish event, Raff is actually following Bürger's example.

The "Lenore" symphonies of Klughardt and Raff did not contribute to the development of the programmatic symphony, though Raff's at least was popular until the end of the nineteenth century. In France the Klughardt and Raff symphonies may have suggested the subject of "Lenore" for the symphonic poem Henri Duparc wrote in 1875. In German-speaking countries, though, no clear tradition of orchestral *ballades* developed. Only a couple of composers worked in the genre, each following a different idea.

In the 1870s Ernst Rudorff (1840-1916) published a suite of movements that takes its name—*Ballade (Introduction, Scherzo, and Finale)*[15]—from its introduction in folk-song style. Julius Röntgen (1855-1932) transferred the idea of Grieg's Ballade to the orchestral medium in his *Ballade on a Norwegian Folk Melody* (1896)[16]; he also chose for his theme a folk melody in changing meter (see Example 8-4), like the ballad "Sjugurd og trollbrura" on which Grieg had recently written his *Romanze with Variations* for two pianos. But Röntgen's flexible variation form owes much more to Brahms, to

Example 8-4. Röntgen, *Ballade on a Norwegian Folk Melody,* Op. 36, mm. 1-36.

[8-4 continued]

whom he dedicated his Ballade, than to Grieg. The Berlin composer Paul Ertel (1865–1933) followed Mihalovich, in a sense, by writing a symphonic poem on the subject of Hero and Leander (1908),[17] but in this work, subtitled "Waves of the Sea and of Love," the narrative of characters is absorbed into a sea-portrait completely impressionistic in style.

Among these various works with little relation to each other may be mentioned one orchestral *ballade* from Finland, the "Ballade" from the *Karelia Suite*[18] (1893) by Jean Sibelius (1865-1957). Sibelius derived the Suite, which from the start has been one of his most popular works, from music he wrote in 1893 for a pageant of medieval Finnish history,[19] and the musical nature of the Ballade is determined by the tableau it originally accompanied. The tableau represented a Finnish king in his castle listening to a minstrel singing, and the Ballade unfolds a long folklike theme, interrupted briefly just before the end by another folklike melody played by the English horn. In the original version, this English horn melody was sung by a tenor to the words of a ballad, "Dansen i rosenlund." Sibelius's Ballade does not represent the story told in an imagined song, as most orchestral *ballades* do, but the singing of a song within a dramatized story.

FRANCE

The orchestral *ballades* written in France, in contrast to those of the German-speaking countries, form a highly unified group; the most obvious sign of that unity, paradoxically, is that they are all based on German literary ballads. The earliest work in the group is Henri Duparc's *Lénore*, after Bürger's ballad, published in 1875. Three years later Vincent d'Indy published *La Forêt enchantée (The Enchanted Forest)*, based on Uhland's ballad "Harald." César Franck, the teacher of both Duparc and d'Indy, followed his pupils into the field in 1882 with *Le Chasseur maudit (The Wild Huntsman)*, based on another ballad by Bürger. (Two French piano *ballades* of German inspiration also come from the same few years: the Fauré Ballade of 1880, inspired—according to the composer—by the "Forest Murmurs" in *Siegfried*, and the Saint-Saëns piano duet, also of 1880, on Heine's ballad "King Harald Harfagar.") A later orchestral *ballade,* somewhat removed from the others in spirit as well as in time, is Paul Dukas's *The Sorcerer's Apprentice*, composed in 1897; but it too stems from a German literary ballad, in this case by Goethe.

The German tradition of literary ballads was far richer than the French, so it is perhaps not extraordinary to find French composers turning to German models for orchestral *ballades*. That several composers who worked closely together (Franck and his pupils) turned to those models at almost the same time may seem to reflect nothing more than a brief shared enthusiasm.

But the enthusiasm can be understood as part of a larger pattern. In the decade after France's defeat in the Franco-Prussian War (1871), French composers—some of whom had taken part in the defense of Paris—were coming to terms with the music of the newly unified German Empire. They were visiting Germany to hear Wagner's music dramas, as well as to meet Wagner and Liszt. They were absorbing Wagner's German legendary themes along with his new musical language. They were studying the symphonic poems of Liszt and finding subjects for symphonic poems and operas in German poetry. Their motivation was at times strongly nationalist (a nationalism defined largely in opposition to German music), but the terms in which French composers conceived of a national French music—including chamber music as well as mythological operas, symphonic poems as well as symphonies—were nonetheless set by the example of German music. The French orchestral *ballades* from around 1880 represent an extraordinary moment of group apprenticeship to a foreign ideal by composers as old—in the case of Franck—as sixty.

Duparc, d'Indy, and Franck

Henri Duparc (1848-1933) met Wagner and heard his music in 1869. Between then and 1885, when he stopped composing, he wrote *Lénore*[20] and other orchestral music, besides the songs for which he is still remembered. Among the four French orchestral ballades, Duparc's *Lénore* is the only one based on a story of love and, appropriately, the one most indebted to the music of *Tristan and Isolde*. One side of this *Lénore* is formed by a cluster of themes evidently representing the heroine's yearning for her dead lover. It is these themes that show the influence of the love music in *Tristan*: the twisting melodic lines, the chromatic counterpoint, the repetitions and rising sequences of phrases and motives (see Example 8-5). The other side of *Lénore* is made up of themes and motives evidently representing the ghost lover's appeals to Lenore to ride into the night with him. These themes derive from a more traditional vocabulary of horn calls and galloping motives.

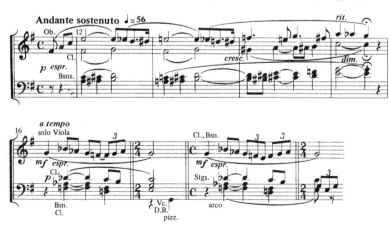

Example 8-5. Duparc, *Lénore*, mm. 12-19.

The programmatic nature and musical form of the work are indebted to Liszt. Duparc does not follow the poem as a progression of episodes or events; instead he represents the two sides of its subject in his two clusters of themes, which contrast with each other in character and tempo (though not in meter). These two clusters together make a progression that evolves as it repeats—very much like the thematic progression in Liszt's Second Ballade. In the fourth and last evolution of the thematic progression, Duparc produces no Lisztian reconciliation of his contrasting themes, but something that fits Bürger's story better: a strident confrontation of themes from each cluster, superimposed against one another in pairs. The ending is more straightforwardly descriptive: Lenore's death is announced by a fragmentation of themes and by a phrase of modal, organlike chords.

Vincent d'Indy (1851-1931) had joined Duparc as a student of Franck several years before he went to Bayreuth in 1876 and heard the first performance of the *Ring* cycle. Though Wagner is reported to have advised him to apply Wagnerian principles to a French subject, he favored subjects and texts by German poets, especially Schiller, in both orchestral and vocal works for most of the next decade. Among his works of this period is *La Forêt enchantée (The Enchanted Forest: Legend-Symphony after a Ballad by Uhland*, 1878).[21] The Uhland ballad, "Harald" (1813), tells of a knight who leads his troops, singing "many a victory song," into a wild forest, where they fall under the enchantment of singing and dancing elves. Only Harald himself resists the spell, until he drinks from a magical spring and falls into a centuries-long slumber.

This Uhland ballad has little in common with "The Minstrel's Curse," except that the singing of songs is an important action in both poems. "Harald" comes closer in theme to Heine's ballad "King Harald Harfagar," on which Saint-Saëns wrote his piano *ballade* at practically the same time that d'Indy wrote *La Forêt enchantée*. The most similar Wagnerian subject is that of *The Ring*, and among Wagner's works it is *The Ring* that d'Indy's music relies on the most. But the Wagnerian influence is only one of many; in some ways and in some passages, Berlioz appears to have been even more influential.

The plan of the work could hardly be simpler: a scherzo-like movement representing the riding and singing knights is followed by a slower movement, distinguished by "magical" instrumental effects, representing the enchanting song of the elves (see Example 8-6). A final section, in changing rhythms, using the themes of the previous movements as well as new material, represents the enchantment of Harald. Nothing more is needed to shape the story of "Harald" in music: it is a ballad without a ballad process, a narrative poem without much narrative mechanism. When d'Indy changed Uhland's title to *The Enchanted Forest*, he revealed that he was attracted to the subject almost entirely by its natural and magical elements, which inspired him to create a lavish orchestral tableau.

Bürger's "The Wild Huntsman" ("Der wilde Jäger," 1785), from which Franck made a symphonic poem (*Le Chasseur maudit*) in 1882,[22] has some of the same narrative and pictorial elements as "Harald"—the forest setting,

Example 8-6. D'Indy, *La Forêt enchantée*, Op. 8, rehearsal-letter K, mm. 35–49.

the horseback riding, the turning of a man into a spirit. It is close in narrative structure and moral message to Bürger's earlier ballad, "Lenore." Franck, trying new musical genres and reinventing his musical language at the age of sixty, may have been following the example or the guidance of his pupils Duparc and d'Indy. But if their orchestral *ballades* influenced his turn to the genre or his choice of poetic model, they do not seem to have influenced his conception of the genre, and they had nothing to contribute to the development of Franck's musical language. *Le Chasseur maudit* is a more compelling work than the *ballades* by Duparc and d'Indy and has rightfully kept a place in the orchestral repertory, while the latter have only occasionally been revived in the twentieth century.

At the front of his published score Franck put his summary of Bürger's ballad.[23] The four short prose paragraphs to which Franck reduced Bürger's long and complicated poem not only provide a guide to the musical sections of his *ballade*, but also indicate how he redefined the story. Bürger's huntsman, for instance, commits a series of outrages against God, animals, and humans. Franck, in his summary and in his *ballade*, retains only the first of these: his huntsman's offense is the sacrilegious act of hunting on a Sunday morning, when he should be in church. In other words, the ballad process of Bürger's poem begins with a complex act of defiance, each part of which contributes something different to the power of the poem, while in Franck's version there is a single act of defiance—and one that not every listener has been able to take seriously.[24] But if Franck exaggerated the importance of sacrilege as a theme in Bürger's poem, he at least chose a theme that was characteristic of Bürger: in "Lenore," for example, the protagonist's refusal to accept the death of her lover is transformed into sacrilege when she declares that she does not believe in God. In Bürger's ballads, then, sacrilege appears not so much as an outrage in itself, but as a sign of a character's unruly temperament, which demands to be subdued.

Franck's *ballade* has a reputation as "blatantly imitative music,"[25] and with reason, but the reputation is deceptive. The crux of "The Wild Huntsman," as Franck himself compressed the story, is an episode that resists musical illustration, and even in the most "blatantly imitative" passages, Franck's descriptive methods are sometimes sophisticated. The opening passage (*Andantino quasi allegretto*) is an example. Franck presents the elements of the conflict clearly: a horn call representing the count's love of hunting and bells representing the call to church. But the significance of the principal theme of the passage—a long theme for cellos, with major and minor inflections—is not so clear. Roger Fiske considers it a "call for a proper sobriety,"[26] yet it opens with a motive closely related to that of the horn call. The passage as a whole, though it presents the elements of conflict, suggests a harmonious world where conflict need not arise.

This introductory passage is interrupted by the main theme of the work, the music of the hunt. But though Franck is moving from a still scene to a galloping one, he keeps the same tempo (while changing meter from 3/4 to 9/8), saving dramatic rhythmic change for the moment of reckoning. This main theme (*L'istesso tempo*) is another "blatantly imitative" passage in that its first phrases are played by unaccompanied horns and all the phrases have galloping rhythms. But it is also a complex musical statement composed of distinct phrases, and it is not clear what each of them represents in the narration. One phrase, which remains insistently quiet as it is heard more and more often, may represent the voice of the count's conscience: Franck's plot summary encourages listeners to hear the voice of conscience in this section of the music. But here, as in the opening section, Franck has sacrificed clarity about details of the plot for clarity in the overall effect: the endless galloping rhythms tell us that, whatever his doubts, the count keeps riding.

A sudden break, during which only a pulsing note from the violas is heard (see Example 8-7), sets the stage for the reckoning. At this point Franck's summary reads: "Suddenly the count is alone; his horse will go no farther; he blows on his horn, and the horn does not sound." The viola notes pulsing steadily through this passage perfectly capture both the cessation of movement and the count's solitude. His fruitless blowing on the horn is a more problematic effect. Since Franck's medium is purely instrumental, he has to sound the horns of the orchestra in order to show them not sounding. He makes the point patiently, giving the muted horns successively weaker blasts (see Example 8-7) and later a single diminishing chord (see Example 8-8).

The moment needs this patient exposition, not only because it is such a difficult action to depict by purely orchestral means, but also because listeners need a chance to do more than simply grasp what is being represented. If they are to find any force and depth in this work, they need to

Example 8-7. Franck, *Le Chasseur maudit*, mm. 246-55.

Example 8-8. Franck, *Le Chasseur maudit*, mm. 268-72.

be able to feel the horror of what the count is realizing at this moment. That horror is not a feeling that the music itself develops; the listener must supply it. As a result, the silencing of the horns in this passage—like the silencing of the oboe at the end of the "Scene in the Country" in Berlioz's *Symphonie fantastique*—may trigger a listener's emotional response at one hearing of the work and not at another, for reasons that have little to do with the quality of performance or even the listener's attentiveness and goodwill.

In the rest of the work Franck's task is more straightforward, and so is his music. The action of inaction—the silencing of the count's horn—is succeeded by an action characteristic of ballads, an action in words: a "lugubrious voice" condemns the hunting count to be hunted himself, chased eternally by creatures from hell. Franck's musical language for this episode

(*Molto lento*) comes from nineteenth-century operatic conjuring scenes, with soft string tremolos setting the mood and a trombone, joined by other wind instruments, representing the voice of doom. Next, according to the plot summary, flames leap up from everywhere, and Franck creates his own version of Wagner's "Magic Fire" music (*Più animato*). Finally, the count is chased by demons, and the parallel of this action to the earlier hunting scene allows Franck to return to his main theme, his exposition, to round off what has become an episodic musical form. The final section (*Allegro molto*; *Quasi presto*), however, is no recapitulation. The main theme is not restated, but reduced to fragments that are thrown together with furious energy. Simply by sticking to his ballad story, Franck arrives at a musical close exhibiting the same processes of fragmentation and transformation, along with some of the same fiery energy, as the reckonings that close the Chopin Ballades.

Dukas, *The Sorcerer's Apprentice*

Like the *ballades* of Franck and his students, *The Sorcerer's Apprentice: Scherzo, after a Ballad of Goethe*[27] (1897) by Paul Dukas (1865–1935) is based on a German literary ballad. Though Dukas wrote his *ballade* a decade and a half after Franck wrote his, *The Sorcerer's Apprentice* (*L'Apprenti sorcier*) has at least one point of stylistic contact with *Le Chasseur maudit*: each has a long main theme embodying the irrepressible movement at the heart of the story. Nevertheless, Dukas's musical language in *The Sorcerer's Apprentice* is strikingly different from Franck's. In fact, finding the most relevant historical context for Dukas's *ballade* is a difficult task, rendered more so by Walt Disney's vivid film animation in *Fantasia* (1940), the memory of which obstructs efforts to hear the music on its own terms, just as the memory of Dukas's music obstructs efforts to read Goethe's poem on its own terms.

Goethe's poem ("Der Zauberlehrling," 1797) is an unusual ballad. Goethe recognized a balladlike theme in a classical source—a story told by Lucian within the dialogue *The Lover of Lies* (*Philopseudēs*)—and, while preserving all the essential details of the story, gave it the symmetrical shape and cautionary-tale emphasis of a ballad. At the same time, by retaining Lucian's first-person narration, he gave "The Sorcerer's Apprentice" an immediacy unusual for a ballad.

Dukas in some respects followed Goethe's poem "verse by verse," as Guy Ropartz writes.[28] The symmetry of the composition, for example, is justly described by Maurice Emmanuel as "deduced from Goethe's ballad."[29] But Dukas's response to the first-person narration was more ambiguous. For the most part, his music traces the course of the story as the apprentice himself experiences it, without any suggestion of a narrator's voice or commentary. But his version is also touched, as several writers have observed, with "ironic and mordant laughter,"[30] implying a narrating persona—something Goethe's narrative structure does not allow—a persona distinct from, and not altogether sympathetic to, the viewpoint of the poor apprentice. That laughter is especially noticeable at the very end—the abrupt last four chords, in fact—exactly the moment when, as Carolyn Abbate has observed, the music extends past the actions and words represented in the poem.[31]

Dukas's musical narration, like that in most symphonic poems, depends on a system of thematic associations. *The Sorcerer's Apprentice* is remarkable in that the themes are all presented in close succession at the beginning of the work and in that those four themes, in perfectly recognizable forms, make up virtually every measure of the work. Dukas identified the themes in a note he wrote at the head of his manuscript score, but did not publish[32]:

The first phrase, given by the violins over the harmonies of the violas and violoncellos, can be named the "Sorcery motive" (see Example 8-9).

Example 8-9. Dukas, *The Sorcerer's Apprentice*, mm. 2–6.

This motive, exhibited at the opening, contains two thematic elements: the first remains almost invariable in the course of the piece, while the second engenders the Scherzo proper.

A second theme, very lively in movement and of an impulsive spirit, characterizes the young apprentice sorcerer (see Example 8-10).

Example 8-10. Dukas, *The Sorcerer's Apprentice*, mm. 14–17.

Finally, a third, more subsidiary idea—a kind of call, vigorously emphatic, sustained by chromatic harmonies—is entitled the "Evocation motive" (see Example 8-11).

Example 8-11. Dukas, *The Sorcerer's Apprentice*, mm. 24–32.

This horn call is interspersed with the various combinations of the two principal themes: at the end, it expresses the idea of *Mastery* when it appears, amplified, in the postlude that restores the calm tempo of the introduction.

Ropartz, perhaps without even knowing Dukas's note, described the introduction of the piece as "like a thematic catalog of the work,"[33] and other writers have described it as a kind of presentation of characters before the curtain rises on the action.[34] But though the introduction does present the themes in a systematic way (which has no equivalent in Goethe's poem), it can still be heard as participating in the action. For if the sounding of the "Evocation motive" at the end of the introduction (*Vif*) is not heard as the apprentice speaking the magic command to the broom, then the slow stirring of the main theme immediately afterward, at the beginning of the "Scherzo proper" (rehearsal-number 6), can hardly be taken to represent the magic power slowly bringing the broom to life.

The distinction that Dukas draws in his note between a theme that "remains almost invariable" and one that "engenders" other music is the key to the narrative method and musical structure of the whole work. The continuity of the story—the embodiment of the broom's activity and the depiction of the apprentice's changing mood—is carried by themes that keep transforming and combining, in particular by the second "element" of the "Sorcery motive," which becomes the main theme of the Scherzo. This theme is never recapitulated; it never appears the same way twice. It is associated with the magical animation of the broom, and its main musical characteristic is its flexibility in conveying a sense of movement. At the beginning of the "Scherzo proper," when this theme represents the first stirring of the broom, it is given a slowly accelerating introduction, and even then, as G. W. Hopkins has demonstrated, the theme itself embodies a further steady increase in momentum.[35] Later, after the apprentice has chopped the broom in two, further transformations of this theme—its lead motive appearing alone, then in parallel tenths, and then the whole theme in canonic imitation (rehearsal-numbers 42–45)—convey, with perfect pacing, the resumption of water-carrying by doubled forces.

At that moment Dukas concentrates everything on clear depiction of the action, leaving it to listeners to imagine the feelings of the apprentice. At other times, though, he suggests the course of those feelings. The fragmentations, reshapings, reorchestrations, and reharmonizations of themes, by which he depicts the building tide of water, also create an impression of the mounting panic of the apprentice. Especially effective in conveying this parallel development are passages in which Dukas combines two themes, the main theme ("Sorcery motive") and the "Apprentice motive," either superimposing them or alternating quickly between them.

The first "element" of the "Sorcery motive," although Dukas says that it "remains almost invariable," actually takes part in the transformations, though much less fully than those other two themes. It is the "Evocation motive" that functions in a drastically different way. It appears four times in the work (at rehearsal-numbers 3, 38, 49, and 55), and though it is not exactly the same each time, it is the least variable of the themes. It is also the most distinctive of the themes—with its characteristic long notes, brass coloring, and whole-tone chords—and the one that Dukas keeps most separate from the other themes. The appearances of the "Evocation motive," as a result, stand out as discrete events in the story, and events of the same kind: the motive represents, in each case, the speaking of a command ("evocation").

If ballads in general rely heavily on actions accomplished through the speaking of words, this ballad of Goethe's is an extreme case: the only spoken words (as opposed to unspoken thoughts) in this text are the four spoken commands that Dukas represents with his "Evocation motive," four words by which characters accomplish, or try to accomplish, actions. The four commands are all different: the first is the apprentice's conjuration that activates the broom; the second his desperate and ineffective command to it to stop; the third (when the two brooms are at work) his desperate call to his master; and the fourth, the master's powerful command, which stops the brooms. Nevertheless, they are all commands, and Goethe's text equates them all as ritualistic utterances by placing them all in the same position within the complex stanzas of his ballad and giving them all the same repeating form of opening: "Walle! walle!"—"Stehe! stehe!"—"Wehe! wehe!"—"In die Ecke, Besen! Besen!"

Dukas responds to that parallel by the extraordinary measure of representing all four utterances with the same theme, a theme with musical characteristics traditional for the representation of supernatural or ritual words—the long notes and brass chords—and with a phrase repetition that implies a repeated word (the musical phrase may even have been suggested to him by a specific word in the text: in the French translation that Dukas printed with his score, it is the second command—"Arrête, arrête!" ("Stop, stop!")—that fits the musical phrase best. The four appearances of the "Evocation motive" are not exactly the same, but somewhat differentiated in keeping with differences in the commands:[36] the motive is most repeated, rising each time in sequence, when it represents the apprentice frantically ordering the broom to stop. But to make the meaning of each appearance clear, Dukas relies less on differences in the form of the theme than on the placement of that appearance in relation to the other themes of the work.

The clarity of the entire narration, in fact, depends on the reciprocal relationship between the appearances of the "Evocation motive" and the transformations of the other themes: the "almost invariable" appearances of the "Evocation motive" mark the stages in the ongoing progression made by the other themes, while the transformations of those themes provide the context for attributing new content to each successive appearance of the

"Evocation motive." The symmetry of the composition, as of the poem, is formed largely by the arrangement of these equivalent commands: the two desperate cries of the apprentice are heard, both at peaks of the hubbub, just before and after the pivotal action of splitting the broom, while the two effective commands— that of the apprentice setting the broom to work and that of the master stopping it—frame the entire action, the entire Scherzo.

Dukas's subtitle "Scherzo" evidently does not refer to the musical form of the work. A better explanation seems to lie in the playful spirit of the music. If Dukas had a technical sense of the term in mind, he may have been thinking of his phrase rhythm, which resembles that of earlier scherzos, especially Beethoven's. The foundation of that phrase rhythm is what Dukas labels "ternary rhythm"; that is, the quick 3/8 measures of the "Scherzo proper" are systematically formed into three-measure groups (with an occasional hemiola). The "true" meter, as Hopkins points out, can be taken as 9/8.[37] These three-measure groups are the musical equivalent of interchangeable parts: all starting on downbeats, often static or self-sufficient in harmony, they are self-contained motives that the composer assembles in endlessly inventive combinations and recombinations. There are no real phrases, no breaths, in the music, not even in the utterances of the "Evocation motive." The musical process of the work seems to be driven by an arbitrary, machine-like energy.

The power and originality of Dukas's work lie precisely in the image that his musical process creates: the sorcerer's apprentice has set loose a machine that runs beyond his control. That image does not come from Goethe. Goethe's apprentice speaks to the broom—and this is the humor of the poem—as to a sentient being, an evil spirit, an adversary. In his battle with the unknown, with his own ignorance, he learns to accept authority. Dukas's *Sorcerer's Apprentice*, fashioned in a different medium, but also in a different age, tells the same story with new significance and new humor. His is a machine-age nightmare. His apprentice feels powerless, not before a being he cannot understand, but before an energy without mind or being, an automaton. Because the music does not distinguish the increasing activity of the broom from the increasing panic of the apprentice, he seems to be caught up in the very movement he is resisting. What is funny in Dukas's version, accordingly, is not the apprentice's language (as it could hardly be in an instrumental medium), but his plight. Dukas's comic technique here fits with the theory of his contemporary Henri Bergson (1859–1941) that comedy arises from an intrusion of the mechanical into human life.[38]

The Disney "Sorcerer's Apprentice," unlike other episodes in the 1940 *Fantasia*, tells the story that its music was actually written to illustrate. This episode of the film, consequently, offers a rare case of a composer's nonverbal narration being interpreted by another nonverbal narration. Disney accepted Dukas's version of the story as a modern-day nightmare of helplessness in the face of an unresponsive, machine-like force. His animation excels precisely at showing the apprentice caught up in the irresistible motion of brooms and water. Within the film tradition, Disney's "Apprentice" can be seen as a successor to the assembly-line sequences in René Clair's *A nous la liberté* (1931) and Charles Chaplin's *Modern Times* (1936). But the comparison to those two classic examples of Bergsonian comedy shows how far Disney changed the tone of Dukas's *Apprentice*. Disney's version of the story is comic only in the sense that he retained the happy ending. He made the story into a portrait of guilt—a feeling that had virtually disappeared in Dukas's version. And whereas the earlier versions—Goethe's as well as Dukas's—had not specified the age of the apprentice, except to call him an apprentice, Disney made him as small as a young child, in effect turning a ballad into a fairy tale.

BRITAIN

British orchestral *ballades* of this period constitute a distinctive repertory in that most of them are based on folk ballads rather than literary ballads, and based on them as songs, not just as stories. These orchestral *ballades* are offshoots of the oldest ballad-collecting movement in Europe. The earliest of them is contemporary with Chopin's piano *ballades*. But the composer of that work had no thought of creating a new genre, and no British composer followed his example for another half-century.

This forerunner, the *Overture to Chevy Chace*[39] by George Alexander Macfarren (1813-1887), was written in 1836 as the overture to an opera, but the composer withdrew it from the opera in a dispute about his billing as composer and had the overture performed independently.[40] The opera was presumably based on the famous British ballad of the same name, and the overture, with its horn calls, threatening interruptions, and martial rhythms, fits the ballad story of a hunt that provokes murderous battle between the houses of Percy and Douglas. Only the somber ending of the story is missing from the overture. The most remarkable feature of the overture is that the tune of the folk ballad appears as one of its principal themes. Macfarren was one of the musicians making the piano arrangements for William Chappell's *Collection of National English Airs* (1839-40),[41] which opens with two different tunes to "Chevy Chace," and he adapted the first of these tunes to a new rhythm for use in his overture (see Example 8-12).

The work, then, is a hybrid of two traditions of opera overture: the quoting tradition of the potpourri overture and the descriptive tradition of the programmatic overture. In its performance history, though, it was always an independent work. At its first performance it was praised as a "piece of descriptive writing."[42] In subsequent years it was conducted in Leipzig by Mendelssohn and in London by Wagner, who admired its "peculiarly wild, passionate character."[43] But for all the success of the *Chevy Chace* Overture

Example 8-12. "Chevy Chace": (*a*) the folk ballad (transposed), from W. Chappell, ed., *Collection of National English Airs,* No. 1 Bis; (*b*) Macfarren, theme from *Overture to Chevy Chace.*

as independent program music, Macfarren's idea of quoting a folk song in the course of a programmatic work seems to have had no influence in the genre where that idea might have flourished: the orchestral *ballade*.

Forty-three years elapsed between the publication of this work and that of the next British orchestral *ballade*. Following the tradition established by then in Germany, France, and elsewhere, it took a literary ballad as its model. *La Belle Dame sans merci: Ballad for Orchestra*[44] (1884) by Alexander Mackenzie (1847–1935) is based on the ballad of that title (1820) by Keats. The most striking feature of Mackenzie's *ballade* is its symmetrical frame, modeled on Keats's framing stanzas. In Keats's opening stanza, the speaker of the poem asks, "O, what can ail thee, knight-at-arms, / Alone and palely loitering?" In the last stanza, finishing his tale, the knight answers: "And this is why I sojourn here / Alone and palely loitering."[45] Mackenzie, accordingly, opens and closes his *ballade* with identical music, a long "speaking" passage, unaccompanied at first, which draws the listener into and out of the tale (see Example 8-13). Arpeggiated melody, often omitting a triadic step and leaping by a sixth, is characteristic of this passage. This stylistic feature may derive from folk music, in particular Scottish folk music, which Mackenzie had spent much time arranging as a young man. Indeed, it is a mark of his style in general, not a distinction of his works on Scottish subjects (such as the "Highland Ballad" for violin and piano, mentioned previously in Chapter 7, note 44).

A few years later another Scottish composer, Hamish MacCunn (1868–1916), wrote two orchestral *ballades* based on British folk ballads. *The Ship o' the Fiend*[46] (1890), based on the ballad better known as "The Daemon Lover" or "The House Carpenter," resembles Brahms's piano *ballade*

Example 8-13. Mackenzie, *La Belle Dame sans merci,* Op. 29, mm. 1–13.

"Edward" in its relationship to the ballad text. This ballad begins, like "Edward," in dialogue, and MacCunn's main theme represents three stanzas of that dialogue in phrases that can almost be sung to the lines of text, the woman's lines in phrases given to the oboe and the lines of the demon lover in phrases given to the French horn.

There is no such close fit of words and melody in *The Dowie Dens o' Yarrow*[47] (1890). This is the work Shaw considered "a predestined failure, since it is impossible to tell a story in sonata form."[48] However overstated that criticism may be in principle, it makes a fair point about this work: the "predestined" form allows the composer to trace most of the story as a sequence of musical vignettes (Shaw concedes the "good musical fight in the middle section"), but not to complete the story on the same terms.

Another composer may have used the generic title "Ballade" in part to justify taking liberty with sonata form—as his professors taught it—in a one-movement orchestral work. Samuel Coleridge-Taylor (1875–1912) wrote his *Ballade in A Minor,*[49] the work that first made him known to the English public, for the Gloucester Musical Festival in 1898, the year after he finished at conservatory. For Coleridge-Taylor, the son of West African and English parents, the word "*ballade*" may have been identified with European music in general, rather than with the music of any one nation. It may consequently have seemed the right title for a work in a cosmopolitan European style, with themes that are forceful, but have no local color (see Example 8-14).

Example 8-14. Coleridge-Taylor, *Ballade in A Minor,* Op. 33, mm. 1-6.

A few years later John McEwen (1868-1948), a Scottish contemporary of MacCunn's, wrote a work that evokes folk song more strongly than any earlier British *ballade*. The work, *Grey Galloway*,[50] was the most popular of McEwen's three *Border Ballads* for orchestra (1905-08). He evokes Scottish folk song so strongly in this work because his melodies rely not on any single element of folk-song style, but on a complex of elements: modes, rhythms, and ornaments.

During World War I, Frederick Delius (1862-1934) wrote a *Ballad for Orchestra* that is not based on ballads of any sort. *Eventyr: Once Upon a Time*[51] is based instead on Norwegian fairy tales, which Delius had read in the celebrated collection by Asbjørnsen and Moe.[52] Evidently for him "Ballad" had become a generic title for narrative instrumental works on legendary subjects. Eric Fenby describes *Eventyr* as Delius's "only work that suggests narrative whilst evoking the spirit of the scene."[53] Of course, a fairy tale in various pertinent ways is not like a ballad: it is not a song or even a poem, it is much more likely to be peopled by children, animals, and imaginary creatures, and its action is determined by a process very different from the ballad process. Nevertheless, Delius's narrative method in *Eventyr* has a place in the history of the *ballade*.

Delius's original indication, "After Asbjørnsen's Fairy Tales," as well as other remarks attributed to him, indicate that he was not retelling one fairy tale in particular, but creating a musical story from the impressions that a number of the fairy tales had made on him.[54] Even so, Fenby—Delius's secretary in his last years—could specify, up to a point, what the music represents:

> The musical interest turns on the play and interaction of two groups of themes; the one, in the strings, expressing the idea of the warmhearted superstitious peasantry in these tales; the other, in the woodwind and brass, the eerie interventions in their lives of the fantastic creatures of Norwegian legend—the trolls, giants, demons, pixies.[55]

Eventyr begins, like many *ballades*, with a suggestion of a narrator's voice—low, modal, and gloomy (see Example 8-15). The unusual thing about this narrator's voice is that it does not reappear at the end of the work, but in the thick of the action, as one character out of many, just before the two

Example 8-15. Delius, *Eventyr*, mm. 1-4.

surprising "wild shouts" of the invisible men's chorus (personifying goblins). It is the "warmhearted" string music of the peasantry that frames the piece. In the sense that fairy tales often tell of humans who leave human society for an adventure among "fantastic creatures" and then return to their own kind, this framing structure supports an interpretation of the work as a single narrative, a model of a fairy tale. But the goblins get the first and last laugh: brief passages of twittering woodwinds frame the "human" frame, mocking the neat compartments of a single narrative and perhaps supporting an interpretation of the whole work as more comment than narrative.

A study of orchestral textures in *Eventyr*—as vivid as those in *The Sorcerer's Apprentice*, but utterly unruly in comparison—would suggest that Delius was drawn to Norwegian fairy tales largely by their mingling of different worlds, their narrative of unclarity. Clearly he had a gift for rendering such unruly subjects in music: several champions of his music have recommended *Eventyr* as one of his finest works.

CHAPTER 9

Orchestral *Ballades* in Slavic Europe

RUSSIA

Considering that folk ballads and poetic ballads were of tremendous importance to the development of Slavic literature early in the nineteenth century[1] and that the piano *ballade* was created in just that period by a Polish composer, Chopin (inspired by contemporary ballads of Polish poets), it is surprising that Slavic composers did not create orchestral works in the genre until late in the century. Perhaps the earliest example is *Toman a lesní panna* (1875) by the Czech composer Zdeněk Fibich. And the first masterpieces, by Tchaikovsky and Dvořák, were not written until the 1890s. All these works are based on ballads written in the early part of the century, important poems from the heyday of the ballad movement in Slavic literature.

Tchaikovsky, *Voevoda*

The "Symphonic Ballade" *Voevoda* (1891)[2] by Piotr Tchaikovsky (1840-1893) is based on Pushkin's 1833 translation of Mickiewicz's 1827 ballad "Czaty" ("Sentry"). In 1877 the poem had been set for baritone and orchestra by Eduard Nápravník (1839-1916),[3] the St. Petersburg conductor who premiered several of Tchaikovsky's operas, and Nápravník's composition could have suggested at least the subject to Tchaikovsky. The poem has been admired as one of Mickiewicz's best ballads;[4] but in choosing that poem for his subject, Tchaikovsky was making this work less accessible to audiences, especially outside of Poland and Russia, than the orchestral works—like *Romeo and Juliet*, *Francesca da Rimini*, and *Manfred*—that he based on classics of European literature. Tchaikovsky's own treatment of his *Voevoda* did not help its cause: at first pleased with it, he turned against it and tore up the score after the first performance. The score was reconstructed from the orchestral parts and published soon after his death.[5]

230

But though it is one of his last and most original works, it has never become one of his popular ones.

For Tchaikovsky, reading the ballad by Mickiewicz was a very different matter from reading those European classics on which he had composed other orchestral works. The ballad was just a few short stanzas (in contrast to whole plays by Shakespeare and Byron, though not so different in length from Dante's telling of the Francesca story); and although Tchaikovsky read the ballad, as he presumably read the other works, in translation,[6] in this case the translation was itself the work of a great poet. The novelty of working from such a model accounts in large part for the originality of *Voevoda* among Tchaikovsky's literary orchestral works: rather than distilling the story of his poetic model, he transformed it whole into symphonic music, at some points responding directly to the poetic lines in musical form.

Consequently, one cannot appreciate Tchaikovsky's achievement in this work without reading the whole poem, even if it must be in translation. Since it was Pushkin's version of the poem that Tchaikovsky had before him, it is Pushkin's Russian, rather than the original Polish of Mickiewicz, that is translated here into English (preserving the stanza structure, but not the meter or rhyme of the Russian):

Voevoda
(The General)

> Late at night, from a campaign
> The general returned.
> He orders the servants to be silent;
> Hurries to bed in the bedroom;
> He pulls back the cover...Indeed!
> There's no one there; the bed is empty.
>
> And, gloomier than black night,
> He lowers his frightening eyes,
> He begins to twirl his gray moustache...
> He throws back his sleeves,
> He goes out, unbolts the door;
> "Hey you," he calls, "You piece of the devil!
>
> "Why is there no dog by the fence,
> And no bolt?
> I'll get you, bastards! Give me my rifle,
> Get a sack and a rope,
> And take my gun down from the nail,
> Follow me! I'll get her!"
>
> The master and the servant crawl below the fence,
> In quiet reconnaissance.

They enter the garden—and through the branches,
On a bench by the fountain,
In a white dress, they see the young lady
And a man before her.

He says, "All is lost,
Everything I used to enjoy
And used to love:
The sighing of a white breast,
The pressure of a tender hand...
The general has bought it all.

"How many years I have suffered through you,
How many years I have searched for you!
You are locked away from me.
He didn't search, he didn't suffer;
He just jingled his silver
And you gave yourself to him.

"I galloped in the gloom of night
To see the eyes of a dear young lady,
To press a tender hand;
To wish her, in her new household,
Many years, much mirth,
And then flee forever."

The young lady weeps and grieves,
He kisses her knees,
And the others look through the branches,
Lowering their rifles to the ground,
They each bite off a cartridge
And ram the shot home with the rod.

They approach carefully.
"My lord, I can't take aim,"
The poor servant whispers,
"It must be the wind, my eyes are teary,
I'm trembling, there's no strength in my arms,
The powder won't go under the hammer."

"Shut up, you robber's spawn!
I'll give you something to cry about!
Sprinkle the powder...Aim...
Aim at her forehead. More to the left...Higher.
I'll deal with milord myself. Quiet!
I'll go first; you wait."

The shot resounded in the garden.
The servant hadn't waited for his master;
The general shouted,
The general staggered...
It seems the servant's shot went wrong:
It hit him right in the forehead.

—translated by Karen Black

For a modern literary ballad, this poem is remarkably free of any distancing archaic tone. Likewise, Tchaikovsky introduces no archaic sound or any other distancing effect into his *ballade*: there is no suggestion of folk song or of a narrative voice, no mediating frame in the music, as there is in piano *ballades* of Chopin and other composers or in certain British orchestral *ballades*. Tchaikovsky presents his story dramatically: the voices heard in *Voevoda* are the voices of the characters. Characters also "speak" in the *ballades* of Franck and Dukas, but only at crucial moments in the story; Tchaikovsky's *ballade* is more like an operatic scene for orchestra.

That scene begins—just as the poem does—in pantomime. According to Tchaikovsky's student and colleague Sergei Taneiev, writing to Tchaikovsky's brother Modest about the work in 1901, this opening of the work "serves only as a preparation for the love episode."[7] It is true that the opening music, representing the general's search for his wife, makes the strongest imaginable contrast to the central episode, which represents the garden meeting of the wife and her former suitor. But the same could be said of the "feuding" theme of Tchaikovsky's *Romeo and Juliet* in relation to the love theme of that work. In *Voevoda*, even more than in *Romeo and Juliet*, the contrast is defined by a distinction between rhythms of movement in the opening episode and rhythms of speech (sung speech) in the love episode.

For over two hundred measures in the opening episode, a scurrying triplet figure, which suggests both the general's hurried search and his rising anxiety, predominates over any slower-moving, more singable line (see Example 9-1). The slower-moving lines, for their part, are formed so that they collaborate with the triplet figure in the representation of movement and mood, rather than standing apart as a voice. Mostly energetic scalar lines, they repeat in rising sequence and combine contrapuntally with their own inversions, dramatizing the general's racing thoughts as the triplet figure alone could not do. The musical material of this episode, in other words, does not just make a contrast with what comes next, but serves to dramatize the opening action of the poem.

Example 9-1. Tchaikovsky, *Voevoda,* Op. 78, mm. 5–12.

Likewise, this musical episode makes its own articulated dramatic progression, rather than forming a simple preparation for the love episode. The progression takes a cyclical form: an action begins quietly, rises in volume and harmonic tension, breaks off, and resumes. The cyclic form in itself is not suggested by any structure in the poem, but it makes an apt musical analogue to the obsessive workings of a jealous mind. Obsessiveness is also portrayed within the first cycle (mm. 1–57) by a tonic pedal (on A) that is maintained for most of the cycle, through a tremendous crescendo and through most of the compact exposition of themes and textures. The second cycle (mm. 57–152) represents a more frantic stage in the same mental process: it begins, abruptly, a half-step higher than the first cycle, it moves to and from pedal points several times, and it takes twice as long over the same themes as the first cycle.

The third cycle (mm. 153–225), while maintaining the triplet figure without break, is otherwise different in content and form from the other two; it represents a new stage in the general's actions. The pedal points and the self-mirroring scale theme are not heard again, but the triplet figure takes over their functions, becoming an ostinato figure that mirrors itself (see Example 9-2), so that it now represents the general impatiently standing, giving orders.

The orders are heard in the form of phrases for the bass clarinet, marked *forte ma espressivo quasi parlando,* and Tchaikovsky provides for the "speaking" quality by giving those phrases the rhythms of interjections (see Example 9-2). While these musical phrases do not

Example 9-2. Tchaikovsky, *Voevoda,* Op. 78, mm. 181–88.

exactly fit the rhythms of the gruff phrases that Pushkin puts into the general's mouth, they are comparably short, abrupt, and uneven lines, evoking the general's voice. By phrase rhythm alone Tchaikovsky marks the general's interjections apart from both the scurrying movement before and the strophic love plaint that follows.

The poem makes a revolving-stage transition, as it were, between the general's scene and the love scene: the reader follows the general and his servant crawling into the garden and sees the wife and lover through their eyes before hearing the lover's words to her. Tchaikovsky's transition follows this model closely. After the general's last phrase, the scurrying triplet figure is slowed to a crawl (mm. 219–25), and the scene is changed (mm. 226–36) to the sounds of the harp and celesta (a newly invented instrument that Tchaikovsky was using here for the first time). A new, slower tempo is established, and the appearance of the new characters is represented by the introduction of one of their themes (mm. 239–71), not yet "sung" in full, but tried out by the woodwinds against unsettled harmonies and a new pedal point (E-flat).

The love scene proper—the lover's speech to the wife—begins with a different theme, in a new key (E minor): the theme for violas and bassoon marked *cantabile, con passione* (mm. 276–90; see Example 9-3). It is a theme that only Tchaikovsky could write, in a quietly intense setting that perfectly fits the lover's self-absorbed opening lines, leaving room for heavier effects later in his speech. Nevertheless, the theme has been criticized, beginning with Taneiev, who wrote:

> It seems to me that the device that Piotr Ilich used in the composition of the middle part is incorrect. It is possible to sing the words of the

Pushkin ballad to this melody, as for instance: [here Taneiev puts the line "Ne iskal on, ne stradal on" (He didn't search, he didn't suffer) to the first eight notes of the melody in Example 9-3]. Evidently the middle part was composed not as an orchestral work, but as a romance. This romance performed by orchestral instruments without words makes a somewhat undefined impression and loses much in this form.

Example 9-3. Tchaikovsky, *Voevoda,* Op. 78, mm. 276–83.

A similar response to the music has led Henry Zajaczkowski, in a recent study, to a different interpretation. He describes the "central episode" as "purposely non-indulgent, rather plain 'love-music' (for it pertains not to a new and growing affection, but to a former love that now seems to be in ruins, however involved the young man obviously still is)."[8] Without conceding that the music is either "undefined" or "plain," we can recognize that these two statements raise crucial questions about the central episode of *Voevoda*. Though there is no reason to credit Taneiev's speculation that Tchaikovsky originally wrote this part of the work "as a romance" (to be sung), there is every reason to think that he had Pushkin's lines in mind as he wrote his themes. It is not only the first phrase of the music that fits Pushkin's poetic structure: Tchaikovsky's whole "speech" for the lover consists of three different themes, each forming a rounded musical strophe, just as Pushkin's speech consists of three poetic strophes. Moreover, he follows Pushkin in the shape of the whole episode: a strophic speech by the lover, followed by a moment of wordless exchange between the lover and the wife. (In Tchaikovsky's music, as in the poem, the wife has no lines of her own to speak). The episode is distinct from the rest of the work in its themes (Zajaczkowski writes that the absence of the general's scurrying music in this section "conveys the two young people's complete unawareness of their potentially dire circumstances"[9]). This distinctness is underlined by the structure of the themes: in the themes of this one episode of the *ballade*, Tchaikovsky has imitated the strophic structure of the poem, giving the impression of a speech—or, as Taneiev would have it, a romance—within the narrative.[10] The lover's speech stands out as the one sustained utterance in both the poem and the music.

Though the themes of that speech are all strophic, Tchaikovsky distinguishes them from one another in character, in the rhythms of their lines, and even in the number of lines, and he makes a more elaborate speech than Pushkin by bringing some of the themes back in new versions. The first strophic theme, in E minor, is followed without transition by the more passionate second strophic theme (mm. 290-311), in D major, played by the oboe. Because this was the theme previewed in the transition to this episode, it now seems to have a special significance in the lover's appeal to his beloved. The first theme then returns in E minor (mm. 312-25), this time given more urgency by a violin accompaniment of abrupt, short scales.

This theme is extended (mm. 326-33), and the extension accelerates into the third strophic theme (*Allegro moderato*, mm. 334-57, still in E minor), which hardly seems to belong to the same speech as the first two, its character is so unimpassioned and its color so bright. Yet it is the theme that most perfectly fits the rhythmic structure of the Pushkin strophe. Perhaps the bright tone represents the lover's ironic wish of "many years, much mirth" to his beloved "in her new household," and, if so, the bassoons' sinister chromatic scale, which interrupts this theme, could suggest the bitterness implicit in that wish. The theme is rounded out by another extension of the first strophic theme (mm. 358-61), then followed by a final version of the second strophic theme (mm. 361-84), now in E-flat major. This richly scored version, its melody carried by the strings in triple octaves, is the climax of the lover's speech. If even this version sounds "rather plain," it does so because Tchaikovsky is still keeping something in reserve for the wordless exchange that follows.

That passage (*Allegro giusto*, mm. 385–425) is marked apart from the lover's speech by its contrapuntal texture and its phrasing—a single long phrase that sequences endlessly higher. Both features signal a change from the representation of words to the representation of the wordless feelings that overwhelm the lover and the wife when he finishes his words. From Pushkin's single, simple line about the wife—"The young lady weeps and grieves"—Tchaikovsky creates a memorable musical image of sobbing and distress (*Moderato*, mm. 402–25): at first G-major and F-sharp major triads alternate in rising and falling arpeggios, and then D-major and F-sharp major triads alternate in uneven rhythms. This passage can hardly be said to make an "undefined impression."

The series of major triads is brought to an end by a single diminished-seventh chord (*Allegro vivacissimo*, m. 426). The diminished-seventh sonority, characteristic of the opening episode of the work, has been virtually excluded from the middle episode, so that this one chord signals the beginning of a new episode. The signal is reinforced a few measures later by the return of the scurrying figure (m. 430). The new episode, relying on the language of references developed in the first episode, is extremely compact. The bass clarinet again represents the general giving orders, this time answered by flute and clarinet, representing the protests of the servant (mm. 434–53). The scurrying figure becomes both faster and quieter as the two take aim (mm. 454–69), and the tense quiet is broken with a tremendous jolt by a chord that marks the shot with which the servant kills the general (m. 470). The remaining moments (mm. 471–510) are filled with stark chords denoting his death.

David Brown aptly notes that these chords "look forward to the world of the Sixth Symphony."[11] To notice the resemblance is to feel the tragic tone that Tchaikovsky brought to the death of the general in *Voevoda*. In doing so he was departing from the literary model he had followed devotedly up to this point. Pushkin's narrator mocks the general's death by mocking his own truthfulness: "It seems the servant's shot went wrong." In contrast, the original version by Mickiewicz, while sensational, is not mocking: "The poor Cossack took aim, the lone blast would not wait, / He fired his gun straight—at the general's head!"[12]

Tchaikovsky, in taking the death seriously, is not faithful to Pushkin's tone, but he is faithful in his own way to the structure of the story that Mickiewicz and Pushkin tell. In terms of the ballad process, the servant's shot is the act of reckoning in the story, and the servant's misaiming—shooting the general instead of the wife—demonstrates that the act of defiance which initiates the ballad process is not the surreptitious meeting of the wife and lover, but the general's defiance of nature in marrying a wife much younger than himself. Pushkin counts on a single response from his readers to that defiance of nature: he portrays the general unsympathetically and the lover and wife sympathetically, and he makes light of, and thereby justifies, the servant's shooting of his master. Tchaikovsky, by contrast, asks his listeners to consider the general's defiance of nature from both sides, to switch from sympathy for the lover and wife—a sympathy he evokes powerfully in the middle episode—to an equally strong sympathy for the general a few moments later.

Voevoda is a difficult work to appreciate fully, even in a persuasive performance.[13] But it would be wrong to blame the difficulty, as Taneiev did, on the themes of the love episode: they grow more compelling on successive hearings. The real difficulty is that Tchaikovsky followed the poem so literally—and with so many kinds of literalness—that the music makes extreme demands on its listeners as readers. One of his kinds of literalness— the most commonplace in program music—was to represent a gunshot with a sudden loud chord. Another kind—not so commonplace—was to follow the narrative progression of the poem practically line by line. Still another kind—with precedents in the *ballade* tradition—was to represent different voices within the narrative by imitating the phrase rhythms and verse structures of the poem. Tchaikovsky's most sophisticated kind of literalness in *Voevoda* was to expect his listeners to follow the poem so closely that, recognizing his one departure from literal imitation of the poem, they turn their sympathies to the general once he is shot.

Within the *ballade* tradition, the literalness of Tchaikovsky's *Voevoda* presents the maximum contrast to the nonspecific narration of the Chopin Ballades. But even when the methods of imitation are most contrasted, the identity of the ballad as a genre creates resemblances: Tchaikovsky, like Chopin, uses strophic themes to represent a speaking voice, though it is the passionate voice of a character rather than the dispassionate voice of a narrator; and Tchaikovsky's ending, like Chopin's, is an abrupt and violent reckoning with elements of his opening music. Tchaikovsky's literal response to the text of Pushkin's "Voevoda" is a literalness specific to the ballad genre, and it is no accident that in that direct response to the poetic text, his *Voevoda* is more closely related to the four orchestral *ballades* of Dvořák, written several years later, than to other programmatic works of his own.

Liapunov, A. S. Taneiev, and Glazunov

In *Voevoda* Tchaikovsky concentrated on the action of his poetic model, giving hardly any attention to the setting. In the international tradition of orchestral *ballades*, that is not at all unusual. But it would be surprising to find a similar concentration in all Russian orchestral *ballades* of the period, when Russian program music in general was filled with scene-painting, and especially with exotic color. In Rimsky-Korsakov's symphonic suite *Sheherazade* (1889), for example, the exotic scene-painting gets the better of the action, though the narrative frame supplements the action of the stories with an action of its own. Equally exotic in setting, but closer to a ballad in its story, is the influential symphonic poem *Tamara* (1884) by Mily Balakirev (1837–1910). The poem by Lermontov, based on Georgian legend, is a kind of Caucasian "Loreley," telling of a queen who lured men to her castle with irresistible song, made love to them, then killed them. Balakirev's version, full of Oriental effects, is more atmospheric than narrative. The Orientalism of this work has no echo in Russian orchestral works that bear the title "Ballade": Russian composers seem to have associated the word with Russian rather than with Oriental folklore. But the programmatic mode that *Tamara* exemplifies—a narration enveloped in scene-painting and atmosphere— prevails in Russian orchestral *ballades* except for Tchaikovsky's.

The Ballade, Op. 2,[14] by Sergei Liapunov (1859–1924), for instance, begins and ends in a dreamy atmosphere. Liapunov was finishing his studies with Tchaikovsky and others at the Moscow Conservatory when he wrote the first version of this work in 1883. But he had gone on to study with Balakirev in St. Petersburg and to collect folk songs in the field with Balakirev and Liadov by 1896, when he finished revising it. Nothing in the score of his Ballade indicates that he used authentic folk songs or drew on a particular ballad story in this work. But the opening theme in particular (see Example 9-4) is strongly colored by the influence of Russian folk song.

The melody expands on a tiny, folklike motive in a rhythm determined by that motive rather than by the meter. The accompaniment adds to the evocation of folk song: a pedal point, a countermelody that mirrors the melody, and a cadence on an open fifth. The somber atmosphere of this opening could foretell a tragic ballad story, but that atmosphere is gradually dispelled as the melody is transposed to higher and brighter keys. The opening of the Ballade sets a scene: the folklike theme suggests it is an open-air scene, and the rising progression suggests a gradual awakening or coming to life. This episode gives way to a more active one, with a bustling new theme (based on the motive of the opening theme) and contrapuntal combinations of all the themes. Liapunov seems to be concentrating the action of his story into this middle section. The ending of the Ballade, a reminiscence on the most sentimental of the themes, is completely removed from action.

If a dreamy ending seems unusual for a *ballade*, Liapunov may have been influenced not only by a Russian tradition of atmospheric program music, but also by new trends in literary ballads. Dreamy endings were characteristic of late nineteenth-century poems that, though they sometimes took the name "ballad," were based in a new way on folk poetry. These were short poetic narratives that conjured up an incident in the life of a hero known from a traditional epic. A "ballad" of this type by the poet, dramatist, and novelist Alexei Tolstoy (1817–1875) provided the model for an orchestral *ballade* by Alexander Taneiev (1850–1918)—the uncle of Sergei Taneiev—a student of

Example 9-4. Liapunov, Ballade, Op. 2, mm. 1-9.

Rimsky-Korsakov and an important administrator in the Russian government who at the same time had an impressive career as a composer. Taneiev's Ballade, published in Moscow and Leipzig in 1907, has title pages in both Russian and French; in Russian the title is given as *Aleša Popovič: Musical Episode...on the Subject of the Poem by Count A. K. Tolstoy*, while in French it is given as *Ballade, After a Poem (Aliocha Popowitch) by Count A. Tolstoy*.[15]

Aleša Popovič is the hero of several medieval Russian *byliny* (epic songs). Alexei Tolstoy's poem relates an episode in which Aleša Popovič abducts a princess and, while carrying her down a river in his boat, seduces her by his marvelous singing. The poem provides the composer with rich musical opportunities: the legendary tone, the gentle movement of the waves, Aleša's harp-playing and singing, the seduction, and the "silence of the river" that "embraces the boat" at the end. Taneiev responded to each of these opportunities with a passage in a different melodic style, harmonic language, rhythm, and orchestral color. The work is notable not so much for these passages individually (Aleša's song, in the manner of Rimsky-Korsakov, is lovely, but hardly seductive) as for the contrasts among them, and

Example 9-5. Glazunov, Ballade, Op. 78, mm. 1–20.

especially for the ending, in which the music of the waves gradually stills all memory of song and passion.

The Ballade, Op. 78,[16] by Alexander Glazunov (1865-1936), another pupil of Rimsky-Korsakov, has a similar ending, but otherwise shows an entirely different conception of the genre. The title page gives no suggestion of a literary model, and the music gives no suggestion of narrative. Its simple ternary form places the work more naturally in the lyrical tradition of piano *ballades* than in any tradition of orchestral *ballades*. But the atmosphere of the music fits into an orchestral tradition: just as Sibelius or Liadov might have done, Glazunov uses a still, repeating viola figure to evoke a magical, nocturnal scene (see Example 9-5).

Within this atmosphere he maintains a beautifully consistent texture, with melodic phrases that play endlessly on appoggiaturas and with a counterpoint of voices that endlessly creates cross-relationships. The middle section has as much continuity as contrast with the opening section, and the work as a whole seems to present an imagined moment rather than an entire action. The musical depiction of imaginary scenes, a practice carried out lavishly in *Sheherazade* and *Tamara*, is perfectly distilled in this Ballade.

CZECHOSLOVAKIA

Fibich, *Toman a lesní panna*

"Toman a lesní panna" ("Toman and the Wood Nymph") is the lead poem in the collection *Echoes of Czech Songs* (1839)[17] by František Ladislav Čelakovský (1799-1852). Čelakovský's folk-song imitations are said to have influenced many branches of subsequent Czech poetry,[18] and the vivid ballad "Toman" inspired two symphonic poems by important Czech composers, the first by Zdeněk Fibich (1850-1900), written thirty-five years after the poem was published, and the second by Vítězslav Novák (1870-1949), written a comparable period later.

The poem tells of a young man who rides off on a summer evening to see his sweetheart, heeding his sister's warning that he should avoid the route through the forest. Arriving at his sweetheart's house, he learns she has rejected him in favor of another suitor. Pale and dejected, he sets out for home at midnight, this time riding through the woods, ignoring his sister's warning and thereby committing the act of defiance that seals his doom. The beautiful wood nymph approaches him on a deer, sings seductively as she rides beside him, and finally takes him into her fatal embrace.

The Czech tradition of orchestral *ballades* began in 1875 with the symphonic poem on "Toman"[19] by Fibich, who led the way for Czech musicians in several genres. His decision to write an orchestral *ballade* accords with his taste for ballads as texts or subjects of songs, opera, and melodrama, and his treatment of the erotic passages of "Toman" foreshadows the later operatic and piano music associated with his love for his pupil, Anežka Schulzová.[20] His extremely literal treatment of Čelakovský's poem was noted by the Czech music critic Václav Novotný in an analytical article published in 1874, before the work was even finished;[21] that literalness set the course for all later Czech composers of orchestral *ballades*.

Fibich's music is not literal in the sense that his themes are tailored to the rhythms of Čelakovský's lines; in fact, two of the themes are preexisting melodies, chosen for their associations rather than their form. Instead, Fibich follows the progression of the poem step by step, so that, as Novotný showed, every passage of the music can be connected to a passage of the poem. As in Dukas's *The Sorcerer's Apprentice*, there is a virtually unchanging theme that represents the most important act of speech in the story: the warning given by Toman's sister not to go through the woods.[22] Other themes, which are subjected to more development, represent characters, actions, feelings, and scenes. These themes include the two preexisting melodies: the festivities at the home of Toman's sweetheart are represented by the melody of a Czech folk dance, and the wood nymph is represented by a melody from a song Fibich had written when he was sixteen, a setting of Heine's "Sommerabend," which tells of a man who comes upon a nymph in the moonlit woods.[23]

Through most of this work, then, Fibich's method is to narrate through a series of short vignettes, each created from discrete musical material. The vignette of seduction at the end, however, works on a different principle and derives considerable power from that change: themes from throughout the work now combine and evolve in a long, breathless passage of impassioned music (see Example 9-6).

Example 9-6. Fibich, *Toman a lesní panna,* Op. 49, mm. 373-94.

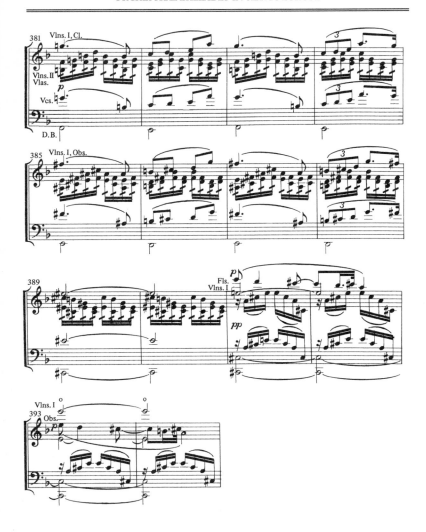

Dvořák, Four Symphonic Poems on Ballads by Erben

Dvořák's four symphonic poems of 1896[24] are based on ballads from the collection *Kytice* (*The Garland*), first published in 1853, by Karel Jaromír Erben (1811–1870). Erben far surpassed Čelakovský in his knowledge of Czech folk song: he had already published the words and melodies of hundreds of Czech folk songs in his own transcriptions by the time he published *Kytice*. His works—both the folk-song transcriptions and his literary ballads based in part on Czech folk songs—were of the greatest interest to Czech composers, especially Fibich and Dvořák. Fibich wrote two concert melodramas on ballads from *Kytice: Štědrý den (Christmas Day)*, published in 1880, and *Vodník (The Water Goblin)* in 1883. Soon afterward, in 1885, Dvořák composed his dramatic cantata *Svatební košile* (usually referred to in English as *The Spectre's Bride*), also on a ballad from *Kytice*. And for the first of his symphonic poems on Erben ballads he chose a text that Fibich had already used for one of his melodramas: "The Water Goblin." For a period of two decades, then, Fibich and Dvořák took turns, in effect, writing orchestral and vocal works based on Czech literary ballads (almost all from Erben's *Kytice*), beginning with Fibich's *Toman a lesní panna* (which Dvořák could have heard performed in 1878), and culminating in Dvořák's four orchestral *ballades* of 1896.[25]

The four Erben poems on which Dvořák based these works are classics of Czech poetry, but they are barely known elsewhere, and not all have been translated into English. Each poem tells a complex story, and Dvořák's music tenaciously follows the progressions of the stories and the language of the poetry. In fact, it would be hard to name any symphonic poem that follows such a complicated story in such detail as *The Golden Spinning Wheel*. That is not to say that the music cannot be appreciated without the poetry in one's head. Dvořák himself had the music published with summaries of the poems (in Czech, German, and English), rather than full texts and translations. But he also took pains to insure that listeners heard the exact points of correspondence between the stories and his music: he supervised the music critic who wrote the program notes for performances of the works in Vienna.[26] His concern does not seem misplaced. In Czechoslovakia, where the poetry itself is taken seriously, these symphonic poems have always been considered four of Dvořák's greatest works, while in other countries they are virtually unperformed, even though they are major orchestral works written by one of the most popular of orchestral composers at the height of his powers.

Clearly, if one is going to understand this music, one needs to begin by understanding the relation of the pieces to their poetic models, and the best preparation for understanding that relationship is the experience of studying other instrumental *ballades*. Furthermore, placing these works within the *ballade* tradition gives one a sense of what extraordinary works they are. For instance, a few earlier composers of *ballades*—such as Tchaikovsky—had shaped themes to conform to the rhythms of lines in their poetic models, but they had done so only at isolated moments in their *ballades*. Dvořák—as his sketches show[27]—did so systematically, so that at practically every stage in his musical narration, important lines of Erben's poetry are rendered in wordless song. This practice, together with Dvořák's faithfulness to the progression and details of the stories he is retelling, places his *ballades* at the extreme of literal representation within the *ballade* repertory.

In a sense, Dvořák's text-bound conception of the *ballade* is the antithesis of Chopin's. But in other respects, his four *ballades* are remarkably comparable to the four by Chopin. In fact, Dvořák was the only composer after Chopin to develop a scheme of thematic structures and thematic processes that characterizes a whole series of *ballades*, while allowing a distinctive musical form to each individual work in the series. Beyond that, Dvořák's is the only set of *ballades* that can stand comparison to Chopin's for beauty, variety, and dramatic power.

Dvořák's thematic scheme is as follows: each *ballade* begins with a musical episode that is complex in form, made up of motives that are subject to development and transformation throughout the work. Later episodes contain, besides those developing motives, autonomous themes—that is, themes that appear in just one form and at just one point in the work. The opening episode is rich in reference: a complex musical statement with large-scale repetitions or returns, it relates the whole first episode of the story. The motives within this musical episode are associated with particular characters in the story and in some cases represent utterances by those characters. When these motives return in readily recognizable form later in the *ballade*, they retain their association with those characters. But the same motives also reappear transformed—redefined, in a sense—and in these transformations they may carry new associations: in *The Golden Spinning Wheel*, as Otakar Šourek points out,[28] the motive representing the king in the first episode is transformed in later episodes to represent the wicked stepmother and the good sorcerer.

The autonomous themes of the later episodes almost all represent utterances by the characters. Many of them are fitted to lines of Erben's poetry representing words spoken—or in some cases sung—by the characters (as opposed to lines of the narrative voice). Some of these themes represent crucial actions accomplished through words. When the poem presents a dialogue of characters, Dvořák creates a dialogue of themes; and when the poetic dialogue takes the form of incremental repetition—the form typical of ballad dialogue—Dvořák subjects his dialogue of themes to varied repetition.

The following analysis of *The Water Goblin* demonstrates the workings of this scheme. Next, shorter commentaries on the other three *ballades* focus on the distinctive features of each.

The Water Goblin

The plot summary of *The Water Goblin* that appeared in German and English at the front of the original (1896) edition of Dvořák's score is given here in its English version (where the title is translated as *The Water-Fay*):[29]

> By the edge of the lake, in the pale moon-shine, the Water-Fay is sitting on a poplar-branch, making himself a coat of green, and shoes of red: he sings at his work, for to-morrow will be his wedding-day. On the

morrow, his chosen victim, a maiden from the village near, rises early from her bed, and says she must wash her clothes in the lake. In vain does her mother try to stay her, telling her of an evil dream she has had in the night; in vain does she warn her that to-day is Friday. Her daughter will not be dissuaded, and goaded on by an impulse she cannot resist, hurries down to the lake.

Scarcely has she dipped one little foot in the water, when the ground gives way beneath her, and the Water-Fay is heard clapping his hands for joy, as he sees his victim sink into the depths.

The maid becomes his wife. But drear and lonely to her are the deep recesses of the lake, where the Water-Fay holds prisoners the souls of drowned men and drowned women, and drear is the lullaby the poor girl sings to her babe, bewailing her own unhappy fate; for her heart is sick with longing for home, and with a passionate desire to see her mother.

The Water-Fay is enraged at her song, and, in his anger, threatens to turn her into a fish. She answers, she will herself turn to senseless stone, unless he give her permission to visit her mother at least once again. Wearied by her ceaseless entreaties, the Fay at last gives in, and sets her free for one day, to revisit the world above; the child he keeps as a pledge of her return. Sorrowful is the meeting between mother and daughter, and endless their tears and lamentations. As twilight comes on, a furious knocking is heard at the door: it is the Water-Fay, come to demand his wife's return. The mother scornfully refuses to let her go. Immediately a frightful storm rises over the lake: something is suddenly dashed with great violence against the door of the cottage: the mother opens it, and finds—the headless body of her daughter's child.

The story has a double ballad process. In the second of the four parts of the poem, there is a reckoning for the maiden's defiance of her mother's warning: she falls into the lake and into the clutches of the water goblin. In the third part of the poem the water goblin sets conditions for her visit to her mother: she not only has to leave her baby behind, but she is not to embrace anyone during her visit and she is to return to the water goblin before the sounding of vespers. These last two conditions, though not mentioned in the above summary, are crucial to the poem (and in turn to Dvořák's music) because it is the young woman's defiance of these conditions in the fourth and final part of the poem that brings on the second reckoning: the killing of her baby.

Dvořák turns the first two parts of the story—containing the first ballad process—into a single, large, symmetrical musical episode. The first section of this episode (*Allegro vivo*, mm. 1–126) represents the water goblin sitting by the lake singing of his coming wedding. A single motive is repeated and playfully developed (but with hardly any departure from its static B-minor harmony) throughout this section (see Example 9-7). Through the entire

Example 9-7. Dvořák, *The Water Goblin*, Op. 107, mm. 9–12.

work, in fact, this water-goblin motive is heard far more often and is transformed in far more ways than any other motive.

A new section, representing the scene between the maiden and her mother, opens with a change to the major mode, a slower tempo, and a folklike clarinet melody (*Andante sostenuto*, mm. 127–46; see Example 9-8).

Example 9-8. Dvořák, *The Water Goblin*, Op. 107, mm. 127–30.

The melody fits the words in which the maiden announces to her mother that she will go to the lake. The minor mode returns for the mother's response: another folklike melody, fitted to the words of the mother's warning and narration of her dream (mm. 151–96; see Example 9-9). These words are of special importance in the story because the daughter's defiance of this warning sets the story in motion, and Dvořák builds the music of the dialogue—and of the whole opening episode—symmetrically around the music of the mother's warning. Further, he gives that music a ritualistic force by presenting the melody three times (once for each verse of the mother's text) and setting the same chromatic counterpoint against it each time, while reorchestrating both the melody and the counterpoint. According to Leoš Janáček, who wrote full and admiring reviews of all four Dvořák *ballades*, the contrapuntal line gives this passage its warning tone, and even certain details of the orchestration illustrate points in the mother's narration.[30]

Example 9-9. Dvořák, *The Water Goblin*, Op. 107, mm. 151–58.

The daughter's defiance of the warning is signaled by the return of her theme, again in B major, more gorgeously scored than before, but now dogged—as Šourek points out[31]—by the distinctive rhythm of the water-goblin motive, ominously beaten on the timpani (mm. 197–216). This musical dialogue of daughter and mother, with its folklike melodies and its symmetries of theme and mode, has less of a speaking tone and more of a ritualistic form than any of the later dialogues in the work. The difference is explained as much by the function of this music in Dvořák's thematic scheme as by the nature of the words represented here. The melodies of this dialogue, even though they were created to fit the particular words spoken by the two characters at this moment in the story, reappear—as Dvořák's thematic scheme dictates—in later episodes, standing for new words. For that reason it makes sense that the themes of this first dialogue are memorable, songful melodies, easily identified with characters and not just with particular words.

At the very moment when this dialogue ends, Dvořák—according to his own account of the work[32]—indicates the daughter's fall into the lake with a loud crash at a deceptive cadence (m. 219). At this point the original tempo returns and the water-goblin motive is heard in a modulating passage—the first so far in the work—that leads, after a couple of falling whole-tone scales that suggest the daughter sinking in the water, to a full statement of the water goblin's theme in B minor (m. 263). Heard against a brass fanfare, that statement, in Dvořák's words, expresses the water goblin's "diabolical delight at having gained the victim who will become his wife." At the height of this statement the trombones introduce a version of the water-goblin motive played on the tonic note rather than the dominant (mm. 283-86). This is the version with which the episode ends (mm. 303-35)—on a quiet note depicting the restoration of calm to the lake—and also the version with which the entire work will end.

To writers beginning with Šourek [33] the return of the water-goblin motive in this scene and at later points justifies analyzing the work in rondo form. On this analysis the work has the peculiarity that modulation occurs only in returns of the rondo theme, while the other themes—the "episodes"—are all harmonically static and stay in the tonic, major or minor. Rondo-form analysis leads John Clapham to call the work as a whole "very strangely proportioned, and rather unsatisfactory."[34]

The tonal and thematic form become altogether more satisfactory when the rondo model is replaced by an analysis of the work as three episodes, of which the first has already been described here. The second and third episodes follow the same tonal plan as the first: they open in the tonic, have a modulating passage in the middle, and end with a full close in the tonic. Thematically, the three episodes have a kind of symmetry: the first and last use the mother's and daughter's themes as well as the water-goblin motive, while the middle episode has largely autonomous themes except for the latter motive. This analysis points up the close correspondence between Dvořák's musical structure and the narrative structure of Erben's poem, in which dialogues of the mother and daughter come before and after the central dialogue of the daughter and the water goblin.

Dvořák's most extraordinary music comes in the middle episode, the scene under the lake. This music is set apart from the rest of the work not only by its unique themes, but also by remarkable thematic processes and by otherworldly harmonies and instrumental colors. The corresponding part of the poem begins with six stanzas—the longest narrative passage in the poem—describing the "joyless, sorrowful" realm of the water goblin. Dvořák renders this passage with six musical stanzas that are alternating versions of the same descending chromatic melody (*Andante mesto come prima*, mm. 336-401). This melody in its original version (mm. 336-43) perfectly fits the words of the first stanza of the poetic passage; it is hardly remarkable in itself, though in its chromaticism it contrasts with the folklike melodies heard earlier. The alternating version (mm. 344-55) combines a chromatic passage of woodwind chords—a kind of harmonic abstract of the chromatic melody—with the water-goblin motive, played by pizzicato strings. When the fifth of these musical stanzas is reached (m. 376), the chromatic melody suddenly surges with feeling and movement, breaking out of the bounds of its original phrases. The poem also becomes heart-rending at the fifth stanza of this passage, announcing that those who enter the "crystal gate" of the lake will never see their loved ones again. The next stanza of the poem pictures the water goblin with his wife, now nursing their baby, and the corresponding musical stanza (mm. 390–401) combines the "joyless" chromatic chords with two simultaneous versions of the water-goblin motive—a weird, three-part texture for the unhappy family of three (see Example 9-10).

Example 9-10. Dvořák, *The Water Goblin*, Op. 107, mm. 390–401.

The tempo relaxes (*Un poco più lento e molto tranquillo*), and a shimmering dominant-seventh chord from the muted strings introduces the wife's lullaby (mm. 404-45). The idea of singing, as opposed to speaking, may be suggested by the folklike quality of the main motive (mm. 408-11); but what the passage really makes vivid is not so much the woman's medium of expression as the complexity of her words and feelings. Successive short phrases express her warmth toward her smiling baby (mm. 412-13), as Dvořák's note in his sketch attests, and her yearning to return to her mother (mm. 414-15). For each new stanza, the lullaby settles down by a half-step on a rich new dominant chord, and this harmonic movement, coming after so much static tonic harmony, makes the lullaby marvelously expressive.

The words that the wife sings enrage her husband and touch off a long dialogue between the two. The water goblin's rage erupts on exactly the same deceptive-cadence progression (mm. 446-50) that had earlier indicated the maiden's fall into the lake. The water-goblin motive is heard throughout this passage and continues as a complement to a new phrase that fits the two stanzas of the water goblin's menacing speech to his wife: "What are you singing, my wife? I do not want your song!" (mm. 464-75; see Example 9-11).

Example 9-11. Dvořák, *The Water Goblin*, Op. 107, mm. 464-66.

Even richer in texture is the wife's reply (*Andante e molto tranquillo*; *Tempo primo maestoso*; mm. 476-508). In the poem this reply—her plea to be allowed to leave the lake and visit her mother—is eight stanzas long, and its urgency could hardly have been conveyed by the means Dvořák used elsewhere in this work: repeating a musical theme once for each new stanza of the poetic speech. In this case, instead, he telescopes the speech, starting with a French horn phrase fitted to her words (mm. 476-79) and adding other phrases—not all fitted to the words—in counterpoint as the first phrase continues. The resulting density of texture suggests not only the urgency of her words, but also the tension between the two characters. In fact, the water-goblin motive is heard beneath the wife's phrases, and her phrases themselves begin to resemble phrases of his: in a new scalar melody of the wife's (mm. 492-95; see Example 9-12), though its first (ascending) phrase is derived from a bass line in her lullaby (mm. 414-15), its second (descending) phrase is very close to the second phrase of the water goblin's menacing words, heard just before (see Example 9-11).[35] This extraordinary moment in the dialogue can only be taken as intentionally confusing, a musical depiction of the moment in an argument when the words and voices of two people in conflict become indistinguishable.

Example 9-12. Dvořák, *The Water Goblin,* Op. 107, mm. 492–95.

The water goblin closes the argument by asserting his authority. Over a portentous dominant pedal, the theme of his previous menacing speech is heard again (*Più mosso,* mm. 509–21), but this time standing for new words: his permission to his wife to visit her mother, under harsh conditions. This speech and the whole middle episode are capped, like the first episode, by a triumphant version of the water-goblin motive (*Andante maestoso meno mosso quasi Tempo primo,* mm. 534–37), but this time the tone of triumph, in B major rather than B minor, is luridly mocking. After that, the music dies away, as the first episode did, to a quiet close on the tonic, while a fragment from the wife's first melody (clarinets and English horn, mm. 542–46), which originally signified her departure for the lake, now signifies her return from it.

Janáček singled out this middle episode—or, more precisely, the lullaby and ensuing dialogue that make up most of it—as unprecedented for "precision, clarity, and truthfulness" in the representation of speech by means of instrumental music.[36] Dvořák's representational means were not in themselves unprecedented. Janáček was especially interested, for his own purposes, in Dvořák's shaping of melodies to fit poetic lines. But that practice can be found in many earlier works, and in imitating the stanza structures of the speeches in Erben's poem, Dvořák was following the practice of Tchaikovsky's *Voevoda* and even, in a way, of Chopin's Ballades. Dvořák's faith in these practices, however, was certainly remarkable. In the middle episode of *The Water Goblin*, faced with a stretch of poetry made up entirely of long speeches, he modeled his musical structures unyieldingly on the verse structures of those speeches, turning the very strictness of control—the repetitiveness of phrases and phrase-lengths—into a source of dramatic power.

The third and final episode is constructed on very different and in a sense more conventional principles. The scene opens at the end of the daughter's visit to her mother, and Dvořák represents this opening by bringing back the melodies of the daughter and mother from the first episode, now arranged into a phrase-by-phrase dialogue and given a new character (*Lento assai*, mm. 549–81). This time, though, there is no exact correspondence between poetic lines and musical phrases, in part because Erben's poetry has a different meter at this point.[37] Instead, by recollecting melodies from the first episode, Dvořák dramatizes the change in the lives of both daughter and mother since they last spoke together. The musical procedure here could be described as thematic transformation, but transformation of a whole dialogue of themes rather than of a single theme.

The following section (*Allegro vivace*, mm. 590–755), which brings the story to its final reckoning, has no stanza structure and no stable key; it is by far the longest stretch of such music in the work. In this section of the poem, the dialogue comes in shorter, more rushed exchanges than before—the fearful daughter pleading to be allowed to go back to the lake, the mother insisting that she stay, then the water goblin, outside their house, demanding that the daughter return to him, and the mother ordering him to be gone. Dvořák uses motives already associated with the characters to represent these brief utterances: the daughter is represented by her pleading scalar theme from the middle episode (mm. 598–601, etc.), the mother by a transformed motive from her narration in the first episode (cellos and basses, mm. 622–33), and the water goblin by a motive from his menacing theme in the middle episode (horns, mm. 660–69, etc.). At the same time, Dvořák introduces motives to represent "sound effects"—sounding actions in the episode: the storm rising over the lake (cellos and basses, mm. 602–05, etc.), the bells ringing for vespers (bell, mm. 634–55), and the knocking of the water goblin on the mother's door (violas and cellos, mm. 658–59, etc.).

All these motives are brought together in a progression that is seamless and frenetic, but not confused or formless. It is organized into complexes of motives, each of which is heard and then subjected to incremental repetition: each repetition is usually a step higher and somewhat changed. The first of these complexes (mm. 590–657) represents the daughter pleading with her mother, while the storm rises and then the bells are heard. The second (mm. 658–721) represents the water goblin's knocking and the rising voices of the daughter and the water goblin. After that the music has reached such a frenzy that only fragments of motives are heard, until a powerful transformation of the water-goblin motive (mm. 734–47) leads into the four chords of reckoning (mm. 748–52), representing the baby's head and body being severed and hurled against the door by the water goblin.

Dvořák arrives at this horrifying climax by exactly the means that Chopin uses in the endings of his Ballades: furious energy, breathless phrasing, and fragmented motives (instead of whole restated themes) throughout the *Allegro vivace* section. But Dvořák moves beyond that climax to an elaborate and subdued resolution unlike anything in the Chopin Ballades. This final section (*Andante sostenuto*, m. 756 to the end) represents the aftermath of the murder, but musically it is no coda: the last of the reckoning chords (m. 752) has brought the music back to the dominant of B minor, and the *Andante sostenuto* section, after a long dominant pedal, gives the final episode—and the entire work—its resolution in that tonic key.

With this section Dvořák also brings Erben's story to its completion. The mother opens her door to find the body of her daughter's child, and Dvořák signifies the fulfillment of the mother's dire dream with a gasping transformation of her theme, played by English horn and bass clarinet (mm. 760–80). But Dvořák also alters and extends the story, as his own account attests.[38] Whereas Erben ends with a gruesome description of the baby's corpse, Dvořák moves from the mother's dream to the daughter's grief (a new line for oboes, mm. 780–88) and ends with the water goblin disappearing into the lake (the chords of the water goblin's realm from the middle episode at mm. 788–96, then the water-goblin motive by itself to the end).

Dvořák's focus on the water goblin at the end is strangely moving. Both narratively and musically it completes the parallel between the first episode and the third: at the end of both episodes the water-goblin motive repeats and dies away, rising like an air bubble, to represent the character's disappearance into the lake. This parallel gives the work a satisfying symmetry; but given Dvořák's amazing fidelity to Erben's poem in the earlier parts of the work, his departure from the poem at the end deserves to be

Zlatý kolovrat.

I.

kolo lesa pole lán,
hoj jede, jede z lesa pán,
na vraném, bujném jede koni,
vesele podkovičky zvoní,
jede sám a sám.

A před chalupou s koně hop!
a na chalupu: klop, klop, klop!
„Hola hej! otevřte mi dvéře,
zbloudil jsem při lovení zvěře;
dejte vody pít!"

Vyšla dívčina jako květ,
neviděl také krásy svět;
přinesla vody ze studnice,
stydlivě sedla u přeslice,
předla, předla len.

— 23 —

understood as more than a device of musical form.

Dvořák's narrative emphasis is in fact different from Erben's throughout the final episode. Erben gives more lines to the mother in that episode than to the daughter and water goblin together, and the discovery of the baby's body by the mother confirms that the driving force of the entire story, in his version, is the mother-daughter conflict, for which the mother bears at least half the guilt. But in Dvořák's final episode, the mother's voice is heard very little, and the return of the water goblin to his own realm at the end confirms that in Dvořák's reading of the story the driving force—the defiance of nature that engenders the ballad process—has been the intrusion by both the daughter and the water goblin into realms where they do not belong. If Dvořák's ending amounts to a reinterpretation of Erben's story, it is a reinterpretation that keeps the story true in its own way to the ballad tradition, since it is common in ballads for the act of reckoning to produce a restoration of the natural order.[39]

The Noon Witch, The Golden Spinning Wheel, and *The Wild Dove*

Dvořák wrote his four symphonic poems on Erben ballads in quick succession: within two weeks of sketching *The Water Goblin*, he sketched *The Noon Witch* and *The Golden Spinning Wheel*, and a few months after orchestrating those works he composed *The Wild Dove*.[40] In all these *ballades* he adhered to the thematic scheme he established in *The Water Goblin*. Beyond that, there is no feature of musical form common to all four works. In fact, Dvořák's four *ballades*, designed in response to four specific poetic models, have greater variety in musical form than the four Chopin Ballades.

In *The Noon Witch* Dvořák was faced with a poem[41] that is not only the shortest of the four by far, but so compact that it moves immediately from the act of defiance to the act of reckoning: a mother, annoyed by the cries of her child when she is trying to do her chores, threatens to call on, and finally does call on, the noon witch to take the child away. In the very next line, to the mother's horror, the witch appears, ready to claim the child. Dvořák expands the narration by repetitions, and these repetitions, without altering the significance of the story, determine the musical form of the work. In the poem, for instance, the mother's rising irritation is traced in a single sequence; but Dvořák makes a repeating episode of it, a repeated exposition in which the repetition reinforces the opposition between the opening music of "the child playing quietly," in C major, and that of the scolding mother, in A minor.[42]

This opposition is reconciled only in the last six measures of the work, when melodic and harmonic motives of the child's music reappear transformed—along with the witch's motive—in A minor. Repetition also allows Dvořák to turn two lines of dialogue, in which the witch and the mother contend over the child's fate, into a powerful dramatic scene; the drama comes precisely from the repeated alternation between the chilling music of the witch and the emotional pleading of the mother. At the end of the work Dvořák expands the narration by adding rather than repeating: after depicting the return of the father to find his wife in a faint and his child dead, Dvořák adds music to express the father's agitation (*Maestoso*, mm. 487–91). But though the phrase has no direct source in Erben's poem, this addition, unlike the one Dvořák made at the end of *The Water Goblin*, is perfectly in keeping with the sensationalism of Erben's ending.

The third of Dvořák's *ballades*, *The Golden Spinning Wheel*, is based on a poem in which Erben crossed the ballad with the fairy tale.[43] The characters come from the world of the fairy tale: the young king who falls in love with the spinning maid, Dornička, whose stepmother and stepsister stab her and leave her for dead so that the king will marry the stepsister instead, mistaking her for Dornička. The magic in the story is also more like fairy-tale magic than ballad magic: a wizard finds the dismembered Dornička, buys back her feet, hands, and eyes from the stepsister, and revives her, and his golden spinning wheel sings a song that reveals to the king his false wife's identity and her crime. The "fairy-tale element," Milada Součkova writes, "determines the whole structure of the ballad."[44] At the same time, the crux of the action allows the story to be called a ballad: the stabbing of Dornička is an act in defiance of the king and of nature, producing its act of reckoning in the form of the spinning wheel's song, which reunites the king with the true Dornička.

As the poem is a ballad with the length and episodic complexity of a fairy tale, Dvořák's *Golden Spinning Wheel* is the longest and richest of his orchestral *ballades*. It is constructed on the same principles as *The Water Goblin*: in the first episode he introduces the motives associated with the main characters and most subject to transformation later,[45] and throughout the work he shapes themes and phrases according to the sound patterns of Erben's lines, so that the list of such themes and phrases is even longer here than in *The Water Goblin*.[46] The first episode, as in *The Noon Witch*, is repeated; but here the repetition is substantially altered, so that the whole repeated musical episode represents the incremental repetition in the opening of the poem: the king rides to Dornička's cottage once by chance and falls in love with her, then rides there again the next day to ask her stepmother's permission to marry her. The succeeding episodes, each itself divided into sections in different rhythms, keys, and characters, represent dialogues structured by incremental repetition, as well as actions in dance and song: the dialogue of Dornička with her stepmother and stepsister leading up to the stabbing; the dance music celebrating the unsuspecting king's marriage to the stepsister; their love music; the negotiations in which the wizard's boy sells the stepsister the golden spinning wheel in exchange for Dornička's missing eyes and limbs; and the song the spinning wheel sings to the king.

In the final episode, it is a lovely touch of irony, and not just a musical rounding off, that the love music of the king and the false Dornička (mm. 662–85) comes back unchanged (except that it is slightly shortened) to mark the restoration of the true Dornička to the king (mm. 988–1005). The whole work, despite its length, is astonishing for its compression, and that compression enables Dvořák to narrate the dauntingly complex story clearly and compellingly: utterance after utterance and scene after scene are evoked in close succession with the deft, vivid strokes of an operatic master.

One episode in the work deserves separate mention here because it has prompted controversy among earlier writers. This is the episode that writers since Janáček have called the "grisly" or "diabolical" or "demonic" scherzo,[47] the scene (*Molto vivace*, mm. 334–576) in which the stepmother and stepsister dress Dornička for her wedding and then stab her on the way to the king's castle. As Antonín Sychra has demonstrated, this music epitomizes Dvořák's method of reconciling narrative program with conventional musical form, since the episode is formally a scherzo, complete with repeats, embedded within the work, and at the same time it follows the third part of the poem stanza for stanza, almost line for line. At the moment of the stabbing, the motive of the king is sounded by trumpets and trombones, simultaneously in two different rhythms against the prevailing meter (mm. 411–18), and Sychra maintains that it is impossible to tell from the music whether the motive here represents Dornička's dying thought of the king—Šourek's reading—or the murderesses' thoughts of their own royal futures. But if Dvořák is following the poem closely here, this appearance of the motive is surely best explained by the ironic words the stepmother and stepsister speak to Dornička as they stab her: "Rejoice now in your royal lord," and so on.

More peculiar, given Dvořák's method, is the little waltzing tune that appears soon afterwards (mm. 452–59, etc.; see Example 9-13). In its instrumentation as well as its notes, the tune is obviously close to the music that represents the song of the golden spinning wheel much later (mm. 856–67, etc.; see Example 9-13). Its appearance in the "scherzo" is peculiar because the poetic text makes no reference to the spinning wheel at that point. But Dvořák, sensitive to the structural correspondence between the stabbing and the revelation of the stabbing—sensitive, in effect, to the nature of the ballad process—plants his own reference to the spinning wheel to make the structure of the story clear in his music.

In *The Wild Dove*, the last of the four *ballades*, themes representing wordless musical sounds play a more important role than themes representing speech. The work opens with a funeral march, the sound to which a young widow accompanies her husband's body to the grave. The

Example 9-13. Dvořák, *The Golden Spinning Wheel,* Op. 109, mm. 452-55 (*above*) and mm. 856-59 (*below*).

long central episode is filled with dance music, representing the wedding festivities when she remarries. And in the last episode, Dvořák depicts the cooing of a wild dove over the first husband's grave (mm. 465-66, etc.), a sound that awakens the wife's remorse for having poisoned him and drives her to drown herself.[48]

There are two speaking episodes in the poem, but even these are one-sided dialogues. When the suitor proposes to the widow (*Allegro,* mm. 70-116), she does not respond to him, but takes three days to leave off grieving: Dvořák represents this change by twice transforming the melody of the funeral march into a dancing flute tune (*Andante, Tempo primo,* mm. 117-41). Likewise, when she hears the wild dove, her verbal response, scolding the dove (mm. 475-76), is less prominent than her nonverbal response, the workings of her guilt, represented by the return of the "curse motive" (mm. 467-73) that Dvořák had planted in the opening episode.[49] The limited musical reference to speech in *The Wild Dove* sets this *ballade* apart musically from the other three.

The funeral march at the opening is repeated, like the opening episodes of *The Noon Witch* and *The Golden Spinning Wheel,* but here too there is a difference. The funeral march theme modulates upward by a half-step as it proceeds, and the repetition, starting at the new tonal level (m. 20), again modulates upward by a half-step. In fact, modulation, especially upward by a half-step, is so pervasive throughout the work that it comes to stand for the changes, beyond human control, that are brought about by time—one of the themes of the poem.

The wedding music (*Molto vivace*; *Un poco meno mosso*; *Allegretto grazioso*, mm. 143–456), rich in styles and balanced by sectional returns, would make a splendid ballet scene. Taking off from just a few lines of the poem, this music goes its own way for much longer than any passage in Dvořák's three earlier *ballades*. But that is not to say he was forgetting about the poem or neglecting the narrative momentum here. The very length of the dance passage indicates the widow's suppression of her guilt for the time being. Suppression of guilt, as has been noted in earlier chapters of this study, is reflected in the lyrical or cheerful interludes of some instrumental *ballades*, including Chopin's. Though it hardly figures in the first three of Dvořák's *ballades*, in *The Wild Dove* he plays up the suppression of guilt, by the novel means of letting it determine the proportions of the whole work.

The most dramatic musical event in this *ballade* comes just after the woman, unable to suppress her guilt any longer, drowns herself. The funeral march is heard (*Andante, Tempo primo*, mm. 499–505) in nearly its original form (though without its original dotted-rhythm accompaniment), for the first time since the beginning. This musical return, like that of the love music in *The Golden Spinning Wheel*, gives force to the changed situation: this time the march music refers to the woman's own funeral. The return of the march music marks the beginning of what Dvořák himself called the "epilogue" of the work. Like the quiet ending of *The Water Goblin*, this epilogue is composed of themes and thematic fragments recalled and transfigured in the hushed aftermath of the reckoning—in this case the frenzied music of the woman's despair and suicide.

Eventually the themes of the work are stilled entirely, and a long passage of functionally unrelated chords begins, played by woodwinds (mm. 537–40). In character and construction, this passage is related to the famous chord progressions that open and close the *Largo* movement of Dvořák's "New World" Symphony. The chordal passage in *The Wild Dove*, connected by its harmonic fluidity to the earlier passages of chromatic modulation, serves as another reminder of Erben's theme of the inexorable changes wrought by time. But whereas Erben put that theme at the center of his poem, where it provides the mechanism of the ballad process, Dvořák refers to it—in harmonically fluid passages—throughout his work, even now after the ballad process is completed.

At this point Dvořák turns away from his human subject: the musical themes, connected to human figures and their affairs, all drop away. As the strings take the chord progression to its nonfunctional conclusion, the cooing of the wild dove is heard again, this time as a purely natural sound, since the story provides no human character to hear a message in it. In an ending unprecedented in the history of the instrumental *ballade*, Dvořák is depicting not so much the restoration of the natural order as the absorption of human tragedy into the processes of time and nature, which create their own peace beyond all reckoning. If the narrating voice in a folk ballad is traditionally detached emotionally from the story it tells, Dvořák achieves another kind of detachment here by moving beyond the events and characters of his story and resting his narration in clear-eyed contemplation.

Like Chopin, Dvořák belonged to a national culture that was largely ignored by the rest of Europe, and his orchestral *ballades*, like Chopin's piano *ballades*, can be considered nationalist works written for an international audience. Modeled on poems that were virtually unknown except to Czech readers, three of Dvořák's four *ballades* were first performed in London and Vienna.[50]

Dvořák's music, however, represents an utterly different solution to the dilemma from Chopin's. Not only is each of his *ballades* modeled on a particular poetic ballad, but each one clings to the sounds of the lines and the narrative progression of that ballad. Dvořák's project, then, was more presumptuous than Chopin's. He counted on his international audience to take an interest in his countryman Erben's poems in order to appreciate the music he based on those poems, just as a decade earlier he had counted on the same interest when he wrote his cantata on Erben's "The Spectre's Bride" and his oratorio on Vrchlický's "St. Ludmilla," both on commissions from England. This presumption, in both vocal and orchestral works, relied on the double nature of the stature he had achieved only after decades of patient work (at an age that Chopin never reached)—winning recognition throughout Europe for his instrumental works in the German tradition at the same time that he was contributing important operas, songs, and other works to the musical culture of his homeland. Among other major late nineteenth-century composers, only Tchaikovsky—belonging to a similarly isolated national culture—likewise proved himself in every available national and international medium, and he too ventured to write a text-bound symphonic work based on a Slavic ballad only when his reputation was long established abroad as well as in his own country.

To say that Dvořák expected his international audiences to take an interest in the Erben poems is to raise the question of how much attention he expected them to give the poems. He did not have the whole poems printed in the scores, even in Czech; and he did not reveal even to his Czech audiences how many of the melodies in his *ballades* he had fitted to Erben's lines, but left his citations of those lines buried in his sketches, as if that practice were a private self-indulgence. Furthermore, as the works were introduced to foreign audiences, he seems to have revised his expectations of how closely those audiences would follow the stories. For the first Viennese performances of *The Water Goblin* and *The Noon Witch*, he sent Robert Hirschfeld, who was writing the program notes, detailed accounts of the poetic programs with musical illustrations.[51] But later, for *The Wild Dove*, he seems to have sent Hirschfeld a briefer description;[52] and for *The Golden Spinning Wheel*, the last of the four works to be performed in Vienna and the most complex in its relation to its poetic model, he sent Hirschfeld the poem with the following disingenuous comment:

> Just as in the case of "The Water Goblin," "The Noon Witch" and "The Wild Dove," I made no attempt to set the whole poem in terms of music, but merely the several *principal protagonists*, in order to express the *character* of its *poetic music*.[53]

This comment is perhaps best understood as Dvořák's attempt to protect himself from any more ridicule of the sort that Eduard Hanslick, the most important Viennese critic, had leveled at his other Erben *ballades*. Hanslick, who had long supported Dvořák as a symphonist following in the footsteps of Brahms, attacked the *ballades* on two grounds: he disliked Erben's poems (he was himself a native of Prague, but he had left long before and apparently never looked back), and he disliked Dvořák's step-by-step adherence to those poems (he said he feared Dvořák was following a "precipitous path" that led "straight to—Richard Strauss"[54]). Dvořák was mistaken to hope he could forestall criticism by denying the close relation of his music to the poems. The less attention one gives the poems, the more one is likely to agree with Hanslick that the music is "all interesting music-making, but bad narration,"[55] while the more intimately one studies the music in relation to the poetry, the stronger and clearer that music appears.

In choosing Czech poems for international audiences, Dvořák was wise to choose ballads, since the whole Western world had learned how to respond to ballads. Like Chopin, he was using a national genre that was at the same time a unifying element in Western culture. But, then as now, a composer who invoked the unity of Western culture was still powerless to make all its constituent national cultures equal in status, and listeners in many countries, following Hanslick's lead, have found Erben's ballads harder to approach and easier to dismiss than they would find ballads in another language. Dvořák, understanding this situation, did not evade it as Chopin had done, but wrote *ballades* that insist on the particulars of Erben's poetry. His triumph is in the musical realm that was within his power: in these works he makes it seem natural that the particular sounds and forms, as well as the themes, of poetry should yield the musical material and forms of a wordless musical narration.

Novák and Janáček

Three important Czech orchestral *ballades* followed Dvořák's in the first two decades of the twentieth century: *Toman a lesní panna* (*Toman and the Wood Nymph*)[56] (written in 1906-07) by Vítězslav Novák, and *The Fiddler's Child* (*Šumařovo dítě*)[57] (written in 1912) and *The Ballad of Blaník*[58] (written in 1920) by Leoš Janáček. Both composers were thoroughly familiar with Dvořák's *ballades*: Novák had been Dvořák's pupil; Janáček had reviewed and conducted those works. But at a time when almost all Czech composers were using Czech ballads as subjects or texts of musical works, Novák and Janáček were evidently responding to a broad stimulus, not just to Dvořák's example, and in fact their *ballades* depart from that example in several respects. In Janáček's case that departure was to some extent determined by his choice of subjects: modern (late nineteenth-century) ballads, as opposed to the classic ballads of Erben. But Novák departs in much the same way from Dvořák's compositional method, in spite of the fact that his subject is another classic ballad: the Čelakovský ballad on which Zdeněk Fibich had written his orchestral *ballade* of the same title decades earlier.

Actually, Novák's title page does not cite Čelakovský's version of *Toman a lesní panna*, but refers simply to "a Czech legend." And though it can be taken for granted that he knew the legend in Čelakovský's version, his way of citing his source gives a clue to his compositional method. Novák does not follow the poem episode by episode, as Fibich did, but instead concentrates on imagining the protagonist's psychological progression, to such an extent that he sacrifices the depiction of all but the basic external events and severely limits the representation of sounding actions. The warning by Toman's sister, for instance, which is the subject of the main theme in Fibich's *ballade* (see p. 244), is suggested in Novák's by only a "key-note" chord within the main theme, a discordant and recurring chord, like the one leading from the introduction into the main theme of Chopin's first Ballade. The only representation of a sounding voice is a calling motive formed by the repetition of a major seventh, first played by the clarinet in the final section of the work, representing the wood nymph calling out to Toman as she rides beside him.

Novák relates the vicissitudes of a passionate soul by transforming and retransforming his long and passionate main theme. To that extent, the programmatic method of this work is not very different from that of his earlier piano *ballade* on Byron's *Manfred* (see pp. 189-90). But in *Toman a lesní panna*, his method is more complicated. As the protagonist's music evolves, it is played off against the music of the wood nymph, a completely distinct music, with its own (whole-tone) harmonic language and its own orchestral colors (flutes, muted strings, horns, and harps). This music, which opens the work, is treated differently from Toman's: it does not evolve; in fact, it is not even a complete theme. The wood nymph is not a character in her own right, but an answer to Toman's need to escape from his own world of unrequited love. Even in the final episode, when the wood nymph is represented by several different motives, including the calling motive, her music does not interact with his, but alternates with it, until, at the climax that signals her fatal embrace, her music disappears and his theme is left to die away.

Janáček, in his two orchestral *ballades*, follows compositional principles that are close to Novák's. He too creates separate musical worlds for different characters in the story, and he too does so by means of separate harmonic languages and orchestral colors. Janáček also concentrates, especially in *The Ballad of Blaník*, on depicting evolutionary processes, though here his means are different from Novák's and different also from Dvořák's in *The Wild Dove*. What is most surprising in these two works, given Janáček's interest in Dvořák's *ballades* and his general interest in correspondences between speech melody and musical melody, is how little he seems to use the lines of his poetic models as models for his musical themes. Instead, he relies—even more than Dvořák did in *The Wild Dove*—on representations of musical sounds within his stories. In both *ballades* his rigor in the treatment of motives and instruments creates a narrative precision comparable to Dvořák's; and if Janáček's narration is harder to follow than Dvořák's, it is no fault of his musical technique, but simply that he strays further from the poetic source than Dvořák does.

In *The Fiddler's Child* he reconstructs the story somewhat, while preserving the spirit of the poem. The poem, by Svatopluk Čech (1846-1908), is a ballad only in the sense that it is a sad story about village life: it has no ballad process. It tells of a village fiddler who has died after a hard life, leaving an infant daughter and his violin. The mayor entrusts both to the care of an old woman. One night the old woman dreams that the dead father appears above the crib, playing his violin and singing a song that beckons his child to a better world. In the morning the mayor finds the child dead and the violin gone and refuses to believe the old woman's tale.

Janáček constructs his whole musical narration around an opposition that becomes explicit only at the end of the poem: between the oppressed poor, who include both the fiddler and the old woman, and the unsympathetic mayor who controls their destinies. From the social commentary implicit in the poem, Janáček creates a musical tension that dominates his version of the story. At the beginning (see Example 9-14) and throughout the work, Janáček represents the poor of the village by a choir of violas, the fiddler by a folklike phrase played on solo violin (allied to the viola choir by its similarity of timbre), and the mayor by a four-note motive that stands apart because it is chromatic, it is heard in unison, and it is played by woodwinds (excluding the oboe, which is reserved for the crying of the infant).[59] The identification of characters with instruments is reminiscent of Dvořák's practice, especially in *The Noon Witch;* but Janáček carries it out much more relentlessly here.

Because the motives associated with the characters remain distinct in color, melodic scale, and texture, Janáček can transform them all (not just the principal motive, as Novák did) and still keep their identities clear. The mayor's motive and the viola choir usually appear together, making a contentious joint commentary on the main story. That main story unfolds partly in the evolutions of the fiddler's theme and partly in a succession of new themes: the fiddler's musical life and his death are recalled; and in

Example 9-14. Janáček, *The Fiddler's Child*, mm. 11–25.

preparation for the fiddler's song, we hear the old woman falling asleep and the child plaintively crying.[60]

In Čech's unballadlike ballad, the fiddler's song is the only utterance by any of the characters, and it is an utterance of an exceptionally complicated nature: it is a song both played and sung; it is the central action of the story, transporting the child out of the world that has treated her father so harshly; and it arises within the old woman's dream. Janáček's method is beautifully suited to do justice to the nature of this song. His representation of it begins with the fiddler's original motive, then grows ecstatic, stretching the intervals of the motive as it leaps higher and higher (see Example 9-15).

The leaps of the solo violin are answered by the whole first violin section, perhaps depicting the fiddler's combination of singing and playing, but also following Janáček's own prescription for keeping a theme distinct in instrumentation, transferring it at most to "the nearest related instruments, from which it takes only some of their shade or their light."[61] In this case the "nearest related instruments," coupled to the solo violin, bestow the most extraordinarily intense light. All the while, other instruments resume the tremolos and punctuating chords of the old woman falling asleep, reminding us of her role as the dreamer of the fiddler's song that we are hearing.

As the song continues (*Con moto*; *Meno mosso*), another transformation of the fiddler's motive, in a more dancing rhythm, suggests the joys of the

Example 9-15. Janáček, *The Fiddler's Child*, mm. 358–62.

heavenly afterlife that the fiddler is promising his infant. Even before this passage is finished, the mayor's motive intrudes, and the remaining few moments of the work are taken up with transformations of that motive. Whereas the poem ends on a note of ironic discord—the poet's own voice is heard siding against the mayor in favor of the old woman's superstitious account—Janáček, characteristically, brings his discord-causing motive to a moving reconciliation. The mayor's four-note motive, sounded again in austere woodwind unison, is repeated and transposed until the strings soften it, join it, and—on the very last note—harmonize it.

In *The Ballad of Blaník* the poem itself has to do with transformations—magical transformations. The legend of Blaník, as retold by several Czech poets and as represented in Smetana's symphonic poem,[62] told of the mountain in which St. Wenceslas and his knights had slept for centuries, armed and ready to battle for their homeland. Janáček's symphonic poem, however, is based on a poem by Jaroslav Vrchlický, published in his *Selské Ballady* (*Peasant Ballads*) of 1885, that incorporates the old legend into a new story. In this story the peasant Jíra, a Czech Rip van Winkle, finds his way into the mountain at its miraculous yearly opening on Good Friday and sees the waiting knights, but at the closing of the entrance he is sealed inside. He falls asleep and then awakens to discover that the knights' weapons have turned into farm tools. Hearing the Passion music again, he makes his way out and finds that he himself has become an old man. Like "The Fiddler's Child," this ballad is a modern reflection on folk legends rather than a ballad in any structural sense.

Janáček, working this time from a poem without a single word of dialogue, used two themes that represent music: a humble hymn tune representing the Passion music that Jíra hears in the distance as he enters the mountain and again years later when he awakens and leaves it, and a second hymn tune, more grandly harmonized and played by harps, representing the imposing sight of St. Wenceslas and his knights. Just as the poem is largely occupied with imagining Jíra's sensations, even this second hymn tune might be taken to represent a tune that Jíra hears—this time in his head—when he comes upon the knights.[63] Jíra himself is represented by a theme that evolves for the entire length of the work: even its first form (see Example 9-16) itself emerges out of the opening figure, a winding figure in waltzing rhythm that captures the character's wandering spirit.

Example 9-16. Janáček, *The Ballad of Blaník*, m. 12.

If in *The Wild Dove* the passage of time brings about the decisive action of the story, in *The Ballad of Blaník* the passage of time *is* the decisive action. Consequently, the longest and most important passage of the work represents Jíra's years of sleep inside the mountain.[64] The passage begins (*Con moto*) with an imaginative depiction of Jíra falling asleep: his theme repeatedly starts and stops, leaving only a single tremolo note sounding during the halts. After this, Jíra's theme and the knights' theme evolve together, representing the two simultaneous processes of change in the poem: the aging of Jíra and the transformation of the knights' weapons into tools. In this remarkable passage—similar to the Fauré Ballade in its parallel evolution of themes—the two themes remain distinct from each other as they evolve, despite changing instrumentation and despite the intrusion of other themes, old and new, including the Passion hymn.

Both themes achieve definitive and triumphant new forms in this passage, but the new forms do not altogether displace the old. The new form of Jíra's theme (*Allegro [con brio]*), expressing the character's joy at returning to the outside world, is stopped short (*Tempo I* before rehearsal-number 25), and a plaintive new mood is established with a clarinet solo, as Jíra sees from his reflection in a stream that he has become an old man. The work ends, after many evolutions, with two recapitulations: the flute version of Jíra's initial wandering music returns (*Tempo I* at rehearsal-number 26), suggesting that despite his shock at the loss of years, he finds the strength to return to his home and life; then the original form of the knights' theme returns (*Meno maestoso*), played once, as before, by the harps, but then immediately afterward by the violins. In this way Janáček not only rejoices in the new condition of the knights' weapons as tools of agriculture, but reenacts their transformation.

These two moments of recapitulation at the end of *The Ballad of Blaník* belong specifically to the *ballade* tradition. They do not constitute a sonata-form recapitulation—the work is no more in sonata form than Chopin's Ballades are. Rather, they appear as sudden, short jolts to our memory, exactly like the moments of recapitulation in Dvořák's *The Golden Spinning Wheel* and *The Wild Dove*—or like the ironic returning lines in Vrchlický's poem that presumably provided Janáček's immediate inspiration. But Janáček's recapitulation of the flute passage in *The Ballad of Blaník* has its own irony, a false innocence of tone, as if Jíra could simply resume the mountain ramble he had begun so many years before. Given that the ballad process is a process of irreversible transformation, recapitulation in ballads is by nature ironic: any words or notes that can be repeated unchanged at the end serve only to measure how much has changed since they were first heard.

If the ironic recapitulation can be considered a technique with which the Czech composers enriched the *ballade* genre, the extreme isolation of themes is another. It is common to *The Ballad of Blaník*, *The Fiddler's Child*, and Novák's *Toman a lesní panna*. Like Dvořák's technique of modeling melodies on poetic lines, it is a technique of highly concrete representation. The taste for concreteness reflects, perhaps, a change in musical representation that was general—not restricted to the *ballade* genre—since the time of Chopin. Janáček's particular way of isolating themes introduced into the *ballade* genre a kind of montage technique that allowed him to display and develop several musical images within a single passage. This technique is in effect the antithesis of Chopin's technique of thematic convergence (one theme turning into another). If Chopin conceived of the *ballade* as a single-threaded narration in the course of which hidden relationships would suddenly appear, Janáček's contribution was to reconceive the genre as a complex narration in which related developments would unfold simultaneously.

In another sense Janáček's narrative structure is simpler than Chopin's: there is no narrative frame, no representation of a narrator's voice, in his *ballades*. In this respect Janáček's *ballades* belong with those of Dvořák, Tchaikovsky, Franck, and Dukas. These works, the masterpieces of the orchestral *ballade* in the late nineteenth and early twentieth centuries, are all characterized by literalness or concreteness in representing the utterances of characters in the stories. In a way, they are the works of this period that are most faithful to the *ballade* tradition of representing sounding words as the crucial actions of ballads.

But they are also the works in which the narrative voice is least often heard. In other orchestral *ballades* of the same period (including those of d'Indy, most British composers, and the Russian composers except for Tchaikovsky), scene-painting and folk song play a greater role than the representation of action, spoken or otherwise, and the narrator's voice is more often heard, generally as part of the mood-setting. In these works the scene-painting impulse of the late nineteenth century is stronger than the narrative tradition of the *ballade*. Common to both groups of works is the pursuit of concrete representation—whether based on a particular story or not. That pursuit seems to have forced composers to concentrate on just one sort of voice—the narrator's or the characters'—in their narratives, sacrificing the rich structure of voices that Chopin achieved by refusing such concreteness.

PART IV

The *Ballade*
Since World War I

Koloubek.

Okolo hřbitova
cesta úvozová;
šla tudy, plakala
mladá, hezká vdova.

Plakala, želela
pro svého manžela,
neb tudy naposled
jej doprovázela. ——

Od bílého dvora
po zelené louce
jede pěkný panic,
péro na klobouce.

PLATE 8. Illustrated first page of "The Wild Dove," from an 1890 edition of Erben's
Kytice.

CHAPTER 10

Martin and the *Ballade* Since World War I

In the history of the instrumental *ballade* from Chopin to the 1990s, World War I falls just past the midpoint. In the latter half of that history—the half that remains to tell—the *ballade* has continued to flourish,[1] but with a difference: since the war there has been a tremendous change in the types of *ballade* composed. The most important postwar *ballades* have been of a type—the concerto *ballade*—that hardly existed before the war, while *ballades* of the type most prominent in the decades just before the war—the orchestral *ballade* on a poetic model—virtually stopped being written after the war. It is natural to consider the war itself or the consequences of the war at least partly responsible for such drastic and abrupt changes.

A couple of reasons can be suggested to explain why, in the aftermath of World War I, composers did not go on writing orchestral *ballades* modeled on the stories of folk or Romantic ballads. As emblems of national culture and national aspirations, those ballads had retained their power over composers and audiences for a remarkable period almost a century in length, but after a war in which nationalist competition had devastated Europe, a war that ended, paradoxically, in the realization of many peoples' aspirations to nationhood, those emblems were neither wanted nor needed as before. It is symptomatic that at the end of the war the composition of *ballades* of all types declined most precipitously in precisely those Central European lands, like Czechoslovakia, that had just won their independence; even Bartók, though he continued collecting folk songs and deriving new inspirations from them in his own music, made fewer folk-song arrangements, and none of ballads, after the war.

The decline of orchestral *ballades* can also be seen as part of the general decline of programmatic music after the war. At a time when more and more composers were reacting against nineteenth-century practices of musical

273

representation, the orchestral *ballade* suffered from its association with the most extreme, most literal of those practices.

Nevertheless, the *ballade* in general has prospered since the war; the title has in fact been applied to a greater variety of music in the twentieth century than it was in the nineteenth. No longer associated particularly with the piano and the orchestra, it has been given to works for any instrument or combination of instruments. The stylistic range within the genre has also increased. In the mid-twentieth century, twelve-tone *ballades* were composed alongside folk-song *ballades* in nineteenth-century styles. Though a good many of these works are worth studying and performing, very few of them demonstrate any fresh thinking about ballads or about the tradition of the instrumental *ballade*. Even more often than in the period before the war, the title "*ballade*" proved to be little more than a convenient answer to the problem of what to name a work of moderate length in one movement. Since the aim of understanding the *ballade* as a genre would not be advanced by considering such works, the present study will not survey the whole range of *ballades* composed since World War I as it has surveyed those from the earlier period. Instead, it will concentrate on two developments that occurred in the genre after the war.

The first is the turn, in a very few orchestral and piano *ballades*, to literary ballads different from the folk and Romantic ballads that had been used before as narrative models, or to new ways of treating folk-song melodies as themes. The second development is the concerto *ballade*, a type of *ballade* whose solo-group texture provided new structures for evoking the voices and episodes of a narration. The concerto *ballade* was the specialty of Frank Martin, whose six Ballades for different solo instruments with orchestra form the most impressive group of *ballades* since Dvořák. The present study concludes with these two developments because they demonstrate that the instrumental *ballade*, though the product of nineteenth-century imaginations, could still stir new ideas long after its heyday; consideration of these new types of *ballade*, consequently, helps in placing the genre within the larger history of musical narration.

ORCHESTRAL AND PIANO *BALLADES*

Two orchestral *ballades* written immediately after World War I in effect concluded the long tradition of orchestral *ballades* on poetic models: Janáček's *Ballad of Blaník* of 1920, described in the previous chapter, and *The Ballad of Reading Gaol*,[2] also of 1920, by the French composer Jacques Ibert (1890–1962). Both works, however, depart from that tradition by being modeled on late nineteenth-century literary ballads that relate only remotely to older balladry. Ibert's *Ballad of Reading Gaol* is modeled on Oscar Wilde's poem of the same title (1898), which narrates the thoughts of a prison inmate as he awaits and witnesses the execution of a fellow prisoner who "had killed the thing he loved, / And so he had to die." The choice of subject and the correspondingly heavy tone of the music may surprise anyone who knows Ibert from such works as the orchestral suite *Escales* or the *Trois Pièces brèves* for woodwind quintet. The poem, for a ballad, is notably lacking in dialogue, lacking in deeds that are accomplished through words. As the narrator says: "We made no sign, we said no word, / We had no word to say." The passages from the poem that Ibert cites at the beginning of his score emphasize the other prisoners' torment as they wait for the dawn of the condemned man's execution day, and Ibert's most notable music in this work—particularly a passage in which a single slow measure of music in 5/4 rhythm repeats and repeats—depicts that waiting. Like Janáček's *Blaník*, then, this work centers on a rendering of the passage of time. The two together bring the speech-depicting tradition of the orchestral *ballade* to a paradoxical close.

Since the composition of these two works, other traditions of orchestral *ballades* have been revived—as in the *Ballade and Passacaglia on a Theme in Swedish Folktone*[3] (1937) by Kurt Atterberg (1887-1974) or the Ballade subtitled "Symphonic Variations on *'Het waren twee Conincskindren'* "[4] (1950) by Henk Badings (b. 1907)—and new musical techniques have been introduced into the genre—as in the twelve-tone *Ballata Sinfonica*[5] (1970) by Sándor Szokolay (b. 1931). But other composers did not take up from Janáček and Ibert the challenge of adapting the narrative tradition of the orchestral *ballade* to the texts of modern ballads.

Among the many piano *ballades* written since World War I, much the same holds true: there has been little return to the narrative tradition begun by Chopin and little exploration of modern literary ballads (or, for that matter, of song ballads). A few piano *ballades*, including an expressionist one by John Ireland (1879-1962) and a delicate twelve-tone work by George Perle (b. 1915),[6] may be considered narrative in the vague sense that they have no large-scale repetitions or recapitulations: Richard Goode, the dedicatee of the Perle Ballade, connects form and narration in that way when he writes of the work that "the narrative, except for one dreamily reminiscent bar near the end, never looks back."[7] For both Ireland and Perle the idea of a musical form that "never looks back" may have belonged to the Romantic heritage they evoked with the title "*ballade*," but in these works they did not use any specific narrative model, let alone that of a ballad.

One piano work that explores a new repertory of folk songs is *North American Ballads*, written in 1978-79 by Frederic Rzewski (b. 1938).[8] Each of these four Ballads is a fantasy on an American protest song. The songs range from the traditional spiritual "Down by the Riverside" to a labor union song from the 1930s, "Which Side Are You On?" Though they vary in origin, they are all songs sung in American social movements in the mid-twentieth century, and it seems likely that Rzewski found them all in the same collection of protest songs.[9] Like Charles Ives or like Roy Harris in his *American Ballads*[10] for piano (1947), Rzewski can harmonize his melodies playfully or ironically without ever mocking the songs. A distinctive characteristic of his Ballads is that through the elaborate variations and minimalist manipulations of the melodies, a memorable four- or five-note phrase can always be heard: the phrase to which the key words of the song are sung. In a deep sense—and not just because they are *ballades* on songs that are not ballads—these works resemble the Grieg Ballade: by relentlessly working over the melody of a song, they dramatize the composer's commitment to the meaning of its words.

Rzewski's Ballads are as political in significance as Grieg's, yet Rzewski does not share the nationalist dilemma of Grieg or Chopin or certain other nineteenth-century composers of *ballades*: as a twentieth-century American composer, he does not face the indifference of international audiences to his native song traditions. On the contrary, mid-century American folk singers popularized songs like "Down by the Riverside" not just in America, but throughout the world (and if two of the songs Rzewski chose—"Dreadful Memories" and "Winnsboro Cotton Mill Blues"—are not known abroad, neither are they known by many Americans). Still, Rzewski faces a comparable dilemma that nationalist composers have recognized since at least the time of Bartók: the dilemma of composers whose political sympathies lead them to deal with folk songs—the music of their compatriots, but not of their own class—but whose own musical medium—the Western classical tradition—does not unite people of all classes, whatever its power to reach elite audiences across international boundaries. Rzewski's technique of dwelling insistently on memorable melodic motives in these Ballads serves as a way of dealing with that dilemma, a means of reaching out to audiences that do not customarily listen to contemporary concert music, or to classical music in general. If Perle's Ballade of 1981 can be said to emulate Chopin's Ballades in refinement of sonority and formal progression, Rzewski's Ballads of practically the same date can be said to emulate their powerful accessibility.

MARTIN AND THE CONCERTO *BALLADE*

Concerto *ballades*, which constitute the one important new category of *ballade* in the twentieth century, have been written in several countries by a number of composers, who in most cases are unlikely to have been influenced by one another. Nevertheless, there is a common pattern: most of these *ballades* are episodic in the sense that they move from one discrete section—discrete in tempo and meter as well as theme—to another without break. Continuity is provided in part by the presence of the solo instrument in every section, and one can ask about each of these *ballades* whether the solo instrument is giving the work a kind of narrator's voice. In that context it is remarkable that the most popular solo instrument in concerto *ballades* is the piano, one of the least vocal of instruments, yet one of the most distinctive-sounding in the company of an orchestra.

Charles Koechlin (1867-1950) may have been following the example of his teacher Fauré in writing his Ballade[11] for piano and orchestra (completed in 1919). His Ballade is like Fauré's not only in its medium and its episodic form, but also in its association of the term "*ballade*" with nature. Koechlin describes the character and structure of the work in an epigraph that speaks of "old legends and ancient little songs" singing "in the forest of memory." The Ballade[12] for piano and orchestra written a few years later (1922) by Koechlin's friend Darius Milhaud (1892-1974) also has a change of meter and tempo for each of its themes, but its symmetry of form prevents it from seeming episodic. The *Concerto Ballata*[13] (1931) for violoncello and orchestra by Alexander Glazunov (1865-1936) is in effect a three-movement concerto without breaks between the movements. The *Scottish Ballad*[14] (1941) for two pianos and orchestra by Benjamin Britten (1913-1976) derives its title from the Scottish folk tunes he takes as themes, giving each, as Donald Mitchell writes, "an unpredictable or even contrary 'reading.'"[15] But the work also fits the formal pattern of concerto *ballades* in what Mitchell calls its "powerful, paradoxical juxtapositions of opposed moods" without breaks between sections.

The Swiss composer Frank Martin (1890-1974) wrote six concerto *ballades* between 1938 and 1972, each for a different solo instrument with a differently constituted orchestra. Two of these works—the Ballades for flute and for trombone—are *morceaux de concours*, commissioned test pieces for the contestants in a musical competition, and those two are much shorter than the other four. Despite this difference, the six works conform to the same conception, Martin's own conception of the *ballade* genre, so that they form a varied group around a single idea, like the four Ballades of Chopin or the four of Dvořák, rather than separate works embodying different ideas, like the three Ballades of Liszt.

Three of Martin's Ballades (including the two competition pieces) were originally composed for the solo instrument with piano, but were orchestrated by Martin almost immediately. In each case the orchestral part is no mere amplification of the original piano part, but creates a distinctive complement to the timbre of the solo instrument. The orchestral versions, then, can be taken as Martin's fuller realizations of his conceptions. The following list of the six Ballades[16] is arranged in order of composition of the original versions, but also includes the orchestral versions:

1938
Ballade for Alto Saxophone and Orchestra (piano, percussion, and strings), commissioned by the saxophonist Sigurd Racher

1939
Ballade for Flute and Piano, commissioned by the *Concours international d'exécution musicale*, Geneva
Version for flute, string orchestra, and piano, 1941
(Version for flute and full orchestra by Ernest Ansermet, 1939)

1939
Ballade for Piano and Orchestra (winds, percussion, harp, and strings)

1940
Ballade for Trombone and Piano, commissioned by the *Concours international d'exécution musicale*, Geneva
Version for trombone and small orchestra (winds, timpani, piano, and strings), 1941

1949
Ballade for Violoncello and Piano
Version for cello and small orchestra (winds, percussion, harp, and strings), 1950

1972
Ballade for Viola, Wind Orchestra, Harp, Harpsichord, and Percussion, commissioned by the Mozarteum, Salzburg

Martin wrote and published program notes for concert or recorded performances of each of his Ballades. These essays make Martin the first composer in the history of the instrumental *ballade* to commit his thoughts about the genre to paper, make him in fact virtually the first person—after a century of instrumental *ballades*—to put any conception of the genre into words. At the same time, Martin's essays make clear how idiosyncratic his approach to the genre was. They reveal that he came to his conception of the genre in the course of responding to a particular commission and to the capacities of the commissioner's instrument—the saxophone—and that he then found it congenial to extend the same conception to very different solo instruments, sometimes with the spur of commissions for those instruments and sometimes without. Some passages from his essay on the Saxophone Ballade make clear how his conception of the genre arose from his desire to take advantage of the character of a particular instrument:

> Of the wind instruments, the saxophone joins the greatest expressive suppleness—a suppleness that allies it, as well as the horn, with the human voice—to the extreme volubility of the flute or clarinet. It is therefore suited to grand lyrical expression as well as to bursts of virtuosity.
>
> This drove me to entrust to it a piece centered on expression more than on any formal element whatever, a piece inspired by the Romantics rather than by the Classics, in short, a *Ballade* that, in a lyrical narrative

style, could make appeal to the particular expressions of that
instrument.

To surround it and support it, I chose an orchestra of strings with
piano and percussion....The piano and percussion, by contrast, could
only help throw into relief this singing voice.

Thus was born this *Ballade* in which the saxophone appears
sometimes elegiac and sometimes explosive [*emporté*].[17]

The starting point for a Martin Ballade, in other words, was not literary:
"No literary theme," he writes of the Piano Ballade, "directed the composition
of this *Ballade*."[18] His starting point was not even an abstract model of the
ballad as a narrative type. Instead, it was the sound of an instrument, an
instrument that suggested the human voice singing, and because it suggested
contrasting expressions of that human voice—lyrical as well as voluble,
elegiac as well as explosive—Martin imagined it to be telling a story. He does
not imply that this imaginary story owed anything to the characteristic
content or form of ballads. In every one of the essays, in fact, he characterizes
his Ballades as extremely free in form, though it is not difficult to find
common formal features among them.[19] We might suppose that Martin chose
the title "Ballade" because it was a title that a century of music had made
available for one-movement works of narrative character, but nowhere does
he mention earlier instrumental *ballades* as models. He cites literary types,
but as vague points of reference, not as specific models: in one essay he
speaks of "the ballads of Ossian," in another of "a transposition into the
domain of pure music of what in poetry would be a story or a dramatic
recitation."

Taken together, his essays suggest that he associated the term *"ballade"*
with a tone more than with any formal characteristic. But it is hard to specify
what that tone might be or when it is most clearly heard in the music. Martin
adopts no "narrating tone" comparable to the one that many twentieth-
century critics have heard at the opening of Chopin's first Ballade. He might
have thought of the *ballade* tone as archaic more than as narrative: in the
notes to the Trombone Ballade he writes of his love for the "archaic
character" of the instrument's construction, and in the Viola Ballade he
employs both the harpsichord (a Mozartian tone in a work written for the
Salzburg Mozarteum?) and the harp (an Ossianic tone?). But aside from these
few choices of instrumental color, there is nothing archaic in the tone of his
Ballades. There is no archaic-sounding musical material—no hint of folk-song
phrasing or harmony, for example—in these works, which are written in his
chromatic mature style.

Martin's Piano Ballade, completed in the opening months of World War
II, will be discussed here, with passing comparisons to his other Ballades. The
Piano Ballade, one of the longer Ballades rather than one of the competition
pieces, is of particular interest partly because it invites comparisons to works

in the long tradition of solo piano *ballades* and partly because, of all the instruments to which Martin gave the task of representing a lyrical, narrating voice within the context of the orchestra, the piano posed the greatest challenge. At the same time, the Piano Ballade is typical of all the Martin Ballades in many respects.

It is typical of Martin's Ballades, for instance, that the Piano Ballade begins with "expressive suppleness," which then yields to "volubility"—to use his terms—though there is no gradual building of momentum as there is in Chopin's Ballades. It is typical, too, that the expressive opening is in arioso style: a long, slow melody in irregular phrases for the solo instrument and a steady accompaniment of slowly changing chords (see Example 10-1).

Example 10-1. Martin, Ballade for Piano and Orchestra, mm. 1–14. Two-Piano version. Copyright 1948 by Universal-Edition, Vienna. Copyright Renewed. All Rights Reserved. Used by permission of European American Music Distributors Corporation, sole U.S. and Canadian agent for Universal-Edition, Vienna.

The melody, like arioso melody in opera, owes its declamatory intensity to its rhythmic irregularity, thrown into relief by the perfect regularity of the accompanying chords, and to its obsessive dwelling on a few notes—often a half-step apart—per phrase. Although characteristic of Martin's Ballades, it is hardly characteristic of the *ballade* tradition in general for a *ballade* to begin with a melodic utterance so completely unlike the strophic melody of a folk song and, what is more, so apparently unsuitable for any kind of thematic transformation. A composer who opens a *ballade* in this way—and who writes of transposing into music "what in poetry would be a story or a dramatic recitation"—is using the freedom of a wordless musical medium to explore narrative in the widest sense and in so doing risks confusing listeners by denying them even the comfort of knowing whether to imagine a narrated story or a dramatized one.

In the opening of the Piano Ballade, as in the openings of other Ballades of Martin, there is at least a clear division into melody and accompaniment that allows one to imagine a singer's voice and an instrumental accompaniment of chords, perhaps strummed on one instrument. The harmony helps keep the two functions distinct: the melody, through all its chromatic twisting, persistently avoids the harmony of the accompanying chords. The resulting harmonic relationship is not bitonal: both the melody and the accompaniment are too chromatic in themselves to establish clearly contrasting tonalities. Rather, there is an effect as of a polarizing force acting between the two parts, holding them in isolation from each other no matter how they move.

Oddly enough, Martin does not use another, cruder device that would dramatize the distinction between melody and accompaniment as a difference of roles: giving one to the solo instrument and the other to the orchestra. Instead, the piano both sings the melody and plays the accompaniment, while the orchestra adds color to the accompaniment, at first subtly with doublings and later more boldly with independent lines. Even in Martin's other Ballades, when he is working with solo instruments that are easier to cast in the role of singer, he does not always treat those instruments in ways that would most obviously approximate the singing voice: the Cello Ballade, for instance, begins with a cello melody in double stops. While choosing the concerto medium for a *ballade*, then, Martin characteristically refuses—from the beginning—to let his representation of narrative fall into any overly specific, simple-minded scheme.

In the Piano Ballade, the opening theme is narrative in function not because it is presented as if by a narrator, but because it is presented as one event within an unfolding story. From the first note, it has such intensity of expression and such freedom and amplitude of development as to suggest the speech of a character caught at a particular moment, in a particular situation. This is a theme we are destined never to hear again in its original arioso rhythm or its original plaintive tone. The amazing thing is that we later hear every note of this extraordinarily long theme in thematic transformation (at rehearsal-numbers 32–42), or rather in a continually evolving transformation that might be compared to passages of "progressive transformation" in Chopin's Ballades. Beyond that, the opening chromatic motive of the theme returns in many new guises, in many new episodes, so that Martin writes that the Ballade is "almost continually dominated" by this theme: "It comes to the point of disappearing completely, but remains underneath like a conducting-wire."[20] The work is narrative—is a *ballade*—in the sense that no theme in it ever repeats or returns as such—just as no moment in a story recurs—yet the action at the outset determines everything that follows.

Even the other important theme of the work, which contrasts with the opening theme in many ways and appears to represent an opposing principle in the narrative, derives from a moment in the opening theme. This other theme, which constitutes the second episode (*Allegro vivace*, rehearsal-number 5), is hardly a theme at all: it has neither a fully formed melody nor a settled texture, though the whole episode is dominated by a skipping triplet rhythm. What defines the theme is a harmonic motive—a major triad alternating with the minor triad a minor third above it—that appears in different forms, both melodic and chordal (see Example 10-2). This two-chord motive was first heard at the climax of the opening theme (rehearsal-number 4), and the tension between its two triads represents, in its own way, the same polarizing force as the harmonic tension between the melody and accompaniment in the opening theme.

Example 10-2. Martin, Ballade for Piano and Orchestra, rehearsal-number 6, m. 4, and rehearsal-number 7, mm. 3–7. Two-Piano version. Copyright 1948 by Universal-Edition, Vienna. Copyright Renewed. All Rights Reserved. Used by permission of European American Music Distributors Corporation, sole U.S. and Canadian agent for Universal-Edition, Vienna.

But it is the simple two-chord motive, not the long opening theme, that is recognizable, thematically transformed, in most episodes of the Ballade. Unsuitable for representing a voice or a character, but succinctly embodying a dramatic tension, the motive—sometimes with its associated triplet rhythm—lends itself to any number of different textures, each of which can suggest a different dramatic situation. In one sequence of episodes, for instance, this motive is transformed into a declamation in double octaves for the piano (rehearsal-number 42), a "sort of funeral march" in triple time (rehearsal-numbers 43–48), and a piano cadenza (rehearsal-number 48).

The cadenza—a characteristic feature of Martin's Ballades—functions as an episode of special importance. The solo instrument, in its solitude, seems more than before to be identified with a character in the story. On the model of cadenzas in arias and concertos, the appearance of a cadenza here signals a decisive turn toward a conclusion. While the cadenza is made up almost entirely of brilliant developments of the two-chord motive, it is interrupted for a somber moment by a quotation from the opening theme, a transposition of four measures taken from the middle of a phrase in the middle of that theme (mm. 16–19, piano part only)—the only exact return of any earlier passage in the Ballade. If the opening theme is the music in this Ballade most representative of speech, this fragmentary reminiscence of that theme represents the only moment of reflection in the work. The moment is brief and isolated, but it breaks the pattern of endless new transformations and thereby allows a final development, when the orchestra returns, in which the opening theme and the two-chord motive are reconciled.

In the context of mid-twentieth-century music, Martin's reliance on thematic transformation as a constructive principle in this and his other Ballades is a throwback to Romanticism, in keeping with his own assertion that the first of his Ballades was "inspired by the Romantics." But it is not a simple throwback: to write a thematic transformation of a theme fifty-two measures long, a transformation that itself undergoes several changes of texture and character, is to go well beyond the conventional understanding of the technique, which is conditioned above all by Liszt's practice. It is to go beyond even the "progressive transformations" of long narrating themes in Chopin's Ballades. It is to give new narrative purpose to the Romantic idea of thematic transformation, so that what in Romantic music marked a particular stage in the progression of a story becomes in Martin's practice a story in itself, with its own stages of progression.

This complicated relation to the Romantic tradition is characteristic of Martin's Ballades in many ways. Writing at a time when narrative instrumental music was unfashionable, especially among Western European composers, because of its representational premises, Martin brought a very modern abstractness to the tradition of the *ballade* and of narrative music in general. His use of the concerto medium in his Ballades, for example, is as modern, complex, and unrepresentational as his use of thematic transformation:

through the solo instrument—even the piano—he suggests the declamatory power of sung narrative, but he does not represent any particular narrative frame or relationship of voices through the structure of solo and orchestra. His whole concept of the *ballade* is more abstract than that of any Romantic composer, even Chopin, himself the Romantic composer most shy of musical depiction. Whereas Chopin in his Ballades creates a musical abstract of the ballad process, Martin combines narrative elements of many musical genres— notably opera and concerto—into a musical progression independent of any one narrative genre. Martin's Ballades are profoundly sympathetic modern reflections on Romantic program music, proposing, in his own distinctive musical voice, a twentieth-century transformation of the Romantic *ballade* into a universal narrative.

CHAPTER 11

Conclusion

All *ballades* belong, if not to the history of musical narrative, then at least to the history of musical representation: even the simplest salon *ballades* remind their listeners of sentimental songs. The most important parts of the *ballade* repertory—including all the *ballades* by major composers—belong to the history of musical narrative in the nineteenth and twentieth centuries. In fact, the *ballade* tradition constitutes one of the most significant chapters in that history. The present survey, which gives the whole repertory the attention previously reserved for certain individual *ballades*, makes it possible for the first time to recognize the significance of that chapter.

Other chapters in the same history—the chapters on subjects long and fully studied, such as the program symphony, the symphonic poem, and Wagnerian leitmotif narration—all deal with systems of signifying motives, that is, musical motives that signify subjects of the narration. What makes the *ballade* distinctive and important in this company is that it has a double system of signification: musical phrases in a *ballade* characteristically represent phrases of song that in turn signify the sung words of a narration. The system is complex and difficult, but also natural. Wordless music is representing in the first place what it represents most easily: other music.

The representation of sung narrative in instrumental music has by no means been confined to *ballades*. In fact, the idea has been cultivated as steadily in other instrumental works as in *ballades*, and techniques for representing sung narrative have developed along parallel lines inside and outside the *ballade* genre. Thus, in the late 1830s, Robert Schumann in his Fantasy, Op. 17, for piano created a musical narrative as personal and as filled with outside references as Chopin's Ballades, written at the same time, were impersonal and nonspecific, but nevertheless a narrative also created out of the phrase structures of song. In its first movement a narrative represented by the evolution of a songlike theme is interrupted by a song of narrative character (a folklike strophic melody "in legendary tone"), then the earlier evolution resumes and culminates, through a process of "thematic convergence" akin to Chopin's, in a phrase from an actual Beethoven song.

285

Likewise, in 1911, barely a decade after Dvořák created wordless themes in his Erben *ballades* to fit lines of Erben's poetry, Enrique Granados composed his *Goyescas*[1] as a kind of wordless opera for piano. Several years later he adapted the music for an actual opera of the same title, keeping large stretches of the music virtually unchanged (as Smetana had done in making an aria out of his own piano Ballade a half-century earlier) and charging a librettist with the task of fitting the text to the existing musical phrases.[2]

Even closer to Dvořák's practice, curiously, are several works written in the same period as Martin's Ballades by Paul Hindemith (1895-1963), notably his *Hérodiade* (1944), subtitled "An Orchestral Recitation of a Poem by Stéphane Mallarmé," a ballet score in which the orchestra "recites the poem…by means of a single melodic line ranging from the lowest to the highest registers of the orchestra and fitted exactly to every syllable of the French text."[3] Such works as these prove that the double system of signification—the idea of evoking narrative through an evocation of song—did not arise solely in response to the challenge of writing *ballades*, but held a wide, general appeal for composers in the past century and a half.

Nevertheless, no other genre of instrumental music has developed to rival the *ballade* in this field of musical representation, undoubtedly because no genre of narrative song other than the ballad has been prominent enough in Western culture to serve as the model for a genre of instrumental music. As a result, the comparable works by Schumann, Granados, Hindemith, and others stand as single, isolated ventures, while *ballades* constitute a tradition.

The present survey of that tradition shows that the idea of representing narrative song in instrumental music fueled the development of the *ballade*; that the *ballade* developed as a coherent genre, not just as a collection of individual experiments; and that the driving idea, as a result, can be treated as an important historical alternative to the idea of musical representation with signifying motives.

From this survey it can be seen that the coherence of the *ballade* genre derives from the persistence of certain compositional problems inherent in the genre, not from any particular solutions to those problems suggested by leading works in the genre. We might expect otherwise, given that this genre, unlike many others, began with its most prestigious works. It is true, nonetheless, that the problems Chopin defined in his Ballades inspired many different solutions in other composers' *ballades*, even piano *ballades*, and hardly any imitations of the techniques he himself developed as solutions to those problems.

One of these problems is characteristic of any representation of narrative song: the problem of working simultaneously on two separate planes of representation: the plane of narrating (the song) and the plane of the story narrated (the content). Many composers of *ballades* distinguished the two planes of representation with two bodies of thematic material, but they shared no common technique for mediating between the two. Chopin distinguished between narrating themes and characterizing themes, mediating between them with new types of thematic transformation—"thematic convergence" and "progressive transformation." But later composers like Franck, Tchaikovsky, Dvořák, Dukas, and Janáček used no themes recognizable as narrating themes; instead they distinguished characterizing themes from themes that embodied characters' utterances, subjecting the former but not the latter to thematic transformation.

Still other composers, writing monothematic *ballades*—generally but not exclusively folk-song variations—faced the same problem in inverted form: how to make the two planes of representation distinct with only one theme. Brahms's solution in his "Edward" Ballade is remarkably like Bartók's in his Ballade on "Angoli Borbála": within a strophic musical form that suggests the narrating song, the composer suggests the drama of the story by driving the theme underground (like Martin's "conducting-wire") in a central interlude and then letting it emerge again with renewed force. The dramatic interplay of folk theme and chromatic bass within the variations of Grieg's Ballade, Op. 24, is yet another technique for suggesting the two planes of representation within a monothematic *ballade*.

The other persistent problem belongs not to all representations of narrative song, but only to *ballades*: how to reflect the ballad process—the underlying plot mechanism of ballads—in a wordless musical composition. Again, Chopin's own solution was rarely imitated; Bülow's Ballade, Op. 11, and the original version of Liszt's Second Ballade are virtually the only piano *ballades* that end, like all of Chopin's, in a whirlwind of musical reckoning. The *ballade* is not a formal type determined by Chopin's response to the ballad process; instead it is a field of formal inventiveness guided by many composers' responses to the ballad process, either as they sensed it from their reading of ballads or as a particular ballad model presented it to them. Within this field, it is noteworthy that among *ballades* complex enough in form to represent the course of a plot (that is, excluding lyrical *ballades*, which are character pieces), most end with the abrupt return of opening material severely transformed. Even a few remarkable strophic works—like the Brahms "Edward" Ballade or the Bartók Ballade on "Angoli Borbála"—embody the ballad process in this way.

The diversity of techniques found within such a long and rich tradition can be sorted by historical period, revealing, incidentally, that different techniques used in one period may reflect a single predilection or habit of thought characteristic of that age. For instance, Dvořák's technique of deriving melodies from poetic lines (in his Erben *ballades*) and Bartók's technique of linking a melodic motive to the crucial word originally sung to it (in his Janko Ballade) can be connected as different forms of the same cryptic literalness of representation. Both forms can be seen as more characteristic of composers at the turn of the century than of composers in either Chopin's age or Martin's.

Finally, the richness and brilliance of the *ballade* tradition over a century and a half can be taken as evidence of a healthy, though largely unrecognized, abundance of methods available to composers in that period for representing narrative in instrumental music. If the most prominent methods have been those relying principally on signifying motives—the methods of program symphonies since Berlioz and of symphonic poems since Liszt—they have not been the only methods. The most important alternative to them has been the representation of narrative through the phrase structures of song, the method pioneered by Chopin in his Ballades and validated chiefly by later works within the *ballade* tradition.

To regard the signifying-motive method and the sung-narrative method as alternatives is not to deny that each method has often infiltrated the genres identified with the other. Signifying motives appear frequently, perhaps inescapably, in *ballades* that relate the stories of particular ballads, and in method Liszt's Second Ballade is as much a symphonic poem as it is a *ballade*. At the same time, song structures play an important role in the narrative method of Berlioz's *Symphonie fantastique*, and a quoted song is the main theme, the main signifying motive, in Liszt's symphonic poem *Tasso*. Moreover, techniques that in Chopin's Ballades are specific to the narrative task of representing a ballad—techniques like "progressive transformation" and "thematic convergence"—appear in other nineteenth-century music—such as symphonic and chamber works of Brahms—without the same narrative significance.

Nevertheless, there are two senses in which it is helpful to regard the narrative method of the *ballade* as an alternative to that of the symphonic poem and program symphony. The first sense is historical. In the period between Chopin's death and World War I, it was not just the subject matter or the symbolic value of ballads that gave the instrumental *ballade* its special appeal to composers who wanted to create national music for their countries. Even the narrative method of the *ballade* was an advantage, in comparison to that of the symphonic poem, in that it provided a way to evoke, in piano or orchestral music, both the telling of national legends and the singing of songs in the national language. The second sense is contemporary. To acknowledge the *ballade* as an alternative to the more celebrated method of musical narration in the nineteenth century is to rescue both methods from too close an identification with the ideologies and aesthetics of that age. It is to recognize what a few *ballades* of recent years have shown: that one of the strengths of instrumental music in any age is its power to remind listeners of story and song and that in any age there is more than one way to summon that power.

Notes

CHAPTER 1 (pages 19-30)

1. The editions are listed in Maurice J. E. Brown, *Chopin: An Index of His Works in Chronological Order*, 2nd ed., rev. ([London:] Macmillan, 1972), p. 73. Scholars have found only one other instrumental *ballade* of comparably early date, the Ballade in Clara Wieck's *Soirées musicales*, Op. 6, also published in 1836 (publication information in ch. 5, n. 1). See Günther Wagner, *Die Klavierballade um die Mitte des 19. Jahrhunderts* (Munich: Musikverlag Emil Katzbichler, 1976), pp. 42, 114-16.

2. *Allgemeine Musikalische Zeitung* 2 (January 1837), p. 26.

3. William S. Newman, *The Sonata Since Beethoven* (Chapel Hill: University of North Carolina Press, [1969]), pp. 9, 37-40, 81-86.

4. See William J. Entwistle, *European Balladry* (Oxford: [Oxford University Press, 1969]; first published 1939), pp. 123-30.

5. Gordon H. Gerould, *The Ballad of Tradition* (Oxford: [Oxford University Press,] 1932), p. 11.

6. Ibid., p. 6.

7. Albert B. Friedman, "Ballad," in *Princeton Encyclopedia of Poetry and Poetics*, enlarged ed., ed. Alex Preminger (Princeton, New Jersey: Princeton University Press, [1974]), p. 62.

8. Chopin, letter to his parents, May 28, 1831, in *Selected Correspondence of Fryderyk Chopin*, trans. and ed. Arthur Hedley (New York: McGraw-Hill, [1963]), p. 82.

9. Letter of January 29, 1831, in *Selected Correspondence*, p. 78.

10. Letter of July 6, 1831, in *Selected Correspondence*, p. 85.

11. See Zofia Lissa, "Du Style national des oeuvres de Chopin," *Annales Chopin* 2 (1957), pp. 121, 150.

12. Letter to his parents, June 25, 1831, in *Selected Correspondence*, p. 83.

13. See Brown, *Chopin: An Index*, p. 29.

14. Brown gives the tune in *Chopin: An Index*, p. 72.

15. Krystyna Kobylańska, in *Frédéric Chopin: Thematisch-bibliographisches Werkverzeichnis* (Munich: Henle, 1979), p. 45, cites three writers who agree on 1831 as the date when Chopin began the Ballade. None of the three (B. E. Sydow, Arthur Hedley, or Maurice J. E. Brown) gives any evidence for that date.

16. Gastone Bellotti, in *F. Chopin: L'uomo* ([Milan:] Sapere, 1974), pp. 350-52, demonstrates the unreliability of a letter from Chopin's editor Schlesinger, claiming to have heard Chopin play the Ballade in 1831. See also p. 610.

17. See Stefania Pawliszyn, "Elementy melodyki ukraińskiej w twórczosci Chopina," in *The Book of the First International Musicological Congress Devoted to the Works of Frederick Chopin*, ed. Zofia Lissa (Warsaw: PWN—Polish Scientific Publishers, [1963]; hereafter referred to as *Chopin Congress: Warszawa 1960*), pp. 361-62, and Jan Prosnak, "Elementy berżeretki francuskiej, 'sztajerka' i folkloru ukraińskiego w twórczosci Chopina," ibid., pp. 375-77.

18. Lissa, "Du Style national," pp. 150-51.

19. On Polish nationalism, see Norman Davies, *God's Playground: A History of Poland* (New York: Columbia University Press, 1984), vol. 2, ch. 1: "Naród: The Growth of the Modern Nation (1772-1945)."

20. J. P. T. Bury, "Nationalities and Nationalism," ch. 9 in *The New Cambridge Modern History*, vol. 10 (Cambridge: Cambridge University Press, 1960), p. 213.

21. See Robert R. Ergang, *Herder and the Foundations of German Nationalism* (New York: Columbia University Press, 1931), p. 150.

22. Bury, in *The New Cambridge Modern History*, vol. 10, p. 216, distinguishes "a linguistic nationalism," inspired by Herder, from a French tradition of liberal nationalism. In Poland, according to Andrzej Walicki, the nationalism that developed after the partitions of the late eighteenth century defined itself more in political than in linguistic terms, but eventually a linguistic and ethnic conception of the nation triumphed. See Walicki's *Philosophy and Romantic Nationalism: The Case of Poland* (Oxford: Clarendon Press, 1982), ch. 4, part 1.

23. Boyd C. Shafer, in *Nationalism: Myth and Reality* (New York: Harcourt, Brace and World, [1955]), pp. 148-49, describes the adoption of anthems and flags, which he calls "the songs and symbols of the faith."

24. Giuseppe Cocchiara, *The History of Folklore in Europe*, trans. John N. McDaniel (Philadelphia: Institute for the Study of Human Issues, [1981]; original Italian ed., 1952), p. 274.

25. These activities are described in chs. 12, 14, and 15 of Cocchiara, *The History of Folklore in Europe*.

26. The standard survey in English is Entwistle, *European Balladry*.

27. See H. Munro Chadwick and N. Kershaw Chadwick, *The Growth of Literature*, vol. 3 (New York: Macmillan, 1940), pp. 774-76, and "Note on English Ballad Poetry," pp. 682-93. The process of defining the genre continues in Lajos Vargyas, *Hungarian Ballads and the European Ballad Tradition*, trans. Imre Gombos (Budapest: Akadémiai Kiadó, 1983), vol. 1, pp. 19-47.

28. Walter Wiora, in *European Folk Song: Common Forms in Characteristic Modifications*, trans. Robert Kolben (Cologne: Arno Volk, [1966]), p. 5, writes: "It is only in the light of a European totality that the part played by each nation and the origins and peculiarities of its songs can be understood."

29. Carl Dahlhaus, *Nineteenth-Century Music*, trans. J. Bradford Robinson (Berkeley: University of California Press, [1989]; original German ed., 1980), p. 37.

30. Günther Wagner, in *Die Klavierballade*, p. 43, traces this practice to James Huneker, *Chopin: The Man and His Music* (New York: Charles Scribner's Sons, 1900; reprinted, New York: Dover Publications, [1966]), ch. 10. A more elaborate proposal is offered in Zdzisław Jachimecki, *Frédéric Chopin et son oeuvre* (Paris: Delagrave, 1930; original Polish ed., 1927), ch. 5. Still others are reviewed in Lubov Keefer, "The Influence of Adam Mickiewicz on the Ballades of Chopin," *American Slavic and East European Review* 5 (May 1946), pp. 38-50.

31. Robert Schumann, in *Neue Zeitschrift für Musik* 15 (1841), p. 142, reprinted in *Robert Schumanns gesammelte Schriften über Musik und Musiker*, 5th ed., ed. Martin Kreisig (Leipzig: Breitkopf & Härtel, 1914), vol. 2, p. 32. The whole sentence reads: "Er sprach damals auch davon, daß er zu seinen Balladen durch einige Gedichte von Mickiewicz angeregt worden sei." In the collection of

Schumann's writings translated by Paul Rosenfeld (Robert Schumann, *On Music and Musicians*, [New York:] Pantheon Books, [1946], p. 43), the sentence is mistranslated so that it refers to the second Ballade only.

32. Lissa, "Du Style national," p. 151. See also Wagner, *Die Klavierballade*, p. 121.

33. See Friedman, "Ballad," p. 62.

34. Eero Tarasti, for instance, relates the musical form of Chopin's Polonaise-Fantasy, Op. 61, to principles of narrative structure in "Pour une Narratologie de Chopin," *International Review of the Aesthetics and Sociology of Music* 15/1 (June 1984), pp. 53–75. Other recent articles that indicate the range of methods being used and repertory being investigated include Owen Jander, "Beethoven's 'Orpheus in Hades': The *Andante con moto* of the Fourth Piano Concerto," *19th-Century Music* VIII/3 (Spring 1985), pp. 195–212, and Anthony Newcomb, "Schumann and Late Eighteenth-Century Narrative Strategies," *19th-Century Music* XI/2 (Fall 1987), pp. 164–74.

35. Wagner, *Die Klavierballade*, pp. 143–52. That list, evidently culled from the nineteenth-century Hofmeister catalogs of music in print, has been an invaluable source for the present study. Less easy to obtain, but also valuable for its list of works, especially because its coverage extends into the first decades of the twentieth century, is a 1934 dissertation at the University of Vienna, Gertrud Axel's *Die Klavierballade*.

36. "Ballade (ii)," in *The New Grove Dictionary of Music and Musicians*, ed. Stanley Sadie ([London: Macmillan Publishers, 1980]), vol. 2, p. 78. A broader survey of nineteenth-century applications of the term *"ballade"* to instrumental works is found in the entry "Ballade (Neuzeit)," section vi, by Wolf Frobenius, in the *Handwörterbuch der musikalischen Terminologie*, ed. Hans Heinrich Eggebrecht (Wiesbaden: Steiner, 1971–).

CHAPTER 2 (pages 31–48)

1. Aside from Schumann's report (discussed in the previous chapter) of Chopin's reference to Mickiewicz, the only clue that may be traceable to Chopin is in a letter of 1839 in which an agent for Breitkopf & Härtel, after negotiating with Chopin, asks the publisher what price to offer Chopin for "a Ballade of the Pilgrims." The letter is quoted and discussed by Jeffrey Kallberg in "Chopin in the Marketplace: Aspects of the International Music Publishing Industry," part 2: "The German-Speaking States," *MLA Notes* 39/4 (June 1983), pp. 812–13. Even if, as can be inferred from the letter, Chopin once referred to the second Ballade by that title, the title itself offers a less specific source for the music than Schumann's remark does. The material cited by Kallberg on this subject suggests to me that the title points not so much to a particular story behind the music as to a patriotic-religious assertion that Chopin evidently decided, in the end, not to make through the publication of his music.

2. On ballad imitation by English poets, for example, see Albert Friedman, "The Difficulties of Imitation," in *The Ballad Revival* (Chicago: University of Chicago Press, [1961]).

3. See, for example, Alan Bold, "Content of the Ballads," in *The Ballad* ([London:] Methuen, [1979]).

4. Bertrand Bronson writes: "Ballad tunes are a part of the general body of folk music, only hypothetically separable from the mass of lyric folksong" ("Ballad," I,6, in *The New Grove Dictionary*, vol. 2, p. 74.) The closeness of particular ballad

melodies to other folk melodies is illustrated throughout Walter Wiora's *European Folk Song*.

5. These three musical types are recognized in the histories of ballad *Lieder* given in most modern musical dictionaries, following the account by Philipp Spitta, "Ballade," in *Musikgeschichtliche Aufsätze* (Berlin: Gebrüder Paetel, 1894), pp. 403–61.

6. "The romantic period of Polish poetry begins in 1822, the date of the publication of the first volume of poems by Adam Mickiewicz (1798–1855). He at once attained a position of leadership in the movement .... Between 1822 and 1830 he published a series of ballads which are on a level with those of Schiller and Goethe." (M. Kridl and Z. Folejewski, "Polish Poetry" in *Princeton Encyclopedia*, p. 651.)

7. Lissa, "Du Style national," pp. 150–51.

8. A tiny survey of Polish song of this period is given by Gerald Abraham in *The New Oxford History of Music*, vol. 8: *The Age of Beethoven 1790–1830*, ed. Gerald Abraham (London: Oxford University Press, 1982), pp. 574–78. A full survey of the subject, with a chapter on ballads and related genres, is offered by Jerzy Gabryś and Janina Cybulska, in *Z dziejów polskiej pieśni solowej* ([Cracow:] Polskie Wydawnictwo Muzyczne, [1960]). The bibliography of *The Age of Beethoven* cites modern sources that make available some of the songs discussed in both surveys.

9. See Julian Krzyżanowski, *A History of Polish Literature*, trans. Doris Ronowicz (Warsaw: PWN—Polish Scientific Publishers, 1978; original Polish ed., 1972), p. 238.

10. See Lissa, "Du Style national," pp. 149–50.

11. Entwistle, *European Balladry*, bk. 2, ch. 2. Erich Seemann, in his introduction to *European Folk Ballads*, ed. Erich Seemann, Dag Strömback, and Bengt Jonsson (Copenhagen: Rosenkilde & Bagger, 1967), pp. xii–xv, excludes Poland from the Nordic, or, as he calls it, "Germanic," tradition. Werner Danckert, in *Das Volkslied im Abendland* (Bern: Francke, [1966]), pp. 167–75, limits the term "Nordic" to Scandinavian ballads.

12. Entwistle, *European Balladry*, p. 195.

13. Erich Seemann, for instance, writes: "Certain themes are particularly frequent in the ballads of the various countries and peoples; thus the South Slavonic ballads often deal with dramatic incidents at weddings" (*European Folk Ballads*, p. xx).

14. Trans. in the editor's Introduction to *Poems by Adam Mickiewicz*, ed. George Rapall Noyes (New York: The Polish Institute of Arts and Sciences in America, 1944), p. 5.

15. Published in Russian in 1928, Vladimir Propp's *Morphology of the Folktale* did not appear in English until 1958. A second English edition (trans. Laurence Scott, rev. and ed. Louis Wagner) was published in 1968 (Austin: University of Texas Press).

16. A. J. Greimas, "Eléments pour une théorie de l'interprétation du récit mythique," *Communications* 8 (1966), pp. 28–59.

17. Gérard Genette, *Narrative Discourse: An Essay in Method*, trans. Jane E. Lewin (Ithaca, New York: Cornell University Press, [1980]; original French ed., 1972); Paul Ricoeur, *Time and Narrative*, trans. Kathleen McLaughlin [Blamey] and David Pellauer, 3 vols. (Chicago: University of Chicago Press, [1984–88]; original French ed., [1983–85]).

18. The heart of this repertory of folk ballads would be those published in Thomas Percy's *Reliques of Ancient English Poetry* (1765) and in Herder's *Volkslieder* (1778–79), some of which are translations from Percy's *Reliques*.

19. Claude Bremond, *Logique du récit* (Paris: Editions du Seuil, [1973]).

20. To Goethe, epic and drama seemed, along with lyric, the natural poetic forms, which he found united with great succinctness in folk ballads. (See *Westöstlicher Divan: Noten und Abhandlungen*: "Naturformen der Dichtung," in *Goethes Werke*, Hamburg ed., ed. Erich Trunz (Munich: C. H. Beck, 1982), vol. 2, pp. 187–88. Since Goethe's time, scholars have continued to be interested in the relationship of ballad and epic (see Vargyas, *Hungarian Ballads*, vol. 1, pp. 19–47), while the term "tragedy" occurs regularly in systems of ballad classification (note, for instance, the important classes "romantic tragedies" and "domestic tragedies" in Albert Friedman's *The Penguin Book of Folk Ballads of the English-Speaking World* (Harmondsworth, England: Penguin Books, 1976; original ed., 1956).

21. For a skeptical account of theories of the "ballad society," see Ruth Finnegan, *Oral Poetry: Its Nature, Significance and Social Context* (Cambridge: Cambridge University Press, [1977]), pp. 250–54.

22. See Gerould, *The Ballad of Tradition*, p. 11: "A ballad is a folk-song that tells a story... objectively with little comment or intrusion of personal bias."

23. Alan Dundes, "Structuralism and Folklore," in *Essays in Folkloristics* ([Meerut, India:] Folklore Institute, [1978]), p. 194.

24. Ibid., pp. 196–97.

25. Adapted from the translation by Dorothea Prall Radin in *Adam Mickiewicz 1798-1855: Selected Poetry and Prose*, Centenary Commemorative Edition, ed. Stanislaw Helsztynski (Warsaw: Polonia Publishing House, 1955), p. 37.

26. Entwistle, *European Balladry*, pp. 198–99. See also Seemann, *European Folk Ballads*, p. xxiii, and Bronson, "Ballad," I, 5–6, in *The New Grove Dictionary*, vol. 2, pp. 73–74.

27. Version of "Barbara Allen" from Ramsay's *Tea-Table Miscellany* (1750), reprinted in Friedman, *The Penguin Book of Folk Ballads*, p. 89.

28. See Bronson, "Ballad," I, 5–6, in *The New Grove Dictionary*, vol. 2, pp. 73–74.

29. The narrative songs in the first volume of Oskar Kolberg's *Pieśni ludu polskiego zebrał i wydał* (Warsaw: J. Jaworsky, 1857) show a great variety of meters.

30. See Krzyżanowski, *History of Polish Literature*, p. 350.

31. See Wiktor Weintraub, *The Poetry of Adam Mickiewicz* (The Hague: Mouton, 1954), pp. 43–44.

32. A somewhat different example is Schumann's 1840 setting of Adelbert von Chamisso's ballad, "Die Löwenbraut." Piano transcriptions of songs offer another possible analogy or even source of influence for the thematic structure of the Chopin Ballades. Most song transcriptions of Chopin's day, however, are based on strophic songs, not on the long, complex ballads of composers like Loewe. Something of an exception is Liszt's transcription of Schubert's "Erlkönig," written at just this time and published in 1838.

33. Friedman, Introduction to *The Penguin Book of Folk Ballads*, p. xiii.

34. Adapted by James Parakilas from the translation by Arthur Prudden Coleman and Marion Moore Coleman in Helsztinksi, ed., *Adam Mickiewicz*, p. 47.

35. Francis B. Gummere, *The Popular Ballad* (Boston: Houghton Mifflin, [1907]), pp. 90–91.

36. Bold, *The Ballad*, p. 29.

37. Johann Wolfgang von Goethe, "Ballade. Betrachtung und Auslegung," in *Über Kunst und Altertum* III/1 (1821), reprinted in *Goethes Werke* (Berlin and Darmstadt: Der Tempel-Verlag, [1967]), vol. 7, p. 212.

38. Axel Olrik, "Epic Laws of Folk Narrative," trans. in *The Study of Folklore*,

294
NOTES

ed. Alan Dundes (Englewood Cliffs, New Jersey: Prentice-Hall, [1965]), pp. 129–41.

39. See David Buchan, *The Ballad and the Folk* (London: Routledge & Kegan Paul, [1972]), pp. 87–88.

40. Flemming G. Andersen and Thomas Pettitt, while attacking Buchan's thesis of ballad re-creation, write: "There can be no doubt that ballads, in Scotland and elsewhere, show the formulaic and structural features Buchan has so carefully analyzed" ("Mrs. Brown of Falkland: A Singer of Tales?" *Journal of American Folklore* 92, no. 363 [January–March 1979], p. 24); and Albert Friedman argues against Buchan that ballads derived their textual patterns largely from their distinctive association of words with tunes ("The Oral-Formulaic Theory of Balladry—a Re-rebuttal," in *The Ballad Image: Essays Presented to Bertrand Harris Bronson*, ed. James Porter [Los Angeles: Center for the Study of Comparative Folklore and Mythology—UCLA, 1983], pp. 215–40).

41. Buchan, *The Ballad and the Folk*, chs. 9–11.

42. Ibid., p. 88. The cited stanza is from the ballad "Child Waters."

43. Olrik's Law of Contrast states that "The *Sage* (folk narrative) is always polarized." See Olrik's "Epic Laws," p. 135.

44. "Without repetition, the *Sage* cannot attain its fullest form. The repetition is almost always tied to the number three." Olrik, "Epic Laws," p. 133.

45. See Gummere, *The Popular Ballad*, pp. 117–34.

46. Buchan, *The Ballad and the Folk*, p. 114.

47. See, for example, the diagram on p. 133 in Buchan, *The Ballad and the Folk*. See also ch. 3 in Mark Booth, *The Experience of Songs* (New Haven, Connecticut: Yale University Press, [1981]).

48. See the chapter on that poem in Earl Wasserman, *The Finer Tone: Keats' Major Poems* (Baltimore, Maryland: Johns Hopkins Press, 1953), especially pp. 68 and 78–79.

49. Ibid., p. 81.

50. Buchan, *The Ballad and the Folk*, p. 135.

51. Schubert's response to the narrative structures of "The Elf-King" is pointed out by Leon Plantinga in *Romantic Music: A History of Musical Style in Nineteenth-Century Europe* (New York: W. W. Norton, [1984]), pp. 119–21.

52. Friedman, *The Ballad Revival*, p. 259.

CHAPTER 3 (pages 49–87)

1. Wagner, *Die Klavierballade*, p. 121.

2. James Huneker, *Chopin: The Man and His Music*, p. 156.

3. Hugo Leichtentritt, *Analyse der Chopin'schen Klavierwerke*, 2 vols. (Berlin: Max Hesses Verlag, 1921–22), vol. 2, p. 1. See also Arthur Hedley, in *Chopin*, rev. Maurice J. E. Brown (London: J. M. Dent & Sons, 1977; original ed., 1947), pp. 173–74, who writes of the first Ballade that the "legendary atmosphere is created in the first bars" and refers to the "'story-telling' G minor theme." More recently, Carl Dahlhaus, in *Nineteenth-Century Music*, p. 148, attributes a "narrative 'ballad tone'" to that theme.

4. Goethe, *Westöstlicher Divan*, pp. 187–88.

5. See Leichtentritt, *Analyse*, vol. 2, p. 1; Hedley, *Chopin*, p. 173. The most extensive development of this idea can be found in Wagner, *Die Klavierballade*, pp. 34–42, 46–47, 106–11.

6. Wagner, *Die Klavierballade*, pp. 34–42.

7. Dahlhaus, *Nineteenth-Century Music*, p. 149.

8. Others who have described the ballad genre, rather than individual ballads, as Chopin's model include Kenwyn G. Boldt, in *The Solo Piano Ballade in the Nineteenth Century* (D.M.A. thesis, Indiana University, 1967), and Neil David Witten, in ch. 6 of *The Chopin "Ballades": An Analytical Study* (D.M.A. thesis, Boston University, 1979). Witten was the first to analyze formal features of the Chopin Ballades as analogous to characteristic narrative techniques of ballads.

9. Dahlhaus, *Nineteenth-Century Music*, p. 105.

10. The passage (*Westöstlicher Divan*, pp. 187–88) reads as follows: "There are only three true natural-forms of poetry: one purely narrative, one inspired by enthusiasm, and one realized in persons: Epic, Lyric, and Drama. These three poetic modes may work together or separately. In the smallest poem one often finds them together, and they bring forth the most wonderful form precisely through this conjunction within the narrowest space, as we see clearly in the precious ballads of all peoples."

11. Schumann in *Neue Zeitschrift für Musik* 15 (1841), pp. 141–42, reprinted in *Robert Schumanns gesammelte Schriften*, vol. 2, p. 32.

12. Friedman, "Ballad," in *Princeton Encyclopedia*, p. 62.

13. Bronson, "Ballad," in *The New Grove Dictionary*, vol. 2, p. 72.

14. The edition of the Chopin Ballades referred to throughout this study is that of Ewald Zimmermann (Munich: Henle, [1967]).

15. Günther Wagner explores the connections of this theme with Chopin's nocturnes in *Die Klavierballade*, pp. 32–34.

16. See Wagner, *Die Klavierballade*, p. 41, and Dahlhaus, *Nineteenth-Century Music*, p. 149.

17. Gerald Abraham, *Chopin's Musical Style* (London: Oxford University Press, [1st ed. 1939; corrected ed. 1960]), p. 72.

18. Schumann in *Neue Zeitschrift für Musik* 15 (1841), p. 142, reprinted in *Robert Schumanns gesammelte Schriften*, vol. 2, p. 32.

19. Hedley, *Chopin*, p. 173.

20. Frederick Niecks, *Frederick Chopin as a Man and Musician* (London: 1888; reprinted, New York: Cooper Square Publishers, 1973), pp. 268–69.

21. Gerould, *The Ballad of Tradition*, p. 11.

22. Of all the specific poetic models that have been proposed for Chopin's Ballades, the one that has been most widely accepted is Mickiewicz's "Świtezianka" as model for the second Ballade (see Jachimecki, *Frédéric Chopin et son oeuvre*, p. 128). The comparison may have been inspired by the similarity in key, rhythms, and textures between the primary theme of the second Ballade and Maria Szymanowska's vocal setting of "Świtezianka" (see the musical example in Abraham, ed., *The Age of Beethoven*, p. 578). The main virtue of this comparison, as Jachimecki makes it, is to point out that the last two phrases of the music (mm. 196–203) suggest the reemergence of the narrator's voice at the end of a ballad.

23. Musical analysts all recognize that the primary themes of the Chopin Ballades are long and complex, but they do not, naturally, agree on exactly what constitutes a theme. My account of the theme in the fourth Ballade is closer to Gerald Abraham's in *Chopin's Musical Style*, p. 108 ("First Subject: a 73-bar working of the 4-bar theme"), than to Hugo Leichtentritt's in *Analyse*, vol. 2, p. 31 (primary theme ending in m. 38, "varied repetition" beginning in m. 59). In the first Ballade I agree with Günther Wagner (*Die Klavierballade*, p. 26) that the theme has a "two-part nature," but his second part (mm. 36–67) begins at what I have called the end of the theme.

24. Dahlhaus, *Nineteenth-Century Music*, p. 148.

25. Gerould, *The Ballad of Tradition*, p. 96. Gerould gives an example of such a passage.

26. Ibid., p. 97.

27. André Gide, *Notes on Chopin*, trans. Bernard Frechtman (New York: Philosophical Library, [1949]; original French ed., 1948), p. 29.

28. The openings of the two themes have a similarity of harmonic-melodic structure that is examined by Leon Plantinga in *Romantic Music*, pp. 200–02. Gerald Abraham argues, furthermore, that the winding phrase of the primary theme has "thrown its tendrils over four bars" of this transformation of the secondary theme. See *Chopin's Musical Style*, p. 56.

29. Just before, in the fourth Ballade, the primary theme reappears, in what might more naturally be called a variation than a transformation. But the word "transformation" in a special sense might be applied to the remarkable passage that leads to that variation: a dream structure that gropes from fragments of the theme into the middle of its stanza.

30. Ballads have always been celebrated for their tragic outcomes, but there were ballads of happy outcome in both the folk and literary repertories known to Chopin. In some repertories the comic ballads may even outnumber the tragic. See D. K. Wilgus, *Anglo-American Folksong Scholarship Since 1898* (New Brunswick, New Jersey: Rutgers University Press, 1959), pp. 263–64.

31. See Edward T. Cone, *Musical Form and Musical Performance* (New York: W. W. Norton, [1968]), pp. 83–84.

32. Buchan, *The Ballad and the Folk*, p. 116.

33. Ibid., p. 114.

34. See ibid., p. 57.

35. Buchan notes that "the binary and annular rhythms in the narrative structure should be considered together because their fundamental relationship... here becomes explicit" (*The Ballad and the Folk*, p. 121).

36. See Leichtentritt, *Analyse*, vol. 2, p. 2; Hedley, *Chopin*, p. 174; Abraham, *Chopin's Musical Style*, p. 155; Franz Eibner, "Über die Form der Ballade Op. 23 von Fr. Chopin," *Annales Chopin* 3 (1958), p. 111, n. 3; Wagner, *Die Klavierballade*, p. 26.

37. Abraham compares the form of the work to that of the first movement of Berlioz's *Symphonie fantastique*.

38. Eibner, "Über die Form der Ballade," p. 110.

39. The motive at m. 243, which comes from mm. 201–02.

40. Abraham demonstrates that such nonmodulating transitions are characteristic of Chopin; see *Chopin's Musical Style*, pp. 83–84.

41. Jim Samson, in *The Music of Chopin* (London: Routledge & Kegan Paul, [1985]), p. 179, likewise recognizes two patterns in tension with each other in the first Ballade: an "overall arch" with the "waltz episode" (mm. 138*ff.*) at its "pinnacle," and a "goal-directed momentum, achieved through waves of tension and release."

42. Buchan, *The Ballad and the Folk*, p. 135.

43. Goethe, "Ballade," in *Goethes Werke* (Der Tempel-Verlag), vol. 7, p. 212.

44. Buchan, *The Ballad and the Folk*, p. 142.

45. Leichtentritt analyzes Chopin's Ballades in *Analyse*, vol. 2, ch. 1.

46. Heinrich Schenker, *Free Composition (Der freie Satz)*, trans. and ed. Ernst Oster, 2 vols. (New York: Longman, [1979]), vol. 1, p. 132. Schenker's graph of the piece appears in vol. 2 as fig. 153, ex. 1.

47. Eibner, "Über die Form der Ballade," pp. 107–12.

48. Douglass M. Green, *Form in Tonal Music* (New York: Holt, Rinehart & Winston, [1965]), p. 298.
49. Wagner, *Die Klavierballade*, pp. 26-28. Other recent writers who have used sonata form, with some reservations, to analyze the first Ballade are Michael Griffel, "The Sonata Design in Chopin's Ballades," *Current Musicology* 36 (1983), pp. 125-36, and Jim Samson, *The Music of Chopin*, ch. 11.
50. Dahlhaus, *Nineteenth-Century Music*, p. 148.
51. George Bernard Shaw, *Music in London 1890-94*, 3 vols. (New York: Vienna House, 1973), vol. 2, p. 87.

CHAPTER 4 (pages 91-129)

1. "Das Wort 'Ballade' trug wohl zuerst Chopin in die Musik über. Übrigens scheint uns nur das Wort neu, die Sache kann man schon in Beethoven und Schubert finden." *Robert Schumanns gesammelte Schriften*, vol. 2, p. 343.
2. Chopin's use of musical genres is discussed by Jeffrey Kallberg in "The Rhetoric of Genre: Chopin's Nocturne in G Minor," *19th-Century Music* XI/3 (Spring 1988), pp. 238-61.
3. The traditions defined here are very much like those defined in Axel's *Die Klavierballade*.
4. The Ballade, Moscheles's Opus 100, was published in the *Mozart-Album* (Braunschweig: J. P. Spehr, [1842]). A critical edition of the work appears in *The Nineteenth-Century Piano Ballade: An Anthology*, ed. James Parakilas (Madison, Wisconsin: A-R Editions, 1990).
5. Charlotte Moscheles, *Recent Music and Musicians, as Described in the Diaries and Correspondence of Ignatz [Ignaz] Moscheles*, trans. A. D. Coleridge (New York: Henry Holt, 1873; reprinted, New York: Da Capo Press, 1970), p. 210.
6. See Roger Fiske, *Scotland in Music: A European Enthusiasm* (Cambridge: Cambridge University Press, [1983]), pp. 116-19.
7. *Robert Schumanns gesammelte Schriften*, vol. 2, p. 343.
8. The D-flat Ballade was published as *Ballade* by F. Kistner in Leipzig and as *Le Chant du croisé: Ballade* by J. Meissonier in Paris, both in 1849. The B-minor Ballade was published by Kistner as *2me Ballade* in 1854. The standard critical edition of both Ballades is that of Imre Sulyok and Imre Mező in ser. 1, vol. 9, of the New Liszt Edition (Budapest: Editio Musica, [1981]).
9. Wagner, *Die Klavierballade*, especially pp. 49-57.
10. The main theme of the Ballade is virtually identical to the A-flat major Piano Piece of 1845, reprinted on p. 164 in the same volume of the New Liszt Edition. On the relationship of the two, see the editors' Preface, p. xv.
11. Among subsequent editors, Vianna da Motta followed the original prints in the Breitkopf & Härtel complete edition, while Sauer for the Peters edition and Sulyok and Mező for the New Liszt Edition gave dynamic and expressive indications for the first phrase without citing their authority.
12. Wagner, *Die Klavierballade*, p. 49.
13. Peter Raabe, *Franz Liszt*, 2nd ed. (Tutzing: Hans Schneider, 1968), vol. 2, pp. 58-59.
14. Wagner, *Die Klavierballade*, p. 53.
15. The first edition of this Ballade, as of the first, gives no dynamic indication for the opening.
16. Humphrey Searle, *The Music of Liszt* (London: Williams & Norgate, [1954]), p. 56. Gertrud Axel, in *Die Klavierballade*, p. 34, also justifies the

repetition in terms of sonata-form tradition.

17. Louis Kentner, "Solo Piano Music (1827–61)," in *Franz Liszt: The Man and His Music*, ed. Alan Walker (London: Barrie & Jenkins, [1970]), p. 97.

18. See Márta Grabócz, *Morphologie des oeuvres pour piano de Liszt* (Budapest: MTA Zenetudományi Intézet, 1986), pp. 160, 165–66, 186–89.

19. My analysis of the work as a developing repetition of a fixed progression agrees substantially with Grabócz's analysis of it as a series of "narrative programs" based on the "thematic complex." I find her idea of considering the *Allegretto* material a "refrain" attractive insofar as that material always rounds off the progression, but it is not the "stable point" that she describes: it undergoes changes, like all the other material of the Ballade. See Grabócz, *Morphologie*, p. 68.

20. Wagner, *Die Klavierballade*, pp. 67–68.

21. The autograph, now in the possession of the publisher Schott in Mainz, contains the first two versions of the coda (along with other rejected passages), but not the final version (or certain other passages of the work in its final form).

22. The autograph does not give the new time signature that is needed for this section nor any indication of tempo or volume.

23. See Joseph Horowitz, *Conversations with Arrau* (New York: Limelight Editions, [1984]), pp. 142–46; Kentner, "Solo Piano Music," p. 96.

24. Hans von Bülow, Ballade, Op. 11 (Mainz: Schott, [1856]; critical ed. in Parakilas, ed., *The Nineteenth-Century Piano Ballade*).

25. See the *Neue Zeitschrift für Musik* 25 (December 15, 1854), p. 274.

26. Letter to Louis Köhler, December 20, 1859, in *Hans von Bülow: Briefe und Schriften*, ed. Marie von Bülow (Leipzig: Breitkopf & Härtel, 1895–1908), vol. 4: *Briefe: 1855–1864*, p. 286.

27. The fragment is printed in the collected edition of Smetana's piano works: Bedřich Smetana, *Klavírní Dílo*, vol. 5: *Skladby virtuosní*, ed. Hana Séquardtová (Prague: Supraphon, 1973), pp. 202–11.

28. See Smetana, *Klavírní Dílo*, vol. 5, pp. lxii–lxiii.

29. See Milada Ladmanová, "Chopin und Smetana," in *Chopin Congress: Warszawa 1960*, pp. 324–28.

30. See Smetana, *Klavírní Dílo*, vol. 4: *Lístky do památníku*, ed. Hana Séquardtová (Prague: Supraphon, 1968), p. lvi. The piece is printed on pp. 47–51.

31. This version, which Smetana wrote in the album of Fröjda Benecke, is printed in Smetana, *Klavírní Dílo*, vol. 5, pp. 212–13. Except for the expression markings, it differs only by a few notes from the comparable passage in the larger fragment.

32. See Nicholas Temperley, "Fryderyk Chopin," in *The New Grove Early Romantic Masters* 1 (New York: W. W. Norton, [1985]), pp. 50–51.

33. Brian Large, *Smetana* ([London:] Duckworth, [1970]), p. 90.

34. Smetana composed the opera in the years 1865–67.

35. This couplet and the following phrase are adapted from the translation by Jindřich Elbl in the libretto of the Supraphon recording LPV 98/100 (1960).

36. See Jaroslav Jiránek, "Beitrag zum Vergleich des Klavierstils von Fryderyck Chopin und Bedřich Smetana," in *Chopin Congress: Warszawa 1960*, p. 312.

37. Published by Breitkopf & Härtel of Leipzig in 1873, the work was reprinted by them in the second volume of Scharwenka's *Pianoforte-Werke zu zwei Händen*.

38. Reinhold Sietz, however, says that the work shows a Brahmsian touch. See his entry on Xaver Scharwenka in *Die Musik in Geschichte und Gegenwart*, ed. Friedrich Blume, 17 vols. (Kassel: Bärenreiter, 1949–68), vol. 11, p. 1606.

39. There were two editions, by Troupenas in Paris and Schott in Mainz.

40. Theodor Kullak, "Lénore: Ballade," Op. 81 (London: Wessel, [1853]; critical

ed., with a translation of Bürger's poem, in Parakilas, ed., *The Nineteenth-Century Piano Ballade*).
   41. Kullak, Ballade, Op. 54 (London: Wessel, [1849]).
   42. See the settings of "Lenore" and other Bürger ballads in *Balladen von Gottfried August Bürger, in Musik gesetzt von André, Kunzen, Zumsteeg, Tomaschek und Reichardt*, ed. Dietrich Manicke, vols. 45 and 46 of *Das Erbe deutscher Musik* (Mainz: Schott, 1970).
   43. Anton Rubinstein, "Ballade: Lénore de Bürger," in *Miscellanées*, Op. 93 (Leipzig: Bartholf Senff, [1873]).
   44. See, for example, Michael R. Katz, *The Literary Ballad in Early Nineteenth-Century Russian Literature* ([London:] Oxford University Press, 1976).
   45. Carl Tausig, "Das Geisterschiff: Symphonische Ballade nach einem Gedicht von Strachwitz," Op. 1 (Leipzig: J. Schuberth, [1860]; critical ed., with the poem in German and English, in Parakilas, ed., *The Nineteenth-Century Piano Ballade*).

CHAPTER 5 (pages 130–51)

   1. Clara Wieck, *Soirées musicales*, Op. 6 (Leipzig: Hofmeister, 1836; facsimile reprint in Clara Wieck Schumann, *Selected Piano Music*, intro. Pamela Susskind, New York: Da Capo Press, 1979; critical ed. in Clara Wieck-Schumann, *Ausgewählte Klavierwerke*, ed. Janina Klassen, Munich: Henle, 1987).
   2. See Joan Chissell, *Clara Schumann: A Dedicated Spirit* (London: Hamish Hamilton, [1983]), p. 44.
   3. Robert Schumann, *Davidsbündlertänze*, Op. 6 (Leipzig: A. R. Friese, [1837 or 1838]). Schumann subtitled the work *Eighteen Character Pieces* in its second edition, published in 1850–51.
   4. The review, written on September 12, 1837, appeared in the *Neue Zeitschrift für Musik* on September 15. It is reprinted in *Robert Schumanns gesammelte Schriften*, vol. 1, p. 250.
   5. Letter of January 5, 1838, reprinted in Clara and Robert Schumann, *Briefwechsel: Kritische Gesamtausgabe*, ed. Eva Weissweiler (Stroemfeld: Roter Stern, [1984]), vol. 1, p. 75.
   6. See the rich account of *Salonmusik* by Hans Heinrich Eggebrecht in *Riemann Musik Lexikon*, 12th ed., ed. Wilibald Gurlitt (Mainz: B. Schott's Sons, 1959–75), vol. 3 (*Sachteil*), p. 834. See also the chapters on salon music in Carl Dahlhaus, ed., *Studien zur Trivialmusik des 19. Jahrhunderts* (Regensburg: Gustav Bosse, 1967).
   7. An example of a piano arrangement of an English opera is F. X. Chotek's "Piano-Excerpt Without Words" of Balfe's *The Mulatto* (Vienna: P. Mechetti, [1847 or 1848]), which includes two ballads.
   8. Henry Cramer, "La Romantique," No. 2 of "Deux Ballades," Op. 91 (Mainz: B. Schott, [1853]; critical ed. in Parakilas, ed., *The Nineteenth-Century Piano Ballade*).
   9. Henri Herz, "Deux Ballades sans paroles," Op. 117 (Mainz: B. Schott, [1841]); Theodor Döhler, "Ballade sans paroles," [Op. 41] (London: Cramer, Addison & Beale, n.d.); Theodor Döhler, "Deuxième Ballade," Op. 55 (Vienna: P. Mechetti, n.d.); Edouard Wolff, "Ballade," Op. 62 (Paris: M. Schlesinger, n.d.); Adolf Gutmann, "Ballade," Op. 19 (London: R. Cocks, [1851]); Julius Schulhoff, "Ballade," Op. 41 (Milan: F. Lucca, n.d.).
   10. Carol Mikuli, "Ballade," Op. 21 (Vienna: Schreiber, [1871]).
   11. Sigismond Thalberg, "Célèbre Ballade de S. Thalberg," Op. 76 (Paris:

Heugel, [1862]; critical ed. in Parakilas, ed., *The Nineteenth-Century Piano Ballade*).

12. The title page with that engraving is reproduced in Parakilas, ed., *The Nineteenth-Century Piano Ballade*.

13. Louis Moreau Gottschalk, "La Savane: Ballade créole," Op. 3 (Paris: Escudier, [1849]; a later edition, by J. E. Gould of Philadelphia, is reprinted in *Piano Music of Louis Moreau Gottschalk*, selected and introduced by Richard Jackson, New York: Dover Publications, [1973]).

14. See the discussion by Gilbert Chase in *America's Music: From the Pilgrims to the Present* (New York: McGraw-Hill, [1955]), pp. 314-15.

15. Gottschalk, "Ossian: Deux Ballades," Op. 4 (Mainz: B. Schott, [1850]; reprinted in *The Piano Works of Louis Moreau Gottschalk*, ed. Vera Brodsky Lawrence, 5 vols., New York: Arno Press and The New York Times, 1969).

16. Gottschalk, "Ballade," in *The Little Book of Louis Moreau Gottschalk: Seven Previously Unpublished Piano Pieces*, ed. Richard Jackson and Neil Ratcliff, preface by Gilbert Chase (New York: The New York Public Library and Continuo Music Press, [1976]).

17. Gottschalk, "Sixième Ballade," Op. 85; "Septième Ballade," Op. 87; "Huitième Ballade," Op. 90; all published in Mainz by B. Schott, 1877; all reprinted in Lawrence, ed., *Piano Works*.

18. See John G. Doyle, *Louis Moreau Gottschalk 1829-1869: A Bibliographical Study and Catalog of Works* (Detroit: Information Coordinators, 1982), p. 263.

19. Printed in César Franck, *Selected Piano Compositions*, ed. Vincent d'Indy (reprinted, New York: Dover Publications, 1976). D'Indy believed the work was published at the time of composition, but could find no record of that publication. See his introduction, p. xxxii.

20. Adolf Henselt, "Ballade," Op. 31 (St. Petersburg: T. Stellowsky, n.d.; Berlin: Schlesinger, n.d.).

21. Teresa Carreño, "Ballada," Op. 15, in *Obras de Teresa Carreño* (Caracas: Ediciones del Ministerio de Educación, 1974), reprinted as Teresa Carreño, *Selected Works*, foreword by Rosario Marciano (New York: Da Capo Press, 1985).

22. Johannes Brahms, *Vier Balladen*, Op. 10 (Leipzig: Breitkopf & Härtel, 1856; the modern edition referred to here is Brahms, *Sonaten, Scherzo und Balladen*, ed. Walter Georgii, Munich: Henle, [1977]). The pieces were composed by mid-October of 1854. Concerning the period of composition, see Wagner, *Die Klavierballade*, pp. 72-77.

23. Max Kalbeck, *Johannes Brahms*, 2nd ed. (Berlin: Deutsche Brahms-Gesellschaft, 1908-22), vol. 1, p. 190.

24. Paul Mies, "Herders Edward-Ballade bei Joh. Brahms," *Zeitschrift für Musikwissenschaft* 2 (1919-20), pp. 225-32. Brahms did write a song setting of "Edward" more than twenty years after publishing his Ballades, Op. 10; but Mies is not referring to that song (the duet that opens his *Balladen und Romanzen*, Op. 75): it has no musical connection to the "Edward" Ballade of Opus 10.

25. In his earlier piano sonatas, Brahms had made related "settings" of poems and songs. See Fiske, *Scotland in Music*, pp. 170-71.

26. Herder's version in *Stimmen der Völker* (1778-79) is his translation of the ballad he found in Percy's *Reliques* (1756). The English version is from Percy as respelled by Friedman in *The Penguin Book of Folk Ballads*, p. 156.

27. Wagner, *Die Klavierballade*, pp. 90, 77.

28. Kalbeck, *Johannes Brahms*, vol. 1, p. 190.

29. Wagner, *Die Klavierballade*, p. 94.

30. Ibid., p. 97.

31. This and the subsequent phrases by Schumann come from his letter of January 6, 1855, to Clara Schumann, published in *Robert Schumanns Briefe: Neue Folge*, 2nd ed., ed. F. Gustav Jansen (Leipzig: Breitkopf & Härtel, 1904), p. 404.

32. See Temperley, "Fryderyk Chopin," in *The New Grove Early Romantic Masters* 1, pp. 50-51.

33. Brahms had already written a piece (in B minor) in homage to Mendelssohn. On the identity of this piece and the possibility of any connection between it and the fourth Ballade, see Wagner, *Die Klavierballade*, pp. 72-73.

34. Kalbeck, *Johannes Brahms*, vol. 1, p. 189.

35. Joachim Raff, "Ballade" in *Album lyrique (Nouvelle Edition)*, Op. 17, vol. 2 (Leipzig: J. Schuberth, [1874]); critical ed. in Parakilas, ed., *The Nineteenth-Century Piano Ballade*.

36. See Margit McCorkle, *Johannes Brahms: Thematisch-bibliographisches Werkverzeichnis* (Munich: Henle, [1984]), p. 29.

37. Raff, "Ballade," No. 1 of *Drei Klavier-Soli*, Op. 74 (Hamburg: J. Schuberth, [1859]), written in 1852.

38. Thomas Tellefsen, "Ballade," Op. 28 (Paris: S. Richault, n.d.).

39. Stephen Heller, *Trois Ballades*, Op. 115 (Mainz: B. Schott, [1866]). "Ballade," No. 1 of *Drei Stücke*, Op. 121, first published in 1867; reprinted in Heller, *Pianoforte Werke zu zwei Händen* (Leipzig: Breitkopf & Härtel, n.d.), vol. 4.

40. The middle section of the Mazurka in A minor (No. 134 in Brown, *Chopin: An Index*), first published in *Six Morceaux de salon* and *Notre Temps*.

41. Ferdinand Hiller, "Ballade," No. 1 of *Sechs Claverstücke*, Op. 130, new ed. (Leipzig: F. Kistner, n.d.). Hiller's earlier "Ballade" is No. 4 of his *Vermischte Claverstücke*, Op. 66 (Mainz: B. Schott's Sons, n.d.).

42. Robert Volkmann, *Ballade und Scherzetto*, Op. 51 (Mainz: B. Schott, [1866]).

43. Josef Rheinberger, "Ballade" in *Drei Charakterstücke*, Op. 7 (Leipzig: E. W. Fritzsch, 1867; reprinted, New York: G. Schirmer, 1882).

CHAPTER 6 (pages 152-67)

1. See ch. 2, n. 4.

2. Reprinted from M. I. Glinka, *Polnoe sobranie sočinenij*, ed. V. Ja. Šebalin et al. (Moscow, 1955-69), vol. 6, p. 78. My information on the piece comes from David Brown, *Mikhail Glinka: A Biographical and Critical Study* (London: Oxford University Press, 1974), pp. 47-48, and from Alexandra Orlova, *Glinka's Life in Music: A Chronicle*, trans. Richard Hoops (Ann Arbor, Michigan: UMI Research Press, [1988]), p. 54.

3. See Orlova, *Glinka's Life*, p. 54.

4. Franz Liszt, *Glanes de Woronince* (Leipzig: F. Kistner, [1849]); critical ed. to appear in the New Liszt Edition, ser. 2, vol. 8.

5. See Zoltán Gárdonyi, "Nationale Thematik in der Musik Franz Liszts bis zum Jahre 1848," in *Liszt-Bartók: Report of the Second International Musicological Conference—Budapest 1961* (Budapest: Akadémiai Kiadó, 1963), pp. 77-87.

6. On the musical sources of *Glanes de Woronince*, see Alan Walker, *Franz Liszt*, vol. 2: *The Weimar Years, 1848-1861* (New York: Alfred A. Knopf, 1989), pp. 46-49. For Liszt's own account of his musical experience in the Ukraine, see Liszt, *Die Zigeuner und ihre Musik in Ungarn*, trans. L. Ramann, vol. 6 of *Gesammelte Schriften von Franz Liszt*, ed. L. Ramann (Leipzig: Breitkopf & Härtel, 1883), pp. 157-160.

7. Four volumes, each titled *Douze Airs nationaux roumains (Ballades, chants de bergers, airs de danse etc.) recueillis et transcrits pour le piano par Charles Mikuli* (Lvov: H. W. Kallenbach, n.d.).

8. István Bartalus, *Gyermek lant, növendék zongora tanúlók számára magyar népdalokból* (Budapest: Rózsavölgyi & Társa, 1860).

9. Vojtech Preisler, *České národní písní, k začátečnímu cvičení na pianě*, Op. 113 (Prague: n.p., n.d.). Johann Karl Eschmann, *Zwanzig gute, alte, deutsche Volkslieder für Pianoforte zu vier Händen, zum Gebrauch beim Unterricht*, Op. 59 (Leipzig: J. Rieter-Biedermann, 1878).

10. Ludvig Lindeman, *Aeldre og nyere norske Fjeldmelodier, samlede og bearbeidede for pianoforte* (Christiana [Oslo]: P. T. Malling, [1853–67]; reprinted with notes by O. M. Sandvik, [Oslo:] Universitetsforlaget, [1963]).

11. Sandvik's notes to the Lindeman collection cite later arrangements of many of the melodies.

12. Number 22 in Lindeman's collection.

13. Halfdan Kjerulf, *Norske Folkeviser* (Oslo: C. Warmuth, [1867]).

14. Edvard Grieg, *25 Norske Folkeviser og Dandse*, Op. 17 (Bergen: C. Rabe, W. Harloff, 1870). Critical editions of all Grieg's piano works appear in Edvard Grieg, *Gesamtausgabe (Complete Works)*, ed. Edvard-Grieg Komitee, Oslo (Frankfurt: C. F. Peters, [1977–]).

15. Grieg, *Sex norske Fjeldmelodier* (Copenhagen: Wilhelm Hansen, [1886]).

16. Johan Svendsen, *Norsk Rapsodi* No. 2, Op. 19 (Oslo: C. Warmuth, [1877]).

17. Grieg, *Altnorwegische Romanze mit Variationen*, Op. 51, for two pianos (Leipzig: C. F. Peters, 1891). Grieg's orchestration of the work was published by Peters in 1906.

18. Kjerulf had harmonized the refrain similarly.

19. Grieg, *Ballade in Form von Variationen über eine norwegische Melodie*, Op. 24 (Leipzig: C. F. Peters, [1876]); critical ed. by Dag Schjelderup-Ebbe in Grieg, *Gesamtausgabe*, vol. 2.

20. An autograph sketch of the work bears the title *Capriccio (Ballade) over en norske Fjeldmelodi i Form af Variation*. See the critical notes to the Ballade in the Grieg *Gesamtausgabe*, vol. 2, p. 231.

21. On the sources of the song, see Finn Benestad and Dag Schjelderup-Ebbe, *Edvard Grieg: The Man and the Artist*, trans. William H. Halverson and Leland B. Sateren (Lincoln: University of Nebraska Press, [1988]), pp. 200–01. See also Lindeman, *Aeldre og nyere norske Fjeldmelodier*, p. xii.

22. This translation is taken from Benestad and Schjelderup-Ebbe, *Edvard Grieg*, p. 201.

23. Ibid., pp. 199–200.

24. See Lindeman, *Aeldre og nyere norske Fjeldmelodier*, p. xii. O. M. Sandvik, the modern editor of the collection, writes (p. iii) of Lindeman's transcriptions as a whole that "they show tonal and rhythmical peculiarities of the folksong, less apparent in the harmonized version which was intended for a wider public."

25. Nils Grinde, "Edvard Grieg," in *The New Grove Dictionary*, vol. 7, p. 719.

26. See, for example, Lindeman's arrangement (Number 319) of "Niels Tallefjoren," a melody that Grieg had used in his *Twenty-five Norwegian Folk Ballads and Dances*, Op. 17.

27. Quoted in Benestad and Schjelderup-Ebbe, *Edvard Grieg*, p. 203.

28. Grinde, "Edvard Grieg," p. 719.

CHAPTER 7 (pages 168–200)

1. Gabriel Fauré, "Ballade," Op. 19 (Paris: Hamelle, 1880). The Hamelle edition of the solo piano version is still available; there are several editions of the version for piano with orchestra.

2. The version analyzed here is the solo piano version. The two versions are so close in their progression, however, that this analysis can be applied to the orchestrated score as well.

3. Letter to Marie Clerc, September 17, 1879, letter 37 in *Gabriel Fauré: His Life Through His Letters*, collected, edited, and introduced by Jean-Michel Nectoux, trans. J. A. Underwood (London: Marion Boyars, 1984); French ed., *Gabriel Fauré: Correspondance* (Paris: Flammarion, 1980). See also Nectoux's introduction to the chapter in which the letter appears.

4. For Florent Schmitt, nonetheless, one passage of the work described a Moslem scene, while another described jousting. See his "Les Oeuvres d'orchestre" in the special Fauré issue of *La Revue musicale* 3/11 (1922), pp. 50–59.

5. Ibid., p. 52.

6. Jean-Michel Nectoux, "Gabriel Fauré," in *The New Grove Twentieth-Century French Masters* (New York: W. W. Norton, 1986), p. 15. See also Joseph de Marliave, *Etudes musicales* (Paris: Félix Alcan, 1917), p. 32, and Jean-Michel Nectoux, *Fauré* ([Paris:] Editions du Seuil, 1972), p. 39.

7. Nectoux, *Fauré*, pp. 36–37.

8. Nectoux, ed., *Gabriel Fauré: His Life Through His Letters*, p. 342.

9. Nectoux, *Fauré*, p. 40.

10. Alfred Cortot, "Le Dialogue du piano et de la symphonie," *Conférencia*, June 1, 1938, p. 698; cited in Pierre Auclert, "La Ballade, Op. 19 de Fauré," *Bulletin de l'Association des Amis de Gabriel Fauré* 15 (1978), p. 4.

11. Claude Rostand describes the difference amusingly in *L'Oeuvre de Gabriel Fauré*, 3rd ed. ([Paris:] J. B. Janin, [1945]), p. 67.

12. See Nectoux, ed., *Gabriel Fauré: His Life Through His Letters*, pp. 65–67.

13. Critical ed. in N. Metner, *Sobranie sočinenij* (Moscow, 1959–63), vol. 2.

14. Camille Saint-Saëns, "König Harald Harfagar (nach H. Heine): Ballade," Op. 59 (Berlin: Bote & Bock, [1880]).

15. Edward MacDowell, *Drei Poesien*, Op. 20 (Breslau [Wrocław]: Julius Hainauer, [1886]; critical ed. in Parakilas, ed., *The Nineteenth-Century Piano Ballade*).

16. Agathe Backer-Grøndahl, "Ballade," No. 5 in *Fantasistykker*, Op. 36 (Oslo: Carl Warmuth, 1895; reprinted in Agathe Backer-Grøndahl, *Piano Music*, new intro. by Charles Slater, New York: Da Capo Press, 1982).

17. Edvard Grieg, "Im Balladenton," No. 5 of *Lyrische Stücke*, Op. 65 (Leipzig: C. F. Peters, 1897).

18. Anton Arensky, *24 Morceaux caractéristiques*, Op. 36 (Source of original publication unknown; reprinted, New York: Edwin F. Kalmus, n.d.).

19. Eugen d'Albert, *Fünf Bagatellen*, Op. 29 (Berlin: Bote & Bock, 1905).

20. Antonín Dvořák, "Selská balada" from *Poetické nálady*, Op. 85 (Berlin: Simrock, 1889; critical ed. of this and other *ballades* in Antonín Dvořák, *Souborné vydání*, Prague: Supraphon, 1955–).

21. Anatol Liadov, "Ballade: Pro starinu," Op. 21 (Leipzig: M. P. Belaïeff, 1890); the subtitle *"Pro starinu"* ("From Olden Times") became the title of the orchestral version that Liadov made later and Belaïeff published in 1906; critical ed. of the piano version in Anatoli Ljadow, *Ausgewählte Klavierstücke*, ed. Christopher Hellmundt (Leipzig: Edition Peters, [1972]); critical ed. of the orchestral version in

A. Liadov, *Sočinenija dlja orkestra / Works for Orchestra*, vol. 1 (Moscow: State Publishers "Music," 1977).

22. The 5/4 meter of the Ballade for piano (Vienna: Universal-Edition, 1916) by the Austrian composer Joseph Marx (1882–1964) probably has no such connection with a particular folk-song tradition, but refers to folk song in general.

23. See Gerald Abraham's entry on "Ljadow" in *Die Musik in Geschichte und Gegenwart*, vol. 8, p. 1062. See also his "Random Thoughts on Lyadov" in his *Slavonic and Romantic Music: Essays and Studies* (New York: St. Martin's Press, [1968]), p. 216.

24. Claude Debussy, "Ballade slave" in *Pièces pour piano* (Paris: Choudens, 1891; several modern reprints).

25. See Léon Vallas, *Claude Debussy et son temps* (Paris: Editions Albin Michel, [1958]), p. 126.

26. Max Reger, "Nordische Ballade" in *Aquarellen: Kleine Tonbilder*, Op. 25 (London: Augener, 1902; critical ed. in Max Reger, *Sämtliche Werke*, Wiesbaden: Breitkopf & Härtel, 1954– , vol. 9).

27. Ferruccio Busoni, *Sechs Stücke für Pianoforte*, Op. 33b (Leipzig: C. F. Peters, 1896; the "Finnish Ballade" is currently reprinted by Edition Fazer, Helsinki).

28. Busoni, *Kultaselle: Zehn kurze Variationen über ein finnisches Volkslied für Violoncello und Pianoforte* (Leipzig: Rudolf Dietrich, [probably 1891]).

29. Alexander Scriabin, *Twelve Etudes*, Op. 8, reprinted in Alexander Scriabin, *The Complete Preludes and Etudes for Pianoforte Solo*, ed. K. N. Igumnov and Y. I. Mil'shteyn (New York: Dover Publications, [1973]).

30. Vítězslav Novák, *Exotikon*, Op. 45 (Vienna: Universal-Edition, 1911).

31. Julius Röntgen, "Ballade," Op. 6 (Leipzig: Breitkopf & Härtel, n.d.).

32. Röntgen, "Ballade (No. 2 in G-moll) für das Klavier," Op. 22 (Leipzig: Breitkopf & Härtel, n.d.).

33. Theodor Kirchner, *Romantische Geschichten*, Op. 73 (Leipzig: C. F. W. Siegel, 1884).

34. Cécile Chaminade, "Ballade," Op. 86 (Paris: Enoch, 1896).

35. Johannes Brahms, *Klavierstücke*, Op. 118 (Berlin: Simrock, 1893; critical ed. in Brahms, *Klavierstücke*, new ed., ed. Walter Georgii, Munich: Henle, [1974]).

36. See McCorkle, *Johannes Brahms: Werkverzeichnis*, p. 472.

37. Kalbeck, *Johannes Brahms*, bk. 4, vol. 2, p. 296.

38. I have been unable to discover whether a score of this Ballade survives. The work is reported in Ferenc Bónis, *Mosonyi Mihály* (Budapest: Gondolat, 1960), p. 33, and listed in the standard Hungarian and foreign music dictionaries. The Mosonyi files of the National Széchényi Library in Budapest, however, contain no reference to it.

39. The review appeared in the *Neue Zeitschrift für Musik* 14 (1841). Wolf Frobenius prints an excerpt from the review on p. 19 of his entry on "Ballade (Neuzeit)" in Eggebrecht, ed., *Handwörterbuch der musikalischen Terminologie*.

40. Henri Vieuxtemps, *Ballade et Polonaise de concert*, Op. 38 (originally published, according to the entry on Vieuxtemps in *The New Grove Dictionary*, in Leipzig around 1860; reprinted, New York: G. Schirmer, 1895).

41. Among the Ballades of Jules de Swert is the "Deuxième Ballade," Op. 12 (Leipzig: Robert Seitz, n.d.).

42. Antonín Dvořák, "Ballade," Op. 15, first published in the Christmas supplement of the *Magazine of Music* (London, 1884).

43. Franz Neruda, "Ballade pour violon, avec accompagnement de piano," Op. 42 (London: Chappell, n.d.); Anton Arensky, "Petite Ballade," No. 1 of *Two Pieces*, Op. 12, for cello and piano (Moscow: P. Jurgenson, n.d.); Jenő Hubay, "Ballade pour violon avec accompagnement de piano," Op. 48, No. 1 (London: Joseph Williams,

n.d.); Christian Sinding, "Ballade," No. 3 in *Vier Stücke...für Violine und Pianoforte*, Op. 61 (Leipzig: C. F. Peters, n.d.).

44. George Henschel, "Ballade pour violon avec accompagnement d'orchestre ou de piano," Op. 39 (Hamburg: D. Rahter, n.d.); Moritz Moszkowski, "Ballade," No. 1 of *Zwei Concertstücke für die Violine mit Begleitung des Pianoforte*, Op. 16 (Breslau [Wrocław]: Julius Hainauer, n.d.); Alexander Mackenzie, "Highland Ballad," No. 1 of *Two Pieces for Violin and Piano*, Op. 47 (London: Novello, Ewer, n.d.); Josef Suk, "Ballade" from *Ballade und Serenade für Violoncell mit Pianoforte*, Op. 3 (Berlin: Simrock, 1900).

45. Pablo de Sarasate, "Ballade pour violon avec accompagnement de piano," Op. 31 (Paris: Durand, Schoenewerk, n.d.).

46. Reinhold Glière, "Ballade pour violoncelle avec accompagnement de piano," Op. 4 (Leipzig: M. P. Belaïeff, 1903).

47. Vítězslav Novák, *Trio quasi una ballata*, Op. 27 (Berlin: Simrock, 1903).

48. See Vladimír Lébl, *Vítězslav Novák* (Prague: Supraphon, 1968), p. 24.

49. Leó Weiner, "Ballada," Op. 8 (Budapest: Rózsavölgyi, 1912). Weiner orchestrated the work as "Ballata per clarinetto ed orchestra," Op. 28 (Budapest: Music Edition, 1954).

50. Joseph Marx, "Ballade" (Leipzig: Schuberthaus, 1912).

51. Philipp Jarnach, "Ballade" (Paris: Durand, 1913).

52. Joseph Bohuslav Foerster, "Ballata für Violine und Orchester," Op. 92 (edition for violin and piano, Vienna and Leipzig: Universal-Edition, [1917]).

53. Sergei Prokofiev, "Ballada," Op. 15 (originally published 1912; rev. ed., ed. F. H. Schneider, London: Boosey & Hawkes, n.d.).

54. Sergei Prokofiev, *Prokofiev by Prokofiev: A Composer's Memoir*, ed. David H. Appel, trans. Guy Daniels (Garden City, New York: Doubleday, 1979), pp. 61–62.

55. Philipp Scharwenka, "Ballade," Op. 94a (Leipzig: Breitkopf & Härtel, 1894).

56. Józef Wieniawski, "Ballade," Op. 31 (Hamburg: August Cranz, 1884; critical ed. in Parakilas, ed., *The Nineteenth-Century Piano Ballade*).

57. Not only narrative *ballades* refer to Chopin's music in this way. The Ballade, Op. 34 (Leipzig: M. P. Belaïeff, 1903), by the Russian composer and pianist Felix Blumenfeld (1863–1931) is a work in variation form that imitates piano styles from several genres of Chopin's music.

58. Bohuslav Martinů, "Ballada—Pod Krzecův obraz—Poslední akordy Chopina," autograph score in the Civic Museum, Polička, Czechoslovakia. The score is catalogued in Miloš Šafránek, *Bohuslav Martinů: Leben und Werk* (original Czech ed., 1961; German trans. [Prague:] Artia, [1964]), p. 378.

59. Anatol Provazník, "Ballade en souvenir du grand maître Fr. Chopin: Drame passionel," Op. 130 (Vienna: Universal-Edition, 1924).

60. Ludomir Różycki, "Ballade," Op. 18 (Cracow: A. Piwarski, 1904).

61. Różycki, "Balladyna: Poème pour piano," Op. 25 (Cracow: A. Piwarski, 1909).

62. Eugen d'Albert, *Vier Klavierstücke*, Op. 16 (Leipzig: C. F. Peters, 1898).

63. George Templeton Strong, "Ballade," Op. 22 [ca. 1885], and "Zweite Ballade," Op. 34 (Leipzig: F. M. Geidel, 1888).

64. Amy Beach, "Ballad," Op. 6 (Boston: Arthur P. Schmidt, 1894; reprinted in Amy Beach, *Piano Music*, intro. Sylvia Glickman, New York: Da Capo Press, 1982).

65. See Friedman, *The Penguin Book of Folk Ballads*, pp. x–xi.

66. Vítězslav Novák, "Ballada, dle Byronova *Manfreda*," Op. 2 (Prague: Fr. A. Urbánek, 1893; critical ed. in Parakilas, ed., *The Nineteenth-Century Piano Ballade*).

67. Enrique Granados, *Goyescas: Los Majos enamorados* (Madrid: Union

Musical Española, 1912–14; reissued, 1972).

68. Noble W. Kreider, "Ballad," Op. 3, printed in vol. 5, no. 40, of the Wa-Wan Series of American Compositions (Newton Center, Massachusetts: The Wa-Wan Press, 1906). Reprinted in *The Wa-Wan Press 1901–1911*, ed. Vera Brodsky Lawrence (New York: Arno Press and The New York Times, 1970), vol. 3, p. 280.

69. Busoni's *Indian Fantasy*, Op. 44 (1915), for piano and orchestra, and the two "books" of Busoni's *Indian Journal*, one for piano and the other (Op. 47) for small orchestra (both 1916).

70. José Vianna da Motta, "Ballada sobre duas melodias portuguezas," Op. 16 (Porto: Moreira de Sá, n.d.).

71. Béla Bartók, *[A] Gyermekeknek* (Budapest: Károly Rozsnyai, [1909–11]; reprints by various publishers).

72. See Bartók, "Contemporary Music in Piano Teaching" (1940), in *Béla Bartók Essays*, ed. Benjamin Suchoff (New York: St. Martin's Press, [1976]), p. 426.

73. See, for example, David Brown, "Mikhail Glinka" in *The New Grove Russian Masters 1* (New York: W. W. Norton, [1986]), pp. 20, 30–31.

74. The text in Slovak and English is given in the introduction to *Piano Music of Béla Bartók*, ed. Benjamin Suchoff, ser. 2 (New York: Dover Publications, [1981]), p. xx.

75. Though this is the only piece in the collection that Bartók named a "ballad," others are based on songs that can be considered ballads. One of these, Number 13 in the Hungarian set ("Megöltek egy legényt"), is called "Ballad" in posthumous editions and in the list of works in Jozsef Ujfalussy's *Béla Bartók*, trans. Ruth Pataki ([Budapest:] Corvina Press, [1971]). This piece of only two stanzas nevertheless resembles the Janko Ballad in its dramatic last phrase.

76. See, for example, "The Relation Between Contemporary Hungarian Art Music and Folk Music," Number 45 in Bartók, *Essays*.

77. Bartók, *Tizenöt magyar parasztdal* (Vienna: Universal-Edition, [1920]).

78. Bartók, "Contemporary Music in Piano Teaching," in *Essays*, p. 429. When Bartók delivered this lecture, he illustrated the quoted sentence by playing this Ballad, among other pieces. See p. 429, n. 1.

79. Bartók, *Ungarische Bauernlieder* for orchestra (Vienna: Universal-Edition, 1933).

80. Bartók, *Hungarian Folk Music*, trans. M. D. Calvocoressi (London: Oxford University Press, 1931; reprinted, Westport, Connecticut: Hyperion Press, [1979]). The melody is number A.II.34a. The text, in Hungarian and English, appears on pp. 112–13.

81. Leoš Janáček, *Sonata per violino e piano* (Prague: Hudební Matice, 1922; rev. ed., ed. Joseph Suk, Miami Lakes, Florida: Masters Music Publications, n.d.). Janáček wrote two other violin sonatas, now lost, in 1880.

82. Jaroslav Vogel, *Leoš Janáček: A Biography*, trans. Geraldine Thomsen-Muchová, rev. Karel Janovický (London: Orbis Publishing, [1981]), p. 213.

83. Vogel, *Leoš Janáček*, p. 214. Milena Černohorská, *Leoš Janáček*, German trans. Adolf Langer (Prague: Statní Hudební Vydavatelství, 1966), p. 40.

84. See Bohumír Štědroň, *Das Werk von Leoš Janáček*, trans. Vladimir Brožovsky (privately published, 1959), pp. 35, 75.

85. Vogel, *Leoš Janáček*, p. 215.

86. Ibid.

87. Claude Debussy, *En blanc et noir* (Paris: Durand, 1915). The idea of considering this movement within the genre of the piano *ballade* was proposed by Gertrud Axel in *Die Klavierballade*.

88. *The Poems of François Villon*, trans. Galway Kinnell (Boston: Houghton Mifflin, 1977), p. 175.

89. Vallas, *Claude Debussy*, p. 408.

90. Letter to Jacques Durand, July 22, 1915, published in *Lettres de Claude Debussy à son éditeur* (Paris: A. Durand, 1927), p. 138.

91. Letter to Jacques Durand, August 5, 1915, ibid., p. 142.

CHAPTER 8 (pages 203–29)

1. The overture was published by itself in a four-hand arrangement for piano: Anselm Hüttenbrenner, *Ouverture zur Oper Lenore und für das Pianoforte zu vier Händen eingerichtet* (Graz: [published by the composer,] n.d.).

2. A review that was reprinted in the first edition of the piano version refers to "two independent editions by the composer for piano and for large orchestra."

3. Hans von Bülow, *Ballade für grosses Orchester, nach Uhlands Dichtung: Des Sängers Fluch*, Op. 16 (Berlin: C. F. Peters, n.d.).

4. See Marie von Bülow, *Hans von Bülow in Leben und Wort* (Stuttgart: J. Engelhorn, 1925), p. 89.

5. See Fritz Martini, "Ohnmacht und Macht des Gesanges. Zu Uhlands Ballade *Des Sängers Fluch*," in *Gedichte und Interpretationen*, vol. 3: *Klassik und Romantik*, ed. Wulf Segebrecht (Stuttgart: Philipp Reclam, [1984]), pp. 322–33.

6. There were song settings by Conradin Kreutzer (1780–1849), Heinrich Esser (1818–1872), and Joseph Gersbach (1787–1830). See Max Friedländer, "Uhlands Gedichte in der Musik," in vol. 1 of *Uhlands Werke*, ed. Ludwig Fränkel (Leipzig: Bibliographisches Institut, 1893).

7. Translation by W. W. Skeat in *The Songs and Ballads of Uhland* (London: Williams & Norgate, 1864), p. 414.

8. See the review (by J. von Arnold?) in *Neue Zeitschrift für Musik* 59/24 (December 11, 1863), pp. 215–16. Bülow was on the editorial board of the journal.

9. Ödön de Mihalovich, *Ballade für grosses Orchester nach Strachwitz' Dichtung Das Geisterschiff* (Mainz: B. Schott, [1879]).

10. Mihalovich, *Ballade nach Paul Gyulai's Dichtung A selló (Die Nixe) für grosses Orchester* (Mainz: B. Schott, [1879]).

11. Mihalovich, *Hero und Leander, nach Schiller's Ballade für grosses Orchester* (Mainz: B. Schott, [1879]).

12. Mihalovich, *La Ronde du sabbat, d'après la ballade de Victor Hugo* (Mainz: B. Schott, [1879]).

13. August Klughardt, *Lenore: Symphonische Dichtung nach Bürger's Ballade für grosses Orchester*, Op. 27 (Leipzig: Ernst Eulenburg, 1875).

14. Joachim Raff, *Lenore: Symphonie (No. 5 in E dur) für grosses Orchester*, Op. 177 (Leipzig: Robert Seitz, 1873; reprinted, Berlin: Ries & Erler, 1881).

15. Ernst Rudorff, *Ballade (Introduction, Scherzo und Finale) für grosses Orchester*, Op. 15 (Berlin: Simrock, n.d.).

16. Julius Röntgen, *Ballade über eine norwegische Volksmelodie für Orchester*, Op. 36 (Berlin: Simrock, 1896).

17. Paul Ertel, *Hero und Leander: Des Meeres und der Liebe Wellen (Schiller-Grillparzer). Sinfonische Dichtung für grosses Orchester* (Leipzig: Otto Junne, [1908]).

18. Jean Sibelius, *Karelia: Suite für Orchester*, Op. 11 (Leipzig: Breitkopf & Härtel, [1906]).

19. See Erik Tawaststjerna, *Sibelius*, vol. 1: *1865–1905*, trans. Robert Layton (Berkeley: University of California Press, 1976), pp. 146–48.

20. Henri Duparc, *Lénore: Poème symphonique pour orchestre d'après la*

ballade de Bürger (Leipzig: F. E. C. Leuckart, [1894–95], and Paris: Alexis Rouart [succeeded by Editions Salabert], n.d.). Further information on publication, along with background and analysis, is given in Nancy van der Elst, *Henri Duparc: L'Homme et son oeuvre* (Thesis, Université de Lille III, 1972).

21. Vincent d'Indy, *La Forêt enchantée: Légende-symphonie d'après une ballade de Uhland*, Op. 8 (reprinted[?], Paris: Heugel, 1892).

22. César Franck, *Le Chasseur maudit*, first published in 1882 by L. Grus, according to Wilhelm Mohr, *Caesar Franck*, 2nd ed. (Tutzing: Hans Schneider, 1969); new ed. by Roger Fiske (London: Ernst Eulenburg, 1973).

23. Roger Fiske reprints Franck's French summary in the Eulenburg edition. The English translation of Bürger's poem by Walter Scott can be found in collected editions of Scott's poetry.

24. See, for example, Laurence Davies, *Franck* (London: J. M. Dent and New York: Octagon Books, [1973]), p. 97.

25. Ibid.

26. Introduction to the Eulenburg score, pp. iv–v.

27. Paul Dukas, *L'Apprenti sorcier: Scherzo d'après une ballade de Goethe* (Paris: A. Durand, n.d.; various reprints).

28. J. Guy Ropartz, "Les Oeuvres symphoniques de Paul Dukas," *La Revue musicale* 166 (May–June 1936), p. 66.

29. Maurice Emmanuel in *Le Monde musical* (July 31, 1935), cited in Georges Favre, *Paul Dukas: Sa vie—son oeuvre* (Paris: La Colombe, [1948]), p. 52.

30. Favre, *Paul Dukas*, p. 52.

31. Carolyn Abbate, "What the Sorcerer Said," *19th-Century Music* XII/3 (Spring 1989), p. 230.

32. Translation by James Parakilas. The French text of the note appears in Favre, *Paul Dukas*, pp. 50–51, as well as in Jacques Helbé, *Paul Dukas 1865–1935* (Paris: Editions P. M. P., [1975]), p. 41. According to these sources, Dukas quotes a later version of the apprentice's theme (the version found four measures after rehearsal-number 17), rather than the first version, which I have given in Example 8-10.

33. Ropartz, "Les Oeuvres symphoniques de Paul Dukas," p. 66.

34. Favre, *Paul Dukas*, p. 50; Helbé, *Paul Dukas 1865–1935*, p. 41.

35. G. W. Hopkins, "Paul Dukas," in *The New Grove Dictionary*, vol. 5, p. 691.

36. Abbate, in "What the Sorcerer Said," compares some of the versions of the "Evocation motive," elaborately explaining certain musical differences in narrative terms, but without observing that each of these versions represents different words in the poetic text.

37. Hopkins, "Paul Dukas," p. 691.

38. See Henri Bergson, *Le Rire* (1st ed., 1900; 8th ed., Paris: Félix Alcan, 1912; English trans. in Wylie Sypher, *Comedy*, Garden City, New York: Doubleday Anchor Books, [1956]).

39. George Alexander Macfarren, *Overture to Chevy Chace*, arranged for piano, four hands (London: Wessel, n.d.), was published in 1841, according to Nicholas Temperley ("George Macfarren" in *The New Grove Dictionary*, vol. 11, p. 425).

40. See Temperley, "George Macfarren," p. 425.

41. *A Collection of National English Airs...Harmonized, for the Pianoforte, by W. Crotch, G. Alex. Macfarren, and J. Augustine Wade*, ed. W. Chappell, 2 vols. (London: Chappell, 1839–40).

42. Review in *The Musical World*, (February 10, 1837), p. 124, cited in Percy M. Young, *A History of British Music* (London: Ernest Benn, [1967]), p. 453, n. 2.

43. See Temperley, "George Macfarren," p. 425.
44. Alexander Mackenzie, *La Belle Dame sans merci: Ballad for Orchestra*, Op. 29 (London: Novello, Ewer, n.d.).
45. Earl Wasserman analyzes the symmetrical construction of the poem in *The Finer Tone*, pp. 65-83.
46. Hamish MacCunn, *The Ship o' the Fiend: Orchestral Ballad*, Op. 5 (London: Augener, n.d.).
47. MacCunn, *The Dowie Dens o' Yarrow: Ballad-Overture for Orchestra*, Op. 6 (London: Augener, n.d.). In Francis Child's standard collection *English and Scottish Popular Ballads*, the title of this ballad is "The Braes of Yarrow."
48. Shaw, *Music in London 1890-94*, vol. 2, p. 87. Shaw's comment is discussed earlier, p. 86.
49. Samuel Coleridge-Taylor, *Ballade in A Minor for Full Orchestra*, Op. 33 (London: Novello, 1899).
50. John McEwen, *Grey Galloway: A Border Ballad for Full Orchestra* (London: Novello, 1910).
51. Frederick Delius, *Eventyr: Once Upon a Time (After Asbjørnsen's Folklore): A Ballad for Orchestra* (London: Augener, 1921).
52. Asbjørnsen and Moe, *Norske Folkeeventyr*, first published 1841-44; many editions in English.
53. Eric Fenby, *Delius* (London: Faber & Faber, [1971]), p. 74.
54. See Rachel Lowe, *Frederick Delius 1862-1934: A Catalogue of the Music Archive of the Delius Trust, London* (London: Delius Trust, 1974), pp. 93-94.
55. Fenby, *Delius*, p. 74.

CHAPTER 9 (pages 230-70)

1. See, for example, Katz, *The Literary Ballad*; Milada Součková, *The Czech Romantics* (The Hague: Mouton, 1958); and the articles "Polish poetry" by Manfred Kridl and Zbigniew Folejewski and "Yugoslav poetry" by Vera Javarek in the *Princeton Encyclopedia*, pp. 651-52 and 903-04.
2. Piotr Tchaikovksy, *Voyvode: Ballade symphonique pour orchestre*, Op. 78 (posthumous) (Leipzig: M. P. Belaïeff, 1897; critical ed. in P. Tchaikovsky, *Polnoe sobranie sočinenij [Complete Edition of Compositions]*, vol. 26, ed. I. N. Iordan [Moscow: 1961]).
3. See Ju. Keldyš, ed., *E. F. Napravnik: Avtobiografičeskie, tvorčeskie materialy, dokumenty, pis'ma* [collected by L. M. Kutateladz] (Leningrad: Gosudarstvennoe Muzykal'noe Izdatel'stvo, 1959), p. 423. I have not been able to examine the Nápravník work for any possible musical influence on Tchaikovsky's *Voevoda*.
4. See Weintraub, *The Poetry of Adam Mickiewicz*, p. 42.
5. See the introduction to vol. 26 of the Tchaikovsky *Complete Edition*, p. xv.
6. According to Prof. David Brown, in a 1989 letter to the present author, Tchaikovsky can be presumed to have read *Romeo and Juliet* and the Francesca da Rimini passage of *The Inferno* in Russian translations and *Manfred* in a French translation.
7. This and subsequent passages of Taneiev's letter are taken from the introduction to vol. 26 of the Tchaikovsky *Complete Edition*, p. xvii. Translations are by Prof. Jane Costlow of Bates College.
8. Henry Zajaczkowski, *Tchaikovsky's Musical Style* (Ann Arbor, Michigan:

UMI Research Press, [1987]), pp. 19, 21.

9. Ibid., p. 21.

10. Tchaikovsky himself later extracted most of this speech and transcribed it for piano, under the title "Aveu passionné" ("Passionate Confession"). The piano piece is published in the Tchaikovsky *Complete Edition*, vol. 53, pp. 229-31.

11. David Brown, "Pyotr Il'yich Tchaikovsky," in *The New Grove Russian Masters* 1 (New York: W. W. Norton, [1986]), p. 221.

12. Adapted from the translation by Arthur Prudden Coleman and Marion Moore Coleman, under the title "Guards," in Helsztynski, ed., *Adam Mickiewicz 1798-1855*, pp. 47-48.

13. A particularly convincing performance of *Voevoda* is that by Claudio Abbado and the Chicago Symphony Orchestra, recorded by CBS (MK 42094).

14. The score I have consulted is Liapunov's own reduction for two pianos, four hands, published as *Ballade pour orchestre*, Op. 2 (Berlin: Bote & Bock, [1897]).

15. Alexander Taneiev, *Aleša Popovič: Muzykal'nyj Èpizod dlja bol'šogo orkestra. Soderžanie zaimstvovano iz poèmy gr. A. K. Tolstago / Ballade d'après une poésie (Aliocha Popowitch) du Cte. A. Tolstoy, pour grand orchestre*, Op. 11 (Moscow and Leipzig: P. Jurgenson, [1907]).

16. Alexander Glazunov, *Ballade pour grand orchestre*, Op. 78 (Leipzig: M. P. Belaïeff, 1903).

17. František Čelakovský, *Ohlas písní českých* (various reprints since the original edition). The volume was translated into German under the title *Widerhall tschechischen Lieder* by Friedrich Karl Pick (Prague: Heller & Stranský, 1919).

18. See Součkova, *The Czech Romantics*, pp. 32-33.

19. Zdeněk Fibich, *Toman a lesní panna*, Op. 49, ed. Ludvík Boháček for the Zdeněk Fibich Society (Prague: Export Artia, 1959).

20. On Fibich's style, see John Tyrrell, "Zdeněk Fibich," in *The New Grove Dictionary*, vol. 6, pp. 521-22.

21. Originally published in *Dalibor* 2 (1874), the article was reprinted in Artuš Rektorys, ed., *Zdeněk Fibich: Sborník dokumentů a studií* (Prague: ORBIS, 1951), pp. 42-56.

22. Novotný writes of the "Warning note" (*Výstražný ton*) in the opening passage of the work.

23. The sources of these two themes are given by Ludvík Boháček in his preface to the score of *Toman a lesní panna*, p. iv.

24. Antonín Dvořák, *The Water Goblin*, described on the autograph as *Vodník, sinfonická báseň (dle K. Jaromíra Erbena) pro velký orkestr* and published as *Der Wassermann*, Op. 107 (Berlin: Simrock, 1896); *The Noon Witch*, described on the autograph as *Polednice, sinfonická báseň (dle K. Jaromíra Erbena) pro velký orkestr* and published as *Die Mittagshexe*, Op. 108 (Berlin: Simrock, 1896); *The Golden Spinning Wheel*, described on the autograph as *Zlatý kolovrat, sinfonická báseň (dle K. Jaromíra Erbena) pro velký orkestr* and published as *Das goldene Spinnrad*, Op. 109 (Berlin: Simrock, 1896); and *The Wild Dove*, described on the autograph as *Holoubek (opus 110) (dle báseň K. Jaromíra Erbena) sinfonická báseň pro velký orkestr* and published as *Die Waldtaube*, Op. 110 (Berlin: Simrock, 1899). For further information see Jarmil Burghauser, *Antonín Dvořák: Thematický katalog* (Prague: Artia, 1960).

25. Other works and projects of Dvořák based on ballads by Erben are described by Jarmil Burghauser in his introduction to *The Water Goblin* in ser. 3, vol. 14 of the Dvořák *Complete Edition*: *A. Dvořák: Souborné vydání*, ed. Otakar Šourek et al. (Prague: Artia, 1958), p. xvi.

26. See John Clapham, "Dvořák's Unknown Letters on His Symphonic Poems,"

Music & Letters 56 (1975), pp. 277–87.

27. See ibid., p. 278. Lists of the points of correspondence between the poems and the music are found in the introductions to the four works in the *Complete Edition* (in the cases of *The Water Goblin* and *The Golden Spinning Wheel*, where the correspondences are most numerous, the lists are given only in the Czech versions of the introductions).

28. Otakar Šourek, *The Orchestral Works of Antonín Dvořák*, abridged English version by Roberta Finlayson Samsour ([Prague:] Artia, [1956]; Czech ed., 1944–46), pp. 331, 332, 335.

29. The only published English translation of the poem, by R. A. Ginsburg in his collection *The Soul of a Century: Collection of Czech Poetry in English* (Berwyn, Illinois: privately published, 1942), breaks off in the middle.

30. Janáček's review of *The Water Goblin* appeared in *Hlídka* (New Series) 2 (1897), pp. 285–92; the passage cited here is found on p. 287. His reviews of *The Noon Witch* and *The Golden Spinning Wheel* appeared in the same volume of *Hlídka*, pp. 454–59 and 594–98 respectively; his review of *The Wild Dove* appeared in *Hlídka* (New Series) 3 (1898), pp. 277–82. The four reviews were reprinted in *Musikologie* 5 (1958), pp. 324–59.

31. Šourek, *The Orchestral Works*, p. 317.

32. See Clapham, "Dvořák's Unknown Letters," pp. 279, 281–82.

33. Šourek, *The Orchestral Works*, p. 314.

34. John Clapham, *Antonín Dvořák: Musician and Craftsman* (New York: St. Martin's Press, [1966]), p. 119.

35. In fact, the whole melody is first heard as a bass line during the water goblin's triumph in the first episode (mm. 261–62), but Dvořák can hardly have expected listeners to retain that association through the intervening music.

36. See Janáček in *Hlídka* (New Series) 2, p. 288. Without having seen either Dvořák's sketches or his letter for the benefit of the Viennese program notes, Janáček did not follow the narrative progression of the passage in every detail as Dvořák himself explained it, but he understood perfectly the principles on which Dvořák was imitating the poem.

37. In fact, each of the four sections of Erben's poem has a different metrical-stanzaic form.

38. See Clapham, "Dvořák's Unknown Letters," p. 281.

39. The mother-daughter conflict may have added to the interest of the story for Janáček, who was engaged in writing *Jenůfa* at the time, while Dvořák's emphasis on the opposition between the human and spirit realms fits with his interest in the story of *Rusalka*, which he set a couple of years later.

40. For precise information on the composition and first performances of these works, see Clapham, *Antonín Dvořák: Musician and Craftsman*, p. 117.

41. A German translation ("Die Mittagsdrude") appears in *Der Blumenstrauss von Karl Jaromír Erben*, a translation of *Kytice* by Eduard Albert (Vienna: Alfred Höller, 1909).

42. See Dvořák's description of the themes in Clapham, "Dvořák's Unknown Letters," p. 282.

43. A translation of Erben's poem by Flora Pauline (Wilson) Kopta appears in her *Bohemian Legends and Other Poems* (New York: Jenkins, 1896).

44. Součkova, *The Czech Romantics*, p. 123.

45. Šourek quotes the themes, pointing out their associations and relations, in *The Orchestral Works*, pp. 331–37.

46. The poetic lines that inspired Dvořák's phrases are listed by Burghauser in the introduction to the score in the *Complete Edition*, p. xi.

47. Janáček in *Hlídka* (New Series) 2, p. 597; Šourek, *The Orchestral Works*,

pp. 333–34; Antonín Sychra, *Antonín Dvořák: Zur Ästhetik seines sinfonischen Schaffens*, trans. Gert Jäger and Jürgen Morgenstern (Leipzig: VEB Deutscher Verlag für Musik, 1973; original Czech ed., Prague, 1959), pp. 124–30.
48. The poem is translated as "The Dove" in Ginsburg, *The Soul of a Century*.
49. Dvořák himself labeled this theme the "curse motive" in his sketch. See Šourek, *The Orchestral Works*, p. 339.
50. The exception, *The Wild Dove*, was premiered by Janáček in Brno.
51. These letters are reproduced in full in Clapham, "Dvořák's Unknown Letters," pp. 279–85.
52. Ibid., pp. 286–87.
53. Ibid., p. 287.
54. From Hanslick's review of *The Water Goblin*, reprinted in Eduard Hanslick, *Die moderne Oper*, vol. 8 [*Am Ende des Jahrhunderts (1895-1899)*] (Berlin: Allgemeiner Verein für Deutsche Litteratur, 1899), p. 217.
55. Ibid.
56. Vítězslav Novák, *Toman a lesní panna: Symfonická báseň dle české pověsti* (Vienna: Universal-Edition, 1919).
57. Janáček, *Šumařovo dítě: Ballada—Sv. Čech* (Brno: Club of the Friends of Art in Brno, 1914; critical ed. by Jiří Vysloužil in the Janáček *Complete Critical Edition*, Kassel: Bärenreiter, 1984).
58. Janáček, *Balada Blanická: Symfonická báseň* (critical ed. by Břetislav Bakala, Prague: Artia, 1958).
59. Janáček explained his system of thematic references in a note written for the first performance, printed in *Hudební revue* 7 (1913-14), pp. 203–05, and translated into English in *Janáček's Uncollected Essays on Music*, ed. and trans. Mirka Zemanová (London: Marion Boyars, [1989]), pp. 80–83.
60. For an authoritative account of the narrative scheme of the work, based partly on Janáček's own description of it in *Hudební revue*, see Vogel, *Leoš Janáček*, pp. 190–93.
61. See Zemanová, ed., *Janáček's Uncollected Essays*, p. 81.
62. Vogel gives the literary background of the legend as well as a full account of Janáček's composition in *Leoš Janáček*, pp. 250–53.
63. Jarmil Burghauser (in *Musikologie* 3 [1955]) connects this theme with a Slovak folk song about going to war, but Bohumír Štědroň is more impressed with the fact that Janáček chose not to use the St. Wenceslas hymn here (see his introduction to the Bakala edition of the score, p. xi).
64. Vogel, in *Leoš Janáček*, p. 252, says that "Janáček gives no indication of the long passage of time during Jíra's sleep." On this one significant point I disagree with his interpretation of the work.

CHAPTER 10 (pages 273–84)

1. Unfortunately, there is no catalog of twentieth-century *ballades* comparable to the catalog of nineteenth-century piano *ballades* at the end of Günther Wagner's *Die Klavierballade*.
2. Jacques Ibert, *La Ballade de la Geôle de Reading* (Paris: Alphonse Leduc, [1924]).
3. Kurt Atterberg, *Ballade und Passacaglia über ein Thema im schwedischen Volkston für Orchester*, Op. 38 (London: Ernst Eulenburg, n.d.).
4. Henk Badings, *Ballade voor orkest: Symphonische Variaties over: "Het waren twee Conincskindren"* ([Amsterdam: Donemus; New York: C. F. Peters], 1950).

5. Sándor Szokolay, *Ballata Sinfonica per Orchestra* (Budapest: Editio Musica, 1970).

6. John Ireland, "Ballade" (New York: Associated Music Publishers, 1931; reprinted in John Ireland, *The Collected Piano Works*, London: Stainer & Bell, [1976], vol. 3). George Perle, "Ballade" (New York: C. F. Peters, [1983]).

7. Richard Goode, liner notes to his recording of George Perle's Serenade No. 3 for Piano and Chamber Orchestra, Ballade, and Concertino for Piano, Winds and Timpani (Nonesuch Digital 79108).

8. Frederic Rzewski, *Squares* and *North American Ballads* ([Tokyo]: Zen-On Music, 1983).

9. *Songs of Peace, Freedom, and Protest*, collected and edited by Tom Glazer (New York: David McKay, [1970]).

10. Roy Harris, *American Ballads* (New York: Carl Fischer, [1947]).

11. Charles Koechlin, *Ballade pour piano et orchestre* ([Paris:] Editions françaises de musique, 1974).

12. Darius Milhaud, *Ballade pour piano et orchestre* [Op. 61], ed. for two pianos, four hands (Vienna and Leipzig: Universal-Edition, 1929).

13. Alexander Glazunov, *Concerto Ballata pour violoncelle (en Ut)*, Op. 108 (Leipzig: M. P. Belaïeff, n.d.).

14. Benjamin Britten, *Scottish Ballad for Two Pianos and Orchestra*, Op. 26 (London: Hawkes & Son, 1946; full score, copyright 1969).

15. Donald Mitchell, liner notes to recording of Britten, *Canadian Carnival, Young Apollo, Four French Songs*, and *Scottish Ballad* by the City of Birmingham Symphony Orchestra conducted by Simon Rattle (Angel Records DS-37919).

16. All six Ballades are published by Universal-Edition, Vienna. Descriptions and information about first performances can be found in the complete list of works in Frank Martin, *Un Compositeur médite sur son art: Ecrits et pensées recueillis par sa femme*, introduction by Bernard Gavoty (Neuchâtel: A la Baconnière, [1977]).

17. Frank Martin, *A propos de...: Commentaires de Frank Martin sur ses oeuvres* (Neuchâtel: A la Baconnière, [1984]), p. 26. Translation by James Parakilas. Martin's essays on his other Ballades are also reprinted in this collection.

18. Martin, *A propos de*, p. 41.

19. See, for example, Bernard Martin, *Frank Martin, ou La réalité du rêve* (Neuchâtel: A la Baconnière, [1973]), p. 145.

20. Martin, *A propos de*, p. 185. This essay, reprinted from the jacket of a recording (Vox/Candide CE 31065), appears in English; the translator is not identified.

CHAPTER 11 (pages 285–88)

1. On the "Balada" movement of this suite, see ch. 7, p. 190.

2. On the relation of the opera to the piano suite, see Charles Wilson, "The Two Versions of *Goyescas*," *Monthly Musical Record* 81 (October 1951), pp. 203–07.

3. Luther Noss, *Paul Hindemith in the United States* (Urbana: University of Illinois Press, [1989]), p. 122.

Books and Articles Cited

Abbate, Carolyn. "What the Sorcerer Said." *19th-Century Music* XII/3 (Spring 1989): 221–30.

Abraham, Gerald. *Chopin's Musical Style*. Corrected ed. London: Oxford University Press, [1960].

Abraham, Gerald. *Slavonic and Romantic Music: Essays and Studies*. New York: St. Martin's Press, [1968].

Abraham, Gerald, ed. *The New Oxford History of Music*. Vol. 8: *The Age of Beethoven 1790–1830*. London: Oxford University Press, 1982.

Andersen, Flemming G., and Thomas Pettitt. "Mrs. Brown of Falkland: A Singer of Tales?" *Journal of American Folklore* 92, no. 363 [January–March 1979]: 1–24.

Auclert, Pierre. "La Ballade, Op. 19 de Fauré." *Bulletin de l'Association des Amis de Gabriel Fauré* 15 (1978): 3–11.

Axel, Gertrud. *Die Klavierballade*. Dissertation, University of Vienna, 1934.

Bartók, Béla. *Béla Bartók Essays*. Ed. Benjamin Suchoff. New York: St. Martin's Press, [1976].

Bartók, Béla. *Hungarian Folk Music*. Trans. M. D. Calvocoressi. London: Oxford University Press, 1931; reprinted, Westport, Connecticut: Hyperion Press, [1979].

Bellotti, Gastone. *F. Chopin: L'uomo*. [Milan:] Sapere, 1974.

Benestad, Finn, and Dag Schjelderup-Ebbe. *Edvard Grieg: The Man and the Artist*. Trans. William H. Halverson and Leland B. Sateren. Lincoln: University of Nebraska Press, [1988].

Bergson, Henri. *Le Rire*. English trans. in Wylie Sypher, *Comedy*. Garden City, New York: Doubleday Anchor Books, [1956].

Boháček, Ludvík. Preface to Zdeněk Fibich, *Toman a lesní panna*, Op. 49. Prague: Export Artia, 1959.

Bold, Alan. *The Ballad*. [London:] Methuen, [1979].

Boldt, Kenwyn G. *The Solo Piano Ballade in the Nineteenth Century*. D. M. A. thesis, Indiana University, 1967.

Bónis, Ferenc. *Mosonyi Mihály*. Budapest: Gondolat, 1960.

Booth, Mark. *The Experience of Songs*. New Haven, Connecticut: Yale University Press, [1981].

Bremond, Claude. *Logique du récit*. Paris: Editions du Seuil, [1973].

Brown, David. *Mikhail Glinka: A Biographical and Critical Study*. London: Oxford University Press, 1974.

Brown, David. "Mikhail Glinka." In *The New Grove Russian Masters* 1. New York: W. W. Norton, [1986].

Brown, David. "Pyotr Il'yich Tchaikovsky." In *The New Grove Russian Masters* 1. New York: W. W. Norton, [1986].

Brown, Maurice J. E. *Chopin: An Index of His Works in Chronological Order*. 2nd ed., rev. [London:] Macmillan, 1972.

Buchan, David. *The Ballad and the Folk*. London: Routledge & Kegan Paul, [1972].

Bülow, Hans von. *Hans von Bülow: Briefe und Schriften*. Ed. Marie von Bülow. 8 vols. Leipzig: Breitkopf & Härtel, 1895–1908.

Bülow, Marie von. *Hans von Bülow in Leben und Wort*. Stuttgart: J. Engelhorn, 1925.

Burghauser, Jarmil, and Otakar Šourek. Introductions to Dvořák, *The Water Goblin*, *The Noon Witch*, *The Golden Spinning Wheel*, and *The Wild Dove*. Ser. 3, vols. 14 and 15, Dvořák *Complete Edition: A. Dvořák: Souborné vydáni*. Ed. Otakar Šourek et al. Prague: Artia, 1958 (vol. 14), 1955 (vol. 15).

Čelakovský, František. *Widerhall tschechischen Lieder*. German trans. of *Ohlas písní českých* by Friedrich Karl Pick. Prague: Heller & Stranský, 1919.

Černohorská, Milena. *Leoš Janáček*. German trans. Adolf Langer. Prague: Statní Hudební Vydavatelství, 1966.

Chadwick, H. Munro, and N. Kershaw Chadwick. *The Growth of Literature*. 3 vols. New York: Macmillan, 1932–40.

Chappell, W., ed. *A Collection of National English Airs...Harmonized, for the Pianoforte, by W. Crotch, G. Alex. Macfarren, and J. Augustine Wade*. 2 vols. London: Chappell, 1839–40.

Chase, Gilbert. *America's Music: From the Pilgrims to the Present*. New York: McGraw-Hill, [1955].

Chissell, Joan. *Clara Schumann: A Dedicated Spirit*. London: Hamish Hamilton, [1983].

Chopin Congress: Warszawa 1960. See Lissa, Zofia, ed., for complete citation.

Chopin, Fryderyk. *Selected Correspondence of Fryderyk Chopin*. Trans. and ed. Arthur Hedley. New York: McGraw-Hill, [1963].

Clapham, John. *Antonín Dvořák: Musician and Craftsman*. New York: St. Martin's Press, [1966].

Clapham, John. "Dvořák's Unknown Letters on His Symphonic Poems." *Music & Letters* 56 (1975): 277–87.

Cocchiara, Giuseppe. *The History of Folklore in Europe*. Trans. John N. McDaniel. Philadelphia: Institute for the Study of Human Issues, [1981].

Cone, Edward T. *Musical Form and Musical Performance*. New York: W. W. Norton, [1968].

Cortot, Alfred. "Le Dialogue du piano et de la symphonie." *Conférencia*, June 1, 1938.

Dahlhaus, Carl, ed. *Studien zur Trivialmusik des 19. Jahrhunderts*. Regensburg: Gustav Bosse, 1967.

Dahlhaus, Carl. *Nineteenth-Century Music*. Trans. J. Bradford Robinson. Berkeley: University of California Press, [1989].

Danckert, Werner. *Das Volkslied im Abendland*. Bern: Francke, [1966].

Davies, Laurence. *Franck*. London: J. M. Dent and New York: Octagon Books, [1973].

Davies, Norman. *God's Playground: A History of Poland*. 2 vols. New York: Columbia University Press, 1984.

Debussy, Claude. *Lettres de Claude Debussy à son éditeur*. Paris: A. Durand, 1927.

BOOKS AND ARTICLES CITED

Doyle, John G. *Louis Moreau Gottschalk 1829–1869: A Bibliographical Study and Catalog of Works*. Detroit: Information Coordinators, 1982.

Dundes, Alan. *Essays in Folkloristics*. [Meerut, India:] Folklore Institute, [1978].

Eggebrecht, Hans Heinrich, ed. *Handwörterbuch der musikalischen Terminologie*. Wiesbaden: Steiner, 1971– .

Eibner, Franz. "Über die Form der Ballade Op. 23 von Fr. Chopin." *Annales Chopin* 3 (1958): 107–12.

Entwistle, William J. *European Balladry*. Oxford: [Oxford University Press], 1939, 1969.

Erben, Karl Jaromír. *Der Blumenstrauss von Karl Jaromír Erben*. German trans. of *Kytice* by Eduard Albert. Vienna: Alfred Höller, 1909.

Ergang, Robert R. *Herder and the Foundations of German Nationalism*. New York: Columbia University Press, 1931.

Fauré, Gabriel. *Gabriel Fauré: His Life Through His Letters*. Collected, edited, and introduced by Jean-Michel Nectoux. Trans. J. A. Underwood. London: Marion Boyars, 1984.

Favre, Georges. *Paul Dukas: Sa vie—son oeuvre*. Paris: La Colombe, [1948].

Fenby, Eric. *Delius*. London: Faber & Faber, [1971].

Finnegan, Ruth. *Oral Poetry: Its Nature, Significance and Social Context*. Cambridge: Cambridge University Press, [1977].

Fiske, Roger. Introduction to César Franck, *Le Chasseur maudit*. London: Ernst Eulenburg, 1973.

Fiske, Roger. *Scotland in Music: A European Enthusiasm*. Cambridge: Cambridge University Press, [1983].

Friedländer, Max. "Uhlands Gedichte in der Musik." In *Uhlands Werke*. Ed. Ludwig Fränkel. Vol. 1. Leipzig: Bibliographisches Institut, 1893. 541–45.

Friedman, Albert. *The Ballad Revival*. Chicago: University of Chicago Press, [1961].

Friedman, Albert. *The Penguin Book of Folk Ballads of the English-Speaking World*. Harmondsworth, England: Penguin Books, 1976.

Friedman, Albert. "The Oral-Formulaic Theory of Balladry—a Re-rebuttal." In *The Ballad Image: Essays Presented to Bertrand Harris Bronson*. Ed. James Porter. [Los Angeles: Center for the Study of Comparative Folklore and Mythology—UCLA, 1983]. 215–40.

Gabryś, Jerzy, and Janina Cybulska. *Z dziejów polskiej pieśni solowej*. [Cracow:] Polskie Wydawnictwo Muzyczne, [1960].

Gárdonyi, Zoltán. "Nationale Thematik in der Musik Franz Liszts bis zum Jahre 1848." In *Liszt-Bartók: Report of the Second International Musicological Conference—Budapest 1961*. Budapest: Akadémiai Kiadó, 1963. 77–87.

Genette, Gérard. *Narrative Discourse: An Essay in Method*. Trans. Jane E. Lewin. Ithaca, New York: Cornell University Press, [1980].

Gerould, Gordon H. *The Ballad of Tradition*. Oxford: [Oxford University Press,] 1932.

Gide, André. *Notes on Chopin*. Trans. Bernard Frechtman. New York: Philosophical Library, [1949].

Ginsburg, R. A. *The Soul of a Century: Collection of Czech Poetry in English*. Berwyn, Illinois: privately published, 1942.

Glazer, Tom, ed. *Songs of Peace, Freedom, and Protest*. New York: David McKay, [1970].

Goethe, Johann Wolfgang von. "Ballade. Betrachtung und Auslegung." In *Goethes Werke*. Vol. 7: *Schriften zur Literatur und Kunst*. Berlin and Darmstadt: Der Tempel-Verlag, [1967]. 212–14.

Goethe, Johann Wolfgang von. *Westöstlicher Divan*. In *Goethes Werke*. Hamburg ed. Ed. Erich Trunz. Vol. 2. Munich: C. H. Beck, 1982.

Goode, Richard. Liner notes to his recording of George Perle: Serenade No. 3 for Piano and Chamber Orchestra, Ballade, and Concertino for Piano, Winds and Timpani. Nonesuch Digital 79108.

Grabócz, Márta. *Morphologie des oeuvres pour piano de Liszt.* Budapest: MTA Zenetudományi Intézet, 1986.

Green, Douglass M. *Form in Tonal Music.* New York: Holt, Rinehart & Winston, [1965].

Greimas, A. J. "Eléments pour une théorie de l'interprétation du récit mythique." *Communications* 8 (1966): 28-59.

Griffel, Michael. "The Sonata Design in Chopin's Ballades." *Current Musicology* 36 (1983): 125-36.

Gummere, Francis B. *The Popular Ballad.* Boston: Houghton Mifflin, [1907].

Hanslick, Eduard. *Die moderne Oper.* Vol. 8: [*Am Ende des Jahrhunderts (1895-1899)*]. Berlin: Allgemeiner Verein für Deutsche Litteratur, 1899.

Hedley, Arthur. *Chopin.* Rev. Maurice J. E. Brown. London: J. M. Dent & Sons, 1977.

Helbé, Jacques. *Paul Dukas 1865-1935.* Paris: Editions P. M. P., [1975].

Horowitz, Joseph. *Conversations with Arrau.* New York: Limelight Editions, [1984].

Huneker, James. *Chopin: The Man and His Music.* New York: Charles Scribner's Sons, 1900; reprinted, New York: Dover Publications, [1966].

Indy, Vincent d'. Introduction to César Franck, *Selected Piano Compositions.* Reprinted, New York: Dover Publications, 1976.

Iordan, I. N. Introduction to Tchaikovsky, *Voevoda.* Vol. 26 of Tchaikovsky, *Polnoe sobranie sočinenij.* [Moscow: 1961].

Jachimecki, Zdzisław. *Frédéric Chopin et son oeuvre.* Paris: Delagrave, 1930; original Polish ed., 1927.

Janáček, Leoš. Reviews of Dvořák, *The Water Goblin, The Noon Witch, The Golden Spinning Wheel,* and *The Wild Dove. Hlídka* (New Series) 2 (1897): 285-92, 454-59, and 594-98, and (New Series) 3 (1898): 277-82; reprinted in *Musikologie* 5 (1958): 324-59.

Janáček, Leoš. *Janáček's Uncollected Essays on Music.* Ed. and trans. Mirka Zemanová. London: Marion Boyars, [1989].

Jander, Owen. "Beethoven's 'Orpheus in Hades': The *Andante con moto* of the Fourth Piano Concerto." *19th-Century Music* VIII/3 (Spring 1985): 195-212.

Kalbeck, Max. *Johannes Brahms.* 2nd ed. 4 vols. in 8. Berlin: Deutsche Brahms-Gesellschaft, 1908-22.

Kallberg, Jeffrey. "Chopin in the Marketplace: Aspects of the International Music Publishing Industry," Part 2: "The German-Speaking States." *MLA Notes* 39/4 (June 1983): 795-824.

Kallberg, Jeffrey. "The Rhetoric of Genre: Chopin's Nocturne in G Minor." *19th-Century Music* XI/3 (Spring 1988): 238-61.

Katz, Michael R. *The Literary Ballad in Early Nineteenth-Century Russian Literature.* [London:] Oxford University Press, 1976.

Keefer, Lubov. "The Influence of Adam Mickiewicz on the Ballades of Chopin." *American Slavic and East European Review* 5 (May 1946): 38-50.

Keldyš, Ju., ed. *E. F. Napravnik: Avtobiografičeskie, tvorčeskie materialy, dokumenty, pis'ma.* Collected by L. M. Kutateladz. Leningrad: Gosudarstvennoe Muzykal'noe Izdatel'stvo, 1959.

Kentner, Louis. "Solo Piano Music (1827-61)." In *Franz Liszt: The Man and His Music.* Ed. Alan Walker. London: Barrie & Jenkins, [1970]. 79-133.

Kobylańska, Krystyna. *Frédéric Chopin: Thematisch-bibliographisches Werkverzeichnis.* Munich: Henle, 1979.

Kolberg, Oskar. *Pieśni ludu polskiego zebrał i wydał.* Vol. 1. Warsaw: J. Jaworsky, 1857.

Kopta, Flora Pauline (Wilson). *Bohemian Legends and Other Poems.* New York: Jenkins, 1896.

Krzyżanowski, Julian. *A History of Polish Literature.* Trans. Doris Ronowicz. Warsaw: PWN—Polish Scientific Publishers, 1978.

Large, Brian. *Smetana.* [London:] Duckworth, [1970].

Lébl, Vladimír. *Vítězslav Novák.* Prague: Supraphon, 1968.

Leichtentritt, Hugo. *Analyse der Chopin'schen Klavierwerke.* 2 vols. Berlin: Max Hesses Verlag, 1921–22.

Lindeman, Ludvig. *Aeldre og nyere norske Fjeldmelodier, samlede og bearbeidede for pianoforte.* Christiana [Oslo]: P. T. Malling, [1853–67]; reprinted with notes by O. M. Sandvik, [Oslo:] Universitetsforlaget, [1963].

Lissa, Zofia. "Du Style national des oeuvres de Chopin." *Annales Chopin* 2 (1957): 100–78.

Lissa, Zofia, ed. *The Book of the First International Musicological Congress Devoted to the Works of Frederick Chopin (Chopin Congress: Warszawa 1960).* Warsaw: PWN—Polish Scientific Publishers, [1963].

Liszt, Franz. *Gesammelte Schriften von Franz Liszt.* Vol. 6: *Die Zigeuner und ihre Musik in Ungarn.* Trans. and ed. L. Ramann. Leipzig: Breitkopf & Härtel, 1883.

Lowe, Rachel. *Frederick Delius 1862–1934: A Catalogue of the Music Archive of the Delius Trust, London.* London: Delius Trust, 1974.

Marliave, Joseph de. *Etudes musicales.* Paris: Félix Alcan, 1917.

Martin, Bernard. *Frank Martin, ou La réalité du rêve.* Neuchâtel: A la Baconnière, [1973].

Martin, Frank. *Un Compositeur médite sur son art: Ecrits et pensées recueillis par sa femme.* Introduction by Bernard Gavoty. Neuchâtel: A la Baconnière, [1977].

Martin, Frank. *A propos de...: Commentaires de Frank Martin sur ses oeuvres.* Neuchâtel: A la Baconnière, [1984].

Martini, Fritz. "Ohnmacht und Macht des Gesanges. Zu Uhlands Ballade *Des Sängers Fluch.*" In *Gedichte und Interpretationen.* Vol. 3: *Klassik und Romantik.* Ed. Wulf Segebrecht. Stuttgart: Philipp Reclam, [1984]. 322–33.

McCorkle, Margit. *Johannes Brahms: Thematisch-bibliographisches Werkverzeichnis.* Munich: Henle, [1984].

Mickiewicz, Adam. *Poems by Adam Mickiewicz.* Ed. George Rapall Noyes. New York: The Polish Institute of Arts and Sciences in America, 1944.

Mickiewicz, Adam. *Adam Mickiewicz 1798–1855: Selected Poetry and Prose.* Centenary Commemorative Edition. Ed. Stanislaw Helsztynski. Warsaw: Polonia Publishing House, 1955.

Mies, Paul. "Herders Edward-Ballade bei Joh. Brahms." *Zeitschrift für Musikwissenschaft* 2 (1919–20): 225–32.

Mitchell, Donald. Liner notes to Britten, *Canadian Carnival, Young Apollo, Four French Songs,* and *Scottish Ballad.* Recorded by the City of Birmingham Symphony Orchestra, conducted by Simon Rattle. Angel Records DS-37919.

Mohr, Wilhelm. *Caesar Franck.* 2nd ed. Tutzing: Hans Schneider, 1969.

Moscheles, Charlotte. *Recent Music and Musicians, as Described in the Diaries and Correspondence of Ignatz [Ignaz] Moscheles.* Trans. A. D. Coleridge. New York: Henry Holt, 1873; reprinted, New York: Da Capo Press, 1970.

Musik in Geschichte und Gegenwart. Ed. Friedrich Blume. 17 vols. Kassel: Bärenreiter, 1949–86.

Nectoux, Jean-Michel. *Fauré.* [Paris:] Editions du Seuil, 1972.

Nectoux, Jean-Michel. "Gabriel Fauré." In *The New Grove Twentieth-Century French Masters.* New York: W. W. Norton, 1986.

New Cambridge Modern History. Vol. 10: *The Zenith of European Power, 1830–70*. Ed. J. P. T. Bury. Cambridge: Cambridge University Press, 1960.

New Grove Dictionary of Music and Musicians. Ed. Stanley Sadie. 20 vols. [London: Macmillan Publishers, 1980].

Newcomb, Anthony. "Schumann and Late Eighteenth-Century Narrative Strategies." *19th-Century Music* XI/2 (Fall 1987): 164–74.

Newman, William S. *The Sonata Since Beethoven*. Chapel Hill: University of North Carolina Press, [1969].

Niecks, Frederick. *Frederick Chopin as a Man and Musician*. London: 1888; reprinted, New York: Cooper Square Publishers, 1973.

Noss, Luther. *Paul Hindemith in the United States*. Urbana: University of Illinois Press, [1989].

Olrik, Axel. "Epic Laws of Folk Narrative." Trans. in *The Study of Folklore*. Ed. Alan Dundes. Englewood Cliffs, New Jersey: Prentice-Hall, [1965]. 129–41.

Orlova, Alexandra. *Glinka's Life in Music: A Chronicle*. Trans. Richard Hoops. Ann Arbor, Michigan: UMI Research Press, [1988].

Parakilas, James. Preface to *The Nineteenth-Century Piano Ballade: An Anthology*. Madison, Wisconsin: A-R Editions, 1990.

Plantinga, Leon. *Romantic Music: A History of Musical Style in Nineteenth-Century Europe*. New York: W. W. Norton, [1984].

Princeton Encyclopedia of Poetry and Poetics. Enlarged ed. Ed. Alex Preminger. Princeton, New Jersey: Princeton University Press, [1974].

Prokofiev, Sergei. *Prokofiev by Prokofiev: A Composer's Memoir*. Trans. Guy Daniels. Ed. David H. Appel. Garden City, New York: Doubleday, 1979.

Propp, Vladimir. *Morphology of the Folktale*. Trans. Laurence Scott. Rev. and ed. Louis Wagner. Austin: University of Texas Press, 1968.

Raabe, Peter. *Franz Liszt*. 2nd ed. 2 vols. Tutzing: Hans Schneider, 1968.

Rektorys, Artuš, ed. *Zdeněk Fibich: Sborník dokumentů a studií*. Prague: ORBIS, 1951.

Ricoeur, Paul. *Time and Narrative*. Trans. Kathleen McLaughlin [Blamey] and David Pellauer. 3 vols. Chicago: University of Chicago Press, [1984–88].

Riemann Musik Lexikon. 12th ed. Ed. Wilibald Gurlitt. 5 vols. Mainz: B. Schott's Sons, 1959–75.

Ropartz, J. Guy. "Les Oeuvres symphoniques de Paul Dukas." *La Revue musicale* 166 (May-June 1936): 61–68.

Rostand, Claude. *L'Oeuvre de Gabriel Fauré*. 3rd ed. [Paris:] J. B. Janin, [1945].

Šafránek, Miloš. *Bohuslav Martinů: Leben und Werk*. [Prague:] Artia, [1964].

Samson, Jim. *The Music of Chopin*. London: Routledge & Kegan Paul, [1985].

Schenker, Heinrich. *Free Composition (Der freie Satz)*. Trans. and ed. Ernst Oster. 2 vols. New York: Longman, [1979].

Schmitt, Florent. "Les Oeuvres d'orchestre." *La Revue musicale* 3/11 (1922): 50–59.

Schumann, Clara and Robert Schumann. *Briefwechsel: Kritische Gesamtausgabe*. Ed. Eva Weissweiler. Vol. 1. Stroemfeld, Germany: Roter Stern, [1984].

Schumann, Robert. *Robert Schumanns Briefe: Neue Folge*. 2nd ed. Ed. F. Gustav Jansen. Leipzig: Breitkopf & Härtel, 1904.

Schumann, Robert. *Robert Schumanns gesammelte Schriften über Musik und Musiker*. 5th ed. Ed. Martin Kreisig. 2 vols. Leipzig: Breitkopf & Härtel, 1914.

Schumann, Robert. *On Music and Musicians*. Trans. Paul Rosenfeld. [New York:] Pantheon Books, [1946].

Searle, Humphrey. *The Music of Liszt*. London: Williams & Norgate, [1954].

Seemann, Erich, Dag Strömback, and Bengt Jonsson, eds. *European Folk Ballads*. Copenhagen: Rosenkilde & Bagger, 1967.

Séquardtová, Hana. Prefaces to Bedřich Smetana, *Klavírní Dílo*. Vol. 4: *Lístky do památníku* and vol. 5: *Skladby virtuosní*. Prague: Supraphon, 1968, 1973.

Shafer, Boyd C. *Nationalism: Myth and Reality*. New York: Harcourt, Brace and World, [1955].

Shaw, George Bernard. *Music in London 1890-94*. 3 vols. New York: Vienna House, 1973.

Součkova, Milada. *The Czech Romantics*. The Hague: Mouton, 1958.

Šourek, Otakar. *The Orchestral Works of Antonín Dvořák*. Abridged English version by Roberta Finlayson Samsour. [Prague:] Artia, [1956].

Spitta, Philipp. *Musikgeschichtliche Aufsätze*. Berlin: Gebrüder Paetel, 1894.

Štědroň, Bohumír. Introduction to Janáček, *Balada Blanická: Symfonická báseň*. Critical ed. Břetislav Bakala. Prague: Artia, 1958.

Štědroň, Bohumír. *Das Werk von Leoš Janáček*. Trans. Vladimir Brožovsky. Privately published, 1959.

Suchoff, Benjamin. Introduction to *Piano Music of Béla Bartók*. Ser. 2. New York: Dover Publications, [1981].

Sulyok, Imre, and Imre Mező. Preface to Ferenc Liszt, *Various Cyclical Works* I. Ser. 1, vol. 9 of *New Edition of the Complete Works* [New Liszt Edition]. Budapest: Editio Musica, [1981].

Sychra, Antonín. *Antonín Dvořák: Zur Ästhetik seines sinfonischen Schaffens*. Trans. Gert Jäger and Jürgen Morgenstern. Leipzig: VEB Deutscher Verlag für Musik, 1973.

Tarasti, Eero. "Pour une Narratologie de Chopin." *International Review of the Aesthetics and Sociology of Music* 15/1 (June 1984): 53-75.

Tawaststjerna, Erik. *Sibelius*. Vol. 1: *1865-1905*. Trans. Robert Layton. Berkeley: University of California Press, 1976.

Temperley, Nicholas. "Fryderyk Chopin." In *The New Grove Early Romantic Masters* 1. New York: W. W. Norton, [1985].

Uhland, Ludwig. *The Songs and Ballads of Uhland*. Trans. W. W. Skeat. London: Williams & Norgate, 1864.

Ujfalussy, Jozsef. *Béla Bartók*. Trans. Ruth Pataki. [Budapest:] Corvina Press, [1971].

Vallas, Léon. *Claude Debussy et son temps*. Paris: Editions Albin Michel, [1958].

van der Elst, Nancy. *Henri Duparc: L'Homme et son oeuvre*. Thesis, Université de Lille III, 1972.

Vargyas, Lajos. *Hungarian Ballads and the European Ballad Tradition*. Trans. Imre Gombos. 2 vols. Budapest: Akadémiai Kiadó, 1983.

Villon, François. *The Poems of François Villon*. Trans. Galway Kinnell. Boston: Houghton Mifflin, 1977.

Vogel, Jaroslav. *Leoš Janáček: A Biography*. Trans. Geraldine Thomsen-Muchová, rev. Karel Janovický. London: Orbis Publishing, [1981].

Wagner, Günther. *Die Klavierballade um die Mitte des 19. Jahrhunderts*. Munich: Musikverlag Emil Katzbichler, 1976.

Walicki, Andrzej. *Philosophy and Romantic Nationalism: The Case of Poland*. Oxford: Clarendon Press, 1982.

Walker, Alan. *Franz Liszt*. Vol. 2: *The Weimar Years, 1848-1861*. New York: Alfred A. Knopf, 1989.

Wasserman, Earl. *The Finer Tone: Keats' Major Poems*. Baltimore, Maryland: Johns Hopkins Press, 1953.

Weintraub, Wiktor. *The Poetry of Adam Mickiewicz*. The Hague: Mouton, 1954.

Wilgus, D. K. *Anglo-American Folksong Scholarship Since 1898*. New Brunswick, New Jersey: Rutgers University Press, 1959.

Wilson, Charles. "The Two Versions of *Goyescas*." *Monthly Musical Record* 81 (October 1951): 203-07.

Wiora, Walter. *European Folk Song: Common Forms in Characteristic Modifications*. Trans. Robert Kolben. Cologne: Arno Volk, [1966].

Witten, Neil David. *The Chopin "Ballades": An Analytical Study*. D. M. A. thesis, Boston University, 1979.

Young, Percy M. *A History of British Music*. London: Ernest Benn, [1967].

Zajaczkowski, Henry. *Tchaikovsky's Musical Style*. Ann Arbor, Michigan: UMI Research Press, [1987].

Illustration Sources

ENDPAPERS: "The Noon Witch," illustration by V. Oliva, from Karl Jaromír Erben, *Kytice,* illustrated edition, ed. E. K. Lišky (Prague: Nákladem Umělecké Besedy, 1890). By permission of Národní Muzeum, Prague.

PLATE 1: Title-page of Camille Saint-Saëns, "König Harald Harfagar (nach H. Heine): Ballade," Op. 59, for piano, four hands (Berlin: Bote & Bock, 1880). By permission of the Library of Congress, Washington, D.C.

PLATE 2: Title-page of the first edition of César Franck, *Le Chasseur maudit* (Paris: L. Grus, 1882). Courtesy of the Eda Kuhn Loeb Music Library, Harvard University.

PLATE 3: Konstanty Górski, *Czaty,* from the Polish weekly journal *Tygodnik Ilustrowany,* 1904, p. 427. Courtesy of Muzeum Narodowe, Warsaw.

PLATE 4: Opening episode of "The Water Goblin," illustration by L. Marold, from Erben's *Kytice,* ed. E. K. Lišky (Prague: Nákladem Umělecké Besedy, 1890). By permission of Národní Muzeum, Prague.

PLATE 5: First page of "The Water Goblin," with illustration by F. Jenewein, from Erben's *Kytice,* ed. E. K. Lišky (Prague: Nákladem Umělecké Besedy, 1890). By permission of Národní Muzeum, Prague.

PLATE 6: Illustration of the final episode of "The Water Goblin" by F. Jenewein, from Erben's *Kytice,* ed. E. K. Lišky (Prague: Nákladem Umělecké Besedy, 1890). By permission of Národní Muzeum, Prague.

PLATE 7: Illustrated first page of "The Golden Spinning Wheel," from Erben's *Kytice,* ed. E. K. Lišky (Prague: Nákladem Umělecké Besedy, 1890). By permission of Národní Muzeum, Prague.

PLATE 8: Illustrated first page of "The Wild Dove," from Erben's *Kytice,* ed. E. K. Lišky (Prague: Nákladem Umělecké Besedy, 1890). By permission of Národní Muzeum, Prague.

Chronological List of
Works Discussed

Following is a list of *ballades* and other closely related instrumental works discussed or referred to in the text. It is by no means an exhaustive list of published *ballades*. Vocal works discussed in the text are not included in this list, but every work mentioned in the text is included in the Index.

Works are listed here in chronological order of publication, since in many cases the publication date is the only ascertainable date. Works that have never been published or that were not published until long after they were written are listed by date of composition, with a parenthetical note in the entry explaining the circumstances. Parenthetical notes are included for other works with complicated or uncertain publication histories.

In the column "Piano and Chamber Works," all works are for solo piano unless otherwise specified. In the column "Orchestral and Concerto Works," all works are for orchestra unless a solo instrument is parenthetically specified. Works published by their composers in two versions, one for piano or chamber ensemble and the other for or with orchestra, are listed in both columns.

The letters ME (Modern Edition) in an entry indicate that the work has been republished in recent years or that the original edition is still available. The numbers at the end of the entry refer to the endnote (5/1 for Chapter 5, endnote 1) that gives information about both original and modern editions. The letter R (Recording) indicates that the work has been recorded; information about the recordings is given in the Discography.

PIANO AND CHAMBER WORKS

1830
Glinka, Mikhail. "Finskaja pesnja." ME; 6/2.

1836
Chopin, Fryderyk. Ballade, Op. 23. ME; R; 1/1.
Wieck (Schumann), Clara. "Ballade," *Soirées musicales*, Op. 6, No. 2. ME; 5/1.

1837 or 1838
Schumann, Robert. "Balladenmässig," *Davidsbündlertänze*, Op. 6, No. 10. ME; R; 5/3.

1840
Chopin, Fryderyk. Ballade, Op. 38. ME; R; 1/1.

1841
Chopin, Fryderyk. Ballade, Op. 47. ME; R; 1/1.
Herz, Henri. "Deux Ballades sans paroles," Op. 117. 5/9.
Mosonyi, Mihály. Ballade (violin and piano). (Composed 1841; unpublished.) 7/38.
Panofka, Heinrich. Ballade (violin and piano). (Published by 1841.) 7/39.

1842
Döhler, Theodor. "Ballade sans paroles," Op. 41. 5/9.
Moscheles, Ignaz. Ballade, Op. 100. ME; 4/4.

1843
Chopin, Fryderyk. Ballade, Op. 52. ME; R; 1/1.

1844
Franck, César. Ballade, Op. 9. (Composed 1844.) ME; 5/19.

ORCHESTRAL AND CONCERTO WORKS

1835
Hüttenbrenner, Anselm. *Ouverture zur Oper Lenore* (arrangement for piano, four hands). 8/1.

1841
Macfarren, George Alexander. *Overture to Chevy Chace* (arrangement for piano, four hands). (Composed 1836.) 8/39.

PIANO AND CHAMBER WORKS

ORCHESTRAL AND CONCERTO WORKS

1844 or 1845
Döhler, Theodor. "Deuxième Ballade,"
   Op. 55. 5/9.

1848–50
Smetana, Bedřich. "Stammbuchblatt"
   (on Schiller's "Der Taucher"),
   intended as Op. 3, No. 3. (Composed
   1848-50.) ME; 4/30.

1849
Fontana, Julian. Ballade, Op. 17. 4/39.
Gottschalk, Louis Moreau. "La Savane:
   Ballade créole," Op. 3. ME; R; 5/13.
Kullak, Theodor. Ballade, Op. 54. 4/41.
Liszt, Franz. Ballade (D-flat). ME; R; 4/8.
Liszt, Franz. "Ballade d'Ukraine," *Glanes
   de Woronince*. ME; R; 6/4.
Wolff, Edouard. Ballade, Op. 62. 5/9.

1850s
Hiller, Ferdinand. "Ballade," *Vermischte
   Clavierstücke*, Op. 66, No. 4. 5/41.
Schulhoff, Julius. Ballade, Op. 41. 5/9.

1850
Gottschalk, Louis Moreau. "Ossian:
   Deux Ballades," Op. 4. ME; R; 5/15.

1851
Gutmann, Adolf. Ballade, Op. 19. 5/9.

1852–57
Mikuli, Carol. *Douze Airs nationaux
   roumains (Ballades, chants de
   bergers, airs de danse etc.)*. 4 vols.
   6/7.

1853
Cramer, Henry. "La Romantique," *Deux
   Ballades*, Op. 91, No. 2. ME; 5/8.
Gottschalk, Louis Moreau. Ballade
   (A-flat). (Composed 1853.)
   ME; R; 5/16.
Kullak, Theodor. "Lénore: Ballade,"
   Op. 81. ME; 4/40.

PIANO AND CHAMBER WORKS

ORCHESTRAL AND CONCERTO WORKS

1853–67
Lindeman, Ludvig. "Sjugurd og trollbrura," *Aeldre og nyere norske Fjeldmelodier*. ME; 6/10.

1854
Henselt, Adolf. Ballade, Op. 31. 5/20.
Liszt, Franz. *2me Ballade*. ME; R; 4/8.

1856
Brahms, Johannes. *Vier Balladen*, Op. 10. ME; R; 5/22.
Bülow, Hans von. Ballade, Op. 11. ME; R; 4/24.

1858
Smetana, Bedřich. Ballade (E minor). (Composed 1858.) ME; 4/27.

1859
Raff, Joachim. "Ballade," *Drei Klavier-Soli*, Op. 74, No. 1. 5/37.

1860s
Carreño, Teresa. "Ballada," Op. 15. ME; 5/21.

1860
Tausig, Carl. "Das Geisterschiff: Symphonische Ballade nach einem Gedicht von Strachwitz," Op. 1 (version for piano). ME; R; 4/45.
Tellefsen, Thomas. Ballade, Op. 28. 5/38.
Vieuxtemps, Henri. *Ballade et Polonaise de concert*, Op. 38 (version for violin and piano). (Published about 1860.) ME; R; 7/40.

1862
Thalberg, Sigismond. "Célèbre Ballade," Op. 76. ME; 5/11.

1860
Tausig, Carl. *Das Geisterschiff: Symphonische Ballade nach einem Gedicht von Strachwitz*, Op. 1 (version for orchestra). (No known publication of this version.) 4/45.

Vieuxtemps, Henri. *Ballade et Polonaise de concert*, Op. 38 (version for violin and orchestra). 7/40.

1863
Bülow, Hans von. *Ballade, nach Uhlands Dichtung: Des Sängers Fluch*, Op. 16. 8/3.

PIANO AND CHAMBER WORKS

1866
Heller, Stephen. *Trois Ballades*,
  Op. 115. 5/39.
Volkmann, Robert. *Ballade und
  Scherzetto*, Op. 51. 5/42.

1867
Heller, Stephen. "Ballade," *Drei Stücke*,
  Op. 121, No. 1. 5/39.
Hiller, Ferdinand. "Ballade," *Sechs
  Clavierstücke*, Op. 130, No. 1. 5/41.
Kjerulf, Halfdan. *Norske Folkeviser*.
  6/13.
Rheinberger, Josef. "Ballade," *Drei
  Charakterstücke*, Op. 7, No. 1. 5/43.

1870
Grieg, Edvard. *25 Norske Folkeviser og
  Dandse*, Op. 17. ME; R; 6/14.
Swert, Jules de. "Deuxième Ballade,"
  Op. 12 (cello and piano). 7/41.

1871
Mikuli, Carol. Ballade, Op. 21. 5/10.

1873
Rubinstein, Anton. "Ballade: Lénore de
  Bürger," *Miscellanées*, Op. 93. 4/43.
Scharwenka, Xaver. Ballade, Op. 8.
  4/37.

1874
Raff, Joachim. "Ballade," *Album lyrique
  (Nouvelle Edition)*, Op. 17, Vol. 2,
  No. 2. ME; 5/35.

1875
Röntgen, Julius. Ballade, Op. 6. 7/31.

1876
Grieg, Edvard. *Ballade in Form von
  Variationen über eine norwegische
  Melodie*, Op. 24. ME; R; 6/19.

ORCHESTRAL AND CONCERTO WORKS

1870s
Rudorff, Ernst. *Ballade (Introduction,
  Scherzo und Finale)*, Op. 15. 8/15.

1873
Raff, Joachim. *Lenore: Symphonie (No.
  5 in E dur)*, Op. 177. R; 8/14.

1875
Duparc, Henri. *Lénore: Poème
  symphonique d'après la ballade de
  Bürger*. 8/20.
Fibich, Zdeněk. *Toman a lesní panna*,
  Op. 49. ME; R; 9/19.
Klughardt, August. *Lenore:
  Symphonische Dichtung nach
  Bürger's Ballade*, Op. 27. 8/13.

PIANO AND CHAMBER WORKS

1877
Gottschalk, Louis Moreau. "Sixième
Ballade," Op. 85. ME; 5/17.
Gottschalk, Louis Moreau. "Septième
Ballade," Op. 87. ME; 5/17.
Gottschalk, Louis Moreau. "Huitième
Ballade," Op. 90. ME; 5/17.

1880s
Henschel, George. Ballade, Op. 39
(version for violin and piano). 7/44.
Moszkowski, Moritz. "Ballade," *Zwei
Concertstücke*, Op. 16, No. 1
(violin and piano). R; 7/44.
Neruda, Franz. Ballade, Op. 42
(violin and piano). 7/43.
Sarasate, Pablo de. Ballade, Op. 31
(violin and piano). 7/45.

1880
Fauré, Gabriel. Ballade, Op. 19 (version
for solo piano). ME; R; 7/1.
Saint-Saëns, Camille. "König Harald
Harfagar (nach H. Heine): Ballade,"
Op. 59 (piano, four hands). 7/14.

ORCHESTRAL AND CONCERTO WORKS

1877
Svendsen, Johan. *Norsk Rapsodi* No. 2,
Op. 19. R; 6/16.

1878
d'Indy, Vincent. *La Forêt enchantée:
Légende-symphonie d'après une
ballade de Uhland*, Op. 8. R; 8/21.

1879
Mihalovich, Ödön de. *Ballade nach
Strachwitz' Dichtung Das
Geisterschiff*. 8/9.
Mihalovich, Ödön de. *Ballade nach
Paul Gyulai's Dichtung A sellő
(Die Nixe)*. 8/10.
Mihalovich, Ödön de. *Hero und
Leander, nach Schiller's Ballade*.
8/11.
Mihalovich, Ödön de. *La Ronde du
sabbat, d'après la ballade de Victor
Hugo*. 8/12.

1880s
Henschel, George. Ballade, Op. 39
(version for violin and orchestra).
7/44.

1881
Fauré, Gabriel. Ballade, Op. 19 (version
for piano and orchestra). (Performed
1881; published 1901.) ME; R; 7/1.

PIANO AND CHAMBER WORKS

ORCHESTRAL AND CONCERTO WORKS

1882
Franck, César. *Le Chasseur maudit*. ME; R; 8/22.

1884
Dvořák, Antonín. Ballade, Op. 15 (violin and piano). ME; R; 7/42.
Kirchner, Theodor. "Balladenmässig," *Romantische Geschichten*, Op. 73, No. 19. 7/33.
Röntgen, Julius. "Ballade (No. 2 in G moll)," Op. 22. 7/32.
Wieniawski, Józef. Ballade, Op. 31. ME; 7/56.

1884
Mackenzie, Alexander. *La Belle Dame sans merci: Ballad*, Op. 29. 8/44.

1885
Strong, George Templeton. Ballade, Op. 22. (Published about 1885.) 7/63.

1886
Grieg, Edvard. "Sjugurd og trollbrura," *Sex norske Fjeldmelodier*. ME; R; 6/15.
MacDowell, Edward. "Ballade," *Drei Poesien*, Op. 20, No. 2 (piano, four hands). ME; 7/15.

1888
Strong, George Templeton. "Zweite Ballade," Op. 34. 7/63.

1889
Dvořák, Antonín. "Selská balada," *Poetické nálady*, Op. 85, No. 5. ME; R; 7/20.

1890s
Hubay, Jenő. Ballade, Op. 48, No. 1 (violin and piano). 7/43.

1890
Arensky, Anton. "Petite Ballade," *Two Pieces*, Op. 12, No. 1 (cello and piano). 7/43.
Liadov, Anatol. "Ballade: Pro starinu," Op. 21. ME; 7/21.

1890
MacCunn, Hamish. *The Ship o' the Fiend: Orchestral Ballad*, Op. 5. 8/46.
MacCunn, Hamish. *The Dowie Dens o' Yarrow: Ballad-Overture*, Op. 6. 8/47.

PIANO AND CHAMBER WORKS

1891
Debussy, Claude. "Ballade slave," *Pièces pour piano*. ME; R; 7/24.
Grieg, Edvard. *Altnorwegische Romanze mit Variationen*, Op. 51 (version for two pianos). ME; R; 6/17.
Mackenzie, Alexander. "Highland Ballad," *Two Pieces*, Op. 47, No. 1 (violin and piano). 7/44.

1893
Brahms, Johannes. "Ballade," *Klavierstücke*, Op. 118, No. 3. ME; R; 7/35.
Novák, Vítězslav. "Ballada, dle Byronova *Manfreda*," Op. 2. ME; 7/66.

1894
Beach, Amy. Ballad, Op. 6. ME; R; 7/64.
Scharwenka, Philipp. Ballade, Op. 94a. 7/55.

1895
Arensky, Anton. "Petite Ballade," *24 Morceaux caractéristiques*, Op. 36. ME; 7/18.
Backer-Grøndahl, Agathe. "Ballade," *Fantasistykker*, Op. 36, No. 5. ME; 7/16.
Scriabin, Alexander. "Alla ballata," *Twelve Etudes*, Op. 8, No. 9. ME; R; 7/29.

1896
Busoni, Ferruccio. "Finnische Ballade," *Sechs Stücke*, Op. 33b, No. 5. ME; 7/27.
Chaminade, Cécile. Ballade, Op. 86. 7/34.

ORCHESTRAL AND CONCERTO WORKS

1896
Dvořák, Antonín. *Vodník, sinfonická báseň (dle K. Jaromíra Erbena)*, Op. 107. ME; R; 9/24.
Dvořák, Antonín. *Polednice, sinfonická báseň (dle K. Jaromíra Erbena)*, Op. 108. ME; R; 9/24.
Dvořák, Antonín. *Zlatý kolovrat, sinfonická báseň (dle K. Jaromíra Erbena)*, Op. 109. ME; R; 9/24.
Röntgen, Julius. *Ballade über eine norwegische Volksmelodie*, Op. 36. 8/16.

PIANO AND CHAMBER WORKS

1897
Grieg, Edvard. "Im Balladenton,"
Lyrische Stücke, Op. 65, No. 5. ME;
R; 7/17.

1898
d'Albert, Eugen. "Ballade," *Vier
Klavierstücke*, Op. 16, No. 4. 7/62.

1900s
Sinding, Christian. "Ballade," *Vier
Stücke*, Op. 61, No. 3 (violin and
piano). 7/43.
Vianna da Motta, José. "Ballada sobre
duas melodias portuguezas," Op. 16.
7/70.

1900
Suk, Josef. "Ballade," *Ballade und
Serenade*, Op. 3 (cello and piano).
7/44.

1902
Reger, Max. "Nordische Ballade,"
Aquarellen: Kleine Tonbilder,
Op. 25, No. 4. (Composed 1897–98.)
ME; 7/26.

1903
Blumenfeld, Felix. Ballade, Op. 34. 7/57.
Glière, Reinhold. Ballade, Op. 4 (cello
and piano). 7/46.
Novák, Vítězslav. *Trio quasi una
ballata*, Op. 27 (piano trio). R; 7/47.

ORCHESTRAL AND CONCERTO WORKS

1897
Dukas, Paul. *L'Apprenti sorcier: Scherzo
d'après une ballade de Goethe*. ME;
R; 8/27.
Liapunov, Sergei. Ballade, Op. 2. 9/14.
Tchaikovsky, Piotr. *Voevoda*, Op. 78.
ME; R; 9/2.

1899
Coleridge-Taylor, Samuel. *Ballade in
A Minor*, Op. 33. 8/49.
Dvořák, Antonín. *Holoubek (dle báseň
K. Jaromíra Erbena), sinfonická
báseň*, Op. 110. ME; R; 9/24.

1903
Glazunov, Alexander. Ballade, Op. 78. R;
9/16.

1904
Różycki, Ludomir. Ballade, Op. 18
(piano and orchestra). R; 7/60.

PIANO AND CHAMBER WORKS

1905
d'Albert, Eugen. "Ballade," *Fünf Bagatellen*, Op. 29, No. 1. 7/19.

1906
Kreider, Noble W. Ballad, Op. 3. ME; 7/68.

1909
Różycki, Ludomir. "Balladyna: Poème pour piano," Op. 25. 7/61.

1911
Bartók, Béla. "Ballade (Pásou Janko dva voli)," *[A] Gyermekeknek* (Slovak set, No. 39). ME; R; 7/71.
Novák, Vítězslav. "Ballade," *Exotikon*, Op. 45, No. 3. 7/30.

1912
Martinů, Bohuslav. "Ballada—Pod Krzecův obraz—Poslední akordy Chopina." (Composed 1912; unpublished.) 7/58.
Marx, Joseph. Ballade (piano quartet). 7/50.
Prokofiev, Sergei. "Ballada," Op. 15 (cello and piano). ME; R; 7/53.

ORCHESTRAL AND CONCERTO WORKS

1906
Grieg, Edvard. *Altnorwegische Romanze mit Variationen*, Op. 51 (version for orchestra). ME; R; 6/17.
Liadov, Anatol. *Pro starinu: Ballada*, Op. 21b (version for orchestra). ME; 7/21.
Sibelius, Jean. "Ballade," *Karelia—Suite*, Op. 11. ME; R; 8/18.

1907
Taneiev, Alexander. *Aleša Popovič: Ballade d'après une poésie du Cte. A. Tolstoy*, Op. 11. 9/15.

1908
Ertel, Paul. *Hero und Leander: Des Meeres und der Liebe Wellen (Schiller-Grillparzer). Sinfonische Dichtung.* 8/17.

1910
McEwen, John. *Grey Galloway: A Border Ballad.* 8/50.

PIANO AND CHAMBER WORKS

Weiner, Leó. "Ballada," Op. 8 (clarinet and piano). R; 7/49.

1912–14
Granados, Enrique. "Balada," *Goyescas: Los Majos enamorados*. ME; R; 7/67.
Metner, Nikolai. Sonata-Ballade, Op. 27. ME; R; 7/13.

1913
Jarnach, Philipp. Ballade (violin and piano). 7/51.

1915
Debussy, Claude. *En blanc et noir* (two pianos). ME; R; 7/87.

1917
Foerster, Joseph Bohuslav. "Ballata," Op. 92 (version for violin and piano). 7/52.

1920
Bartók, Béla. "Ballade (Tema con variazioni)," No. 6 of *Tizenöt magyar parasztdal* (version for piano). ME; R; 7/77.

1922
Janáček, Leoš. "Ballade," Sonata (violin and piano). ME; R; 7/81.

1924
Provazník, Anatol. "Ballade en souvenir du grand maître Fr. Chopin: Drame passionel," Op. 130. 7/59.

ORCHESTRAL AND CONCERTO WORKS

1912
Janáček, Leoš. *Šumařovo dítě: Ballada—Sv. Čech*. ME; R; 9/57.

1917
Foerster, Joseph Bohuslav. "Ballata," Op. 92 (version for violin and orchestra). 7/52.

1919
Koechlin, Charles. Ballade (piano and orchestra). (Completed 1919; published 1974.) ME; R; 10/11.
Novák, Vítězslav. *Toman a lesní panna: Symfonická báseň dle české pověsti*. R; 9/56.

1920
Janáček, Leoš. *Balada Blanická: Symfonická báseň*. ME; R; 9/58.

1921
Delius, Frederick. *Eventyr: Once Upon a Time (After Asbjørnsen's Folklore): A Ballad*. ME; R; 8/51.

1924
Ibert, Jacques. *La Ballade de la Geôle de Reading*. R; 10/2.

PIANO AND CHAMBER WORKS

ORCHESTRAL AND CONCERTO WORKS

1929
Milhaud, Darius. Ballade, Op. 61 (piano and orchestra). 10/12.

1931
Ireland, John. Ballade. ME; R; 10/6.

1931
Glazunov, Alexander. *Concerto Ballata*, Op. 108 (violoncello and orchestra). R; 10/13.

1933
Bartók, Béla. "Ballade (Tema con variazioni)," No. 1 of *Magyar parasztdalok / Ungarische Bauernlieder* (version for orchestra). ME; R; 7/79.

1937
Atterberg, Kurt. *Ballade und Passacaglia über ein Thema im schwedischen Volkston*, Op. 38. 10/3.

1938
Martin, Frank. Ballade for Alto Saxophone and Orchestra. ME; R; 10/16.

1939
Martin, Frank. Ballade for Flute and Piano. ME; R; 10/16.

1939
Martin, Frank. Ballade for Piano and Orchestra. ME; R; 10/16.

1940
Martin, Frank. Ballade for Trombone and Piano. ME; R; 10/16.

1941
Martin, Frank. Ballade for Flute, String Orchestra, and Piano (version with orchestra). ME; R; 10/16.
Martin, Frank. Ballade for Trombone and Small Orchestra (version with orchestra). ME; R; 10/16.

1946
Britten, Benjamin. *Scottish Ballad*, Op. 26 (two pianos and orchestra). ME; R; 10/14.

337

CHRONOLOGICAL LIST OF WORKS

PIANO AND CHAMBER WORKS

ORCHESTRAL AND CONCERTO WORKS

1947
Harris, Roy. *American Ballads.* ME; R; 10/10.

1949
Martin, Frank. Ballade for Violoncello and Piano. ME; R; 10/16.

1950
Badings, Henk. *Ballade voor orkest: Symphonische Variaties over: "Het waren twee Conincskindren."* ME; 10/4.
Martin, Frank. Ballade for Violoncello and Orchestra (version with orchestra). ME; 10/16.

1954
Weiner, Leó. "Ballata," Op. 28 (version for clarinet and orchestra). ME; 7/49.

1970
Szokolay, Sándor. *Ballata Sinfonica.* ME; 10/5.

1972
Martin, Frank. Ballade for Viola and Orchestra. ME; R; 10/16.

1983
Perle, George. Ballade. ME; R; 10/6.
Rzewski, Frederic. *North American Ballads.* ME; R; 10/8.

Discography

The following discography is not an exhaustive list of recorded *ballades*, but an aid in finding recordings of the less familiar *ballades*. Accordingly, all works for which recordings have been found are listed below, alphabetically by composer, but works that have been recorded more than three times are simply marked "Numerous recordings." The listings of recordings include both currently available and out-of-print items. The entry for each recording includes the recording title if it differs from the titles of the works recorded; the performers; and the recording label, number, and year.

Bartók, Béla. "Ballade (Pásou Janko dva voli)," *[A] Gyermekeknek* (Slovak set, No. 39).

Numerous recordings.

Bartók, Béla. "Ballade (Tema con variazioni)," No. 6 of *Tizenöt magyar parasztdal* (version for piano).

Numerous recordings.

Bartók, Béla. "Ballade (Tema con variazioni)," No. 1 of *Hungarian Peasant Songs (Magyar parasztdalok)* (version for orchestra).

Budapest Philharmonic Orchestra, conducted by János Sándor. Hungaroton (LPX 11319), 1970s.

Beach, Amy. Ballad, Op. 6.

On "The American Romantic."
Alan Feinberg, piano.
Argo (430 330–2), 1990.

Brahms, Johannes. *Vier Balladen*, Op. 10.

Numerous recordings.

Brahms, Johannes. "Ballade," *Klavierstücke*, Op. 118, No. 3.

Numerous recordings.

Britten, Benjamin. *Scottish Ballad*, Op. 26 (two pianos and orchestra).

> Peter Donohoe, Philip Fowke, pianos; City of Birmingham Symphony Orchestra, conducted by Simon Rattle.
> EMI (4XS 37919), 1982.

Bülow, Hans von. Ballade, Op. 11.

> On "Bayerns Schlösser und Residenzen."
> Werner Genuit, piano.
> BASF (BF 21108, KBF 21108), 1973.

Chopin, Fryderyk. Ballade, Op. 23.

> Numerous recordings.

Chopin, Fryderyk. Ballade, Op. 38.

> Numerous recordings.

Chopin, Fryderyk. Ballade, Op. 47.

> Numerous recordings.

Chopin, Fryderyk. Ballade, Op. 52.

> Numerous recordings.

Debussy, Claude. "Ballade slave," *Pièces pour piano*.

> Numerous recordings.

Debussy, Claude. *En blanc et noir*.

> Numerous recordings.

Delius, Frederick. *Eventyr*.

> Numerous recordings.

Dukas, Paul. *The Sorcerer's Apprentice (L'Apprenti sorcier)*.

> Numerous recordings.

Dvořák, Antonín. Ballade, Op. 15 (violin and piano).

> Alfred Csammer, violin; Sontraud Speidel, piano.
> Corono (SM 30003), 1971.

Dvořák, Antonín. "Selská balada," *Poetické nálady*, Op. 85, No. 5.

> 1. Radoslav Kvapil, piano.
>   Supraphon (1 11 0566), 1972.
>
> 2. Gerald Robbins, piano.
>   Genesis (GS 1019), 1972.

Dvořák, Antonín. *Vodník*, Op. 107.

> Numerous recordings.

Dvořák, Antonín. *Polednice*, Op. 108.

> Numerous recordings.

Dvořák, Antonín. *Zlatý kolovrat,* Op. 109.
Numerous recordings.

Dvořák, Antonín. *Holoubek*, Op. 110.
Numerous recordings.

Fauré, Gabriel. Ballade, Op. 19 (piano).
Numerous recordings.

Fauré, Gabriel. Ballade, Op. 19 (piano and orchestra).
Numerous recordings.

Fibich, Zdeněk. *Toman a lesní panna*, Op. 49.
Prague Symphony Orchestra, conducted by Vladimír Válek.
Supraphon (1110 3913), 1986.

Franck, César. *Le Chasseur maudit.*
Numerous recordings.

Glazunov, Alexander. Ballade, Op. 78.
USSR TV and Radio Large Symphony Orchestra, conducted by Odysseus
Dmitriadi.
Melodiya (C10 15745, 15746), 1980.

Glazunov, Alexander. *Concerto Ballata*, Op. 108 (violoncello and orchestra).
Boris Pergamenschikow, violoncello; Bavarian Radio Symphony Orchestra,
conducted by David Shallon.
Schwann Musica Mundi (CD 11119), 1987.

Gottschalk, Louis Moreau. "La Savane: Ballade créole," Op. 3.
1. On "The World of Louis Moreau Gottschalk."
Eugene List, piano.
Vanguard (VSD 723–724), 1973.

2. On "Louis Moreau Gottschalk: Klavierstücke."
Klaus Kaufmann, piano.
Koch Schwann Musica Mundi (310 035), 1990.

Gottschalk, Louis Moreau. "Ossian: Deux Ballades," Op. 4.
On "Gottschalk: Ten Characteristic Pieces."
Amiram Rigai, piano.
Musical Heritage Society (MHC 2161), 1975.

Gottschalk, Louis Moreau. Ballade (A-flat).
On "Music of Louis Moreau Gottschalk."
Leonard Pennario, piano.
Angel (S-36090), 1975.

Granados, Enrique. "Balada," *Goyescas: Los Majos enamorados.*
Numerous recordings.

Grieg, Edvard. *25 Norske Folkeviser og Dandse*, Op. 17.

   1. On "Edvard Grieg: The Complete Piano Music," vol. 6.
   Eva Knardahl, piano.
   BIS (CD-108), 1978.

   2. Kjell Baekkelund, piano.
   Norsk Kulturråds Klassikerserie (NFK 30053), 1983.

Grieg, Edvard. *Ballade in Form von Variationen über eine norwegische Melodie*, Op. 24.

   Numerous recordings.

Grieg, Edvard. *Altnorwegische Romanze mit Variationen*, Op. 51 (two pianos).

   On "Grieg: Piano Music for Four Hands."
   Kjell Baekkelund, Robert Levin, pianos.

   Etcetera (KTC1004), 1982.

Grieg, Edvard. *Altnorwegische Romanze mit Variationen*, Op. 51 (version for orchestra).

   Philharmonia Orchestra, conducted by Raymond Leppard.
   Philips (6514 203, 7337 203), 1982.

Grieg, Edvard. "Im Balladenton," *Lyrische Stücke*, Op. 65, No. 5.

   Numerous recordings.

Grieg, Edvard. "Sjugurd og trollbrura," *Sex norske Fjeldmelodier*.

   On "Edvard Grieg: The Complete Piano Music," vol. 6.
   Eva Knardahl, piano.
   BIS (CD-108), 1978.

Harris, Roy. *American Ballads*.

   Numerous recordings.

Ibert, Jacques. *La Ballade de la Geôle de Reading*.

   Louisville Orchestra, conducted by Jorge Mester.
   Louisville Orchestra (LS-736), 1974.

Indy, Vincent d'. *La Forêt enchantée*, Op. 8.

   On "Vincent d'Indy: Five Tone Poems."
   Orchestre philharmonique du pays de la Loire, conducted by Pierre Dervaux.
   Arabesque (8097–2), 1981.

Ireland, John. Ballade.

   1. On "John Ireland: Piano Music," vol. 3.
   Eric Parkin, piano.
   Lyrita (SRCS.89), 1978.

2. On "John Ireland: Piano Music," vol. 2.
Alan Rowlands, piano.
Lyrita (RCS 23), [no date].

Janáček, Leoš. *Šumařovo dítě (The Fiddler's Child)*.

1. Brno State Philharmonic Orchestra, conducted by Břetislav Bakala.
Supraphon (SUA 10053), 1950s.

2. Brno State Philharmonic Orchestra, conducted by Jiří Waldhans.
Supraphon (SUA ST 50894), 1967.

3. Brno State Philharmonic Orchestra, conducted by František Jílek.
Supraphon (1110 2840), 1981.

Janáček, Leoš. *Balada Blanická*.

1. Brno State Philharmonic Orchestra, conducted by Břetislav Bakala.
Supraphon (SUA 10053), 1950s.

2. Brno State Philharmonic Orchestra, conducted by Jiří Waldhans.
Supraphon (SUA ST 50894), 1967.

3. Brno State Philharmonic Orchestra, conducted by František Jílek.
Supraphon (1110 2840), 1981.

Janáček, Leoš. "Ballade," Sonata (violin and piano).

Numerous recordings.

Koechlin, Charles. Ballade (piano and orchestra).

Bruno Rigutto, piano; Monte-Carlo Philharmonic Orchestra, conducted by
Alexandre Myrat. XDR (4XS-37940), 1983.

Liszt, Franz. "Ballade d'Ukraine," *Glanes de Woronince*.

1. Toos Onderdenwijngaard, piano.
Editio Laran (ST 5055), 1984.

2. Robert Black, piano.
Orion (ORS 84463), 1984.

Liszt, Franz. Ballade (D-flat).

Leslie Howard, piano.
Hyperion (CD A66301), 1988.

Liszt, Franz. *2me Ballade*.

Numerous recordings.

Martin, Frank. Ballade for Alto Saxophone and Orchestra.

Marcel Perrin, saxophone; Nuremberg Symphony, conducted by Urs
Schneider.
Colosseum (SM 525), 1970s.

Martin, Frank. Ballade for Piano and Orchestra.

1. Sebastian Benda, piano; Chamber Orchestra of Lausanne, conducted by
Frank Martin.
Jecklin Disco (JD 529-2), 1970s.

2. Jean-François Antonioli, piano; Turin Philharmonic, conducted by Marcello Viotti.
Claves (D 8509), 1985.

Martin, Frank. Ballade for Flute and Piano.

Numerous recordings.

Martin, Frank. Ballade for Flute, String Orchestra, and Piano.

Numerous recordings.

Martin, Frank. Ballade for Trombone and Piano.

1. Christian Lindberg, trombone; Roland Pontinen, piano.
BIS (258), 1984.

2. Davis Shuman, trombone; Leonid Hambro, piano.
Golden Crest (RE 7011), 1962.

Martin, Frank. Ballade for Trombone and Small Orchestra.

Armin Rosen, trombone; Chamber Orchestra of Lausanne, conducted by Frank Martin.
Jecklin Disco (JD 529-2), 1970s.

Martin, Frank. Ballade for Violoncello and Piano.

1. Klaus Heitz, violoncello; Monica Hofmann, piano.
Musical Heritage Society (MHS-3916), 1978.

2. Maxine Neuman, violoncello; Yolanda Liena, piano.
Opus One (123), 1980s.

3. Henri Honegger, violoncello; Frank Martin, piano.
Jecklin Disco (JD 563-2), 1989.

Martin, Frank. Ballade for Viola and Orchestra.

Ron Golan, viola; MIT Symphony Orchestra, conducted by David Epstein.
Pantheon (D-0981X).

Metner, Nikolai. Sonata-Ballade, Op. 27.

1. Vladimir Pleshakov, piano
Orion (OC-673), 1970.

2. Malcolm Binns, piano.
Peral (SHE 535), 1977.

Moszkowski, Moritz. "Ballade," *Zwei Conzertstücke*, Op. 16, No. 1 (violin and piano).

Charles Treger, violin; Maria Szmyd-Dormus, piano.
Muza (SXL 0908), 1970s.

Novák, Vítězslav. *Trio quasi una ballata*, Op. 27 (piano trio).

Czech Trio.
Supraphon (1 11 1089), 1972.

Novák, Vítězslav. *Toman a lesní panna.*

  Czech Radio Symphony Orchestra of Prague, conducted by Josef Hrnčíř.
  Panton (11 0067), 1977.

Perle, George. Ballade.

  Richard Goode, piano.
  Nonesuch (79108-4), 1985.

Prokofiev, Sergei. "Ballada," Op. 15 (cello and piano).

  Dimitri Ferschtman, cello; Ronald Brautigam, piano.
  Etcetera (KTC 1059), 1988.

Raff, Joachim. *Lenore: Symphonie (No. 5 in E dur)*, Op. 177.

  Berlin Radio Symphony Orchestra, conducted by Matthias Bamert.
  Koch Schwann Musica Mundi (CD-311013), 1988.

Różycki, Ludomir. Ballade, Op. 18 (piano and orchestra).

  Barbara Hesse-Bukowska, piano; Polish Radio National Symphony
  Orchestra of Katowice, conducted by Jan Krenz.
  Olympia (OCD 306), 1988.

Rzewski, Frederic. Ballad No. 3, "Which Side Are You On?" *North American Ballads.*

  Frederic Rzewski, piano.
  Vanguard (VA 25001), 1980.

Schumann, Robert. "Balladenmässig," *Davidsbündlertänze*, Op. 6, No. 10.

  Numerous recordings.

Scriabin, Alexander. "Alla ballata," *Twelve Etudes*, Op. 8, No. 9.

  Numerous recordings.

Sibelius, Jean. "Ballade," *Karelia—Suite*, Op. 11.

  Numerous recordings.

Svendsen, Johan. *Norsk Rapsodi* No. 2, Op. 19.

  On "Rapsodies norvégiennes."
  Bergen Symphony Orchestra, conducted by Karsten Andersen.
  Norsk Kulturråds Klassikerserie (NKF 30 006), 1974.

Tausig, Carl. "Das Geisterschiff: Symphonische Ballade," Op. 1 (piano).

  On "Romantic Transcriptions."
  Rian de Waal, piano.
  Etcetera (ETC 1016), 1983.

Tchaikovsky, Piotr. *Voevoda*, Op. 78.

  Numerous recordings.

Vieuxtemps, Henri. *Ballade et Polonaise de concert*, Op. 38 (version for violin and piano).

> Arthur Grumiaux, violin; Dinorah Varsi, piano.
> Musique en Wallonie (6806 059), 1974.

Weiner, Leó. "Ballada," Op. 8 (version for clarinet and piano).

> On "Clarinet Recital."
> Kálmán Berkes, clarinet; Zoltán Kocsis, piano.
> Hungaroton (SLPX 11748), 1975.

Index

Ballad of Blaník, The
(Vrchlický/Janáček), 263, 267-69,
274-75
Ballad *Lieder,* 32-34, 40-45, 126-27
Ballad process, defined 34
Ballad of Reading Gaol, The
(Wilde/Ibert), 274-75
Ballade, instrumental
melodies in bare octaves, 56-58,
148-50
musical forms. See Sonata form;
Ternary form; Variation form
"narrative tone," first cited 49
as nationalist genre, 26, 177-79,
187-200, 262-63
refrain structure, 197-98
sextuplet rhythm, 40-41, 54-55,
124, 188
as title for instrumental music, 19, 49,
91-92, 114, 125, 135, 186, 274
Ballade, in medieval French poetry, 199
"Ballade Against the Enemies of France"
(Villon), 199-200
"Ballade contre les ennemis de la
France." See "Ballade Against the
Enemies of France"
Ballade de la Geôle de Reading, La. See
Ballad of Reading Gaol, The
"Ballade of the Pilgrims" (Chopin), 291
ch. 2/n. 1
"Ballade d'Ukraine" (Liszt), 154-56
Ballads, folk. See also Nordic ballad
tradition
melodies, 32, 40, 152
oral composition, 31, 45-48
prosody, 40
Ballads, literary
new trends in late nineteenth
century, 177, 191, 240, 264,
274-75
prosody, 40
set as accompanied songs, 40-45,
126-27
"Balladyna" (Słowacki/Różycki), 187-88
Ballata Sinfonica (Szokolay), 275
"Barbara Allen" (British folk ballad),
36-38, 40
Bartalus, István (1821-1899)
Children's Lyre, 156-57
Bartók, Béla (1881-1945), 22, 192,
196-97
Ballad: Theme with Variations
(*Fifteen Hungarian Peasant*

Songs), 194-96, 287
Ballad (*For Children*), 192-94, 287
"Free Variations" (*Mikrokosmos*),
194
Hungarian Folk Music, 194
The Miraculous Mandarin, 196
Battle pieces, 51, 199
Beach, Amy (1867-1944)
Ballad (Op. 6), 188-89
Beethoven, Ludwig van (1770-1827),
56, 91, 93-94, 224, 285
Pastoral Symphony, 51
Piano Sonata (Op. 109), 167
"Belle Dame sans merci, La" (Keats),
47, 226
Belle Dame sans merci, La (Mackenzie),
226
Beregszászy, Lajos, 196
Bergson, Henri, 224
Berlioz, Hector (1803-1869), 19, 28,
71, 216
Harold in Italy, 20, 56
Symphonie fantastique, 20, 51, 56,
68, 71, 219, 288
Blanc et noir, En (Debussy), 199-200
Bold, Alan, 146
Bopp, Franz, 25
Border Ballads (McEwen), 228
Borodin, Alexander Porfirievich
(1833-1887), 179
Brahms, Johannes (1833-1897), 28
Ballade (Op. 118, No. 3), 182-84
Four Ballades (Op. 10), 139-50,
226-27, 287
Bremond, Claude, 35
Brentano, Clemens, and Achim von
Arnim
Des Knaben Wunderhorn, 25
Britten, Benjamin (1913-1976)
Scottish Ballad (Op. 26), 277
Bronson, Bertrand, 40
Brown, David, 238
Brown, Maurice, 28-29
Buchan, David, 46-47, 72-74, 81, 84
Bülow, Hans von (1830-1894)
Ballade (Op. 11), 114-17, 287
Ballade, after "The Minstrel's Curse"
(Op. 16), 205-09
Bürger, August Gottfried, 19, 32
"Die Entführung" ("The Abduction"),
125-26
"Lenore," 21, 27, 35-39, 126-27, 203,
205, 210-11, 214-18

Gutmann, Adolf (1819–1882)
  Ballade (Op. 19), 136, 299 ch. 5/n. 9
Gyermekeknek. See *For Children*
Gyulai, Paul
  "The Water Nymph" ("A sellö"),
  209–10

Hanslick, Eduard, 263
"Harald" (Uhland), 214, 216–17
Harris, Roy (1898–1979)
  American Ballads, 276
Hedley, Arthur, 57
Heine, Heinrich, 32, 128
  "König Harald Harfagar," 177, 214,
  216; illus. facing p. 16
  "Sommerabend," 244
Heller, Stephen (1813–1888), 148
  Ballade (Op. 121, No. 1), 149–50
  Three Ballades (Op. 115), 149–51
Henschel, George (1850–1934)
  Ballade (Op. 39), 185, 305 ch. 7/n. 44
Henselt, Adolf (1814–1889)
  Ballade (Op. 31), 138
Herder, Johann Gottfried von, 19, 24–25,
  156
  "Edward," 139–43
  "The Elf-King's Daughter" ("Erlkönigs
  Tochter"), 38, 64
Hero and Leander (Ertel), 213
Hero and Leander (Mihalovich), 210
"Hero und Leander" (Schiller), 112, 210,
  213
Hérodiade (Mallarmé/Hindemith), 286
Herz, Henri (1803–1888)
  "Deux Ballades sans paroles"
  (Op. 117), 136, 299 ch. 5/n. 9
"Highland Ballad" (Mackenzie), 185, 226,
  305 ch. 7/n. 44
Hiller, Ferdinand (1811–1885), 148
  Ballade (Op. 66, No. 4), 150, 301
  ch. 5/n. 41
  Ballade (Op. 130, No. 1), 150
Hindemith, Paul (1895–1963)
  Hérodiade, 286
Hirschfeld, Robert, 262–63
Holoubek. See *Wild Dove, The*
Hopkins, G. W., 222, 224
"House Carpenter, The" (British folk
  ballad), 226
Hubay, Jenö (1858–1937)
  Ballade (Op. 48, No. 1), 185, 304
  ch. 7/n. 43

Hugo, Victor, 32
  "La Ronde du Sabbat" ("The Witches'
  Sabbath"), 210
Huneker, James, 49
Hungarian Peasant Songs, Fifteen
  (Bartók), 194–96
Hüttenbrenner, Anselm (1794–1868)
  Overture to Lenore, 205

Ibert, Jacques (1890–1962)
  The Ballad of Reading Gaol, 274–75
  Escales, 275
  Trois Pièces brèves, 275
"Incremental repetition," first cited 47
Indy, Vincent d' (1851–1931)
  La Forêt enchantée (Op. 8), 214,
  216–17
Ireland, John (1879–1962)
  Ballade, 275
Ives, Charles (1874–1954), 276

Jachimecki, Zdzisław, 290 ch. 1/n. 30,
  295 ch. 3/n. 22
Janáček, Leoš (1854–1928)
  on Dvořák's *ballades,* 249, 255, 259
  The Ballad of Blaník, 263, 267–69,
  274–75
  Ballade (Sonata for violin and piano),
  197–99
  The Fiddler's Child, 263, 265–67
  Jenůfa, 311 ch. 9/n. 39
Jarnach, Philipp (1892–1982)
  Ballade, 185

Kalbeck, Max, 139, 142, 147, 184
Kalevala (Finnish epic), 181
Kallberg, Jeffrey, 291 ch. 2/n. 1
Karelia Suite (Sibelius), 214
Keats, John
  "La Belle Dame sans merci," 47, 226
Kentner, Louis, 103–04
"King Harald Harfagar" (Heine/Saint-
  Saëns), 177, 214, 216; illus. facing
  p. 16
Kirchner, Theodor (1823–1903)
  "Balladenmässig" (Op. 73, No. 19),
  182
Kjerulf, Halfdan (1815–1868)
  Norwegian Folk Ballads, 157–58
Klughardt, August (1847–1902)
  Lenore (Op. 27), 210–11
Knaben Wunderhorn, Des (Arnim and
  Brentano), 25

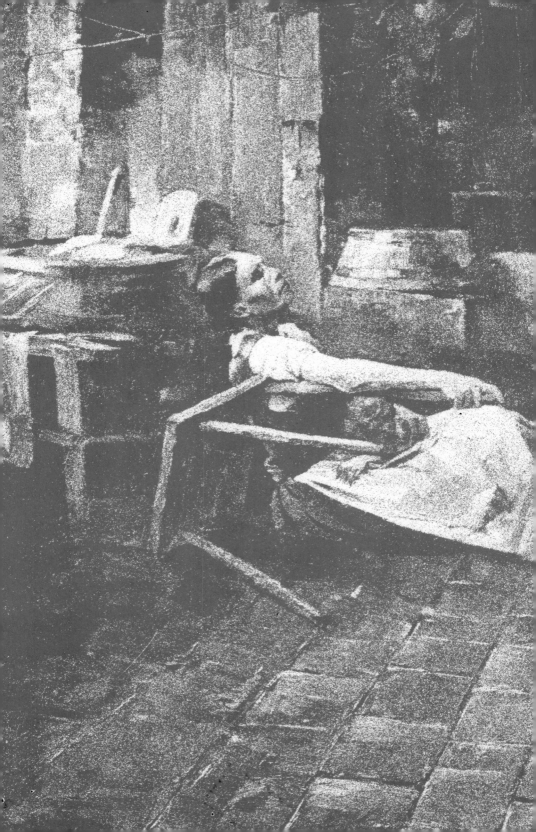